MAN AND MANKIND: CONFLICT AND COMMUNICATION BETWEEN CULTURES

COMMUNICATION AND INFORMATION SCIENCE

A Series of Monographs, Treatises, and Texts

Edited by
MELVIN J. VOIGT
University of California, San Diego

Man and Mankind:
Conflict and Communication between Cultures

by Edmund S. Glenn, *University of Delaware*
with Christine G. Glenn, *Good Samaritan Hospital,*
Portland, Oregon

ABLEX Publishing Corporation
355 Chestnut Street
Norwood, New Jersey 07648

Copyright 1981 by Ablex Publishing Corporation.
Second Printing 1982.

Printed in the United States of America.

ISBN: 0-89391-068-6

Library of Congress Cataloging in Publication Data

Glenn, Edmund S.
  Man and mankind.

  (Communication and information science)
  Includes index.
1. Intercultural communication. 2. Culture conflict.
3. Acculturation. 4. Social role. 5. Sex role.
I. Glenn, Christine G. II. Title. III. Series.
HM258.G53   306   81-3474
AACR2

All quoted passages are reprinted here
by permission of the author/copyright holder.
The author expresses his gratitude for
the permission granted.

ABLEX Publishing Corporation
Norwood, New Jersey

*To Marjorie and to our children,
with gratitude for their patience and encouragement.*

Contents

Introduction

Man's relations with his surroundings ("transactions" would be the word used by Dewey) build up through the accumulation of his experience, his knowledge, his expectations, i.e. the structure which may be considered as his personal culture. This is "Man."

As man lives, his experience expands. The human group which influences an adult and which an adult must take into account is broader than are the surroundings noticed by a child. Little by little the environment becomes what we call *a* particular culture. The concept applies even to the physical surroundings, since the culture of the group mediates most of the experiences of each man within nature.

The situation of human groups has much in common with the situation of individuals. As they grow and expand, they come into contact with other human groups. The experience of culture contact becomes one of the most important sources of the information on which is based the knowledge they acquire—and also of the conflicts from which they suffer. This is "Mankind."

Are there "superior" and "inferior" cultures? The words of this comparison are largely meaningless. One must specify, "superior" or "inferior" at what? Every culture is well adapted to *its* environment and every culture undergoes an experience of maladaptation if the environment changes. The basic environment of a given human population may be more or less "broad" i.e. it may require the ability to handle more or less information to arrive at adaptation. Culture contact is generally easier for those groups whose store of information is richer.

The methods for organizing information differ depending on the amount of information to be organized and on the numbers of people to whom the information is to be *communicated*. An overall methodology of the acquisition and storage of information is used in this book as a *paradigm*. The forms of the paradigm are used to compare and to describe different cultures and sub-cultures.

Three main polar oppositions define the forms of the paradigm:

(1) The associative-abstractive. Knowledge acquired through a largely spontaneous experience within an environment is associative. Such a knowledge fits closely with the feelings of individuals and the shared preoccupations of small or relatively small groups. The codification of thought into precise meanings and well organized lexicons is carried out by abstraction. The results of abstraction do not reflect the spontaneous experience of small groups, but the specifically stated systems of knowledge of large groups—potentially of all mankind.

Although differences along the associative-abstractive dimension are used in characterizing cultures, all cultures need and possess both types of elements.

(2) Universalism-Patricularism. Universalism sees the world through the conceptualizations reflected in the definitions of words. It is abstractive; it does not care for all those experiences which make one person different from another. It knows "dog" but not "Fido" or "Mandy." In opposition, particularism does not know "man" or "woman," but "Dick" and "Jane." It is usually associative, reflecting personal lives and personal feelings. However it can also be abstractive where it reflects episodes of action undertaken specifically to test theories or in furtherance of the promises of theories.

Another important opposition falling under this categorization is that between faith in language (Russians) and faith in action (Americans).

(3) Broadening vs. narrowing the frame of reference. Policies may aim at broadening or at narrowing the frame of reference. The Roman empire made it possible for men of very different backgrounds to say "cives Romanus sum"—"I am a Roman citizen, I obey the same law, I belong." Hitler restricted belonging, and mutual understanding, to people of the same ethnic origin. Where one broadens culture through the expansion of common learning, the other narrows it by accepting information only from those sharing a common origin or a supposedly unchangeable body of "truth."

Different subcultures of the same culture often differ along this dimension. Within the broadly educated upper middle class women and men meet often in the context of professional roles rather than in the context of sexually assigned positions. Among the narrowly educated, relationships to which sex or sexual traditions are irrelevant occur less frequently.

1

THE ANALYSIS
OF INTERCULTURAL
COMMUNICATION

with Christine G. Glenn

Human commonality and human diversity

Communication among men is made possible by their having something in common; it is made difficult by the differences which exist among them. That much is obvious. Where the difficulty arises is in discovering and describing the elements of commonality and of difference, and in doing so in a way capable of explaining misunderstandings and pointing towards understanding.

The first question which we must therefore ask is, what general approach to his issue will we take? That is, how can we determine the commonalities and differences which are most relevant for understanding communication? In the analysis of the similarities and the differences between human groupings there appear to be three general approaches. They are:

1. The functionalistic approach, following in the main the work of Malinowski. The rationale of functionalism is that all cultures must provide for a number of social needs, from child rearing to religion. Each such universal need provides an organizational dimension; the different ways in which the needs are met become the values of the dimension.
2. The values approach, used by researchers such as Kluckhohn and Strodtbeck (1961), and Condon and Yousef (1975). The main thrust of this appraisal

is the analysis of the value orientations which govern how given peoples judge various aspects of the human experience. For example, with respect to nature, the orientation of some cultures may be governed by the expectation that man can dominate nature and that any behavior which leads to such a domination should be valued positively. The feeling in other cultures may be that man should find a way to attain harmony with nature. In still other cultures, the main feeling is that man is likely to be dominated by nature and must take steps to propitiate nature or to learn to accept nature's decrees.

3. The cognitive approach, suggesting that different cultures structure knowledge differently and that these differences will largely determine many aspects of behavior and communication, e.g., the topics which are felt to be worth talking about, the organization of information during communication, the types of information which are accepted as evidence for any given opinion. This is the general approach taken in this book

Cultures, individuals, situations: a statement of the problem

The field of cognition can be defined as the study of human information processing (Neisser, 1967). Very basically, it is concerned with the question, how do men think? How is informational input, such as sensory or proprioceptive stimulation organized into events such as thoughts, images or memory traces which "make sense" (a phenomenological event) to the interpreter? This book will not concern itself with the entire field of cognition. We must therefore ask how a cognitive approach to intercultural communication can be achieved; or, more basically, what a cognitive approach means. Two distinctions are important in this regard. The first is that between cognitive processes and the products of cognition. With regard to the processes, it will be argued that it is possible to talk of cognitive styles, that is, patterns of thinking or ways of organizing information which become habitual and which can be used in a number of situations and on numerous types of information (e.g., Kagan et al., 1963). Turning to the product of cognition, it becomes clear that individual events are generally not evaluated or interpreted in isolation. They are more generally organized with other events, forming more or less extensive networks or cognitive structures. These structures can be concepts, or beliefs, or complex systems of interrelated beliefs. It is obvious that cognitive processes and cognitive products are logically distinct but psychologically intertwined; the product is a reflection of the process. The distinction, however, remains a powerful heuristic and will be retained.

The second distinction which is inherent in a cognitive approach is that of the level of analysis. An analysis of communication can focus on a single interpersonal situation or dialogue, on an individual and his typical cognitive styles, on a social group and styles which are shared within it, on an entire culture and its styles, and, some argue, even on the intellectual development of the species. Each of these, e.g., the situation, the individual, and so on, can therefore be taken as the unit of analysis. The examination of each unit or level will provide different information relevant to communication. The most basic level is that of the single event or situation. It is a truism to state that the topic or event which is discussed will influence the types of information presented and the way in which they are organized. The next level of analysis takes the individual as the focus. Each individual has learned through his or her own experiences how to interpret various situations or types of information. To the extent that each person's experiences and abilities are uniquely his or hers, they will be private and perhaps unusual or even incomprehensible to others. However, to the extent that individuals share certain experiences, their interpretations will be similar. This immediately takes us to the next level, that of social groups; there are numerous gradations at this level. Members of social groups (e.g., the family, a religion, a culture) will tend to develop similar cognitive structures because of shared experiences. It is therefore possible to speak of collective structures or representations; the importance of this construct for the understanding of cultural differences and similarities cannot be overstressed. For that reason, it is valuable to quote at length the definition given by Lévy-Bruhl (1910):

> The representations we call collective, to define them roughly without going too deep into the matter, can be recognized on the basis of the following characteristics: they are shared by the members of given social groups; they are transmitted from generation to generation within such groups; they dominate individual minds, in which they generate feelings of respect, or fear, or of adoration, etc. for their contents. They do not depend on the individual for their existence. It is not that they imply a collective subject distinct from the individuals making up the social group, but they have characteristics which cannot be accounted for by the sole consideration of individuals. Thus language, even though it exists strictly speaking only within the minds of the individuals who speak it, is none the less clearly a social reality, based on a set of collective representations. It dominates individuals, it is in existence before their births, and it survives their deaths.

Kroeber (1917) took a similar stand in his article on the superorganic and in his later works, as did White (1949). There exist patterns of behavior and belief characteristic of collectivities. The description of such patterns, both from a static and an evolutionary point of view, presents characteristics which can be explained without a necessary recourse to individual psychology.

We are now in a position to return to the issue of how a cognitive approach can be applied to the analysis of intercultural communication. First, a cognitive model is developed that will stress the process over the products of cognition. In particular, we present psychological parameters on dimensions which characterize patterns of thought. Of course, as processes can only be known through their products, frequent references are made to particular beliefs.

Second, the model concentrates on collective modes of thought, emphasizing the patterns which are typical of large cultural groups. Again, digressions into individual psychology are made, as the two areas cannot be completely separated.

A word on direction

In concluding this brief introduction, it may be valuable to make explicit two major assumptions that underlie what has already been said and that provide the meta-theoretical basis of the formal model which is presented in the third chapter.

The first assumption relates to the general approach; it has already been noted that the emphasis is on cognitive processes rather than on cognitive products. One might well ask whether or not this was an arbitrary decision. In fact it was not. The reason for it is that an emphasis on the products is necessarily static; it will produce dimensions along which concepts, beliefs, institutions, etc., can be placed. The issue that is being raised here is the question of the nature of description versus that of explanation in the social and behavioral sciences. An emphasis on the products will be descriptive, while explanation requires that the origin of cognitive products be determined. Thus, only by understanding the process, i.e., how people organize information, can we understand the products and make predictions about how an individual or a culture will react to new situations. The ability to make predictions is central to an explanatory theory.

The second assumption deals with the nature of cognition. Let us begin with a statement which is tautological but possibly heuristic: All areas of study which deal with human thought and/or with the way it is manifested in concepts and conceptual systems (e.g., psychology, sociology, sociolinguistics, anthropology, epistemology)are closely related; these areas differ primarily in their choice of a unit of analysis. While few would openly disagree with such a statement, its implications for the subject matter of these disciplines and for their interrelationships is not obvious. This statement is the working premise of this book.

A corollary of this assumption (and there are supporting data for it) is that there are a finite number of cognitive laws which hold for all questions dealing with human learning; these cognitive laws or principles are applicable in each of these disciplines. Stated differently, there are certain basic learning mechanisms which govern how individuals organize their experiences into concepts, the ways in which these concepts can be reorganized into more abstract concepts, and the ways in which these concepts can be organized into conceptual systems. These conceptual systems and modes of thought are reflected in the behavior of individuals, in the collective behavior of societies and cultures, and in the institutions of social and cultural groups. What is being proposed is that cognition be regarded as a hierarchical process in which principles that can explain how an infant grasps his or her first scheme can also be applied to explain creative scientific discoveries, the development of social and cultural institutions and of political and social movements, etc. No claim is being made here for a complete theoretical system; this book will not answer all the questions of the social or behavioral sciences and may in fact raise as many as it attempts to answer. However, it attempts to take the above statement about the interrelationship of these disciplines seriously and to begin in some way to arrive at a theoretical system which can provide some answers and a context within which such issues can be raised.

The organization of the book

The second chapter presents the derivation of the model which presides over the body of the analysis. The purpose of that chapter is twofold: (1) to acknowledge and to specify the debt to earlier thought and research; and (2) to refer to a body of data without which the theory itself could be considered unsupported. Following its antecedents, the model itself is presented in chapter 3.

The fourth chapter presents a theory of human cognition, and also deals with the main psychological implications of the model. This is followed by a chapter on the manner in which the model might influence linguistic analysis.

Chapter 6 shows that the social class subcultures in the contemporary United States fit in with the analysis and support its suggestions. Chapters 7 and 8 deal with the very controversial and very important question of collective cognitive pathology. Chapter 8 also takes up the political implications of the work.

The following group of chapters present summary analyses of some of the main families of cultures.

Chapter 12 presents some conclusions and touches upon the question of social morality.

2

DERIVATION OF THE MODEL

with Christine G. Glenn

A first step towards a cognitive analysis of culture and culture change

Understanding communication calls, first of all, for an understanding of the manner in which people acquire, organize, and transmit information. The method by which this understanding will be sought in the present analysis is based on a hypothetical question: what can be the operations by which culturally characteristic beliefs and behaviors can be acquired? Furthermore, what operations can explain the transmission of culture from generation to generation? What changes in the organization of information can lead to historically observed changes in beliefs and behaviors? Is there such a thing as a dominant direction of cultural evolution? If so, what is it and why is it? What causes conflicts between cultures, and what makes the resolution of such conflicts possible? Are there types of culture? If so, are they sufficiently distinct to permit the development of a typology of cultures? On a slightly different but very necessary level: what parts or areas of culture are to be selected as sources of data?

The last question can be answered only in a somewhat arbitrary manner. There is no program of cultural analysis that can be established as the only proper and legitimate one. The program ultimately selected must be due to a hunch—hopefully educated—of the researcher. The main guiding line is the level at which the analysis is to take place. In

7

the present case the level is that of very broad generality, similar from that point of view to Parsons and Shils' (1950) general theory of action.

Three areas of culture are examined:

1. The world view and the psychological-cognitive operations which can lead to it.
2. The semantic organization of communication and the type of argumentation which leads to the acceptance or rejection of propositions.
3. Institutions and their functioning.

A major methodological point is that the descriptions selected as characteristic must be the same for all three of the areas above. The characteristics selected will appear as polarities between mechanisms of learning and of structuring knowledge. The first polarity is that between learning by association and organizing knowledge by abstraction (Glenn, 1973, 1974). Detailed analyses concerning such polarities are presented in chapter 4; in the meantime the contrasting characteristics of each polarity are presented through its use in the analyses of cognitive phenomena. What must be borne in mind is that the analyses must be applicable to (1) learning, (2) communication, and (3) social organization.

A second point is an obsession with parsimony: descriptions of types of action familiar in the literature are reduced to as few as possible.

The associative-abstractive polarity

A first example of culturally characteristic world views that can be tied to a manner in which thought can be generated and expanded can be taken from Frazer's analysis of magic (1922).

Contagious Magic proceeds upon the notion that things which have once been conjoined must remain ever afterwards, even when quite disserved from each other, in such a sympathetic relation that whatever is done to the one must similarly affect the other. Thus the logical basis of Contagious Magic . . . is a mistaken association of ideas. . . . The most familiar example of Contagious Magic is the . . . sympathy which is supposed to exist between a man and any severed portion of his person, as hair or nails; so that whoever gets possession of human hair or nails may work his will, at any distance, upon the person from whom they were cut. This superstition is world-wide. . . .

Again magic may be wrought on a man sympathetically, not only through his clothes or a severed part of himself, but also through the impressions left by his body in sand and earth. In particular it is a world-wide superstition that by injuring footprints you injure the feet that made them. Thus the natives of South-Eastern Australia think that they can lame a man by placing sharp pieces of quartz, glass, bone, or charcoal in his footprints. Seeing a Tatungoland man very lame, Dr. Howitt asked him what was the matter. He said "some fellow put bottle in my foot". . . .

Similar practices prevail in various parts of Europe. . . . A German huntsman will stick a nail taken from a coffin into the fresh spoor of the quarry, believing that this will hinder the animal from escaping. The aborigines of Victoria put hot embers in the tracks of animals they were pursuing.

Frazer mentions the mechanism of association. Its presence seems evident. The only question which calls for an immediate answer is that of what can be associated with what else. One of the manners in which selections can be made is propinquity: things which are experienced together either because they are perceived (or, more generally, sensed) together, or because they are remembered together, or again because the sight of one coincides with the memory of another.

The enormous extent of the cultures in which examples can be found eliminates any possibility of a diffusion process. The origin appears to be much simpler: that there are regularities within the transactions between man and his environment and that these regularities are sufficiently widespread to induce similar associations in different cultures. Yet the environment is not sufficiently regular to eliminate randomness: Association as a basis of the world-view is reasonably trustworthy only within inextensive environments. Species ranging through many different environments, such as man, need something else—at times *with* association, and at times *instead of* association.

The title of this section suggests that the something in question is abstraction. A definition may be to the point. Külpe (1904) described abstraction as a mechanism which allows the subject to decrease the salience of some elements of knowledge, while increasing that of others. A more modern theory based on Russel's theory of types distinguishes between an object language—about things and low in abstractions—and various levels of meta-languages—statements about other statements, becoming more abstract by moving away from things and toward statements about statements which themselves are statements about statements. There is no contradiction between the two definitions. Both lead to a selection of elements towards which attention should be directed, and elements which should be disregarded, at least within the context in which abstraction is carried out.

Let us now present an example. Any *concept* will do. Let us take the concept of "citizen." We understand that a citizen is a human being. Our attention is directed towards those characteristics by which a citizen is distinguished from other human beings. An opposition, or a basis for selection, such as healthy–unhealthy, is declared irrelevant to the determination of citizenship, no matter how important it may be to the people concerned. The things to look for are elements capable of defining or describing the political area of the culture concerned—for instance that of the United States. Voting is one of the points which may serve to determine who is and who is not a citizen. At the present moment sex is *irrelevant* to the definition of citizenship. Before the first World War, sex was *relevant* since women could not vote. If the example is well chosen, abstraction consists in removing from existing associations elements which are deemed irrelevant; furthermore, the progressive development of the abstractive part of a culture appears to be carried out by the additional removal of an increasing amount of associations. The passage of time, at least in some contexts, tends to make concepts leaner and more precise.

This is the exact opposite of the associations presented as examples earlier in this section. There, each conditioning led to the inclusion of other inputs from the environment, and the question of relevance was disregarded.

Another item to be noted is that the examples of association were taken from cultures which might be termed "early" or "relatively undeveloped." The place of the western examples can be suggested by the fact that Bacon approved of the treatment of cuts by placing clean tallow between the wound and the bandage. He also mentioned as a remedy the placing of tallow on the blade of the knife by which the wound was inflicted—a clear example of association. He did say that he was not sure of the value of this second therapy, but then, Bacon was Bacon. Thus, in the case of western cultures, associations of this type appear frequent in the past and lose ground with the passage of time. The suggestion is one of the direction in which cultures evolve: from association towards abstraction. So far this is only hinted, even though it appears that associations must be established before being subjected to abstractive analysis and critique.

Divergencies in world views

Divergencies between the ways in which preliterate cultures on the one hand, and "modern" cultures on the other tend to organize the knowledge and the images each has of the world can be seen in an analysis of the Ojibwa by Hallowell (1958):

Ever since linguists began to study the Algonkian family of languages, to which the speech of the Ojibwa belongs, it has been established that nouns fall into two classes, distinguished by different plural suffixes. These classes were labelled "animate" and "inanimate" because the objects to which they referred appeared to approximate the animate-inanimate dichotomy of Western thought. . . .

Since stones are animate, I once said to an old man: "Are *all* the stones we see about us here alive?" He reflected a long while and then replied, "No! But *some* are." This qualified answer . . . indicates . . . that the Ojibwa are not animists in the sense that they dogmatically attribute living souls to inanimate objects such as stones. The hypothesis which suggests itself is that the allocation of stones to an animate grammatical category may be a factor in a cognitive "set." It leaves a door open that on dogmatic grounds our naturalistic orientation keeps shut tight. Whereas we would never expect a stone to manifest animate properties of any kind under any circumstances, the Ojibwa recognize, a priori, potentialities of animation in certain classes of objects under certain circumstances. The Ojibwa do not perceive stones, in general, as animate any more than we do. The crucial test is experience. It is asserted by informants that stones have been seen to move, to open and close their 'mouths' (a hole in the stone), that some stones manifest other animate properties.

The organization of the manner in which knowledge of stones is integrated in the overall world view is abstractive in the case of the modern or Western culture: Impressions of animation among stones are rejected a priori as irrelevant. The Ojibwa world view is associative: It is based on associations appearing within the experiences of individuals and including, in all probability, elements derived from dreams.

The contrast can also be described as an opposition between a theoretic point of view—a general theory of the constitution of the world defining stones as inanimate—and empirical bias, accepting of all kinds of experience (Scribner, 1979).

Using other terms, the western organization appears universalistic, expressing a universal belief about stones. The preliterate organization is particularistic, based on particular experiences of particular individuals and stating no universal law. (Particularism–universalism, and association–abstraction should not be fully equated. The difference between the two contrasts is discussed later.)

It may be useful, even if somewhat premature, to point out the advantages and drawbacks of the two polar oppositions governing the organization of information. The abstractive approach is capable of organizing much richer amounts of information (or the description of much broader environments) than the associative approach. Once an item is described as a stone, there is no more need to seek additional information concerning animation in the case of particular stones. On the other hand, the expression of the individuality of experience is made more difficult; beliefs and dreams involving animate stones are no longer fully acceptable.

Association and abstraction in communication

Analyses in sociolinguistics, particularly those of Bernstein (1964a, b), distinguish two types of communicative usage. One is restricted coding: Cliches, idioms, and ready-made figures of speech predominate and there are relatively few expressions in which words are freely combined in new or novel manners. The other is generalized coding: words are combined relatively freely among themselves and subject to the rules of syntax, and the repetition of previously used or ready-made expressions becomes the exception.

The significance of this comparison to the development of different capabilities in communication is shown by the presentation of a similar analysis by Glenn (1969, 1973):

Let us . . . compare two seemingly synonymous sentences:
(a) It is nice weather we're having.
(b) Maximum temperature in the 70°'s, clear, wind moderate, southwesterly, 10 mph.
The first sentence may be used to convey information about the weather, but, statistically speaking, it is much more likely to be used as a conversational gambit "to make conversation," "to talk about the weather," or "to break the ice."

It may be shown that it typifies a style of expression in which statements are taken as units (syntagms) lacking in inner subdivision and structure and also lacking criterial boundaries defining the limits of their relevance.

First of all, in most such openings both parties are equally aware of the prevailing weather and, therefore, there is no need to convey information about it. The real meaning of the sentence is to convey and to establish an appropriate degree of friendship and of solidarity between the speakers. Thus:

(1) The meaning of the sentence cannot be derived from the general system of the language by breaking it into its lexical, syntactical, and conceptual elements, obtaining the meaning of each of them and re-synthesizing the whole. The understanding of the sentence can be obtained only by becoming familiar with the entirety of the cultural situations within which it may be used, and with the responses that are expected after sentences such as this one are used as signals.

(2) The full meaning of the sentence cannot be grasped without the knowledge of the circumstances under which it is being used. The same opening may have different implications if used by a man trying to strike a conversation with a young woman and if used by a minister to one of his parishoners.

(3) There is no clearly perceptible difference in meaning if one or some of the elements of the sentence are changed. (a') It is beautiful weather we're having has the same meaning as (a).

(4) There is no precise limit to the efficacy of such an utterance; the response of the listener may vary all the way from a rejection of the overture to the establishment of an enduring and intimate friendship.

Thus (a) can be said to be syntagmatic (because it is a unit incapable of meaningful subdivision at the semantic level); holophrastic (because even though a unit, it carries the full meaning of the proposition "Let's be friends, to the extent to which the situation permits it or calls for it"), and associative (because it lacks criterial boundaries and because it carries a considerable potential of ambiguity, the extent of the friendship preferred being left imprecise).

Sentence (b) which could have been taken from a weather report, can be placed in opposition to the first one on each of the above points:

(1) It can be understood by breaking it into its linguistic and conceptual elements.

(2) Its meaning is the same regardless of the conditions of utterance.

(3) There are clearly perceptible differences if terms are substituted: (b') . . . temperature 95° . . . has a meaning different from that of (b).

(4) Its meaning is strictly limited. Thus (b) (the weather report) is a paradigmatic statement, since each word of the sentence may be subsumed under a superordinate paradigm. Temperature, e.g., may be meaningfully incorporated as a unit in innumerable statements. . . . The sentence and each of its elements are semantically precise and the structural parts are relatively independent—set apart unambiguously by criterial boundaries.

The usage exemplified by (a) [is] more associative . . . and the usage exemplified by (b) [is] . . . more abstractive." (Glenn, 1973)

Another point is that (a) is relatively private: Even though the figure of speech used is widespread, the situation is not fully understandable without the inclusion of elements particular to each case in which it is used. The situation under (b) is paradigmatic: To understand it the subject must understand an entire conceptual code shared within the society concerned. This obviously makes the situation public.

Types of legal organization

The first distinction to be discussed, made by Sir Henry Maine (1861), concerns the nature of law. Maine distinguished between societies governed by the *law of status* and societies governed by the *law of contract*.

The core of the law of status is constituted by a nexus of traditional relationships making up the relative and generally asymmetrical positions of the members of society. The main purpose of the law, which usually consists of implicit but thoroughly internalized traditions, is to preserve such networks of social relationships. Family or clan relationships often play a large role in the question of status; in many cases disputes are viewed in terms of opposition between clans or families. In a case of dispute, the relative social positions of the disputants must be taken into account. Law based on ascribed status reflects associative thought as the individual is never clearly separated from his or her group; thus the boundary between the individual and the group is unclear. Moreover, the distinction between criminal law and the law of torts is at most embryonary: A delinquent action is often considered as impinging upon the interests or the status of those involved rather than as an infraction against general rules. Again, this can be seen as resulting from associative thought; any behavior, whether it is a crime or not, is defined in terms of the participants who become associated with each other via the act, and not in terms of a set of principles which apply equally to all people. The basis of the law of status is found in particular social relationships.

The core of the law of contract is the clear statement of either general or particular obligations and rights. In its general aspects it prescribes penalties or rewards to the perpetrators of specific actions, regardless of who they might be. Thus, it is abstractive and universalistic. It is abstractive because the definition of what is relevant and what is irrelevant to judgment is very specific, i.e., only the actions which occasion the legal procedure are regarded as relevant to a decision; all other characteristics are deemed irrelevant. It is universalistic because the laws are stated in general terms which can be applied in a number of different instances; moreover, they are based on principles which are equally binding for all people regardless of other characteristics, e.g., status. Thus, law is based on the concept of "any person" having entered into the contract rather than on the totality of a person's individuality.

A law which affirms the relevance of the social status of individuals appearing as contestants before a judicial or quasi judicial procedure determines a resolution of the case on the basis of the *ascription* to them of rights and obligations appropriate to their station. A law which rejects status as irrelevant and concentrates on allegations of specific deeds and undeeds, proceeds on the basis of a search for the *achievements* of such persons within the context of the question under consideration.

Types of social organization

We turn now to a discussion of social types and the theory of Tönnies (1887), who distinguishes two main types of social organization: *Gemeinschaft or community*, and *Gesellschaft or society*. This is closely related to the area of law which is in fact a formalization of the social organization.

Gemeinschaft is based on generally implicit, traditional and/or affective bonds. Social solidarity is felt rather than decreed; it finds its expression in a feeling of common belonging, at times in friendship—or, as it is seldom emphasized, in enmity—both of which can be ritualized. Thus, it is diffuse, affectively expressed; in the terminology of this work, it is associatively based.

Gesellschaft is based on explicit laws. The very explicitness of laws and regulations makes it impossible to take into account the vagueness of feelings; in consequence society seeks to be affectively neutral. It is this explicitness, formally defining the boundaries of the society and of behavior within it, which argues for considering this form of organization as abstractive.

The opposition between the two may be illustrated between a sense of belonging and the legal right to belong, for example, citizenship. Glenn (1970a) extended the difference between community and society to that between nationality in the ethnic sense and state in the legal sense. A nation is defined by a common cultural background; within a nation a person is defined by (i.e., associated with) his background, including all the conscious or subconscious habits and traditions characteristic of the background. A state is defined by explicit laws of citizenship and changing one's citizenship is a legal or contractural matter.

It may not be too early to note that the Gemeinschaft form is particularly suitable to relatively small and ethnically homogenous human groupings, and the Gesellschaft form to large, mobile, and pluralistic groupings.

Is there a direction of evolution?

Werner (1961) interprets the passage from less developed to more developed types of cognition in terms of five pairs of polar opposites: (1) syncretic–discrete, (2) diffuse–articulated, (3) indefinite–definite, (4) rigid–flexible, and (5) labile–stable.

The beginning items of each pair are associative, and the terminal items are abstractive. Some difficulties arise in regard to the last two items: how can thought, and in particular associative thought, be at the same time rigid and labile? And how can abstractive thought be at the same time flexible and stable? The answer is that associative thought lacks the mechanisms necessary to integrate novel information. In consequence, it clings rigidly to past habits and established structures. On the other hand, it is also capable of accepting new associations without bringing about any inner consistency between them and the fabric of older beliefs. This makes it at the same time rigid—incapable of an orderly transformation of existing structures, and labile—likely to take off in the direction of a new association without the realization of inner contradictions. By contrast, abstractive thought is flexible, because it is endowed with mechanisms capable of assimilating the novel or of accommodating to it; it is also stable because partial transformations may be carried out without disturbing the overall method of approach.

This difference between associative and abstractive thought is related to the amount of information which can and needs to be incorporated into the cognitive structures, and to the organization of information connected with each style. Associative thought is marked by ill-defined relationships between elements. Only a relatively small amount of information can be remembered in an amorphous state. As the amount of information increases, it becomes necessary to organize knowledge, usually in hierarchical structures obtained through abstraction. Hierarchical structures are capable of incorporating new information into a relevant niche, while remaining stable in its other parts.

The differences between association and abstraction in structuring information determine a direction of evolution: from less information to more information, from the weak structures of associative chains towards the stronger structures of hierarchies.

Why?

In the early stages of cultural development, as seen in history and prehistory, mankind was organized in small communities. The relationship between a society's size and the nature of its conceptual outlook was noted by Durkheim (1933):

> In a small society, since everyone is clearly placed in the same conditions of existence, the collective environment is essentially concrete. It is made up of beings of all sorts who fill the social horizon. The states of conscience representing it then have the same character. First, they are related to precise objects, as this animal, this tree, this plant, this natural force, etc. Then, as everybody is related to these things in the same way, they affect all consciences in the same way. The whole tribe, if it is not too widely extended, enjoys or suffers the same advantages or inconveniences from the sun, rain, heat, or cold, from this river, or that source, etc. The collective impressions resulting from the fusion of all these individual impressions are then determined in form as well as in object, and, consequently, the common conscience has a defined character. But it changes its nature as societies become more voluminous. Because these societies are spread

over a vaster surface, the common conscience itself is obliged to rise above all local diversities, to dominate more space, and consequently to become more abstract. For not many-general things can be common to all these diverse environments. It is no longer such an animal, but such a species: not this source, but such sources: not this forest, but forest *in abstracto.*

Communication within small communities is likely to reflect the needs and the usages of what is called in recent sociological usage *high shared context* groups.

We can think of *shared context* as a continuum, with "high shared context" at one end and "low shared context" at the other. High context communication (restricted code in Bernstein's sense) is appropriate when there is considerable overlap of experience between communicators, and low context communication (elaborated code in Bernstein's sense) when little experience is shared. (Erickson, 1972)

An expansion of the social frame of reference, either because of an increase in the size of the population, or because of an increase in the diversity of experiences which need to be reported, leads to a decrease in the proportion of the context shared between subgroups of the community and between its individual members. Common meanings based on common experiences can no longer insure the commonality of meanings in language, ritual, law, and ultimately in a world view, based on commonly accepted definitions. A codification of culture by such shared definitions calls for a development of explicit rules, including statements about language. This, by definition, amounts to the development of abstraction.

The cultural development which results from such codifications can be tied to the historical appearance of identifiable codifiers: Confucius, the Buddah, Manu, Zaroaster, Solon, Socrates, and Plato.

A statement of the cultural-communicative needs in such situations can be taken from Confucius:

Tseu-lu said (to Confucius): "The Lord of Wei intends to place government in your hands. What do you consider the first thing to be done?" "The main thing is to correct the use of titles," answered the master. And he added: "If titles are not correct, words cannot conform to truth; if words do not conform to truth, the affairs (of state) have no success. . . . That the Wise Man commit no error in his words, that is sufficient." Good order depends entirely upon the correctness of language. (Granet, 1950)

Abstractive universals

It was suggested above that the increase in the number and the diversity of human encounters made it necessary to codify the culture in general and more particularly to codify communication. As words are the main tools of communication, the meanings of words need to be defined to make possible communication within low shared context groups.

This, in fact, is what Confucius called for. An example of a much more radical abstractive universalization can be found in Plato (Phaedo).

Have sight and hearing any truth in them? Are they not, as the poets are always telling us, inaccurate witnesses? And yet, even if they are inaccurate and indistinct, what is to be said of the other senses?—for you will allow that they are the best of them?

"Certainly," he replied.

Then when does the soul attain truth?—for in attempting to consider anything in company with the body she is obviously deceived.

"Yes, that is true."

Then must not existence be revealed to her in thought, if at all?

"Yes." . . .

. . . Well, but there is another thing, Simmias: Is there or is there not an absolute justice?

"Assuredly, there is."

And an absolute beauty and an absolute good?

"Of course."

But did you behold any of them with your eyes?

"Certainly not."

Or did you ever reach them with any other bodily sense? (and I speak not of these alone, but of absolute greatness, and health, and strength, and the essence or true nature of everything). Has the reality of them been perceived by you through the bodily organs? or rather is not the nearest approach to the knowledge of their several natures made by him who so orders his intellectual vision as to have the most exact conceptions of that which he considers?

"Certainly."

And he attains the knowledge of them in their highest purity who goes to each of them with the mind alone, not allowing when in the act of thought the intrusion of sight or any other sense in the company of reason, but with the very light of the mind in her clearness penetrates into the very light of truth of each. . . .

"There is an admirable truth in that, Socrates," replied Simmias.

And shall we proceed a step further and affirm that there is such a thing as equality, not of wood with wood, or of stone with stone, but that, over and above this, there is equality in the abstract? Shall we affirm this?

"Affirm, yes, and swear to it," replied Simmias, "with all the confidence in life." (Plato, B. Jowett translation, 1871)

Sympathetic magic, discussed in an earlier section, originated in the uncritical acceptance of experience, including the experience of one's own dreams and thoughts. Socratic and Platonic universalism was derived by abstraction, one example of which was the rejection of sensorial inputs. The corpus to which the abstractive mechanism was applied was described as another, purer world; a position which would not be easily acceptable today. The source of the thought which Socrates and Plato analyzed and refined is the same culture which the majority accepted without questioning. The manner in which they proceeded was thoughtful conversation—the same method by which, according to Piaget (1946, 1960, 1962, 1970), children resorb their egocentrism.

Conversation means words and words stand for universals: perfect equality, not only equality of wood with wood or stone with stone.

Abstractive rationalism (universalism) as guide for action

The basic tool of universalism is reason. It may be expected that the reorganization of knowledge according to its tenets will stress logic at the expense of experience in the elaboration of programs of action. An example may be found in Plato's *Laws*, a proposed constitution for a new city-state to be founded overseas.

The city should be placed as nearly as possible in the center of the country; we should choose a place which possesses what is suitable for a city, and this may be easily imagined and described.

The universalist always refers to his ideas as "well known" or "obvious," and to ideas contrary to his own as "incorrect"—but a comment on the lines above, made some twenty-five hundred years after they were written, is ". . . alas! that he took for granted precisely what we should like to know. . . ." (Mumford, 1961).

Then we will divide the city into twelve portions, first founding temples to Hestia, to Zeus, and to Athene, in a spot which we will call an Acropolis, and surround with a circular wall, making the division of the center city and country radiate from this point. The twelve sections shall be equalized by the provision that those which are good land shall be smaller, while those of inferior quality shall be larger. The number of lots shall be 5040, and each of them shall be divided into two, and every allotment shall be composed of two such sections, one of land near the city, the other of land at a distance. . . . And they shall distribute the twelve divisions of the city in the same way in which they divide the country, and every man shall have two habitations, one in the center of the country, the other at the extremity.

The program prescribes not only what is needed by the "public sector," but also the way in which private lives should be ordered: The public sector cannot operate with perfect smoothness, at the level which a theory unencumbered with reality requires, unless private idiosyncrasies are subordinated to it. Otherwise differences between the particulars subsumed under them become too important.

Let me first give the law of marriage in a simple form, which may be as follows: A man shall marry between the ages of thirty and thirty-five, or, if he does not, he shall pay such and such a fine, or shall suffer the loss of such and such privileges. This would be the simple law about marriage.

This simple law does not, however, satisfy the universalistic mentality, not because it is an invasion of privacy (such a criticism would be particularistic), but because it is a simple prescription, which might express an associative wisdom and not universalistic reason. The latter calls for a logical argumentation going back to the first axioms:

The double law would run as follows: A man shall marry between the ages of thirty and thirty-five, considering that after a sort the human race naturally partakes of immortality, of which all men have the greatest desire implanted in them; for the desire of every man that he become famous and not lie in the grave without a name, is only the love of continuance. Now, mankind are coeval with all time, and are ever following, and will ever follow, the course of time; in this way they are immortal, leaving children behind them, with whom they are one in the unity of generation. And for a man voluntarily to deprive himself of this gift of immortality, as he deliberately does who will not have a wife or children, is impiety. He who listens to the words of the law shall be free, and shall pay no fine; but he who is disobedient, and does not marry, when he has arrived at the age of thirty-five, shall pay a yearly fine of a certain amount, in order that his celibacy may not be a source of ease and profit to him; and shall not share honors which the young men in the state give to the aged.

What must be rejected are particular departures from the universal and timeless idea. One such departure is unexplained riches for some and unexplained poverty for others.

The first and highest form of the state and of the government and of the law is that in which prevails most widely the ancient saying that, friends have all things in common. Whether there is now, or ever will be, this communion of women and children and property, in which the private and the individual is altogether banished from life, and things which are by nature private, such as eyes and ears and hands, have become common, and in some way see and hear and act in common, and all men express praise and blame, and feel joy and sorrow, on the same occasions, and the laws unite the city to the utmost,—whether all this possible or not, I say no man, acting upon any other principle, will ever constitute a state more exalted in virtue, or truer or better than this.

Plato, contrary to some lesser men, had doubts as to the possibility of bringing such an ideal to life. So he proceeded to describe the next best thing:

Let them at once distribute their land and houses, and not till the land in common, since this sort of a constitution goes beyond their proposed origin, and nurture, and education. But in making the distribution, let the several possessors feel that their particular lots also belong to the whole city. . . . And in order that the distribution may always remain, they ought to consider further that the present number of families should be always retained, and neither increased nor diminished. This may be secured for the whole city in the following manner: Let the possessor of a lot leave the one of his children who is his best beloved, and one only, to be the heir of his dwelling, and his successor in the duty of ministering to the gods, the family and the state, as well the living as those who are departed; but of his other children, if he have more than one, he shall give the females in marriage according to the law to be hereafter enacted, and the males he shall distribute as sons to such citizens as have no children . . . [so] that the number of 5040 houses shall always remain the same. . . . In such an order of things, there will not be much opportunity for making money; no man either ought, or indeed will be, allowed to exercise any ignoble occupation. . . .

Further, the law enjoins that no private man shall be allowed to possess gold and silver, but only coin for daily use. . . . Wherefore our citizens . . . should have a coin passing current among themselves, but not allowed among the rest of mankind; with a view, however, to expeditions and journeys to other lands—for embassies or for any other occasion which may arise for sending out a herald, the state must also possess common Hellenic currency. If a private person is ever obliged to go abroad, let him have the consent of the archons and go; and if when he returns he has any foreign money remaining, let him give the surplus back to the treasury, and receive a corresponding sum in the local currency. And if he is discovered to appropriate it, let it be confiscated, and let him who knows and does not inform, be subject to curse and dishonor equally with him who brought the money, and also to a fine not less in amount than the foreign money which has been brought back. . . . No one . . . shall lend money upon interest. . . . And let every possession of every man . . . be publicly registered with the archons whom the law appoints.

What strikes in this program is the total lack of recognition of particulars and of the differences which they introduce. This applies to people who may not accept either giving their children for adoption, or who may have too many children to compensate exactly for the low number of children in other families. It applies also to topography: the new emplacement may or may not be suitable for a circular city. Why 5040 households? Because 5040 is the factorial of 7, and 7 is a lucky number. We are still close to numerology, which tries to read the future through mathematical operations.

Obviously, the total disregard of the particularity of human individuals calls for a modification of the proposed structure in the direction of particularity. The need for particularization can be met (with the usual imperfection) in two ways. The first one is based on the roles played by universalism and particularism. The opposition between the two was described so far as the derivation of concepts from associative clusters; this meant a movement from the particularities of individual or small group experiences towards definitions applicable in broader environments. The resulting paradigms can be subdivided into forms expressing attempts to adjust theory to practice. The resulting particularization can be described as neo-particularism: It is based *not* on a lack of universal categories, but on relegating those categories to the status of hypotheses which must be verified through action, that is to say under the influence of the particular circumstances under which the action is carried out. The mechanism which this process introduces is logical multiplication which provides the possibility of coming down from broad classes to individuals or other particulars. The result of the application of logial multiplication is the definition of particulars in a manner which ties them to the broader (universalistic) classes. In this manner the appropriateness of such particulars to actions undertaken within an environment makes it possible to determine the validity of the universals, or structures of universals, of which such particulars are examples.

The entire process is dominated by abstraction. An example of the mechanism is science. Its core is the evaluation of universalistic hypotheses (Pribram, 1945) by concrete and therefore particularized action. The process can be defined as neo-particularism: a process relying on particularism, not because appropriate universals were not yet developed, but because they needed validation or, possibly, transformation. What information is relevant is to a large extent determined by the universals under investigation.

This distinguishes this kind of particularism from paleo-particularism, which dominates learning at a stage at which abstractive universals have not yet been developed. The difference between paleo-particularism and neo-particularism may be illustrated by two examples. Let us begin with paleo-particularism:

Swinging-Lance used to have power from Life-Giver and also from Spruce before he gave it all up to become a Christian. He got power from Spruce in this way. There was one spruce standing close to the top of the mountain. Down below there was an ice-cold spring of water. Swinging-Lance knew that the tree was up there. . . . One time, just before high winds came from the east . . . that tree was acting funny. It moved like a masked dancer coming up to the fire. Swinging-Lance looked at the spring. There was this same tree growing at the spring. He looked up at the mountain where it had been. The tree was gone from there. Just oaks were growing up there. He drank from the spring. He thought and thought about it. He could not put it out of his mind. The tree was the same one. It looked the same, like a masked dancer's headdress waving to the east. (Opler, 1969)

Here is an absolute particular: an event and its consequences—magic power to the witness—with no attempt at placing it within a grid of universal ideas or general laws, with the possible exception of the transductive attitude according to which every particular happening can be associated with another particular happening.

Neo-particularism or nominalism can be contrasted with paleo-particularism as being a state of affairs within which universal concepts are known and used, but only *as mediators, not as statements of conclusions.*

The . . . scholastic doctrine, . . . taught that the heavenly bodies are un-alterable and incorruptible. This belief seems to have rested on the assumption (*fact*, as it then appeared) that the motions of the heavenly bodies were circular. The "elements"—of fire, air, water and earth—of which all sublunary objects were compounded, moved in straight lines towards the places proper to them, fire and air "upwards," water and earth "downwards." The elements thus have "contraries," away from which they move; all straight line movements, it was held, imply the existence of such a "contrary." But the heavenly bodies move in circles, thus their movement shows them to be without a "contrary." And that which is without a contrary must be exempt from generation and corruption, since, according to Aristotle, all generated objects proceed from their contraries and are corrupted again into contraries. . . .

It therefore follows that heavenly bodies are incorruptible. . . . Their circular movement is the only kind of movement "proper" to such perfectly realized creatures as the heavenly bodies; circular movement being held, it must be remembered, to be inherently "noble," "perfect." (Willey, 1953)

Galileo weakened the scholastic hold on the culture of the time not by using a logical argument against it, but by relying on careful observations and experiments. He rolled objects down an inclined plane, threw them down from the leaning tower of Pisa, and, above all, he observed the firmament through the telescope he had invented. He found mountains on the moon and spots on the sun, proving false the belief in their perfection. Even more, he rejected the Socratic-Platonic method of approaching problems through the mind alone. His method was observation, and all observations are particular happenings.

Galileo came after Plato, and the Greek philosophers had come after mythopoeic thought. This, again, suggests a developmental sequence of paleo-particularism–universalism–neo-particularism. Galileo's and Copernicus' rejection of the existing dogma did not take them back to the kind of particularism illustrated by the beliefs of the Ojibwa. Their particularism was of the kind which uses measurement, that is to say that is highly abstract.

The sequence paleo-particularism–universalism–neo-particularism may be considered as developmental: The lack of fit between a universalistic theory and the environment is solved in a manner which increases the amount of knowledge.

Another way in which the perception of an incongruity within the world view of the culture can be removed, may be described through Weber's categories of traditional, bureaucratic and charismatic leadership.

Tradition is associative: It perpetuates ways of doing which are not based on abstractive system-building, but on the randomness of history.

Bureaucracy is (or tries to be) rational, i.e., to function under the guidance of a system of abstractive rules.

Charisma is irrational by definition. It has no fixed place in history. It can appear before the development of a bureaucracy, or after it. It is often violent and always marked by excess. It is also associative.

Benedict's definition (1934) of the Dionysian type of cultures, as opposed to the Apollonian, shows that the earlier named are charismatic, and the latter ones sufficiently calm to permit reflection and either to maintain tradition or to develop new behaviors through abstraction.

Charismatic behavior only seldom characterizes the continuities of cultures; in most cases it represents more or less ephemeral social movements. As such it is analyzed in the chapter on social movements as associative reactions.

A summation

Several polarities between culturally determined behaviors were mentioned earlier. Most of them can be subsumed under the broader and more parsimonious polarity between association and abstraction.

This applies even to the contrasting ways of deriving identity on the basis of either ascription or achievement (or, of course, of various levels of coordination between the two). The polarity between the domination of ascription and the domination by achievement points out another facet of cultural development, which reinforces the general approach in which psychosocial transformations are tied to increases of the amount of information which must be organized within the context of different types of environment. The facet in question is the extent of the division of social labor. Where the division of social labor calls for a relatively small number of accepted definitions of social usefulness, ascription tends to be the dominant mechanism of social identification. Fixity and lack of change facilitate the play of self-fulfilling prophecies, each individual has his or her place in society, the overall picture is clear and, to a large extent, unchanging from generation to generation. The social coordinates of a person's birth defines what that person will do.

Where the number of activities is great, the role of self-fulfilling prophecies is bound to decrease. There appear professions, or socio-economic niches, which did not exist at the time of earlier generations. The ascription to the son or daughter of the father's and mother's places is no longer possible. The need for new types of labor open the possibility for an individual to select a new social niche, as long as his or her level and type of achievement fit the needs of the new society.

As for the needs of the society itself, the division of labor leads not only to the definition of new social identities, but also—at slightly later stages—to the development of a multiplicity of temporary roles which facilitate the smooth functioning of society and, at the same time, diffuse the subject's sense of identity. A person is not only a computer programmer, but also a commuter: two roles requiring different skills and conferring different kinds of prestige (Zijderveld, 1970).

An example of the frictions which may arise in contacts between people used to abstractive separations between affectively neutral role-behaviors and people used to affective and associative human relationships may be taken from Triandis et al. (1972). Greek domestics employed by Americans in Greece were described either as friendly, honest, willing to go beyond the required amount of work to help their employers, or as surly, lazy, and dishonest. The difference does not appear in most cases to be attributable to differences among the Greeks, but rather to the difference in the manners in which the servants are treated by their employers. Americans following the usual American practice of considering the relationship as limited to the appropriate and quasi-contractual roles of employers and employees were treated with suspicion and unfriendliness: The abstractiveness of their behavior did not meet the expectations of the Greeks. The latter were adapted to a more associative and affective culture, with strongly defined in-groups and out-groups. In such a context employers and employees should form an in-group—even if not an equalitarian one—and look upon one another as "whole persons" rather than as mere embodiments of roles. Those Americans who adapted to the degree of association called for were treated by their domestics with a friendliness going beyond the strict interpretation of their duties.

The polarity between ascription and achievement can be included under the more general evolution from association to abstraction, even if it does specify the area within which the concepts involved are particularly appropriate for the carrying out of analyses.

The situation is different in the case of particularism and universalism. The passage from paleo-particularism to universalism is an example of the passage from association to abstraction. But the passage from universalism to neo-particularism also depends on a renewed application of the abstractive mechanism. It seems in this case that analysis should be carried out in terms of three poles (paleo-particularity–universality–neo-particularity) rather than on a bipolar continuum. This question is explored in the next chapter.

There remains the question of charisma. The evolution in this case (if, indeed, the concept of evolution is appropriate) is in the direction of greater associativity, as a reversal of the more general tendency leading to the development of abstractive concepts. Since the "normal" pattern of change is based on an increase in the information to be organized, it may be assumed (pending a more thorough analysis) that charismatic movements lead to a decrease in the amount of information which the culture is capable of handling and to the exclusion (possibly through censorship) of some or many sources of information.

3

THE MODEL

with Christine G. Glenn

This chapter presents a model of information development and integration. The model provides a context for integrating the polarities described in the last chapter and the data presented for each polarity. The basic assumption underlying the model is that cognitive processes derive information from three separate sources. Each source provides certain limitations upon thought, and each provides a characteristic impetus to its development. Furthermore, each can be seen as conflicting to some degree with the two other ones. Before providing a rationale for the model, it may be useful to list the three selected sources. The rest of this chapter further defines these sources and examines their relationship to the concepts developed in the last chapter. The sources are:

1. The individual subject, characterized by the particularity of experiences, desires, wishes and dreams—and in slightly different terms, by the uniqueness of the way in which the conscious and subconscious are combined in every person.
2. The social group, characterized by public knowledge as opposed to private knowledge. The social group requires that its participants observe rules of mutual intelligibility—e.g., rules of logic as defined by the group.
3. The environment within which and upon which humans act. The main effect of the environment is to impose limits on the possibilities of action—of separating what can from what cannot be done.

It is hoped that the derivation of the model will establish the congruence between the influence of each area and one of three main epistemological styles:

1. *The intuitive.* Knowledge is sought through private experience. The individual subject absorbs and transforms information at both the conscious and the subconscious levels, and in consequence, is not always aware of how he or she arrived at some beliefs. Items of knowledge whose origins are unclear, are intuitions. Royce (1964) points out that the opposite of intuitive insight is the *absence* of insight; in this intuitionism differs from rationalism, as the latter admits the existence of illogical as well as of logical thought.
2. *The rational.* The rational approach seeks knowledge through the application of logical rules to an area of study.
3. *The empirical.* The empirical approach seeks validation through demonstration. The usefulness of ideas must be tested by applying them in the environment.

A theory of meaning

Zvegincev (1957; Glenn, 1959) sees linguistic meaning as the result of three main influences. Each can be viewed as exercising mutually divergent pulls. These are:

1. The structure of a particular language;
2. general (i.e., pan-cultural or humanely universal) laws of logic and thought;
3. the objective correlation to reality.

FIGURE 1:

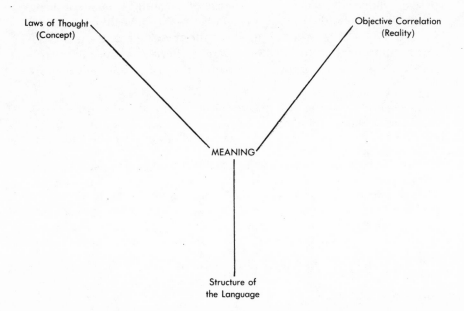

Laws of Thought (Concept)

Objective Correlation (Reality)

MEANING

Structure of the Language

Glenn (1973; 1974) transformed the Zvegincev model because of the following considerations:

1. The structure of one particular language as opposed to the universal laws of human thought (to the extent to which the latter can be discovered) amounts to the opposition between the idiosyncratic and the universal. It was natural for Zvegincev, whose main preoccupation was with lexicography, to place given natural languages—Russian, English, French, etc.—in a polar position. However, in the context of a preoccupation with a general theory of human behavior, natural languages represent the behavior of large groups, and therefore cannot be placed at an apex standing for the particular. Dialects, jargons, and passing linguistic fads would come closer, since they are spoken by fewer people and may have shorter histories. The ultimate particular, however, is the individual, and the ultimate particular in communication is the attempt to communicate the ineffability of personal experience. In consequence, the apex will be given the title of SUBJECTIVITY.

Clearly, complete subjectivity is not communicable, and the context of the definition of the model is communication. In consequence what will be discussed is not the pole itself, but rather the tendency to reach it—or better, to reach for it. Practically speaking this will often mean the communicative characteristics of small intimately acquainted groups, with a high level of shared contextual background.

2. There exist different systems of logic, and the general laws of human thought (if they exist) are unknown. However, since apex (1) was defined on the basis of the greatest possible communicative particularity, apex (2) should be defined as the greatest possible communicative universality. A symbolic system shared by as many people as possible, both in space and in time, would have to be characterized by total symbol stability across subjects and in time; in other words the meanings attached to its symbols would have to be invariant, constant in time, and the same for all communicating subjects. The ltter desideratum suggests the title of CO-SUBJECTIVITY—something which many subjects share identically, and to which they react identically.

3. "Reality" is a tempting title for the third apex: Unfortunately reality is not fully knowable. The best that can be hoped for are identical actions on the part of different subjects under given sets of circumstances, for example, the identical performance of experiments, with complete replicability of results (Bridgman, 1949). Another way of putting it may be that at this apex identical events or situational constraints lead different subjects to identical nonverbal behaviors. This apex, therefore, stands for behavior which is marginally influenced by subjective considerations but reflects, to the extent of the possible, total OBJECTIVITY.

Knowledge capable of being expressed symbolically, and the

symbolic systems which express it, can be seen as being derived from these three sources of information, the subjective, the co-subjective, and the objective. Systems and particular instances may be expected to differ in terms of the degree to which each is influenced by the separate apexes. This can be pictured as:

FIGURE 2:

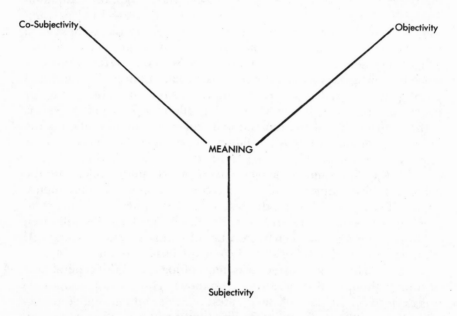

An important hypothesis is that each of the apexes implies requirements which are not compatible with the requirements implied by the other apexes. The next order of business is to show, how this model of meaning can be applied to an analysis of cultures and communication.

The tension between subjectivity and co-subjectivity

To examine the tension between subjectivity and co-subjectivity, one must examine situations in which the influence of the object apex is nil or minimal.

At the subjective apex (even if it is admitted that the apex represents not so much an isolated subject as small intimate groups), expression is restricted to the syntagmatic style, namely, a focus on the particular. One example might be a lovers' tête-à-tête. The emphasis is not on the physical world, but on establishing a private social relationship.

The situation is different as one moves toward the co-subjective apex. Here expression suggests signals defining actions to be undertaken identically and collectively. An example may be an army close order drill (Glenn, 1973).

Even in such simple situations there appears an important contrast between the subjective and the co-subjective: The subjective expressions are of indefinite duration and have unclear meanings. By way of contrast, the collective *rhythm* of a drill is more tightly defined. Note that in neither case is there anything which might be considered a reference to the outside world (i.e., to entities other than the subject or subjects). In Werner's sense (1961), the subjective example is diffuse, and the co-subjective one is articulated.

Related to the army drill is dance. Here groups of people can come together and act similarly. The extreme importance of dance and of ritual in preliterate cultures suggests a festal origin for communication. True enough, much of dance and most of ritual have referents outside the performers *themselves*. But it seems that the elements making collective action possible—rhythm in the first place—are more basic than the representative symbolizations involved.

The subjective—co-subjective dimension cannot be arbitrarily divided into "subjective behaviors" and "co-subjective behaviors." The comparison of behaviors must always be relative. For example, collective dances reflect a greater co-subjective influence than the private swayings or romantic promenades of a couple. Yet dances are often used to create feelings of oneness within a group. As will be discussed later in this chapter, dances and music are in part a reflection of in-group feelings and are a response to needs for subjectivity. An area which reflects the co-subjective pull to a greater extent than dance is mathematics. Consider the expression, $y = f(x)$. It can be said to refer to the objective world, but only in a minimal fashion: All of its symbols can be tied to variables in the external world, be they physical, economic, or other. Yet it is quite obvious that what is involved in mathematics is only marginally the physical entities which can be calculated; the gist of the mathematical approach is a certain way of thinking, and, at that, a way of thinking which is identical across subjects for any given operation. A point worth noting is that most branches of mathematics were developed before ways of applying them to problems of the objective world were known. An example of this historical anteriority is the title of "imaginary numbers" which was first used to describe what today are called negative numbers. As the practical application of the latter became more evident, the title was shifted to its present usage, that of numbers containing the operator $i = \sqrt{-1}$. In the context of this new definition, imaginaries appeared to be merely intellectual curiosities; their application in vectorial calculus and the application of vectorial calculus to physics came later.

Clearly mathematics has gone much further than rhythm in the direction of co-subjectivity: the number of people capable of following a rhythmic exercise—a dance or march, for example—is limited. The simultaneity which characterized the relatively primitive co-subjectivity of rhythm is no longer a condition of co-subjectivity in mathematics. This is because acting out a rhythm in common is usually tied with a shared affective state. Mathematics is affectively neutral (which makes it more abstractive than rhythm); it is capable of notation, and in its written form it carries identity of behavior over time; it is thus capable of being shared (at least potentially) by an unlimited number of individuals. Note that while rhythm is also capable of notation in music, music may mean different things to different listeners. The emotions it engenders are extremely private: as does all art, it reflects subjective influences as well as co-subjective ones.

The need for the evolution from subjectivity (or something close to it) towards co-subjectivity can be traced to the broadening of the social frame of reference.

Mutual intelligibility depends on the sharing of experiences; it makes little sense to talk about color with the congenitally blind. People whose experiences are similar—in limiting cases quasi-identical—can communicate with ease and in depth. Sharing experiences is easiest for those living together, or, at one step removed, for those belonging to the same social group. This suggests that communication will be easiest within small in-groups of people having associated for long periods of time. Within such social context the "units" of experience which must be named may be quite extensive. At the same time the verbal definitions of such units need not be precise; in many cases a simple allusion exchanged between intimates may bring about a wealth of common memories, of common intents—of common meanings.

The enlargement of the social frame of reference calls for the ability to communicate with strangers. The "bits" of experience shared among many become smaller. The need for defining the boundaries of units of meaning becomes greater. What corresponds to each word or expression must be precisely conceptualized.

Thus, the enlargement of the social and cultural frames of reference calls for the codification of language. Words and expressions are given the necessary constancy across subjects (and potentially in time) by being defined at a meta-language level.

The presence of codification is necessary for all social groups. However, the degree to which it is pursued and formalized varies. Furthermore, there have been periods in history during which the need for codification was consciously felt and expressed by the culture's philosophers and thinkers. Expressions of the need for codification can be found in the development of all great civilizations, Eastern as well as Western. In spite of such common needs, the extent of abstraction by which the codification is obtained differs from culture to culture.

The Greek philosophers, and the western civilization of which they were the initiators and the earliest spokesmen, went much further in the direction of co-subjectivity than did the divilizations of the East. The content of the wisdom of the East must be experienced to be known. The relation of master and disciple is extremely important in the transmission of wisdom; the participants live and experience together. Assuredly, their common experience is something else than that of everyday life; it is directed towards understanding, and often bolstered by meditation on written texts. At the same time it goes less far in the direction of co-subjectivity than does the knowledge of the West, transmitted mainly by the printed word in a manner which often makes any actual acquaintance between master and disciple unnecessary (see Northrop, 1953). Here again, mathematics considered as a language is an example of the highest level of abstraction.

It appears clear in the light of these considerations that the transformation of the communicative style, from subjective to co-subjective, is a consequence of social transformations. It is also a condition making such social changes possible.

Yet if social communication needs determine a movement from subjectivity toward co-subjectivity in some societies, psychological needs determine movements in the opposite direction in the very same societies. Central to these needs is the need for expressing the inexpressible—the ineffability of personal experience.

In the same way in which the evolution toward co-subjectivity determines universal concepts through abstraction from particular experiences, the reaction against this evolution seeks to derive the feeling of particularity and even uniqueness by suggesting associations. The prime examples of this technique can be found in fiction and in poetry: The very fact that fiction should be written—and read—is an example of the need for particularity, for fiction is almost always about supposedly particular individuals.

Let us look at some examples:

Trampling my shadow's bones into the concrete with hard heels and then I was hearing the watch, and I touched the letters through my coat. (William Faulkner, *The Sound and the Fury*)

The uniqueness of the combination of words suggests to the reader that he also participates in uniqueness, that the incommunicable has been communicated to him. The case is even clearer in poetry—perhaps because poetry gives the reader an even greater possibility of interpreting what he reads in his own manner, making it by definition unique and yet preserving the illusion of there being an interlocutor, the poet.

> Our boat is asleep in Serchio's stream,
> It sails are folded like thoughts in a dream,
> The helm sways idly, hither and thither;
> Dominic, the boatman, has brought the mast,
> and the oars, and the sails; but 't is sleeping fast,
> Like a beast, unconscious of its tether (P. B. Shelley, *The Boat*)

Thorne (1970) points out that the essence of the poetic style is the violation of the syntactical rules by which grammatically well-formed sentences are generated in systems such as Chomsky's (1965): Inanimate objects, such as boats, do not sleep. This violation permits the creation of a "new" language which can express things inexpressible in Standard English.

A second kind of "new" language is found in linguistic fads. Normal sentences such as "see you later" can be transformed in a number of ways which preserve their general form while modifying their meaning slightly, e.g., "see you at five," "see you at home." Stereotypic sentences of linguistic fads, however, cannot be transformed but must be understood and used in their totality, e.g., "see you later, alligator." While the possibility of substitution has been lost, an immediate expression of human warmth has been added. Linguistic fads are used by in-groups and are employed in part to define in-groups, characterized by a maximum of similarity between co-subjects (Glenn, 1973).

Let us note however, that while a maximum of similarity between subjects gives meaning even to somewhat cryptic expressions, the extent of the populations among which such expressions can be used is reduced.

Mukařovski (1953) describes devices such as adding the rhyme *alligator* as foregrounding an expression, giving it salience. Foregrounded expressions lose their salience through repeated usage; they become backgrounded, either falling into disuse or becoming idioms. Few know nowadays that "he's no great shakes" started in life as "he's no great Sheik" in the days when to be a Sheik or a Sheba was to be foregrounded socially. The multiplicity of such dead bones of former foregroundings shows both that the need for associative particularization is a constant one—and that it can never be finally satisfied.

Poetry and linguistic fads are not the only areas in which we can examine a pull away from shared co-subjectivity to more personal and private feelings of subjectivity. Similar situations may be found in crowd-reactions to the eloquence of charismatic leaders, and in the ability of strongly rhythmic music, such as that of martial marches or of dance, to create feelings of solidarity among those marching or dancing to it, or simply listening while almost feeling the corresponding kinesthetic experiences.

Such feelings may go from the quasi-private sharing within a couple—"they are playing our tune"—to the almost public emotional solidarity which surfaces at the playing of national anthems or which conjoins the members of one generation at the playing of dance music in a style characteristic of its time.

The importance of music as a means for sharing in-group feelings has been noted by others:

> So Elvis Presley came, strumming a weird guitar and wagging his tail across the continent, ripping off fame and fortune as he scrunched his way, and, like a latter-day Johnny Appleseed, sowing seeds of a new rhythm and style in the white souls of the white youth of America, whose inner hunger or need was no longer satisfied with the antiseptic white shoes and whiter songs of Pat Boone. "You can do anything," sang Elvis to Pat Boone's white shoes, "but don't you step on my Blue Suede Shoes." (Eldridge Cleaver, *Soul on Ice*)

Such musical fads may be referred to as "near public" because of the clear indication that the solidarity of the in-group calls for the rejection of the out-group. To be truly public, sharing must be open to all. This unavoidably robs it of personality. The very intensity of personal involvement in an in-group prevents the broadening of the in-group into extensive co-subjectivity: The equilibrium between the needs of subjectivity and those of co-subjectivity is often an uneasy one. Sharp oppositions between in-group and out-groups are expressions of the difficulty involved.

Coincidence of the evolution from the associative towards the abstractive with the evolution from paleo-particularism towards universalism

Let us have another look at the process of conceptualization. Concepts can be defined in terms of a network of sign-significate inferences (Bruner et al., 1956). The use of any concept therefore implies a set of information including observable properties in the case of concrete objects, functional attributes, positive or negative connotations, etc. The very use of a concept therefore carries with it a set of inferences.

Similarly, the act of categorization results in a set of inferences. For example, to tell someone that a sparrow is a bird implies that a sparrow is an animal with wings, a beak, etc.

The manner in which such networks of inferences become parts of public rather than private knowledge is agreement on the placement of criterial boundaries delimiting the content of the category. This amounts to abstraction and the elimination of the particularity of individual experience as irrelevant to the process of inference. It also amounts to universalization (at least to a degree), by the very fact of making public knowledge possible.

This process is not limited to concrete words. The definition of social concepts is similar though sometimes more implicit. For example, the way in which Greeks regard authority figures depends on whether the authority figure belongs to the in-group or the out-group. Such figures are typically seen as concerned and benevolent persons when they belong to the perceiver's in-group; they are seen as competitive when they belong to an out-group (Triandis et al., 1972).

Obviously two in-groups would make different inferences, i.e., harbor different conceptualizations of an authority figure which belongs to one of them but not to another. The definition of a common network of inferences, i.e., a common conceptualization, can be made possible only through the elimination of the in-group–out-group difference. Conversely, the definition of such common conceptualizations perforce leads to the elimination of at least some of the barriers separating the groups.

Thus abstraction and universalization coincide—at least up to this point.

The tension between co-subjectivity and objectivity

The essence of the tension between co-subjectivity and objectivity is that between theory and action.

Broad co-subjectivity means a broad sharing of symbols and meanings—not the "truth" of these meanings or their applicability in action directed at objects. It consists of sets of culture specific beliefs. An example of co-subjective belief systems which are not closely tied to the objective world, is myths. Every culture has its own myths. Myths vary widely from culture to culture, even when they are derived from the same objective reality. Consider for example two sun myths. In Hawaii, the sun was believed to be so lazy that it rushed across the sky in three or four hours, so as to be able to sleep longer. This did not allow the tapa cloth to dry properly. Mauii, a culture hero, solved the problem by fashioning sixteen ropes to tie the Sun's sixteen legs. Mauii caught the sun and tied it to a tree. He and the sun then worked out a compromise: The sun was set free in return for shining longer (Eliade, 1963).

A second example is the Greeks' sun myth. According to this myth, the sun was a golden chariot pulled by four horses and ridden by Apollo. Let us note in passing that the extent to which the Greeks used war chariots was probably minimal, but they were in contact with cultures which made great use of these implements.

It is important to note that while each myth may possess a poetic beauty, there is no compelling reason to adopt one over the other. Thus, if one believed in the story of Mauii, there is no clear reason to give it up for a belief in Apollo. This indicates that many of the co-subjective beliefs of a culture are limited in their co-subjectivity, that is, in the possibility of being shared universally. There are two ways in which belief systems can become suitable for increased acceptance. The first is a pull from co-subjectivity to a broader co-subjectivity via increased abstraction. The second is a pull from co-subjectivity to objectivity via empirical demonstration. While the latter mechanism is more relevant to this section, both will be discussed briefly.

The first mechanism requires the broadening of co-subjective beliefs. This is done by basing the beliefs on increasingly general underlying principles; there is an attempt to logically prove the validity of the beliefs. Beliefs are no longer presented as a series of descriptive statements as in a story, but are presented as a logical argument in which conclusions logically follow from previous premises. The two sun myths can be compared to the Aristotelian theory. It is based on the assumptions that the physical world is imperfect, yet perfection must exist elsewhere as we have the concept of perfection. It must therefore reside in the heavens. Furthermore, there are only two geometric figures which are perfect, i.e., without eccentricities; these are the circle and the sphere. Therefore, all celestial bodies are perfect spheres moving in perfect circles. Note that this view depends on a systematic and impersonal logic to a greater extent than the sun myths. This led to its acceptance beyond the confines of ancient Greece. It achieved an extent of co-subjectivity to which neither the myth of Mauii nor the myth of Apollo's golden chariot could pretend. Note that this view is not "correct," as based on later findings; yet it is co-subjectively appealing.

The second mechanism by which co-subjective belief systems can achieve wider acceptance or applicability involves the use and incorporation of objectively-derived information as a source of validation. This is central to the relationship between the co-subjective and objective apexes. To readers immersed in the highly pragmatic culture of America it will seem obvious that a belief system which can explain or make sense of one's observations is more attractive or valid than one that does not. The theory that the earth is round is more attractive than one stating that the world is flat because of what each can explain, not because either in isolation is more logically perfect.

The appeal of the objective as a means for validating co-subjective beliefs should be obvious. However, it should not be overstated. Changing one's conceptual system is a difficult process and there is a great deal of psychological inertia to overcome. Historically, changes were often long, difficult, and even bloody. One example was the opposition to the recognition of the sun rather than the earth as the center of our planetary system. Kuhn (1973) has more recently documented the difficulty in changing scientific conceptual systems. It is often difficult to determine what are the relevant observations or how to evaluate them. The ascendency of a given scientific paradigm over another is typically determined by the scientific commmunity as a whole and over time.

The difficulty in changing conceptual systems indicate the extent of the possible antagonism between theoretical formulation and observation. It is hardly necessary to indicate the possible harmony between the two; most observations are undertaken to verify rather than to disprove theories. They are guided by theoretical thought, and in most cases support it. Nonetheless, where repeated disagreement between observation and experiment makes a theoretical paradigm untenable, new theoretical formulations become the new orthodoxy—i.e., the new co-subjectivity. The dialectical relationship of thesis–antithesis–synthesis is even clearer between co-subjectivity and objectivity than between subjectivity and co-subjectivity.

This discussion of the co-subjective–objective polarity has focused on the validation of co-subjective theories by objective information. Movements in the reverse direction are also possible. Fortuitous observations can serve as the impetus for new codifications, i.e., co-subjective formulations. For example, Columbus' fortuitous discovery of America required the recognition of vast new lands and the incorporation of this information into the Europeans' conception of the world. The discovery of penicillin was also fortuitous. It created the context for later conceptual breakthroughs in understanding the biochemical mechanisms underlying penicillin's effectivenss and, more generally, in understanding the metabolism of bacteria and the specific effects of various antibacterial agents. A point to be noted is that the twentieth century co-subjective system was ready to incorporate antibiotics in the world view. Penicillin was in use in Poland in the seventeenth century. However, there was no niche for it in the systematic world view, and it fell into disuse instead of becoming conceptualized.

We are now at a point at which we can examine the co-subjective–objective dimension in terms of the polarities described in the last chapter. With regard to co-subjectivity—objectivity processes, movement in either direction involves abstractive thought. For example, in order to examine a codified theory in terms of objective data, it is necessary to define what part of the objective world one is to examine. Objects must be broken down into components or traits and the traits which are relevent are examined. The process of breaking down or categorization is the hallmark of abstractive thought. A quintessential example of objective scrutiny is the process of measuring. Measurement can only be obtained by isolating the variable to be measured. If one has a theory concerning the relationship between height and weight, people must be examined in terms of height and weight only; race, religion, color of eyes, personal mannerisms must all be regarded as irrelevant. Thus all other associations must be ignored. The same process characterizes movement from objective observations to co-subjective theories. For example, if one has made a number of observations and wishes to develop a conceptual framework capable of organizing them, it will be necessary to identify shared dimensions. For example, the category of bird can only be developed after different birds have been observed. The process of categorization will involve making some attributes salient and therefore central to the concept, while others will become irrelevant. Thus wings are a salient feature of birds while the color of wings is not. Again, this process is abstractive.

A second problem to be considered is the relationship between the co-subjective–objective dimension and the universalistic–particularistic polarity.

The objective apex refers to transactions between the individual and the environment; this necessarily implies actions of some sort. Action is unavoidably particularized, as it necessitates interaction with specific objects at specific times. Therefore, the objective apex must coincide with particularism of one or another kind. It was noted earlier that a distinction can be made between paleo-particularism, the focussing on the particular without any awareness of category boundaries and of the logic of classes, and neo-particularism, the focussing on the particular joined with an awareness of categories and of the logic of classes, the latter being capable of providing hypotheses as to what to examine. This distinction is very important at this juncture. An awareness of conceptual systems is the result of thought guided by a highly developed co-subjectivity, i.e., by formalization instigated to allow and expand communication. Objectivity guided by co-subjectivity leads to neo-particularism;

it calls for the possibility of replicability. In its most structured form, replicability takes the form of experimentation, which is very clearly guided by co-subjectivity. Of course, most action is not subject to the rigorous standards of experimentation; nonetheless, most of us do expect a degree of consistency in our transactions with the physical world. If we see a tree in a certain place in the morning we fully expect it to be there in the evening; we are guided by concepts of physical permanence. The extent to which such beliefs dominate thinking depends on the culture. In consequence the encounters between different subjects and the same objective environment may be registered in a variety of ways. In preliterature cultures

> an object is not thought of as the sum of all sense data connected with it. A mountain is not thought of as a unified whole. It is neither static, nor is it a series of inherently connected impressions. It is a continually changing entity from which one is repeatedly subtracting and to which one is repeatedly adding. In the case of the idea of a tree this lack of unification is, of course, even more marked. The talk of a tree being the same when it is constantly undergoing transformations is based on an assumption which the man of action simply does not make. . . . He conceives the possibility of imagining it having an entirely different appearance on the following day. (Radin, 1953)

A cognitive situation of this type cannot be understood as a wrong theory coming into conflict with objective inputs. There is no wrong theory in this case, but rather an absence of theory. "True" knowledge is unlikely to be derived from closer observation; before experiments can be devised a theory must be developed.

There are some fields which deal with the objective world which must be particularistic. Furthermore, some of these must be neo-particularistic. For example, engineering, as exemplified in bridge building, is based on theoretical knowledge. In spite of that, each bridge is a particular, designed to meet the specific conditions of its purpose and its site. It must lean in the direction of neo-particularity and objectivity.

Other fields have weaker objective constraints. They can therefore vary in their emphasis on universalistic or particularistic reasoning. Differences between practices can be more easily attributed to cultural differences. One such field is that of public administration.

In cultures tending towards universalism, uniform practices prevail. It appears inconceivable to the French that the territorial subdivisions of the postal service might not coincide with the boundaries of townships or states. In the neo-particularistically inclined United States the postal service often disregards boundaries established for other purposes: to reach the suburban subdivision of Glen Farms, in Cecil County, Maryland, mail must be addressed to Newark, Delaware, of which Glen Farms is factually a suburb. Pragmatic convenience prevails over conceptual orderliness in some cultures; conceptual orderliness prevails in other ones.

In summary, the objective apex involves particularistic thought while the co-subjective apex tends toward universalism. A culture's understanding of the objective world can be either paleo-particular or neo-particular, depending upon the extent to which abstractive thought is emphasized in the culture and correspondingly on the extent to which the co-subjective apex is developed and influences the perception of the objective.

The tension between subjectivity and objectivity

The tension between these two apexes will often appear as that between desires or thoughts untainted by attempts to analyze them logically or to test them empirically, and the possibilities of their relization. It reflects the subject's self-image and the world's constraints. In situations in which desires map easily onto possibilities, the tention between the apexes is weak. Conversely, when there is no easy or obvious match, the tensions will be experienced more radically.

The degree of tension generated is related in part to the size and the development of a society. In small homogeneous communities, there are relatively few dominant roles. These roles can be internalized easily by an individual, and one's status is thereby determined in one's own eyes and those of the community. Furthermore, the environment is organized so that the roles can be carried out. In these communities, private desires and socially acceptable action tend to be in harmony. In larger communities, there are many more possibilities or choices of action and individuals tend to play many roles. This may result in the poor or incomplete internalization of roles. In these situations, the possibility for tension is greater. If the tension is too great, individuals may attempt to resolve it by temporary escapism or permanent withdrawal from the given environment, by promoting another form of community including the formation of gangs (Thrasher, 1927; Yablonsky, 1962), by following religious or political messianism (Cantril, 1941), or by searching for counter-cultural attitudes (Roszak, 1969).

In terms of the polarity discussed earlier, the subjective and objective apexes reflect associative and abstractive processes respectively. The subjective apex includes the composite of numerous experiences, of the feelings and goals they engender, and of the private thoughts which can result from them. All thoughts and feelings can be entertained. This composite is necessarily diffuse. Ambiguities exist and need not be recognized. For example, the desire to do something is always accompanied by the idea or the possibility of not doing it. Often a desire for an object or action is accompanied by a fear of the same object or action. As long as one remains within the confines of the subjective there is no impetus for resolving such ambiguity. The need for resolution or clarification only arises when there is a need to conceptualize or communicate one's perceptions (a pull to the co-subjective) *or* when there is a need to act (a pull to the objective). The diffuse organization of information at the subjective apex is the mark of associative thought. As one moves to the objective pole, ideas must be tested against the objective environment; this requires action. An action necessarily requires a decision, i.e., the definition of the action to be undertaken. While all ideas can be entertained, all actions cannot be performed. Furthermore, the environment will reinforce or allow some actions and not others. In constant and often subtle ways, the environment will reinforce certain courses of action over others. Patterns of behavior will emerge. These patterns are well defined in the sense that action A means doing one thing and not doing another at that time and place. This delineation is a mark of abstraction—one action has been abstracted out of a myriad of possible actions.

It should be noted that the results of abstraction at the co-subjective apex are different from those at the objective apex. The co-subjective world requires communication and results in the need and the tendency to define and conceptualize. Symbols are attached to concepts and logical operations emerge to manipulate symbol systems. For example, words are attached to objects and grammars develop to organize words. There is a conscious component to the use of symbols.

The objective world requires possible or acceptable action. While it requires choices between actions, it does not in itself require conscious conceptualizations. One can behave without symbolically representing the reasons for the action or all the cues which triggered the action.

The relationship between the three apexes and associative and abstractive processes can be represented in the following diagram.
FIGURE 3:

As one moves from subjective sources of information to either those of co-subjectivity or objectivity there is a concomitant need for abstractive thought. As one moves in the opposite direction, there is an increase in associative thought. Abstractive thought characterizes movement in either direction between the co-subjective and objective apexes. If developed to its fullest extent, movement between these two apexes describes theory building. Theory guides action which provides new observation; the observations are used to change or modify the theory; the new theory guides new actions, etc.

The three medians: Subjectivity and theoretical systems defining reality

The preceding sections discussed the tensions between the three apexes of the model, each representing a different informational source and impetus for thought. The following sections define the model more completely by discussing the tensions along the medians.

The first median begins with the subjective apex. This apex represents the particularity of each individual. The point opposite this apex dissects the co-subjective—objective dimension. Points along this dimension are influenced by co-subjective and objective experience. They therefore reflect attempts to develop symbol systems incorporating objective information. A point along this continuum can therefore represent theoretical systems defining "reality."

The inherent conflict between such theoretical systems and the subjective apex should be apparent. Any theoretical system is by definition an attempt to generalize across a number of specific situations. As such it will lose the uniqueness of any particular experience; conversely, the subjective is a composite of unique personal experiences.

As an example of this conflict, one can examine the role of expertise in society. The training of specialists is abstractive, as the problems to be solved by them and the manners of their solution are delimited and well defined. This can be contrasted with the lack of boundaries which characterizes charismatic leadership. Charismatic leadership is based on the uniqueness of the leader, who in turn extolls the uniqueness of the in-group members.

Historically, the two polar opposites in the field of educational ends are: to awaken charisma, that is heroic qualities or magical gifts; and to impart specialized expert training. The first type corresponds to the charismatic-

type of domination; the latter type corresponds to the *rational* and bureaucratic (modern) structure of domination. The two types do not stand
opposed, with no connections or transitions between them. The warrior
hero or the magician also needs special training, and the expert official
is generally not trained exclusively for knowledge. However, they are polar
opposites of types of education and they form the most radical contrasts. . . .

The charismatic procedure of ancient magical asceticism and the hero
trials, which sorcerers and warrior heroes have applied to boys, tried to
aid the novice to acquire a "new soul," in the animistic sense, and hence,
to be reborn. Expressed in our language, this means that they merely
wished to *awaken* and to test a capacity which was considered a purely
personal gift of grace. For one can neither teach nor train for charisma.
Either it exists *in nuce*, or it is infiltrated through a miracle of magical
rebirth—otherwise it cannot be attained.

Specialized and expert schooling attempts to *train* the pupil for practical
usefulness for administrative purposes—in the organization of public authorities, business offices, scientific or industrial laboratories, disciplined
armies. In principle this can be accomplished with anybody, though to
varying extent. (Weber, 1951)   The efficiency of specialized expertise is undeniable. The reverse of the coin is that it confronts the
individual with a fragmented picture of reality.

The modern mind was conformed to the pluralization of the world
through specialization which cuts reality into little pieces, each piece being
the domain of a relatively small group of experts. These experts discuss
the theories within their own little group where they apply their own
"secret language." (Zijderveld, 1970)

The role of experts is not limited to discussions incomprehensible to the layman. They also take or determine decisions which confront laymen, and which they often understand no better than the
discussions which led to them. They feel faced with incomprehensible
abstractions instead of being faced with human motivations, which one
has at least the illusion of understanding. Their own daily routine is
fragmented into roles—breadwinner, commuter, spouse,
citizen—seemingly unconnected among themselves.

There may ensue various forms of reaction—against bureaucracy and against abstractive rationality itself:

A curious element of this anarchism is the inability or unwillingness to
distinguish between authoritarianism and authoritativeness. When I visited
a number of communes in the company of a highly experienced organic
farmer, we found that many commune members resented and would not
accept his advice on quite elementary but serious mistakes they were making in their first attempts at vegetable gardening. They accepted and loved
the man as a person, but mistrusted any knowledge not gained by their

own trial and error. Some communes have had to suffer epidemics of hepatitis or dysentery because of a stubborn unwillingness to adopt fundamental health precautions that had not grown out of their own experience. (Zablocki, 1971)

The rejection of the knowledge of others, no matter how authoritative, is often accompanied by a willingness to accept one's own experience in the most uncritical manner:

The antinomian strain in communes, in most cases, comes from the psychedelic experience. The individual "sees" that moral codes are games, that all morality is relative and arbitrary, and that the ultimate force behind all morality is not authority but love. Love is seen as an active force, holding things together, and, in so far as a member is judged, it will not generally be so much by his actions as by his vibrations. (Zablocki, 1971)

There is little realization that love within the in-group often leads to hate for the out-group. In the absence of all critical control, such hatred is *felt* to be fully justified. The main thing to be feared is depersonalization. The main thing to be trusted is one's own feelings of goodness.

Tension between ideology and privatism

Ideology is co-subjective—at least to the extent to which it is shared. Concentration on one's private life calls for a synthesis between the subjectivity of wishes and desires, and the objectivity necessary to manipulate the outside world, the world whose objects may be people as well as things. Thus ideology and privatism stand at the opposite ends of a median of the triangle, and may be expected to be mutually antagonistic.

FIGURE 4:

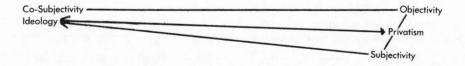

An example may be the situation in Eastern Europe, particularly among the young. They are prone to commit what in Soviet parlance is the sin of "indifferentism": an attitude of deliberate disinterest towards the ruling ideology, and, for that matter, towards ideology in general:

> If they aren't interested in defecting, these relatively sophisticated young East Europeans aren't much interested in Communist theology either. They laugh openly at the formal indoctrination they are given. A young Czech whose duty it has been to teach ideology to young army officers in Prague reports that his classes are devoted to discussing sports. (Kaiser and Morgan, 1973)

What people are interested in are: the struggle for a flat, a job, and adequate living. Once these basics obtained, many young people seek

> widening contacts with Western ideas, fashions and fads. At the most superficial level, blue jeans, wide watch bands and mini-skirts are the most prized items in clothing collections. (Kaiser and Morgan, 1973)

A movement in the opposite direction can be found in America and in Western Europe, where a surfeit of consumers' goods leads to a hunger for ideology. The contrast between the consensus of the 1950s and the conflict of the 1960s and to some extent even the 1970s illustrates this tendency. Explaining it on the basis of Viet Nam leads, at best, to the identification of a precipitating cause: It applies only to the United States, whereas the search for ideology or at least for a cause affected the entire Western world, and in particular the youth of western countries (Glenn, 1969).

A better explanation is found in the following:

> The January 1969 issue of . . . Fortune magazine published the results of an in-depth survey of young people between the ages of eighteen and twenty-four. The study indicated that about 750,000 of the nation's 6.7 million college students now "identify with the New Left," and that two-fifths of the group—about 3 million—"are defined . . . mainly by their lack of concern about making money." (Newfield, 1969)

The polarity between ideology and privatism can be identified with the opposition between collective and self-orientation in the context of large and relatively mobile societies. It is unlikely to be strong in small or fragmented societies in which private lives are thoroughly imbedded in the life of the group, without *necessarily* giving rise to any consciously formulated ideology. Among the youth of the 1960s joining the Establishment is often accompanied by a refusal to conceptualize anything beyond the level of pragmatic necessity.

Tension between social identity and pragmatic requirements

The middle of the side leading from subjectivity to co-subjectivity can be interpreted as the synthesis between the social definition of identity and the interiorization of this identity by the self: in Mead's terms (1934) as the self presented by the generalized other. This social identity may be in agreement or in conflict with the possibilities of pragmatic action, represented in the model by the objective apex. Conflict is particularly likely in times of rapid technological change: For example, the problems of relocating labor in new industries cannot be limited to their purely economic aspects.

FIGURE 5:

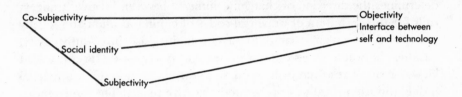

An example of conflicts arising along this dimension may be the feelings of alienation of Appalachian coal miners relocated in textile and electronic industries after the closing of some mines. The self-definition of these men was destroyed by incompatibility between two inputs: on the one hand the traditional self-image and social image of the miner, which includes such characteristics as courage and physical strength, and on the other the requirements of the new jobs to which strength and courage were irrelevant, but which called for patience and dexterity—traditionally women's virtues in the sub-culture.

A more far-reaching example of conflict along this dimension is the contemporary situation of women. The shift from jobs associated with muscle power to jobs associated with brain power makes them the equals of men in many occupations, i.e., at the objective apex. However, women's sense of identity derived from both subjective and co-subjective practices still differs vastly from men's self-images. The resulting conflict tends to erode both the situation at the objective apex (for example, by job discrimination) and in the area of identity definition. There is a clear kinship between the polarity described above and the opposition between ascription and achievement.

Development and evolution

The model presented above is based on three main and three subsidiary polarities. The dialectical opposition within each of these suggested tensions might be resolved either through compromises leading to cultural stability, or through syntheses representing new forms of behavior and leading to cultural evolution.

The main cause of evolution (where it does take place) appears to be the amalgamation of relatively small communities into broader societies, followed in some cases by an increase in social mobility within such societies. The resulting increase in contacts between individuals determines the direction of change; commerce between relative strangers calls for the definition of universal codes of communication and legally permissible behavior, that is to say to an increase in co-subjectivity. Clashes between different co-subjective systems—different world views—may be resolved by a recourse to the arbitration of an impartial judge: the scientifically apprehended objective reality. The *resultant* discovery of new ways of behaving in contact with objects (science, technology, economic and administrative organization) lead to new subjective experiences. These, in turn, must be codified in up-datings of the co-subjective system.

Thus, in addition to swings back and forth along each of the polarities, there may develop a clockwise rotation around the model triangle. This rotation should be visualized as increasing the size of the illustrative figure. From a small triangle, in which the distances between the apexes are minimal, and in which stable accommodations between the three requirements of meaning are likely to prevail, the transformation leads to a large triangle, in which the distances between apexes are sufficient to accentuate their mutual incompatibility. Cultures to which the latter illustration applies become instable. They tend to develop in the direction of greater abstraction (as indicated above). However, such overall development may be interrupted by reactions leading temporarily towards greater associationism and subjectivity. Nazism was only the most striking of such regressive episodes.

FIGURE 6:

Instable Cultures

Stable Cultures

The area of each triangle is illustrative of the total amount of information available to the culture.

Conclusions

The preceding section concludes the derivation and the presentation of the model. The question now is whether the model can be helpful in analyzing the patterns of thought underlying cultural differences and conflicts, whether the latter occur between or within national cultures.

This is done in two groups of chapters. The first group is intended to specify the psychological, sociological, political, and linguistic implications of the model. The second group contrasts a number of cultural types by actual examples, bearing on the cultures of societies and on the cultural bases of social movements.

4

A COGNITIVE THEORY—PSYCHOLOGICAL IMPLICATIONS OF THE MODEL

with Christine G. Glenn

Cognitive psychology is based on the assumptions that individuals develop internal representations of their environment, and that these representations are used to interpret all new experiences. The perception or interpretation of all situations or experiences is therefore a joint function of the situation and the individual's related knowledge. Bartlett (1932) defined these representations as schemata which he considered as organized sets of experiences. Piaget (1962) described this process as the assimilation or interpretation of experiences in terms of existing schemata, and the accommodation or modification of schemata in light of slightly diverging experiences. Transactional psychologists (Cantril, 1950; Kilpatrick, 1961) described the encounter between subject and object as a transaction in which the precise influence of each component on the transaction cannot be completely determined.

An example of this process can be taken from visual perception.

The sizes of the objects we see are not communicated to us directly. What the eye senses is the aperture of the angle between the eye itself and the extremities of the object being perceived. Objects of different sizes may subtend the same angle, since the extent of the aperture is caused not only by the size but also by the distance of the object. From a strictly optical point of view, everything we *see* is ambiguous. Yet what we *perceive* is seldom ambiguous. There must be cues which enable us to select between various possible interpretations.

Cantril, Ittelson, and Kilpatrick (Ittelson and Kilpatrick, 1961) built an experimental room with slanting walls, floor and ceiling. The different elements of the structure were so placed as to subtend the same angles in the eyes of a viewer as would the elements of a "normal" room. The experimental structure was perceived as normal, even though the subjects were aware of the conditions of the experiment. However, after an apprenticeship during which the subjects bounced balls, touched points on walls with a pointer, and in general acted physically within the distorted room, their perception of it changed and they saw it as it was.

This experiment, and many more like it, show that

1. perception depends on the subject and not only on the object;
2. the contribution of the subject to the total transaction depends, at least in part, on the previous experience of the subject, i.e., on memory;
3. different subjects, and the same subjects at different times, may bring different contributions to cognitive transactions.

These points—made in the context of an experiment which invariably surprises even people fully aware of the setup—are much easier to accept if one thinks, not in terms of the usual interpretation of knowledge, but in those of adaptation. Doing so brings in an additional understanding that

4. the same subjects, facing the same object, may participate in different transactions, depending on the cognitive context they bring to the situation. For example, subjects aware of the distorted nature of the room at the conceptual level, find the room to be normal at the perceptual level.

This suggests the possibility of cognitive conflict within individuals as well as between individuals. The question is discussed later in this chapter.

Equilibrium with what?

Equilibration, in the Piagetian sense, means the development of the subject towards the ability to organize ever increasing amounts of information and to adapt to increasingly broader environments.

The model in the preceding chapter suggests that the search for adaptation proceeds in three different directions, based on three different types of transactional definition. It was noted earlier that it is not possible to eliminate fully the influence of either the subject or the object from any transaction, and that it is impossible to fully determine the share of each in any given transaction. However, it is possible to define broad qualitative categories based on probable subject behavior at each of the three apexes of the model triangle.

1. *Objectivity* is shaped to the maximum possible degree by the object and to the minimum possible extent by the subject. The definitions of transactions tend to be dominated by the characteristics of the object. This means that different subjects can act in an identical manner in the context the same object—or that a description of the object can be constant across many or all subjects.

A paradox should be noted at this point. The domination of a transaction by the object means a good adaptation of the subject to the object; this, in turn, suggests the capacity of the subject to manipulate the object or the environment. Object-dominated cognitions lead to the possibility of subject-dominated behavior. A comparison between play and actions directed at the environment may serve as an example. The transactions of play are clearly more subject dominated than similar behaviors directed at reality. Yet play comes earlier in man and in most vertebrates than actions which are "for real." Groos (1898, 1901) considered play as a pre-exercise of behaviors used by the subject after the latter has adapted to a broader range of reality, or acquired a richer repertory of object dominated transactions.

A point to be noted is that the feedback at the objective apex comes mainly from the environment.

2. Where objectivity calls for the broadest possible contact between the subject and the environment, *co-subjectivity* calls for adaptation to a portion of the environment: the human group to which the subject belongs. There are many areas of behavior which call for similarity between the co-subjects and which are only marginally connected with the broader environment. Many cosmologies which united (or still unite) peoples and societies have been found erroneous or irrelevant in the context of a broader environment. However, error or irrelevance does not necessarily lead to the elimination of beliefs, as it might be expected if the only bases for judgment have been objective ones. The co-subjective cannot be denied. Let us go back to a type of situation found often in preliterate cultures.

> As he was paddling upstream, Ewangi was pulled out of his canoe by a crocodile and was never seen again. The news of his disappearance reached Dido village. War canoes were sent to the spot. One of the men who was in the canoe with Ewangi at the time of his death and a man who lived on the shore at this point were arrested, accused of witchcraft and condemned to death. (G. Hawker, quoted by Lévy-Bruhl, 1910)

Actions of this type suggest poor objective adaptation. Yet such an adaptation must have been sufficient for the population concerned; otherwise the community characterized by the belief that saurians are dangerous only when used by a witch could not have survived. The why of such beliefs is that they can be shared. The sharing of beliefs may be more useful from the co-subjective point of view than it is harmful within the context of objectivity.

3. *Subjectivity* characterizes behaviors and beliefs calling for a minimum of contact with the object and a maximum of freedom for the subjects to seek within themselves the feedback generated by their own thought and affect. Dreams are a prime example; love, hate and even artistic creation also fall in this category. Finding friends and lovers often proceeds through a search for common feelings; at the same time this community must differ from the overall attitudes of the entire culture. Friends and lovers must not only become tied among themselves, they must also be separated from the mass of the total population.

The process of adaptation, which is at the same time the process of acquiring knowledge, calls for trading off between adaptations to different environments: subjectivity and co-subjectivity in the example above.

The next problem is to examine this question in connection with the mechanisms of association and abstraction.

Association and abstraction

The subjective, co-subjective, and objective apexes were presented as a description of a minimum number of areas of adaptation necessary for the description of cognitive and adaptative processes in humans. The next point to be examined is whether the model postulating the three areas of adaptation can or cannot be described in terms of the two mechanisms of association and abstraction. The phenomenon in terms of which an answer to this question will be sought is that of language, or rather of a minimum language or minimum system connecting a lexicon and a grammar.

We must first note that the terms "associative" and "abstractive" can be interpreted in a narrow or in a broad sense. Interpreted in their narrow sense, they define two learning mechanisms which are distinct and mutually exclusive. Interpreted in a broader sense, they define general ways of thinking. In the latter context, they are relative terms; arguments can be regarded as more or less associative or abstractive. The purpose of this section is to define both terms first in their narrow sense, and later in their broader sense.

Advances in cognitive psychology have shown that it is heuristic and valid to conceptualize thought in terms of information and information processing (e.g., Neisser, 1967). In this context, learning can be defined as the process by which one unit of information (e.g., a sensation, stimulus, word, action, idea) becomes connected in memory with another unit of information, or, in some situations, the process by which informational units of a given class become connected with units from the same or from a different class. Associative learning and abstractive learning constitute two qualitatively different ways of connecting informational units in memory.

Before facing the question of definition, it can be said that associative theories are currently in disfavor in many areas of psychology. For example, associative theories are generally regarded as inadequate to account for the development and use of language (e.g., Bever et al., 1968). To argue that any theory is inadequate to account for certain observations is, of course, not equivalent to saying that it is wrong. The theory in question may simply not be applicable to the data under consideration, but may be important for understanding other kinds of data; or the theory may be relevant for the issues being studied, but it is either being applied improperly or must be modified in some way. This distinction while self-evident when stated explicitly is often ignored.

In an attempt to prove the inadequacy of associative theories in linguistics, Bever et al. (1968) attempted to define the most basic assumption underlying associative theories.

Associative principles are rules defined over the "terminal" vocabulary of a theory, i.e., over the vocabulary in which behavior is described. Any description of an n-tuple of elements between which an association can hold must be a possible description of actual behavior.

Stated differently, the basic assumption is that the connection between elements or units of information cannot introduce any information beyond that contained in the units themselves. Thus, the connection or link in memory between two associatively connected informational units, A and B, is not labeled; A and B are simply associated with each other or listed. There is nothing in an associative theory which would allow us to define the nature of that connection.

If we accept this definition of associationism, the question of the adequacy of such theories remains. Presenting an example from Chomsky, Bever et al. (1968) argue that associative principles cannot explain how humans learn even the simplest grammars. The "language" they present is a mirror image language. The only two elements in this language are "a" and "b"; the grammar defines well formed strings as all sequences of a's and b's which are immediately followed by the reverse of that sequence. Thus, "aa" is a well formed sentence, as is "abba," "abbaaaabba," etc. In order to either generate or recognize well formed strings in this language, it is necessary to appreciate the relation between the right and left halves of the sentence strings. Thus, a minimal requirement for understanding is to have the concept of middle. However, the concept of middle cannot be reduced to associations between a's and b's; that is, it cannot be described by a series of terminal elements or informational units in the theory. It is in a sense new information. More specifically, this new information defines a nonassociative link between informational elements, i.e., a labeled link or connection. Because it cannot be reduced to a series of associations between elements, it cannot be generated from a theory solely based on the associative schema. As humans are obviously capable of learning this type of information, it is clear that an associative theory alone is inadequate for the characterization of human learning.

It may be useful at this point to characterize the type of learning necessary for learning or understanding a mirror image language. One can, in fact, argue that such learning rests on a single theoretical assumption, which we can label the abstractive metaprinciple:

> Abstractive principles are rules which define a specific or labeled relationship between the elements or terminal vocabulary of a theory. The relationship between elements cannot be reduced to a list of elements.

The labeled relationships necessary for understanding a mirror image language are relatively simple. Abstracted relationships or abstractions may be more complex. Logically, they can include (1) any dimension which equates or contrasts two or more elements (e.g., semantic features such as big, narrow, beautiful); (2) any dimension specifying the relationship of one element to another (e.g., hierarchical relationships such as "a robin is a bird; hands are parts of the body"); (3) rules which specify relationships between several elements (e.g., linguistic rules such as those defining a sentence or proposition; or mathematical and logical rules).

If the abstractive metaprinciple is accepted, it is still necessary to question its adequacy as a learning mechanism. In fact, it can be shown that abstractive theories are also necessarily inadequate in themselves as explanations for many types of learning. As an example, we can return to an examination of the mirror image language presented above. But let us change the task slightly. Instead of attempting to describe what an individual must know either to generate or to recognize acceptable strings, let us assume that the task is to learn a series of well formed strings of a's and b's. One can assume that after learning several strings, the learner will become aware of the structure of the strings and will use that knowledge to learn later strings. Thus, when presented with the string "abaaaaba," the learner may learn "abaa" and then produce the sequence again in reverse. Thus, he or she will use the abstractive relationship between the first half of the series and the second half to learn and reproduce the sequence. Note, however, that the learner's first task is to commit the sequence "abaa" to memory. This can only be done by associatively connecting each element to the next; that is, no abstractive or labeled relationship exists between the first "a" and the "b" in the above string. The relationship between them can be reduced to a list. Thus, an abstractive learning mechanism alone cannot account for the learning of a series of arbitrarily connected elements, while an associative learning mechanism can. While this example of associative learning may be trivial, there are many instances in everyday life in which we remember nonconceptually organized lists, e.g., grocery lists, social security numbers. Furthermore, this type of learning may serve numerous functions within the learning and thinking processes. For example, associative learning may serve to "hold" units together in memory before an abstractive relationship is determined. It is, therefore, necessary to incorporate this type of learning into a complete theory of learning.

In associative learning, units are connected into informational clusters primarily because they occur together in time or space. Thus, the primary boundary on what is learned is the spatiotemporal context. Informational clusters which are learned in different contexts can become associatively connected by chaining; that is, two informational clusters may be connected because of shared units. For example, if an A-B cluster and a B-C cluster have been learned, A may become associated with C. There are no conceptually defined boundaries to an associative cluster of units; that is, there are no criteria for limiting what can become associated with what. In contrast, abstractive learning is based on the abstraction of a relationship between items. The definition of that relationship provides clear boundaries for what can be included in a cluster and what cannot be, i.e., all and only those informational units which contain the relationship can be included. Thus, abstractive learning is not particular to a given situation but is situation independent. Furthermore, it is marked by the search for clear boundaries defining informational structures.

It should be apparent that associative and abstractive learning are separable and mutually exclusive, as neither can be reduced to the other. Furthermore, their postulation constitutes both the necessary and sufficient conditions for explaining learning, at least in those contexts in which knowledge is communicable in one or another language. Thus, both types of learning were necessary to explain how mirror-language strings could be learned when neither mechanism alone could do so; together they were sufficient to explain such learning functionally.

As defined in their narrow sense and discussed above, associative and abstractive thought constitute two separate learning mechanisms. In any given situation, both mechanisms may be functioning to some degree.

In the broader sense of the terms, they refer to general modes of reasoning or thought and are relative terms rather than absolute terms. Associative reasoning is marked by "arbitrary" ties between informational units. Abstractive reasoning is marked by (1) the definition of information which is relevant to a given situation, and (2) the definition of the relationship between informational units.

The organizing character of abstraction is fully evident in experiments on concept formation, such as those of Sakharov (1930), Vygotsky (1962), and Bruner et al. (1956). In these experiments the subjects are asked to distinguish between relevant and irrelevant items of information within an array presented at the beginning of the experiment. The solution of the problem is obtained through the elimination of irrelevant associations.

Association and abstraction appear to be complementary mechanisms for the acquisition and the organization of knowledge. New items are incorporated primarily by association. However, association depends to a large extent on random coincidences and lacks organization. Large amounts of information cannot be retained and utilized in a largely amorphous state; organization, generally of a hierarchical nature is necessary. Abstraction provides the mechanism for such an ordering of knowledge, defining the imbrication of classes and the mutual relevance and irrelevance of items. Concepts, contrarily to associative clusters, never appear as isolates but as parts of networks of relations—in their simplest way as Piagetian groupings.

The primary process for the acquisition of knowledge appears to be associative. Abstraction appears as the primary process for the organization of knowledge. This is in agreement with Bartlett's analyses of memory (1932).

Opposition between association and abstraction

The complementarity of the roles played by association and abstraction should not lead to losing sight of the opposition between them. This antagonism is shown by one of the Bruner et al. experiments (1956).

In a first experiment in concept formation, Bruner et al. used an array of geometric shapes printed on cards. Every card had one element shared with the other cards, but no two cards were identical. Subjects were shown a sample card having some elements defining a concept within the mind of the experimenter; the card also carried information considered by the experimenter as irrelevant. The task consisted in determining which printed cues were a part of the concept and which were not. The subjects received the information necessary by stating whether other cards did or did not have the attributes characterizing the concept; in each instance the experimenter stated whether the subject's hypothesis was or was not correct. In a second experiment, Bruner et al. used pictures of people instead of abstract geometrical shapes.

> The design of the thematic material . . . was governed by two requirements. The first was to parallel the structure of the abstract cards as closely as possible. The second was literally to make the instances of this array reek with meaning. To achieve the first objective, instances were again constructed of two figures: a large one and a small one, an adult human being and a child. As in the abstract material each of these figures had three attributes, varying in two values. The adult figure could be either a man or a woman. The second attribute was dress: the adult, whether man or woman, was either in night dress or in day dress. Finally, the adult figure was either smiling and giving a gift or was frowning with arms clasped behind the back. In shorthand terms, then, the adult figure varied in the three attributes of sex, dress, and affect. So, too, the child figure. . . .
>
> A word should be said about the thematic material. It is characteristic of each instance of the array that it seems to be evocative of a little story or theme. Here is the figure of a father in night dress giving a little boy a present and the little boy has his eyes cast down and his hands behind his back. As one subject said about this instance, "It looks as if Daddy bought the wrong present for junior." . . . In sum, it is characteristic of instances of this sort that they have the power of evoking thematic imagery about the overall nature of the "parent–child" situation portrayed. The purpose of the experiment was carefully explained, subjects being told what a conjunctive concept was and given some examples of possible concepts such as "all cards with a woman" or "all cards with a child in night dress."
>
> What of the performance on the two kinds of tasks? . . . First, in terms of the average number of choices per problem to attain the concept, there is a considerable and statistically significant difference between the two groups. The Abstract Group required . . . an average of 6.1 choices per problem. The corresponding number of choices for the thematic group was 9.7—half again as many choices. The range of choices required for the abstract group was from 5.0 to 7.2 choices; for the subjects of the thematic group from 7.0 to 11.75. The number of redundant choices fits

the same pattern: 1.0 per problem for the abstract group, 3.9 for the thematic group. (Bruner et al., 1956)

The gist of the experiment is to show that the intrusion of task-irrelevant associations decreases the efficiency of the task-relevant applications of the abstractive mechanism. Indeed, the two mechanisms are at the same time complementary and antagonistic.

Another point to be noted is that Vygotsky's experiments (1962) show that children are not able to solve his concept formation problem. The difficulty does not lie with the development of associations but rather with the elimination or subordination of irrelevant associations, that is to say, the application of the abstractive mechanism. This is fully in keeping with Piaget's findings on progressive development of decentration, that is to say, with the progressive subordination of egocentric attitudes. It would appear that abstraction is more difficult to apply than association.

(A caveat must be entered here to avoid misunderstandings at further stages of exposition. It will be shown—indeed, if it has not been shown already—that preliterate and archaic cultures tend to be more associative and less abstractive than "modern" cultures. This, however, may not indicate that subjects belonging to "modern" cultures are necessarily more adept at original reasoning. Concept formation was used above as an example of abstractive thought. "Modern" subjects are characterized by cognitive cultures rich in conceptualization and therefore in abstraction. Yet most concepts known to them are not derived from the mechanisms described by Vygotsky and Bruner; they originate in most cases not in original analyses, but in explanations offered by an older generation. Yet, a fact remains: modern man is exposed to abstractive reasoning. This is bound to provide tools and habits making abstraction easier.)

Anxiety and toleration of ambiguity

The adaptation of a subject to his or her usual environment consists to begin with in the search for regularities within that environment. These regularities may appear as the formation of associations between signs and significates or between signs and patterns of operations undertaken by the subject in response to such signs.

The part of learning which is concerned with the finding of significant regularities of this type can be accounted for by the mechanisms of conditioning. Nothing more would be needed if one of the three following situations were prevailing:

1. If the environment of the subject were narrow and unchanging; this would bring about a situation in which every acquisition of an association could be fully trusted and never call for a restructuration of the subject's knowledge.

2. If the subject were provided with strong biological filtering mechanisms which would lead to the noticing of only those signs which reliably forecast the outcome needed by the subject. Examples of such filtering mechanisms are easily found in the behavior of lower animals; for instance frogs can see only objects in motion and are likely to starve if caged with paralyzed insects of the kinds constituting their regular diet.

3. If there was no language needing a grammar as well as a lexicon.

None of the situations above prevails in the case of a wide ranging species such as man. Regularities may be learned, but the expectation is that such simple associations between sign and significate may be misleading if and when the subject's environment changes or broadens.

Examples of the consequences for the subject of ambiguous or contradictory stimuli have been demonstrated in the laboratory:

> N. R. Shenger-Krestnikova . . . elaborated a conditioned food reflex in a dog to a circle of light projected on a screen in front of it. Differentiation of the circle from an ellipse of the same size and intensity was afterwards tried, i.e., the circle was always accompanied by feeding; the ellipse, never. Differentiation was thus elaborated. The circle called for the food reaction, but the ellipse remained without effect, which is . . . the result of the development of an inhibition. The first ellipse was markedly different from the circle (the proportion of axes was 2:1). Afterwards as the form of the ellipse was brought closer and closer to that of the circle, we obtained more or less quickly an increasingly delicate differentiation. But when we used an ellipse whose two axes were 9:8, i.e., an ellipse which was nearly circular, all this was changed. We obtained a new delicate differentiation which always remained imperfect, and afterwards not only disappeared spontaneously, but caused the loss of all earlier differentiations, including even the less delicate ones. The dog which formerly stood quietly on his bench, was now constantly struggling and howling. (Pavlov, 1928)

Even more destructive results were obtained by Maier (1939) on rats. The animals were made to jump at two cards with two distinctive designs. One of the cards was hinged at the top in such a way as to swing back under the impact of the jumping rat, letting it through to a platform on which food was available. The other card was fastened at both top and bottom in such a way that the jumping rat felt its impact on an immovable object and fell into a net. Once the behavior of the animal indicated that a set of expectations had been established, the cards were interchanged in an irregular pattern. Even where the consequence of the jump was a painless arrival at a store of food, the rats refused to eat, attempted to escape, and showed other signs of anxiety. In the case of some of the animals, the end result was a catatonic seizure.

Similar consequences of ambiguity are found in humans:

> A young man who had fairly well recovered from an acute schizophrenic episode was visited in the hospital by his mother. He was glad to see her and impulsively put his arm around her shoulders, whereupon she stiffened. He withdrew his arm and she asked, "Don't you love me any more?" He then blushed, and she said, "Dear, you must not be easily embarrassed and afraid of your feelings." The patient was able to stay with her only a few minutes and following her departure he attacked an aide. (Bateson, et al., 1956)

What kinds of strategy are open to the subject in order to avoid such catastrophic reactions? At first glance, and speaking broadly, two possibilities seem open:

1. To develop a system of conceptualizations. Such systems are capable of eliminating many ambiguities, as they focus the observations of the subject on many coordinated cues instead of depending on one, or at best a small number of indices.
2. To retreat from the object-dominated end of the transactional continuum towards the subject-dominated one. Responses which are mutually exclusive at the level of action (or of adaptation to the object) need not exclude one another in the context of subject-domination, that is to say, within the thoughts, the musings, and the dreams of the subject. This ability to surmount contradictions by the use of free imagination within the proper domain of the subject is exemplified by belief in such half human and half animal beings as mermaids, centaurs, or satyrs.

Even laboratory pigeons exposed to irregular reinforcement in a conditioning experiment retreat towards subject-dominated rituals consisting of stereotyped sequences of motion (Skinner, 1948; Ferster and Skinner, 1957).

The first of the alternatives noted above is unlikely, particularly in situations demanding an immediate decision by a subject acting alone. The fact that the second alternative appears in laboratory animals devoided of speech makes particularly likely its application in the case of subjects endowed with speech and capable of engaging in subject-dominated action through the medium of speech. The following is an example of an attempt to integrate a mildly anxiety producing situation in the overall fabric of the subject's knowledge or world-view:

> At 4;6 . . . I pointed out to J. the rushing stream at the foot of the mountain and told her to be careful: "Do you know what my little negress friend did? She rolled right to the bottom of the mountain into the lake. She

rolled for four nights. She scraped her knee and her leg terribly. She did not even cry. They picked her up afterwards. She was in the lake, she couldn't swim and was nearly drowned. At first they couldn't find her, and then they did."—"How do you know all that?"—"She told me on the boat." (the boat on which J first saw a negress). (Piaget, 1962)

An important point in this story, which applies also to the ritualized "superstition" behavior in pigeons, is its creative role. Incidents or behaviors which did not exist earlier are invented or created by the transactional conjunction between new inputs from the environment and the subject's own activity close to the pole which the subject can dominate.

Similar compoundings, including the projection of the self upon another real or imagined actor, appear in dreams:

One night I dream that I see on a bookseller's counter a new volume of one of those collectors' series which I am in the habit of buying. . . . The new collection is entitled "Famous Orators," and the first number bears the name of Dr. Lecher.

On analysis it seems to me improbable that the fame of Dr. Lecher, the long-winded speaker of the German Opposition, should occupy my thoughts while I am dreaming. The fact is that a few days ago I undertook the psychological treatment of some new patients, and I am now forced to talk for ten or twelve hours a day. Thus I myself am a long-winded speaker. (Freud, 1950)

What is the function (if any) of such associative clusters derived from retreats from the reality of object-dominance to the fancy of subject-dominance? The main function appears to be to cushion the subject from the anxiety which is often produced by an ambiguous reality.

Yet it seems quite unlikely that dreams alone could suffice to provide the reassurance needed by the subject. Reinforcement is needed; furthermore, reinforcement must be sufficiently constant to accomplish the task. It is only when individual dreams become collective myths, that is to say, when the sharing of beliefs leads to joint participation in rituals carried out in accordance with enduring rules, that co-subjectivity becomes sufficiently strong to be able to alleviate doubt.

Preliterate cultural behavior—and in a way approved behavior in all cultures—may be divided into three main streams: (1) objective behavior which, in the case of preliterates, is largely unchanging and unlikely to lead to anxiety producing situations, (2) co-subjective behavior so extensive in time and so intensive in feeling as to become the main preoccupation of the societies concerned, and (3) subjective behavior largely directed at obtaining rewards defined by the co-subjective sense of values.

The experience of satisfactory participation in ritual leads to the same result as does habitual success in any field; it leads to adjustment at a relatively high level of tolerance of new ambiguities.

Balance and imbalance

The three statements at the end of the preceding section describe a state of relative equilibrium in the process of adaptation of man to society and of society to the environment. The formulation below may clarify the nature of the equilibrium.

1. A feeling of individual freedom can be compounded from two elements: (a) the internalization by the subject of the cultural world view, and (b) the ability on the part of the subject to evade social pressure by blocking the channels of communication by which society might become aware of an area of the subject's independence.
2. A feeling of collective freedom can also be compounded from two elements: (a) the adaptation of society to its environment, and (b) the blocking of the channels of communication through which might penetrate information contradicting the culture's world view.

In both cases the elements under (a) call for a broadening of the flow of information, while the elements under (b) call for the narrowing of such channels. Strategies under (a) are developmental; strategies under (b) are defensive and potentially regressive. Situations in which (a) is likely to be selected are those in which the level of anxiety is moderate; strategies under (b) imply a high level of anxiety.

Several examples of high anxiety caused by contradictory information were given earlier. An example of low anxiety is to the point. In experiments on perceptual illusion the subjects may know the reality and perceive an object contradicting their knowledge. The understanding of the concept of "illusion"—an abstraction of a higher order—is generally enough to eliminate anxiety.

Derivation of the objective

Objectivity was defined in the preceding chapter as a situation of maximum consensus among as many subjects as possible. "As many as possible" is an expression which calls for additional definition. It will be taken here in a sense fitting the problems of the twentieth century; as a consensus shared by members of different national cultures and defining something which might be called a "pan-culture" within the area of knowledge and behavior in which a trans-cultural consensus can be found. Science is the most obvious example, mainly because its consensus calls for the careful observation of objects; the last word being taken in the sense of portions of the nonhuman and the human environment sufficiently stable and sufficiently detached from affectivity to make possible the extension of the participation to all knowers—at least theoretically.

The basis of an objective consensus should be the same as that of most consensual situations: a similarity between the experiences from which different subjects derive the same conclusions. Yet such is not always the case in the derivation of the objective. Broadly speaking, there are two ways in which objective adaptation may be obtained.

1. *From the subjective to the objective.* The first way is through direct contact with the environment which is largely mediated by the social world. For example, the infant develops concepts of physical objects and physical permanence as he manipulates and observes objects. Similarly, individuals learn specific information about their particular environments, e.g., the location of objects, their relationship to others, the particular characteristics of each object. Objective knowledge derived in this way is inductive. Individuals experience particular objects and situations and develop concepts of varying degrees of abstractness to account for the experiences. This route can be schematized as moving directly from the subjective to the objective. The individual attempts to codify knowledge received in this way so that it can be transmitted to others; this amounts to a move from the objective to the co-subjective. Voyages of discovery may be one example.

A particularly important case of the direct move from the subjective to the objective is learning by doing which is the main way by which much of the practical knowledge is transmitted from generation to generation in preliterate cultures (Cole and Scribner, 1974). Such a transmission through shared action to shared memories and shared patterns of behavior leads to what Scribner has called the "empirical bias" (Scribner, 1979).

2. *From the subjective to the co-subjective, and from the co-subjective to the objective.* Most knowledge about the environment, including the purely physical environment, is not obtained by the direct route. Instead, it is derived from a retreat towards the subjective, and from there to the co-subjective where it forms co-subjectively agreed knowledge lacking objective verification. A broadening of the environment leads either to a social movement aiming at a narrowing of the understanding of the environment (a question which is discussed in chapter 7) or to a transformation of the culture in the direction of the objective. Transformations may at first be directed at a part of belief, but partial changes

often call for adjustments which may affect the entire system of the world view.

A schematic representation of the process by which a new shared world view may be evolved is as follows: in a first step, a selected group of observers (i.e., a specialized sub-culture) derives universal concepts through induction and communicates these concepts to the culture. In a second step members of the culture acquire the knowledge of such concepts and use this knowledge in the shaping of their particular encounters with the environment. Such a process is clearly deductive.

One of the most debated problems in philosophy is whether we derive our knowledge from innately known universals in the direction of experienced particulars, or whether we derive the universals which underlie the words of the language from summations of particular experiences. In fact, we do both. New generations deduce behavior appropriate to particular experiences from the universals taught to them in the context of explanations of the meaning of words; in turn, the particular experiences of what has become an earlier generation are codified in the universals to be taught to the next new generation.

Thus, each culture systematizes to varying degrees the knowledge of the environment of which it is aware. This system is then transmitted to younger individuals joining the culture. It follows that most of an individual's objective knowledge is influenced by the co-subjective. Knowledge transmitted in this way is deductive from the individual's perspective. The individual is provided with concepts about the world which he or she then applies to particular situations. This route can be schematized as moving from the subjective to the co-subjective to the objective.

Reality is somewhat more complex than simplified schemas. Statements presenting the development of ideas in a purely deductive and co-subjective manner can, in fact, be influenced by subjective associations. A classical illustration is the often described dream of the famous chemist Kekule.

The gross formula of benzene, C_6H_6, was known, but the manner in which the molecules were bound together remained a mystery. Kekule, among others, was working on the problem. One night, upon falling asleep, he dreamt of a fire. Little by little the dancing flames changed into snakes, which then grabbed their tails with their mouths, forming dancingly rotating rings. Upon awakening, Kekule tried a ring formula for benzene, with three double bonds assumed not to remain in a fixed position but to rotate among the carbon atoms. This formula, ⬡ ,fits the known properties of the compound and is, of course, in use today.

Snakes are widely recognized as symbols of the male organ,

rings as symbols of the female one. It is likely that if Kekule had lived after Freud, rather than before, he might have abstained from making public the amusing story of the dream which led to his discovery. As for the mechanism, it is probably based on the coincidence in time of two preoccupations: research and sex. Upon awakening, abstraction took over from association, and whatever was irrelevant to the chemical problem was eliminated.

The example indicates that the induction of physical laws, i.e., the passage from experience to pattern recognition to law codification, is marked by fluctuations between associative and abstractive thinking. This can be schematized as movement from the subjective apex to the objective–co-subjective dimension, the position along the dimension being determined by the degree of experimentation and of codification involved. The presence of the associative is indicated by the lack of logical rules for discovery and by the often "strange" connection of ideas that are intermediary in the abstraction of clear, logical, and codifiable laws. The abstractive is marked by the individual's recognition of patterns and laws in the environment and/or the individual's behavior which reflects the use of rules or laws.

The discovery of new knowledge by deduction proceeds differently. During this process, the individual has a set of rules which he or she has typically learned from others. The identification of new information consists of applying these rules and pursuing them as far as possible. An example can be taken from organic chemistry. The minimal grammatical rules of chemical symbolization are based on the tetravalence of carbon, C, the bivalence of oxygen, O, and the monovalence of hydrogen, H. Given this minimal rule, we can represent propylalcohol as:

$$\begin{array}{ccc} H & H & H \\ | & | & | \\ H-C-C-C-O-H \\ | & | & | \\ H & H & H \end{array}$$

by permutation, we obtain isopropyl alcohol, the usual rubbing compound:

$$\begin{array}{c} H \\ | \\ H-C-H \\ H-C-O-H \\ H-C-H \\ | \\ H \end{array}$$

by adding one carbon and the appropriate number of hydrogen atoms, we obtain butyl alcohol:

$$
\begin{array}{c}
\text{H H H} \\
| \quad | \quad | \\
\text{H-C-C-C-C-O-H} \\
| \quad | \quad | \quad | \\
\text{H H H H}
\end{array}
$$

The number of possible combinations, permutations, and additions is infinite, leading to the formulae of compounds some of which exist in nature, while others are new to the natural order but can be synthesized, and still others can exist as concepts in the mind but must remain without physical counterpart because the operations necessary for their synthesis are beyond the state of the art. By applying these rules, one can identify an infinite number of substances.

What we have here is an order of creativity which is entirely abstractive, quite different from the mechanism of the associative–abstractive cycle, and yet capable of greatly expanding the possibilities of human action and the limits of human knowledge.

Note that conceptualization at the co-subjective apex is always crystal clear and free from difficulties. It is, moreover, truly co-subjective, being identical for any person conversant with the rules.

The passage to the actual synthesis of new compounds, or to the analysis of existing ones—i.e., action closer to the objective apex—is frought with difficulties. The substances worked upon have none of the clarity of the formulae which represent them. Operations fail. While some of the properties of the compounds can be deduced from their formulae, others cannot; nothing in the formula of ethyl alcohol, C_2H_5OH, suggests its ability to induce drunkenness, while methyl alcohol, CH_3-OH, induces blindness and death. Worse still, some chemists have a hardly describable laboratory sense which leads them to success; others are deficient in this quality. Success at intuition typically involves associative as well as abstractive reasoning.

The influence of different types of co-subjectivity

Different types of individual behavior can be traced to different organizations of the co-subjective environment. While this appears to be evident, a few examples may be to the point as illustrations of the mechanism.

We might begin with a micro-environment leading to micro-linguistic behavior. In considering the case, it may be well to bear in mind that at the beginning of language acquisition words do not "stand" for things, but that things "stand" for words: Things stimulate verbal responses which can be reinforced by social approval if the "right" word is chosen.

The case is that of an American boy aged three. He was aware of the superordinate category "car," which he divided into three subclasses: "Nash," "stationwagon," and "taxi cab." His family owned two Nash sedans of widely varying vintages, 1949 and 1956, very different in appearance one from the other. The boy infallibly recognized and named all Nashes of intervening models, in spite of considerable differences in styling, and the resemblance of the various year models with cars of different makes but similar styling. Nash-Rambler stationwagons were lumped under "Nash"; attempts on the part of the parents to suggest that they were both Nashes and stationwagons were met with anxiety reactions, culminating in tears. Stationwagons of other makes were identified as "stationwagons." All sedans of other makes were called "taxi cabs."

Obviously, the child had learned to focus his attention on those perceptual cues which were shared by Nashes of various vintages, at the expense of cues such as fast-back vs. square-back which would appear more obvious to adults.

This selection of cues may be explained by the micro-linguistic environment, which was as follows: The subject had just begun to participate in conversations with three older siblings. The name of the family make, Nash, often recurred in these conversations. It was frequently opposed to "stationwagon," because shortly before the subject had become a participant in his siblings' conversations there had existed a possibility of buying either a new Nash sedan, or a stationwagon of another make, which was the preference of the children. "Taxi cab" was used to identify strange cars which were occasionally used to return home from downtown trips by bus.

It appears that the boy had organized his perceptual classification of the object-world in such a manner as to avoid negative feedback to his verbal behavior (Glenn, 1959). Later development made necessary an abstractive reclassification, in order to pass from a micro-linguistic to a macro-linguistic environment in which the words expressing the hierarchy of classes were different.

The importance of this type of hierarchical organization of conceptualization has been demonstrated by Deese (1965). He found that free association of American adults with words as stimuli tends to elicit responses consonant with an abstract organization of concepts in classes, rather than the remembrance of past experiential associations. For example, "white" is more likely to call for "black" than for "snow." Such associations may be said to express the paradigmatic organization of the conceptualization of a world view, rather than the syntagms of experiential happenings.

This result is particularly interesting in view of a study by Ervin (1961) which showed that the associations of children tend to be dominated by syntagms, and that the proportion of such syntagms decreases with age, while that of paradigmatic associations increases.

The considerations presented above suggest that the outreach from egocentrism (so often associated with young age by Piaget) towards socialization is accompanied by—or perhaps conditioned by—a resorption of random associations in favor of abstract structures expressing the formalization of collective experience.

Another way of putting it is that the outreach from the subjective towards the co-subjective is dominated by abstraction. This is implied by the partial resorption of egocentrism: Collective definiteness is obtained through the progressive elimination of the idiosyncratic. Clearly, the larger the social frame of reference, the more idiosyncratisms will need to be smoothed out; this, in turn, means a more abstract organization of thought. Ambiguities which could not be resolved in the outreach from the subjective apex towards the objective one because of the likelihood of overwhelming anxiety, and which did not need to be resolved at the subjective apex, are eliminated at the co-subjective level by the elaboration of common conceptualizations based on common abstracting. If the world can be conceived of as a collection of definite things, it is not because it *is* so and is apprehended as such, but because shared language calls for shared definitions, i.e., for an agreed manner of placing criterial boundaries and subdividing the continuum of direct experience. The organization of knowledge may call for structures more complex than can be expressed by a single grouping of superordinate and subordinate classes.

An example may be to the point. A statement such as "my cousin is my best friend" is impossible in Chinese (Metraux, 1954). It seems that the pertinent universe of discourse is dominated by a single inflexible grouping, which distinguishes between "relatives" and "non-relatives," with cousins falling under the former, and friends under the latter. By contrast, in English it is possible to say "from the point of view of affect, X is my friend; from the point of view of kinship, he is my cousin," making meaningful statements such as "my cousin is my best friend" or "a boy's best friend is his mother." Instead of one dominant grouping determining most mind-sets, there develop matrices of many secant groupings engendering and being engendered by multiple mind-sets (Glenn, 1970a).

The passage from the simplest to the most complex of the levels of organization illustrated by the examples is a passage from the subjective (and syntagmatic) to the abstractive (and paradigmatic) with a higher level of abstraction. A simple hypothesis concerning this development is that it is an adaptation from mechanisms sufficient for ordering relatively small amounts of items, to mechanisms capable of handling large amounts of items.

Egocentrism and centration on stimuli

Kagan, Moss & Sigel (1963) obtained experimentally the manifestations of two cognitive styles. In a classification task, some subjects projected their personal preoccupations on a stimulus array; some others paid more attention to the stimulus material and demonstrated finer and "more objective" differentiations. Had the young boy with Nashes been classified on the basis of such criteria, the first phase of his system of classification would have been identified as egocentric—incapable of going beyond personal experience—while his later classification, which is also the one used by the society at large, could be accepted as objective (at least within the culture under consideration).

Furthermore, the first phase is associative, since it is based on associating words (responses) to perceptual stimuli. The final phase is abstractive, since it derives from the elimination of purely personal experiences.

A similar interpretation applies to the prejudiced vs. the open minded types of personality in Allport's study of prejudice (1954). The prejudiced individual bases his social perceptions on beliefs which precede the contact with the stimulus object; the open minded individual observes the stimulus. A similar statement can be made in regard to the field-dependent field-independent categories of Witkin et al (1954, 1962).

Scribner (1979) has provided some clear examples of abstractive and associative reasoning. In several studies, members of various cultures were asked to solve theoretical problems. One example is the following: "All people who own houses pay a house tax. Boima does not pay a house tax. Does Boima own a house?" She found two kinds of responses. The first she labeled theoretic. This is marked by reasoning from the information given. An example is the following response. "If Boima does not pay a house tax, he cannot own a house." The second form of reasoning she labeled empiric. This is marked by using information that was not included or by refusing to reason through the problem because the individual did not have firsthand experience with the situation. Two examples are: "Boima does not have money to pay a house tax," or "I do not know because I do not know Boima."

It should be clear that the terms theoretic and empiric refer to abstractive and associative reasoning, respectively. The first requires a clear demarcation between information which is relevant to solving the problem and that which is not. The demarcation is present in the statement of the problem. A solution requires that the individual understand the "arbitrary" boundaries of the problem and identify the logical relationships which exist between propositions and use them to solve the problem.

The main point is that if solutions can be obtained, it is because the boundaries are not arbitrary, but characteristic of the cultures and subcultures forming the context of the problems. This will be illustrated in the chapter on preliterate cultures.

What can be stated at this point is that the structure and the content of cultures and of individual cognitive sets depends on the history of individual and cultural cognitive development. The logics governing the acquisition of knowledge by direct experience and by exposition to the verbal structures of an earlier generation are not the same. Pure empiricism is often alogical; this can be seen in the ethnocentrism of cultures which may have acquired the capability of subtle logical reasoning in areas with which they are familiar, but which cannot extend such reasoning to subject-matters with which they are not acquainted. The present situation in Iran is a case in point: even though Shi'ite theology is genuinely subtle in the medieval manner, at one time many Iranian students expressed the certainty that Khomeini was a C.I.A. agent. Where the existing conceptual structure is insufficient, people tend to use a primitive associationism which brings together items not because they have something genuinely in common, but because they ellicit similar feelings in the observers.

The logic of pure universalism in which more or less valid classes are learned verbally is two-valued: items either do or don't belong in specific classes. The logic of the objective apex is again different, often multi-valued; things are not this or that, but can be considered as this or that to a greater or lesser degree.

In any case, knowledge obtained from particular experiences, and knowledge obtained from universal conceptualizations guided by language are often handled in different manners, with a possible difference between the resulting conclusions.

Cultures and individuals

Some of the experiments mentioned in this chapter dealt with cultures, others referred to individuals belonging to the same cultures.

Presumably individuals exposed to similar experiences may either broaden their knowledge or cling to sets of narrow and simplistic beliefs, in fact to a retreat from possible experience.

The suggestion that rigid retreatism may be the result of earlier scars in the cognitive structure can be usefully compared with Goldstein's studies (1963) of brain damaged individuals. When the researcher deliberately left a pad and pencil on the table in such a way that the pencil was at an angle to the pad, both being at non-right angles to the edge of the table, he observed many of the subjects surreptitiously trying to introduce greater orderliness in the objects, by placing the pad perpendicularly to the edge of the table and the pencil parallel to the edge of the pad. Apparently the slightest deviation from the simplest possible arrangement led to anxiety and the fear of a "catastrophic reaction" on the part of individuals whose mental functioning was impaired.

There can be great similarities between the behaviors of individuals incapable of solving some cognitive problems even if the causes of this incapacity may be entirely different. The egocentric approach of a child or an impaired individual and the ethnocentric behavior of representatives of cultures with conceptual structures insufficiently developed to handle problems of that type may be very similar. However, such similarities do not extend to the entire ranges of behavior of children, neurotics and preliterates. Where similarities exist, they can be due to weaknesses of subjects or to the difficulty of the problems, due to their strangeness in the context of the subjects' culture.

5

LINGUISTIC IMPLICATIONS

Cognitive analyses involving comparisons between languages unavoidably call for an examination of the Sapir-Whorf hypothesis. A statement of the hypothesis can be found in the following quotation from Whorf's works:

> I find it gratuitous to assume that a Hopi who knows only the Hopi language and the cultural ideas of his own society has the same notions, often supposed to be intuitions, of time and space that we have and that are generally assumed to be universal. In particular, he has no general notion or intuition of TIME as a smooth flowing continuum in which everything in the universe proceeds at an equal rate, out of a future, through a present, into a past; or, in which, to reverse the picture, the observer is being carried in the stream of duration continuously away from a past and into a future.
>
> After a long and careful analysis, the Hopi language is seen to contain no words, gramatical forms, constructions or expressions that refer directly to what we call "time," or to past, present, or future, or to enduring or lasting, or to motion as kinematic rather than dynamic (i.e. as a continuous translation in space and time rather than as an exhibition of dynamic effort in a certain process), or that even refer to space in such a way as to exclude that element of extension or existence that we call time, and so by implication leave a residue that could be referred to as "time." (Whorf, 1956)

Whorf notes that an expression such as "ten days" cannot be directly translated into Hopi, in which cardinal numbers can be used only in respect to entities which can be perceived simultaneously, as in "ten men." For entities which follow one another, as days do, only ordinal numbers are applicable—"the tenth day."

Two questions may be asked at this juncture: (1) Is it possible

73

for humans not to have the intuition of time? and (2) Is it possible to derive an understanding of a culture's world view from the examination of its language?

An answer to the first question can be derived from the work of Piaget (1946). Genevese children between the ages from 4 to 8, are given a task to perform, for example (a) to draw lines as rapidly as possible, and (b) to draw lines as carefully as possible, which means that they must spend more time per line. The time allowed for the two tasks is the same, as measured by the experimenter. The subjects are then asked which one of the two tasks (a) or (b) took more time. Two thirds of the children answer that (a) took longer "because there are more lines," or "because I was drawing faster." Thus what is estimated is not time as it is understood by adults of the same culture as that of the young subjects, but the intensity of the personal involvement in the task. Whorf suggests that the same criterion, that of personal involvement in the events discussed, is also characteristic of Hopi thought.

As for the second question, we must mention some of the criticisms of Whorf's approach. For example, Lennenberg (1953) criticized Whorf's approach on the grounds that the only way in which the latter obtained indications of the cognitive processes of the peoples he studied were through language. Thus, in a way, he was comparing language with language, whereas the proper procedure would be to compare linguistic behavior with nonlinguistic behavior so as to establish a correlation between mutually independent observations.

Since language permeates most of human behavior, a strict adherence to Lennenberg's criterion would restrict research to some possibly marginal types of the manifestations of a culture. Nevertheless, the validity of his criticism must be recognized. It is hoped that the difficulty might be overcome not by direct comparisons of linguistic and nonlinguistic behaviors, but by the comparison of diverse types of linguistic and nonlinguistic behaviors to the analytical model derived in Chapter 3.

Form and content: langue and parole

The triangular model has been derived from a theory of meaning. Meaning can be conveyed in a multiplicity of ways, some of which can be considered to be symbolic systems (different languages, including such specialized systems as mathematics, scientific notations, shared forms of artistic understanding, nonverbal but systematized types of bodily motion, etc), while others, such as possibly transcultural facial expressions of feeling, can hardly be considered as cultural data. However, the proportion of systematized behaviors is so great that the analysis of meaning permeates all or almost all the activities of the species. While there is no theoretical reason for concentrating on common language, a practical approach to analysis is bound to center around this most commonly used tool of communication, that is to say the various natural languages. Thus the first question is the manner in which language appears in the context of each of the three apexes.

Let us begin with the subjective apex. The apex itself can hardly be reached, except perhaps by psychoanalysis: The way in which an individual communicates with himself, or even the question whether the flow of thought within a mind can be considered as communication, is often beyond the reach of the analyst. What can be reached by research is the area of the triangle close to the subjective apex: This, as it was noted earlier, amounts to determining the characteristics of communication within small and strongly cohesive groups. Te characteristic of such groups that is the most likely to shape communication within them is a situation in which very large areas of personal experiences are in fact shared among the members of the group. This means that the "bits" of meaning which are communicated may be proportionally large, and that they can be expressed very economically, in ways of speaking often hermetic to nonmembers of the group. The linguistic category which best fits these characteristics is the *idiom*—a way of speaking the meaning of which cannot be derived from analyses based on grammars and lexicons. In point of fact, conversations within small groups with high shared contexts may be replete with expressions which do not appear as idioms at first glance, but which are used as if they were idioms: syntagmatically and with meanings understandable only within the groups. Any use of proper names as similes or metaphors provides examples of such in-group expressions.

If idioms are a characteristic of subjectivity, the characteristic of linguistic usage close to the co-subjective apex can be described through groupings of paradigms, in such a manner that the meaning of every expression can be obtained by comparing it to the description of linguistic regularities which by that time have become a system of rules. Such systems of rules include the definitions of all the words of a language in terms of other words of the same language. From the philosophical point of view, a collection of such systematizations defines the *essences* of the things to which the concepts expressible in the language are supposed to correspond. Such a correspondence defines the *connotation* of the parts of the symbolic system under consideration, the word "connotation" being taken in its logical sense of definition rather than in the usual manner in which connotation stands for the expression of the feelings and the associations brought about by the word*—something which would fit the subjective apex.

If connotation and essences are the business of the co-subjective apex, *denotation* and *existence* are those of the objective apex. The only legitimate words in the context of the object are those which can be used in the description either of the objects themselves or of the manipulation of objects by the subject.

It appears at this point that the triangular model can be used in differentiating types of linguistic usage. The question is now that of determining the kind of linguistic data that can be analyzed with the help of the model. More precisely the question becomes that of the level of linguistic analysis upon which will bear the application of the model.

Ever since de Saussure, linguists have used his distinction between *langue*, which can be described as the system of transformations capable of generating all the grammatically acceptable statements in a given language, and *parole*, made up of all the bodies of actual statements made in the language. On the basis of this distinction the differences between statements may be either *linguistic*, contrasting what can and what cannot be said in different languages, or *stylistic*, contrasting what was actually said or written either in different languages, or by different speakers within the same language.

Within contemporary linguistics, and in opposition to classical philology, most analyses of ways of speaking tend to emphasize the *langue* at the expense of the *parole*. Even Whorf (1956) based his theory on the question of the possibility or impossibility of expressing something in a given language: This was evident in the quotation in the preceding section.

Clearly, what Whorf describes in this passage (and in many others) is a difference between languages, in the sense of *langue*. The question is one of linguistic necessity and not merely of stylistic preference.

As for the description of this difference in terms of the model, we may say that the Hopi are much more concrete, that they lack the very abstract notion of time, and concern themselves with the psychological experience of duration, in which the time lapsed is not abstracted from the feeling engendered by the effort called for by the subject's action. Thus their *langue* may be described as coming closer to the subjective apex than, for example, English, or, as Whorf put it in the descriptions of many contrasts of this type, Standard Average European, or SAE.

---

*Connotation is taken in the usual sense in Osgood's semantic differential.

However, similar cognitive differences can be found among the speakers of the same language. A first example may be the difference between the poetic and the scientific uses of symbols, and to the corresponding difference between poets and scientists. A less obvious but more important difference may be found in the analyses of different styles in the same language, as described by Bernstein (1964a,) Cohen (1969), and Glenn (1969, 1973). The rationale of correlating styles with the categories of the model is that different speakers of the same *langue* may be subjected more or less frequently to the styles defined by the model; this would lead to different patterns of enculturation.

As soon as the question of frequency is introduced, it becomes evident that we are no longer dealing with the *langue* (a system of possibilities and impossibilities) but with the *parole* (which can define a system of probabilities).

In the case of the *parole* a distinction must be drawn between the content and the form of statements. Such a distinction is not necessary in the context of the *langue*, which deals exclusively with the forms of linguistic expression. Analyses of the cognitive influence of language must deal with both the *langue* and the *parole*; this means that in analyses of corpora of the *parole* only the form and not the substance must be taken into consideration. Otherwise there would be no parallelism between analyses dealing with the *langue* and those dealing with *parole*.

Stylistic differences within one language

An analysis of the distinction between a syntagmatic–associative style and a paradigmatic–abstractive one by Glenn (1969, 1973) was included in chapter 2. Bernstein's position (1964a, b) is essentially similar, except for the nomenclature; he identifies the two styles as restrictive coding and elaborated coding.

Cohen (1969) analyzed the cognitive styles of children from families in which various social functions were stable, each person being assigned stable roles in respect to one another, and of children from "shared function" families, in which mutual roles, responsibilities and functions were unstable. She found that the overall cognitive style of the first group was analytic (abstractive in the nomenclature of this study), while that of the second group was relational (associative in the nomenclature of this study).

From the point of view of linguistic expression, the analytic (abstractive) group generally uses an elaborated code (paradigmatic–abstractive) with grammatically complex constructions. The expression of the relational (associative) group is dominated by a restricted code (syntagmatic–associative), with grammatically simple expressions and a frequent use of idioms. In the case of the abstractive group, words usually have formal meanings, e.., money: coins, cash, currency; wine: port, sherry. In the case of the associative group, words have meanings specific to certain contexts; they are concrete with much use of visual and tactile symbols, e.g., money: green, bundle, trash; wine: blood, slop, molasses. In the abstractive group "token into type" constructions are relatively rare and used for new developments; in the associative group they are frequent and used even for old objects. The style of the abstractive group is depersonalized: meaning is not dependent upon extraverbal context. The style of the associative group is personified; meaning is dependent on time, place, authority, and other social relationships between communicants.

These stylistic-expressive patterns (presented here in an abbreviated form) are parallelled by other cognitive traits. In the abstractive (analytic) group the mode of abstraction is stimulus centered, with sensitivity to parts of objects, awareness of obscure, abstract, and nonobvious features (Kagan et al., 1963), and many manifestations of field-independence in Witkin's sense (Witkin et al., 1954, 1962). In the associative (relational) group the mode of abstraction is self-centered, with sensitivity to global characteristics, awareness of obvious, sensed features, and field-dependence. Word associations tend to be paradigmatic for the abstractive group, syntagmatic for the associative group. In geometric form drawing tests, the abstractive group takes into account relative differences in ratios of shorter and longer sides; the associative group shows little evidence of perception of relative differences.

In the TAT, the abstractive group comes up with relatively constricted stories containing much description of the properties of the stimuli and minimal creative thematic material; the stories of the associative group present much creative thematic material and little sensitivity to properties of the stimuli. Rorschach responses show high stimulus differentiation, a greater reaction time, and a more reflective attitude for the abstractive group; the associative group shows a minimal stimulus differentiation, quicker responses—the time required for response to global characteristic is less—and a more impulsive attitude.

To sum up, the correlation between styles of expression and cognitive styles is striking. Also, the abstractive group seems to be more objective, and de-centered, in Piaget's sense; the associative group more subjective and egocentric.

Stylistic considerations involving several languages

Glenn (1954, 1955, 1966) used a modified type of the translation method to compare diplomatic English, French, and Russian.
Instead of taking a sample sentence in English and comparing it with
the way in which it would have to be expressed in another language (as
Whorf did) he compared actual original texts in the three languages
with their actual translations, using parts of the proceedings of the
Security Council of the United Nations as a corpus. This procedure
made it possible to take into account not only linguistic necessities but
also the stylistic preferences of native speakers of the three languages.

The main problem in comparing originals and translations is
to determine whether observable differences are meaningful. In order
to do so, it is necessary to distinguish several levels of meaning. Glenn
used two levels in his analyses: immediate meaning and latent meaning.

> To attempt to define meaning is to attempt the impossible. But it can be
> said that two expressions have the same meaning if their utterance results
> in the same change in behavior [on the part of listeners]. . . .
>
> Such an approach to meaning brings in the possibility of observing
> meaning, i.e., observing behavior brought about by communication. Yet
> one should not oversimplify: assuming that one begins to observe behavior
> at the moment of utterance, when can one safely terminate observation?
> I may approach a man on campus and say "Excuse me, Dr. Jones, my
> watch has stopped. Could you tell me the time?" I can also say "Hey,
> buddy, got the time?" The chances are that Dr. Jones will react by telling
> me the time—in either case. Thus what might be called the *immediate*
> meaning of the two expressions may be the same. However, if my name
> comes up at some later date in a conversation in which Dr. Jones partic-
> ipates, his attitude may differ according to the expression I have used. We
> may call *latent* the level of meaning which may give rise to specific behavior
> at a later moment. To have identical meaning, expressions must coincide
> in both their immediate and their latent effects. (Glenn, 1965)

It often happens that the immediate meaning can be respected
in translation only at the cost of distorting the latent meaning. The
following analysis is based on Pribram's (1945) parameter of universalism–nominalism.

> The President, a Belgian, says, "*Aucune proposition n'etant faite dans ce sens,
> j'en deduis. . . .*"
>
> The last word becomes "I assume" in the English translation. "I deduce"
> would have been stiff, "I conclude" almost impolite, implying that no
> change of opinion or of interpretation on the part of the Council would
> be welcome. "I assume" is correct because that is the word which an Eng-
> lish-speaking chairman would have chosen in all probability, and also be-
> cause, in nominalistic or hypothetical reasoning, one acts upon assumptions.

Assumptions become certainties only after action has resulted in their verification.

The President could not have used the French equivalent of "I assume." If one considers that reason is capable of reaching entirely valid conclusions, one does not act upon assumptions. "*Je suppose*" would have implied that the members of the Council have not made their positions sufficiently clear to allow the President to reach a clear conclusion.

The Russian translation uses "*zaklyuchaiyu*"*—"I conclude." The strength of this word may be best evaluated by the participle form "*zaklyuchonnyi*" which means a prisoner and is often used in the subsequent remarks of the Soviet delegate. (Glenn, 1954)

The preceding passage suggests that Russian and French come closer to the co-subjective pole (dominance of pure reason or of the shared symbolic system) that does English; the latter tending towards the objective apex (verification of hypotheses through action). Furthermore, reliance on universalism or co-subjectivity appears to be greater in Russian than in French. This suggestion is confirmed by a number of other passages.

The matter is before the Council. . . ." appears in Russian as "Vopros, stoyashchyi pyered Sovyetom. . . ."

There could have been a full stop after the English clause. Not so after the Russian one, which literally means "the question, standing before the Council. . . ." Thus the Russian draws attention to the clause which must necessarily follow, while the English draws attention away from it. Let us see how this looks in the context of the complete sentence: "The matter is before the Council to decide" is the English text, and "Vopros, stoyash-chyi pyered Sovyetom, Sovyet dolzhen razryeshit' sam" (the question standing before the Council, the Council itself must decide) is the Russian one. The English text draws attention to the situation or the circumstances, and merely identifies the substance involved—a decision to be taken by the Council; the Russian merely identifies the circumstances and insists on the substance. . . .

Thus what the Russian places in the principal clause and at the principal center of attention, is a decision of a political nature, possibly with far reaching consequences and doubtlessly connected with the broad picture of the political organization of international life; what it places in the subordinate clause are the procedural facts which govern the immediate actions of the Council. What the English places in the principal clause are precisely those immediate considerations connected with the means of action; what it places in the subordinate clause is the reference to a more distant and broader goal. (Glenn, 1966)

---

*Since it is expected that many of the readers may not be linguists, the transliteration used in the texts is one which gives the best approximation of Russian sounds for speakers of English, and not the one most often found in linguistic publications.

The selection of what appears as a subject and what appears as a predicate follows the same pattern as the choice of what is placed in the principal and what in the subordinate clause, with recurring inversions between the English and the Russian texts. For example, "The important point is the desire of a number of delegations" appears as "The desire of a number of delegations is the important point." In this and in many other examples the Russian subject refers to the substance of the debate, thus suggesting that the substance in question can be easily grasped by the mind. The English subject refers to the procedural circumstances, suggesting that, in a procedural body, the mind should grasp first the presently applicable procedural status, as a means for taking action on the substance (Glenn, 1966).

The full value of this pattern of inversion may be better grasped in the light of other divergencies, in which Russian differs from both English and French. In this pattern, the Russian fails to make the distinction between the fact—or alleged fact—and statement about fact. The other two languages are careful to voice this distinction.

For example, "vmyeshatyel'stvo . . . nye sootvyetstvuyet dyestvityelnisiyi" (the interference . . . does not correspond to reality) becomes in English "the allegation of interference . . . was not in accordance with the facts."

> The word "allegation" was added by the translators, to eliminate a connotation which would be only too obvious in English—and in French, where the translation is "réfutait les allégations selon lesquelles . . . s'imisceraient. . . ."
>
> Elsewhere the French "la conclusion presentée par le représentant. . . . précise que. . . ." (The conclusion presented by the representative . . . clearly states . . .) becomes in Russian "iz slov predstavityelya . . . stanovitsya yasnym" (from the words of the representative . . . it becomes clear). In this case the translation seems to imply that saying "the statement is clear"—with no connotation of the acceptance or the rejection of the statement on the part of those to whom it is addressed—is the equivalent of "the statement makes it clear", which suggests acceptance on the part of the audience. (Glenn, 1966)

The failure to distinguish between fact and statements about alleged fact conveys an impression of absolute certainty; this fits with the belief that thought, and in particular one's own approach to thinking, is capable of fully reaching reality. As such it is an example of extreme universalism or co-subjectivity.

A similar example dealing with Spanish was communicated by Jean Tanner (personal conversation, 1980). Costa-Rican respondents were asked if a report on the project of an open university was acceptable. More than half dealt not with the report but with the pros and cons of the project itself. The question of the similarities between the East European and the Iberic cultures is a promising area of research.

In the preceding example, French and English took the same position opposed to the one reflected by the Russian text. This is by no means always the case. The following pattern of divergence between English and French can be noted.

The English text is replete with sentences in the passive voice, e.g., "The suggestion of the . . . delegate is that. . . ." These appear both in the original and in translations. The corresponding French almost invariably is in the active voice, and identifies the actor as grammatical subject: "The . . . delegate suggests that. . . ."

The French style makes it possible for the listener to build up an image of the delegate—an enduring reality—and perhaps to evaluate his or her consistency or inner logic throughout the suggestions advanced. The style used in English discourages such an approach; each suggestion is viewed punctually. The style fits with a possible admonition; forget about the delegate, consider the suggestion on its merits.

> Summing up the choices of subject in the three languages, we see in Russian a preference for abstract entities of great scope, in French for individual actors, and in English for "cases", i.e. situations or sets of circumstances, in general fairly specific and limited in scope. Within the three preferences, the French one leads to the selection of subjects intermediate in scope (for example in probable extension in time, and in importance) between the other two. Furthermore, the insistence on the individual (in preference to either broad principle or specific circumstances) has for effect drawing attention to the manner in which each individual relates generalities to particulars. (Glenn, 1966)

From parole to langue

In the case of one of the divergencies between Russian and English mentioned in the preceding section, that of the inversion of subject and nominative predicate with the verb *yavlyatsya* used as copula, the matter in Russian is not one of stylistic preference but one of linguistic necessity. With this particular copula, it is compulsory in Russian to use the equivalent of "the Middle East question is the first point on the agenda"—the equivalent of "the first point on the agenda is the Middle East question" is not acceptable (noting that the mark of the predicate in Russian is not the relative placement in the sentence, but the instrumental case ending). A point to bear in mind is that the grammatical rule defining this necessity is unstated in Russian grammars, and can be given a definite form only with difficulty (Glenn, 1973). The

distinction between the linguistically necessary, the stylistically preferable, and the possibility of a free choice of different styles is by no means
as clear as it might appear.

The Russian covert linguistic category determined by what can
be used as subject and what must appear in the predicate can be more
easily stated in semantic than in grammatical or lexical terms. Thus, the
subject must be the one of the two entities which comes closer to the co-
subjective apex, i.e., which can be more easily given a determinate meaning by people unaware of the particular objective and subjective circumstances surrounding the event.

In a similar manner, it can be suggested that the fact (noted by
Whorf, 1956) that Hopi verbs have validity forms rather than tenses
makes the Hopi form of expression come closer to the subjective or
associative pole than do "corresponding" expressions in what Whorf
calls the Standard Average European languages. Hopi verbs carry a
greater amount of information about the subject—the degree of certainty—than do European verbs; conversely, the latter make statements
which seem fully determined by the object and quasi-independent of
the subject.

Hopi metaphysics . . . imposes upon the universe two grand cosmic forms,
which as a first approximation in terminology we can call MANIFEST and
MANIFESTING (or UNMANIFEST) or, again, OBJECTIVE and SUB-
JECTIVE. The objective or manifested comprises all that is or has been
accessible to the senses, the historical physical universe, in fact, with no
attempt to distinguish between present and past, but excluding everything
that we call future. The subjective or manifesting comprises all that we
call future, BUT NOT MERELY THIS; it includes equally and indistin-
guishably all that we call mental—everything that appears or exists in the
mind, or, as the Hopi would prefer to say, in the HEART, not only the
heart of man, but the hearts of animals, plants, and things, and behind
and within all the forms and appearances of nature in the heart of nature,
and by implication and extension which has been felt by more than one
anthropologist, yet would hardly ever be spoken of by a Hopi himself, so
charged is the idea with religious and magical awesomeness, in the very
heart of the Cosmos itself. The subjective realm (subjective from our
viewpoint, but intensely real and quivering with life, power, and potency
to the Hopi) embraces not only our FUTURE, much of which the Hopi
regards as more or less predestined in essence if not in exact form, but
also all mentality, intellection, and emotion, the essence and typical form
of which is the striving of purposeful desire, intelligent in character, toward
manifestation—a manifestation which is much resisted and delayed, but
in some form or other is inevitable. It is the realm of expectancy, of desire
and purpose, of vitalizing life, of efficient causes, of thought thinking itself
out from an inner realm (the Hopian HEART) into manifestation. It is

in a dynamic state, yet not a state of motion—it is not advancing toward us out of a future, but ALREADY WITH US in vital and mental form, and its dynamism is at work in the field of eventuating and manifesting, i.e., evolving without motion from the subjective by degrees to a result which is the objective. In translating into English, the Hopi will say that these entities in the process of causation "will come" or that they—the Hopi—"will come to" them, but, in their own language, there are no verbs corresponding to our "come" and "go" that mean simple and abstract motion, our purely kinematic concept. The words in this case translated "come" refer to the process of eventuating without calling it motion—they are "eventuates to here" (*pew'i*) or "eventuates from" (*angoö*) or "arrived" (*pitu*, pl. *öki*) which refers only to the terminal manifestation, the actual arrival at a given point, not to any motion preceding it. (Whorf, 1956)

Clearly, Whorf had to call upon more than conjugation on the basis of validity forms to arrive at an intimate understanding of Hopi thought, and of the preoccupation with the subjective and the associative which the linguistic form itself imposes on its speakers. Nevertheless validity forms are part and parcel of the picture, and perhaps the most obvious manifestation of the fusion between subject and object in a single statement—something which is far from being specific to Hopi, or even to Amerindian languages.

For example, in classical Turkish the dubitative suffix *miš* had to be added to verbs or nouns if the information conveyed by them had not been acquired by the speaker by direct apprehension but by less trustful means, such as hearsay.

Tilting in the direction of the subjective apex can be effectuated by a variety of means. For example, pronominal rules show the opposite tendencies of English and of Navaho:

A simple illustration is found when we try to translate the English phrases *his horse* and *his horses* into Navaho, which not only lacks a plural category for nouns (Navaho translates equally English *horse* and *horses*) but lacks as well the English distinction between *his, her, its*, and *their* (Navaho may be translated, according to context, *his horse* or *horses, her horse* or *horses, its horse* or *horses* and *their horse* or *horses*). These Navaho forms make difficulties in English also because Navaho makes a distinction between a third person (the bì- in) psychologically close to the speaker (e.g. *his*—that is, a Navaho's—*horse*) as opposed to a third person psychologically remote (e.g. *his*—that is, a non-Navaho's—*horse*). (Hoijer, 1954)

Associative and abstractive tendencies in languages: a discussion

The examples in the preceding section show that different languages make it necessary or desirable to specify one or another type of phenomena. More precisely, the linguistic examples of associativity showed a preoccupation with the relationship between the subject and the object, absent from more abstractive languages.

A number of linguists and anthropologists, including Whorf, saw this as an example of superiority on the part of associative languages.

> It takes but little scientific study of preliterate languages, especially those of America, to show how much more precise and finely elaborated is the system of relationships in many such tongues than in ours. By comparison with many American languages, the formal systematic organization of ideas in English, German, French or Italian is poor and jejune. Why for instance, do we not, like the Hopi, use a different way of expressing the relation of the channel of sensation (seeing) to result in consciousness, as between "I see that it is red" and "I see that it is new?" We fuse the two different types of relationships into a vague sort of connection expressed by "that" whereas the Hopi indicates that in the first case seeing presents a sensation "red" and in the second that seeing presents unspecified evidence from which is drawn the inference of newness. If we change the form to "I hear that it is red" or "I hear that it is new," we European speakers still cling to our lame "that," but the Hopi now uses still another relater and makes no distinction between "red" and "new," since, in either case, the significant presentation to consciousness is that of a verbal report, and neither a sensation per se nor inferential evidence. Does the Hopi language show here a higher plane of thinking, a more rational analysis of situations, than our vaunted English? Of course it does. In this field and in various others, English compared to Hopi is like a bludgeon compared to a rapier. (Whorf, 1956)

The association of the subject and the object in statements conveying information about the two is likened by Whorf to the theory of relativity, which has shown that statements neglecting the influence of the mode of observation upon the observed fail to fit the facts in complex situations. He goes on to suggest that relativity might be more easily expressible in the logic inherent in Hopi than in the one inherent in European languages.

Whether such is or is not the situation, it is difficult to say. What is certain is that the speakers of Hopi—and for that matter the nonspeakers of mathematics—have discovered neither Einsteinian nor Newtonian physics. The discovery of these scientific paradigms would not have been possible if one had not built upon the preceding one: Einstein is inconceivable without Maxwell, Maxwell without Newton, Newton without Galileo, and Galileo without Aristotle, and this not in spite of but because of the differences between them.

What associative languages do (at least as exemplified above) is to express states of consciousness as states of consciousness. As such they cannot be faulted. What abstractive languages do is to present statements of opinion as if they were statements of fact. As such, they can be faulted, and it is precisely this fault finding which sets in motion the intellectual curiosity which ultimately leads to research. This, according to Northrop (1953) is the particular genius of the western cultures and of their languages: Their syntax makes them affirm more than is known, thus it calls for a critical examination of what is said, not only in its social context, but also as to what they affirm. This may be the origin of the creativity and the instability—Northrop calls it the revolutionary character—of western civilizations.

Once again, bringing in a contrast may be useful. Albert (1964) states that in Burundi

> speech is explicitly recognized as an important instrument of social life; eloquence is one of the central values of the cultural world-view; and the way of life affords frequent opportunity for its exercise. . . . The importance of speech for survival and success as well as the primacy of esthetic-emotive values in speech behavior follow directly from Rundi causal theory. In the universe at large and in society, personal power is the sole or chief causal force; it is conceived as directed by the actor's free choice; choice is viewed as dependent on emotional dispositions, assumed to be unstable and changeable. . . . Since emotion is the spring of action and since emotion is much affected by esthetic factors, manipulation of emotions by esthetic devices is the principal business of speech behavior. . . . Labelling a man a liar does not result from his tendency to falsify factual statements, but rather denotes breaking promises. . . .
>
> The key concept for appreciating the norms and values associated with the uses of language is *ubgenge*, "successful cleverness." *Ubgenge* chiefly applies to intellectual-verbal management of significant life-situations. Situational adaptability is a permanent condition of action. Hence, the specific manifestations of *ubgenge* are numerous and diverse. The cleverness of a rogue; the industriousness of a virtuous man whose overlord gives him a cow as a reward for virtue; the skill of a good psychologist-rhetorician in persuading a generous, impulsive—or thoroughly inebriated—superior to give him a cow although he had done nothing to earn it; the skill of a medical curer; the success of a practical joker who has victimized some simple-minded peasant or feeble-minded boy, the wise and just judgments of the *abashingantahe*, the 'elders' in courts and councils; and the technological accomplishments of Europeans are all equally good examples of *ubgenge*. (Albert, 1964)

There is much in common between *ubgenge* and the skill of the sophists as criticized by Socrates in Plato's dialogues, particularly the *Protagoras* and the *Gorgias*: a skill so dependent on the subject and so little dependent on the object that it cannot possibly lead to finding truth about the latter. The practice of such a skill may be contrasted with Socratic inquiry into "the true essence of all things," as exemplified in the quotation from the *Phaedo* in chapter 2. Again, it is precisely because few would accept today Plato's theory of ideas that we can see to what extent this theory has been fecund, by generating inquiry to justify opposition to its own contents.

Difference, deficiency—or both?

One of the most controversial questions in socio-psycholinguistics is that of the contribution of language to the poor school performance of lower class children. Two basic positions emerge (with some simplification):

1. The deficiency hypothesis. Lower class children speak a dialect which does little to prepare them for the abstractive thinking required to achieve well in a school environment (Bernstein, 1964a, b, 1970; Cohen, 1969; Deutsch, et al., 1967, 1968)
2. The difference hypothesis. Children from lower class backgrounds, particularly Black and Puerto Rican children in the United States, speak a different language or dialect than do the school teachers to whom they are exposed, and than is required by the school. This brings about obvious difficulties. (Labov, 1969, 1970).

The first point which should be made is that the two hypotheses are by no means irreconcilable. Difference does not exclude deficiency, and deficiency implies difference; the school child may be faced with both orders of difficulty at the same time. This is obvious with Puerto Rican children, whose native tongue is a dialect of Spanish, and can be easily established in the case of the speakers of Black English Vernacular (BEV) or Nonstandard Negro English (NNE).

Let us take a few examples from the latter. Compare:

> "he my friend," with
> "he be my friend."

The first expression is punctual ("he is my friend now"), the second one durative ("he is always my friend"). This implies a syntactic–semantic rule which does not exist in Standard English. The presence of such a rule is bound to cause difficulties within an environment which does not require the expression of the distinction between the punctual and the durative, calling for "he is my friend" in either case. Obviously enough, the availability of the rule does not imply any deficiency.

Another example may be the use of the double negative, "he

ain't seen nothing." It has been said that the use of the double negative predisposes to logical weakness. Yet the multiple negative is the rule in Slavic languages; for example the equivalent Polish would be "on nie widział niczego"—"he not seen nothing." This did not prevent the development of the Warsaw school of mathematical and linguistic logic, which was extremely fecund; names such as Tarski, Kozakiewicz, and Pelc come to mind.

The situation in regard to the double negative is ambiguous in French. Strictly speaking—or rather etymologically speaking—double negatives are ungrammatical. The translation of the sentence in the preceding example of "il ne voit rien." "Rien" comes from the Latin *res*—thing—and at the origin it was used to add emphasis to the sentence: "he doesn't see a thing." However in contemporary French it means "nothing," and a slangy expression of the same thing is "il voit rien" ("he sees nothing"), satisfying the French tendency toward progressive sequences (Bally, 1944). Thus contemporary French does use the double negative, while being considered by those who speak it as the most logical language in the world.

These examples suggest that differences do not necessarily point to obvious deficiencies.

At the same time the model suggests that *all symbolic systems, including all natural languages, must be deficient from one or from another point of view.* If indeed meaning is the compromise between the divergent demands of subjectivity, co-subjectivity, and objectivity, all utterances must be deficient in regard to at least two of these requirements.

A strategy for determining the deficiencies of any symbolic system may consist in comparing some such systems among themselves to determine (1) what can be expressed in some systems, but not in other ones; or, failing this, (2) what is actually expressed in a corpus representative of given systems, and fails to be expressed in representative corpora of other systems.

Since a linguistic example would be more to the point, the strategy is applied below to a comparison of English and French, an example which is likely to arouse fewer emotions than might comparisons between Black English Vernacular and Standard English.

In English adjectives precede the nouns they modify. In French, they generally follow them. Thus

black table

would be normally translated into French as

table noire.

What is the degree of accuracy of such a translation? The question may be explored by comparing the two expressions with their "equivalents" in one of the Slavic languages in which adjectives may either precede or follow nouns.

Again we will take Polish. [Russian would yield identical results, but is slightly more ambiguous on one point, as the phrase "Stol chyornyi" when used by itself, not as part of a sentence, takes on the semantic value of "the table is black," because of the customary ellipse of the verb *to be* (*byt'*).]

In Polish,

black table

is either

czarny stół, equivalent of black table,

or

stól czarny, equivalent of table noire, or table black.

There is a very definite semantic difference between the two Polish phrases. The earlier one is *descriptive*; for example:

przy ścianie stał czarny stół: by wall stood black table

(there are no articles in Polish). The latter one is *classificatory*; for example:

stół czarny jest tani, a stół biały drogi: table black is

cheap (but) table white expensive

Does this difference between descriptive and classificatory meaning carry into French and English, the two languages under consideration?

Let us take French first. There is a number of situations in which the order adjective–noun is used. Take for example "une jolie fille" (a pretty girl) or "un pauvre homme" (a poor man). The latter—a classic example in the teaching of French—means "a man pitied by the speaker, for whatever reason, not necessarily because of impecuniousness." As such it can be contrasted with "un homme pauvre"—a man poor—which definitely refers to a member of the subclass "with little or no money" of the superordinate class "man."

This seeming flexibility of French to take one or the other approach is limited. One can say "la belle femme" (the beautiful woman) but not "le rouge vin" (the red wine), except through poetic license, as in "red is the wine."

In theory, there are no situations in which the sequence noun–adjective is used in English. Yet if one stands near a cafeteria line one often hears "coffee, black, please." The glottal stop (if present) simply means that the speaker is ready to accept awkwardness in order to express the classificatory intent.

What this example suggests is that English is deficient in the ease with which attention can be directed to the permanent, co-subjective imbrication of concepts. French is deficient in the flexibility with which an expression can be adapted to the subjective or objective context of the utterance.

The suggestionof this example is borne out by more general analysis. Vinay and Darbelnet (1960) point out:

> Linguistic representation can be carried out either at the *level of reality*, using *word-images*, or on that of *understanding*, using *words-signs*. We call *word-sign* everything that tends toward abstract signs, that is to say toward what the number is in the language of mathematics, and that speaks more to the mind than to the senses.
>
> Terms such as "dress rehearsal," "way station," "unveil" (a statue), "unseat" (a member of Parliament) have a greater image value than their French equivalents: "répétition générale," "arrêt intermédiaire," "inaugurer," "invalider." Likewise in "He swam across the river: il traversa la rivière á la nage" . . . the word "nage," the image value of which is no lesser than that of "swim," is subordinated to the abstract term "traverser" (to cross). In other words, the English sentence is organized around a word-image and the French one around a word-sign.
>
> By level of reality we understand the level at which linguistic representation borders concrete reality. The level of understanding is the level of abstraction to which the mind rises to consider reality from a more general viewpoint.

Diplomatic translators working from English into French frequently complain of the imprecision of the former: Too much of the meaning is left to the context. It may be to the point to note in this respect that the juridical concept of "the intent of the legislator" i.e., of the interpretation of a statute in the light of the context of its adoption, is not accepted in French jurisprudence; the latter assumes that the meaning of laws can and must be made unequivocal.

It is not that English lacks the vocabulary necessary for precision; complete dictionaries are often half again as thick for their English–French as for their French–English volumes. However, as Vinay and Darbelnet (1960) point out, the richness of English is mainly in concrete, descriptive terms.

The question is not so much one of language (*langue*) as one of linguistic usage (*parole*). Not far from where I live there is a road sign saying "NARROW BRIDGE." Yet there is no narrow bridge, and in fact no bridge at all for the traffic to cross. What is narrow is an underpass under a railroad bridge, the width of which is irrelevant. Frenchmen to whom the sign was shown are either shocked or amused—but always incredulous, even in the face of evidence.

An example of difficulty in communication between Americans and Frenchmen may be to the point:

Once the conventions of privacy have been breached, the interviewer must still deal with the special French conventions of cognition. The metaphysics which endows the external world with activist attributes of its own also creates new problems of question formulation for an American more accustomed to more empirical habits of thought. In the earliest interviews, I was baffled by the recurrent request from respondents to state precisely various questions that seemed to me already precise. It required much conversation and reflection before I realized that, for the French, precision has a quite different and special meaning, a literally Cartesian meaning. What makes questions *"précise"* for Frenchmen is their capacity to frame the object of reference in a specific context (*"bien délimité, dans un cadre qui est propre"*). The object of reference, to be clear, must be perceived as discrete—with external boundaries sharply defined ("circonscrire l'objet")—in the conventional vocabulary of French philosophy.

French insistence upon a discrete, disengaged object of reference underscores their revulsion against relationships without clearly circumscribed boundaries. The language abounds in pejorative expressions to express this horror of inadequate distentiation—*"dans le jus," "dans le sirop," "dans la soupe"* [all three of which project the image of an immersion on a gooey liquid and signify both discomfort and failure]. These images convey vividly the sense that fluidity (*"des idees floues"*) is the enemy of clarity. Other expressions of distaste for "fuzziness" are *"dans le cirage," "dans le coton,"* and *"dans la vaseline,"* where the soft and shapeless mass without defined margins provides the antonym of clarity and precision. Proper perception of persons and objects requires that "one can see all around them" and thereby position oneself at an appropriate distance. (Lerner, 1956)

This is obtained, not by taking such objects one by one ("crossing bridges when one comes to them"), but by locating each item in respect to a general scheme and avoiding coming up to bridges one may not wish to cross.

A comparison between the dominant styles in French and English suggests that each has distinctive qualities and compensating faults: in other words that either is deficient in respect to the other from one or another point of view.

We can now go back to a comparison of the Black English Vernacular with Standard English. BEV is distinguished not only by different syntactic rules, but also by a lack of the type of literature which would enhance co-subjective or objective precision. True enough, a fairly extensive body of poetry (much of it good) and fiction exists. However, as was shown in chapter 3, the existence of such a body of literature enhances rather than diminishes the subjective character of expression. In consequence, it may be expected that BEV is deficient in some communicative characteristics, without necessarily being deficient in all of them.

In fact, as suggested by a number of sociolinguists (e.g., Labov, 1969, 1970) BEV can be superior in a number of situations, particularly in the use of genuine eloquence within the in-group. However, this point of superiority implies a weakness of the abstractive mechanisms leading to the possibility of broadening communication beyond the cultural limits of the in-group.

Language cannot be evaluated from any single point of view. It was noted earlier, in the example of talking about the weather, that using language to establish interpersonal relations, and using it to convey information are different things. A dialect may be superior in one case, and poorly adapted to the other case.

Conclusions

Technical requirements in linguistics make it necessary to provide descriptions of languages which ignore the contexts within which languages are used. Such context-free descriptions are legitimate, but their validity is obviously limited, since language is unavoidably used in a context. Analyses aimed at the problems of language within culture must take context into account.

Obviously, this is a complicating factor. One strategy capable of partly overcoming unavoidable complications is the comparative method, in which the forms of expression used in different languages in identical contexts are compared among themselves. Some examples of the application of this method were briefly presented in this chapter. The results of such comparisons suggest that actual linguistic behaviors, and the characteristics of natural languages which influence them, may tilt towards one or another of the apexes of the semantic triangle presented in chapter 3. The actual significance of such tilting can be evaluated by comparisons with the tilting found in cultural or sociological descriptions of the populations concerned, rather than in attempts to establish one-to-one correspondences between linguistic and nonlinguistic behaviors. This applies particularly to studies concerning the Sapir-Whorf hypothesis.

6

SOCIOLOGICAL IMPLICATIONS: STRATIFICATION

with Bonnie Chirlin

Introduction

The purpose of this chapter is to show that social behavior tending towards the associative polarity and social behavior tending towards the abstractive polarity form *syndromes*, i.e., that they are not restricted to one particular frame of reference but that they tend to dominate behavior in a variety of contexts. The background against which this proposition will be examined is that of social stratification in the United States in the third quarter of the 20th century.

This stratification can be described in terms of (1) a *lower class*, characterized primarily by sporadic employment and a considerable amount of social disorganization; (2) a *working class*, characterized by normally stable employment in the blue collar hourly wages trades; (3) a *lower-middle class*, characterized by salaried employment of a white collar subprofessional or submanagerial type; and (4) an *upper middle class* characterized by university education and deriving its livelihood from the professions or from managerial positions. The (5) *upper class*, characterized by wealth will not be discussed as such, as it lacks homogeneity, and as data concerning it are scant. Nevertheless a few mentions of it will appear in quotations from the literature.

The expectation is that the tendency towards abstractiveness increases with the socioeconomic status, at least up to the level of the upper-middle class. The rationale behind this expectation is the basic hypothesis put forward in chapter 2 and based largely on Durkheim's theses (1893, 1933): that the development of abstractive thought is made necessary by increases in what he calls social density, that is to say the product of the size of a society by the mobility which prevails within it. Under the circumstances, it may be expected that the strata of society characterized by the greatest mobility and provided by their education with the broadest preparation for handling a diversity of social and subject matter situations ought to be also the ones best prepared for abstract thinking. More precisely, such strata ought to be the most ready to define personal identity, both their own and that of the people with whom they come into contact, according to the abstractive criteria of personal achievement rather than the associative criteria of ascription of global characteristics to groups defined in terms of their birth or sex. It may be useful in this connection to note that ethnic prejudice correlates inversely with the level of education (Allport, 1954).

Within such a context the attitudes of the upper class may be expected to be somewhat ambiguous. On the one hand members of this class are often geographically mobile and even cosmopolitan; on the other the factor of inheritance and of birth plays an important role in their self-definitions.

Patterns of identity definition

The associative–abstractive polarity may be illustrated by the way in which members of the various social classes define their personal identities. In general, lower- and working-class people identify both themselves and others by ascription, while those of the middle classes seek identity primarily through achievement. Ascription is associative, as it bases identity definition upon birth. In other words, a person is identified through association with a particular group, and the consequent assumption is that his or her behavior will follow the patterns characteristic of the group. In contrast, identification by achievement involves the abstraction of a specifically defined attribute, generally occupation, from the person as a whole and even more from the group within which the person originates. For example, a working-class person would be likely to identify him- or herself by race, nationality, or religion; he or she would also often reside in an ethnically defined neighborhood. Middle-class persons would be likely to identify themselves by profession, and to reside in neighborhoods defined by the level of income.

Miller and Riessman (1969) underscore the imbeddedness of the working man in his group:

Traditional practices . . . are very strong in working class families. The pattern is patriarchal, extended (with many relevant cousins, grandparents, and aunts and uncles) and delineated by sharply separated sex roles. The family is not child-centered . . . but parent-centered and controlled. Traditional values of automatic obedience by children are expected to be the norm even if not always observed in practice. (Duvall, 1946; Miller and Riessman, 1969)

The two central characters in Whyte's *Street Corner Society* (1943) provide good examples of associative group-imbeddedness and abstractive achievement orientation. Although both Chick and Doc grew up in an Italian working class neighbourhood, Doc remained a street corner boy while Chick went on to law school and a promising political career. The different careers of Doc and Chick can be better explained by the way in which each identified himself and others than by any significant difference in native intelligence and ability:

Chick and Doc also had conflicting attitudes toward social mobility. Chick judged men according to their capacity for advancing themselves. Doc judged them according to their loyalty to their friends and their behavior in their personal relations. (Whyte, 1943)

Doc's identification with his group—or "gang" without the pejorative connotations—was such that he was not able to abstract or separate himself from it:

Both the college boy and the corner boy try to get ahead. The difference between them is that the college boy either does not tie himself to a group of close friends or else is willing to sacrifice his friendship with those who do not advance as fast as he does. The corner boy is tied to his group by a network of reciprocal obligations from which he is either unable or unwilling to break away. (Whyte, 1943)

Gans (1962) presents a similar picture, describing the Italian American working-class subculture of the West End of Boston as a peer group society. He notes that not only individualism in the sense of self-reliance and self-control of one's life is deemphasized in this culture, but that people can function as individuals only within the peer group:

Yet the peer group is important not only because it provides this much desired companionship and the feeling of belongingness, but because it also allows its members to be individuals, and to express that individuality. In fact, it is only within the peer group that people can do so. (Gans, 1962)

To be an individual within such a context means to find a group which recognizes the subject as a whole person, distinguished from others by idiosyncrasies, allowed a specific place within the group on the basis of peculiarities, and fully accepted as a specific character. Individualism in this sense is fully consonnant with a Gemeinschaft type of social organization; individuals must enter into a group association before they can act out as individuals (collective orientation). This may be contrasted with the middle-class individualism, which is based first of all on a separation from the group of origin carried out in the course of a search for an occupation. Middle-class people also need and form peer groups, but there is a significant difference. While members of the working class seek identity within one closely knit peer group based primarily on kinship or on neighbourhood of origin, those of the middle class tend to be function-oriented and use a number of groups in order to satisfy a variety of needs:

> In the lower-middle-class, and more so in the upper-middle-class, people move in a larger number of peer groups, often formed to pursue specific interests and activities. The West End pattern, in which people spent most of their spare time within the confines of one peer group, is not found here. Consequently the influence of the peer group on the life of the middle-class is much less intense. (Gans, 1962)

The difference between working- and middle-class individualism as it relates to the peer group can be illustrated in terms of Gans' polarity between person-orientation (ascription) and object-orientation (achievement). He notes that object-orientation involves the striving towards the achievement of an "object" or purpose; if one can speak of individualism in this connection it is because the object in question is in general voluntarily selected by the subject. Self-identity is derived from the recognition by others of the subject's ability to achieve his or her objective goal. Such a self-identity is only partial, since the person has in general several goals; the corresponding abilities are in general recognized by different groups of people. Only the subject (and often his or her spouse) is aware of the combination of such diverse partial identities: this is the essence of a Gesellschaft type individualism. In contradistinction, the predominant aspiration in person-oriented individualism is the desire to be an accepted and identifiable member of the group:

> The object-oriented people will join a group in order to achieve a common purpose; the person-oriented ones use the group to become individuals. (Gans, 1962)

To the middle class, the group or rather groups are *a posteriori* to the definition of identity; to the working class the group is *a priori* to the definition of identity. Since children and adolescents follow a pattern of identity definition through the group, in a manner somewhat similar to that of the working-class Gemeinschaft, it seems probable the young growing *into* middle-class patterns must undergo an abstractive transformation, which is a part of their educational process and at least a contributing cause to the crises of adolescence.

Once again, Whyte's and Gans' observations point in the same direction. In *Street Corner Society*, Doc can be described as person-oriented, while Chick is object-oriented. Doc's corner-gang grew out of the habitual association of members over a long period of time and remained an integral part of its members lives, while Chick's club was originally formed for a specific purpose—the social betterment of the members and the improvement of Cornerville.

The peer group of the working-class individual also serves as a vehicle of social control. The West End could be described as a Gemeinschaft, as behavior within it is regulated by a common understanding and a fear of "what others will think," rather than by any explicit code:

> Since everyone knows everyone else, life is an open book, and deviant acts are hard to hide. This means that such acts are either committed outside the reaches of the group—as in the case of adolescents who do their misbehaving outside the West End—or they are not committed at all. (Gans, 1962)

In contrast the middle and upper classes place most emphasis on controls from within. Banfield (1968) notes that, in rearing his children, the upper-class individual stresses

> the idea that one should govern one's relations with others (and, in the final analysis, with one's self) by *internal* standards rather than by an externally given code ("not because you're told to but because you take the other person into consideration"). (Banfield, 1968)

This type of control requires the ability to emphatize (abstractive), a quality which Gans found to be lacking in the working-class individual.

Since the working class as a whole is not achievement-oriented, most working-class individuals are not socially mobile. Even more important, they do not wish to be. Gans rejects the popular notion of the working class as constantly striving to attain a middle-class way of life:

> More important, the West Enders were not frustrated seekers of middle class values. Their way of life constituted a distinct and independent working-class subculture that bore little resemblence to the middle-class. (Gans, 1962)

While members of the middle-class seek identity by achievement or occupation, those of the working class have no real concept of a "career":

Indeed, the difference between the West End and the middle-class person is perhaps nowhere greater than in his attitude toward the career. The idea that work can be the central purpose in life, and that it should be organized in a series of related jobs that make a career is virtually nonexistent among the second generation. (Gans, 1962)

Thus the working-class individuals are unable to abstract their work from their identity as peer group members. For example, Gans observed that even those who moved into professional occupations were more often concerned with using their skills on behalf of the peer group society than in the achievement of professional perfection:

But while these lawyers do want to maximize both income and status, their primary reference group is still the peer group society. As a result, they are person-oriented service agents and have no desire to be object-oriented practitioners of "the law." (Gans, 1962)

In this case "class" must be defined in terms of life-style, rather than by education, income, or occupation.

Middle-class individuals gain the respect of their peers through movement upward, while upward mobility represents a break with the peer group for the working-class individual. For instance, Gans noticed that those West Enders who aspire to the middle class had first to separate themselves from close friends and relatives, and were often rejected by their former associates:

Achievement and social mobility . . . are group phenomena. In the current generation, in which the Italian is still effectively limited to blue-collar work, atypical education and occupational mobility by the individual is frowned upon. (Gans, 1962)

Whyte's observations are similar. In *Street Corner Society* (1943), Doc was not able to separate himself from his corner boys, and thus to exercise his native ability for personal advancement. It appears that working-class peer group community and upward mobility are mutually incompatible in terms of life-styles.

Members of the upper and the upper-middle classes often need to be alone in order to express their identity. In Banfield's words (1968):

The upper-class individual is markedly self-respecting, self-confident, and self-sufficient. . . . He does not mind being alone: indeed he requires a great deal of privacy.

This description is in marked contrast with Gans' observations (1962) of the working-class West Enders:

West Enders live within the group; they do not like to be alone. . . . Indeed, for most West Enders, people who have been trained from childhood to function solely within the group, being alone brings discomfort and ultimately fear.

Gans points out that teenagers in the West End are active when they are in company of their peers, but quite passive when alone:

Their mildnes is due to the fact that they exist only partially when they are outside the group. In effect, the individual personality functions best and most completely among his or her peers. (Gans, 1962)

Likewise, Whyte (1943) points out that separation from the group may have far-reaching effects, including psychosomatic episodes. On separate occasions, two of the characters he describes suffered from nightmares and from dizzy spells when they were temporarily cut off from interaction with the peer group. Both were suddenly "cured" when the situation returned to normal:

When Long John was once more interacting with Doc and Danny with great frequency, his mental difficulties disappeared, and he began acting with the same sense of assurance that had previously characterized his behavior. (Whyte, 1943)

Similarly, in discussing the incidence of emotional disturbance and mental illness in the suburb of Levittown, New Jersey, Gans (1967) points out that the working-class women who had left the peer group community in order to move to the suburbs numbered among the more troubled Levittowners.

The associative difficulty of separating the individual from the group and the function from the individual leads to

the general inability to understand bureaucratic behavior and object orientation. This encourages the development of a conspiracy theory to explain the outside world and breeds suspicions that are frequently inaccurate. As a result, the already existing gap between the working class and the broader society is widened.

Much of the time, the working class can protect itself from real or imagined injury by minimizing its dependence on the larger society. But this solution, which may work in prosperous times and in periods of social stability, is not always effective. In depressions, emergencies, and periods of rapid social change . . . the many indirect relationships to the larger society become apparent, mainly as they are being interrupted or altered. It is at these times that normal methods . . . go awry, and the gap between the working class and the larger society—notably the government—threatens to become harmful to both. The former is hurt by its inability to understand and deal with the changes that are taking place; the latter, by its inability to develop methods to solve the resulting problems. (Gans, 1962)

In 1974 and 1975 violent riots were tearing apart Boston over the question of school integration. The parts of the city most strongly affected were working-class neighborhoods, in particular South Boston, which, although Irish and not Italian, shares many characteristics with the old West End. The courts, which had decreed integration in the name of the abstractive principles of the broader Gesellschaft, did not understand that the penetration of an associative Gemeinschaft by strangers threatens the very identity of the members of the latter. The members of the associative Gemeinschaft do not understand that strangers can be accepted on an abstractive basis, in their role of fellow students. To accept them in this manner would call for a change in the determination of one's own identity, in the direction of the middle-class way of conceiving of the self as a locus of different roles pertaining to different social groupings, rather than as a representative of a preexistent and predetermined community.

The culture of poverty

Both the working class and the middle classes form peer groups and derive their feelings of personal identity from the feedback individuals obtain from such groups. The difference between them is that in the working class the individual grows into a preexisting group, while in the middle classes the individual joins groups or forms them as he or she acquires the mastery of corresponding occupational or social skills.

In contrast, lower-class persons rarely develop any attachment to a particular group. In the *Unheavenly City*, Banfield (1968) implies a connection between the very poor sense of self-identity found in many lower-class individuals and the lack of any stable relationships:

> The lower-class individual has a feeble, attenuated sense of self. . . . He feels no attachment to community, neighbors or friends.

In *The Violent Gang*, Yablonsky (1970) refutes the notion of the lower-class gang as a cohesive, tightly organized group, and applies the term *near group* (as opposed to true group) to them. He states that

> an essential element in a normal group is that its members agree upon and are able to fulfill certain prescribed norms or standards of behavior.

The lower-class gangs studied by him are sorely lacking in these qualities:

> Unlike a true group, near groups, I found, characteristically have the following properties: (1) the roles of the members are not precisely defined; (2) the organism has limited cohesion and tends to be impermanent; (3) there is a minimum consensus among the participants about the entity's

norms; (4) the members and participants are constantly shifting; (5) leadership is often vague and confused.

Yablonsky's picture of the lower-class violent gang as a "paranoid pseudocommunity" contrasts sharply with Whyte's portrayal of Doc's working-class corner-boy gang as a tightly knit group with precisely defined roles and obligations.

Lewis (1966) arrives at similar though more general conclusions:

When we look at the culture of poverty at the local community level, we find poor housing conditions, crowding, gregariousness, but above all a minimum of organization beyond the level of extended or nuclear family. Occasionally there are informal, temporary groupings or voluntary associations within slums. The existence of neighborhood gangs which cut across slum settlements represents a considerable advance beyond the zero point of the continuum that I have in mind. Indeed, it is the low level of organization which gives the culture of poverty its marginal and anachronistic quality in our highly complex, specialized, organized society.

Even the family is loosely organized:

On the family level the major traits of the culture of poverty are the absence of childhood as a specially prolonged and protected stage in the life cycle, early initiation into sex, free unions or consensual marriages, a relatively high incidence of abandonment of wives and children, a trend toward female- or mother-centered families and consequently a much greater knowledge of maternal relatives, a strong predisposition to authoritarianism, lack of privacy, verbal emphasis on family solidarity which is only rarely achieved because of sibling rivalry, and competition for limited goods and maternal affection.

Another associative trait noted by Lewis and also in somewhat different contexts by Drake and Cayton (1962), Davis and Dollard (1940) and Schneider and Lysgaard (1953) is the strong present orientation of the lower class (and, to a lesser extent, of the working class), as opposed to the deferred gratification pattern characteristic of the middle classes. The latter is abstractive, as it requires the deliberate setting aside of existing impulses.

The very concept of a culture of poverty has come under attack on the part of a number of social scientists (cf. Leacock, 1971). It is quite possible that the very incisiveness of the phrase "culture of poverty" has something to do with the controversy. A less striking expression, such as "lower class subculture," might have been more apt to bring out the many points of agreement on facts between the proponents and the opponents of the concept.

The more thoughtful of the critics stress the point that the main characteristics of lower class behavior are due not so much to any intrinsic cultural organization within the class as to the interaction between this class and the broader society within which it is immersed. This is something which I find easy to accept. There are no such things as "adaptation" or "inadaptation," but only adaptation, or lack of it, to specific environments. Under such circumstances the pathology, whether apparent or real, which is observed in the lower class must be due not only to the characteristics of this class, but also to the environment with which it interacts. This is fully recognized by Lewis (1966):

> The culture of poverty is both an adaptation and a reaction of the poor to their marginal position in a class-stratified, highly individuated, capitalistic society. It represents an effort to cope with feelings of hopelessness and despair which develop from the realization of the improbability of achieving success in terms of the values and goals of the larger society.

The nature of the interaction is clearly put by Wright (1971):

> An urban world is a social context in which stranger relations predominate, and an urban man is someone capable of perceiving and acting in ways appropriate to living with strangers.

Folk man and Urban man

A stranger, in this sense, is someone with whom ego entertains relations limited to the definition of the social roles involved. This may mean professional interactions, service of specifically defined public servants to the public at large, common obedience to rules governing behavior in public places (e.g., traffic rules for public thoroughways), service by specifically trained professionals, etc. Contacts are abstractive and affectively neutral, at least to a considerable extent.

An "urban man" is someone aware of the structures of society needed by him and of the behaviors called for in order to obtain what he needs. He establishes relations with others on a role-to-role basis and can, at least in theory, survive in the Gesellschaft without ever depending on a friend or on close and affective relationships.

Folk individuals function poorly in the midst of strangers. To function fully they need human surroundings dominated by person-to-person relations. This may provide them with the affective possibilities they crave. Human surroundings are satisfying only if the abstractive boundary between professional roles and affective relations is left unclear.

In Wright's words (1971), the urban man, living in a world of strangers, "does not interact so much with people as he does with categories . . . waitresses, bus drivers, teachers, salesclerks and the like."

This leads to two important consequences. On the one hand, the avoidance of loneliness requires specific actions undertaken for the purpose and specific social skills making such undertakings possible. On the other hand, thinking of others in terms of categories makes it possible to think of oneself in a like manner. Identity is no longer defined by birth or by an inherited place in society. The individual can think of him- or herself in terms of categories or roles and strive to acquire a role which appeals to him or her. To a large extent the folk man is created by the group into which he is born; urban man creates himself.

Doing so is by no means easy, the more so that the two types of person, meaning the two manners of defining identity, compete one against the other. Still, the technological revolution (like the development of cities in the Middle Ages) leads to enormous increases in the number of professional definitions of social roles—and social identity definitions. The accumulation of individual potentialities makes possible the liberation of marginal groups, of which blacks and women are the clearest examples in the United States. Newly created socioeconomic roles do not lend themselves to the play of self-fulfilling prophecies by which desirable economic and social niches could be reserved to the heirs of previous holders. Computer programming cannot be inherited because there were no computer programmers in the preceding generation. Empty niches of this kind became, at least in part, open to competition. The number of identity defining skills has enormously increased.

Yet this liberating transformation is not without drawbacks. Skills define identities. People without skills have no sociably acceptable identities. This is the gist of the culture of poverty.

Once again, one must note that the essence of subcultural behavior can be understood as deriving not only from the context of individual life within specified groups, but mainly as imposed by the interaction of such groups within the broader society.

So far, the picture seems clear. On the one hand there is the folk man whose characteristics fit those of the lower and, eve more, those of the working class. His manner of determining identity, both for himself and for others, is associative: based on immediately given experience, holistic, carrying for intimates the full histories of previous encounters and incapable of situating the stranger. On the other hand there is the urban man, whose characteristics fit those of the middle classes. His manner of determining identity is abstractive: based on the conceptualization of roles.

Yet, a number of questions call for discussion. First of all, is the choice between the two types more or less free or accidental, or is the relative dominance of the urban man the result of a pervasive and perhaps irreversible sociocultural evolution? Wright (1971) seems to lean in the direction of the first alternative:

I want to suggest, too, that personal worlds are not a thing of the past, that they are not necessarily fading away, nor do they represent only small remnants left over in so-called "underdeveloped" countries or "backward" regions of developed ones. On the contrary, I would guess that may be 70 to 80 percent of the world population today live in personal worlds.

While I tend to agree with Wright as to the relative proportion of the associative and the abstract types in the world population, I hold with Durkheim (1893) that the increasing number of contacts between men and the increasing division of labor exercise a dominant influence on the evolution of societies and their cultures. This influence leads necessarily in the direction of the abstract man: Each new occupation offers him new and necessarily categorial ways of defining himself; at the same time the multiplication of human contacts deprives the individual subject of the time it takes to develop person-to-person understanding, thus forcing him or her to depend on the more rapid mechanism which consists in placing the other in some appropriate and previously conceptualized category. There is nothing wrong with such a process, as long as one remembers that categorization can be no more than the beginning of acquaintance.

I do not share the currently fashionable sorrow at the thought of the possible passing of the folk man. I hold with Gans (1962)

that what I have called the professional upper-middle-class subculture is more desirable than all the rest. If cultures can be compared in the abstract, without concern for the opportunities that encourage them, and the social conditions necessary for their existence, I believe that this culture provides a fuller, more diverse life, a greater range of choices of behavior in all major spheres of life, and the ability to deal more adequately with changing conditions and problems than do any of the other subcultures. It is by no means perfect, but it is more desirable then the others.

A second question is that of the difference between the working and the lower class. While both exhibit the characteristics of what Wright calls the folk man, the difference between their patterns of behavior is often striking. Where the working-class man is closely tied to his family and also in many cases to his union, the lower-class man shuns stable attachments.

He is unable to maintain a stable relationship with a mate; commonly he does not marry. He feels no attachment to community, neighbors, or friends (he has companions, not friends), resents all authority. . . . and is apt to think that he has been "railroaded" and to want to "get even." He is a nonparticipant: he belongs to no voluntary organizations, has no political interests, and does not vote unless paid to do so. (Banfield, 1968)

The basis of the difference may well be economic, particularly in the case of the urbanized working or lower class. In those cases where urbanization took place under conditions of equilibrium between the skills available to the immigrant and the needs of the job market—and, one might add, where ethnic discrimination was not sufficiently severe to prevent the entry of the immigrants into the job market—relatively stable communities of the working class could become established. Where those conditions were lacking, disorganization was likely.

The question whether the lower-class subculture—the culture of poverty—is sufficiently ingrained in a mass of the population to perpetuate itself even in the face of improving circumstances, or whether pathological patterns affect only some of the families in the poverty level, is a controversial one. There is no doubt that some upward mobility is present; there is also no doubt that patterns which become habitual are hard to break. Beyond this, one can only refer to the literature, in particular to Lewis (1966), Banfield (1968), Polansky et al. (1972), and Leeds (1971).

A question of particular importance in the context of the present study is whether the symptoms of tension found in the lower-class culture can be correlated with Dionysian traits. At first glance it appears that they can; the prevalence of drug abuse, of violence, of search for excitement, suggest that such is the case.

Cantril (1963), in analyzing a lynching mob of the thirties, finds that it is dominated by people in the "lowest economic brackets": 19 unemployed, 13 laborers, 8 farmers, 8 skilled workers, 3 salaried people, 4 owners of businesses, 3 miscellaneous.

At least 11 of the active participants in the riot are known to have had previous police records. Nine had been in the hands of the law for stealing, fighting, or bootlegging.

The acknowledged leader of the mob, Lank Smith, was a man 40 years old who could neither read nor write. He had no particular profession but occasionally did a little cattle trading and "bronc Bustin'" in rodeos. He drank a great deal. (Cantril, 1963)

When lower-class people emerge from their isolation, it is often to join a messianic movement, such as that of Father Divine (Cantril, 1963) or of some of the storefront churches. Such movements are described in the next chapter as Dionysian–associative reactions.

Particularism

The structuring of the social world in terms of kin or acquaintance suggests particularism in the Weberian sense, or paleo-particularism in terms of this study: social structures based on categories or roles suggests universalism.

Such suggestions are borne out by other observations. For example lower-class individuals, and to a lesser extent representatives of the working class, see authority in terms of permanent status. Nurses often report difficulties with patients and in particular with male patients belonging to those classes, who often feel diminished by acknowledging the authority of a woman. Middle-class people tend to see authority in functional terms; it is legitimate where it serves a function, "gets things done." The assumption of authority by a person in a specific functional situation does not permanently enhance the status of that person nor does it diminish the status of those who accept it.

Where most commercial exchanges engaged in by the middle class tend to be functional, impersonal, and universalized—as is shopping in a department store—business establishments in slum areas tend to cater to a restricted public of acquaintances and to carry a social meaning going beyond the abstractive specificity of business transactions:

> Many business establishments are so thoroughly acknowledged the property of a single minority group that customers outside the group seem like intruders. When I first went into the Addams area, I entered several places where I was asked "Whatta you want?" as if I were lost. What I did not know was that these places are almost never confronted by someone they have not known for years and that they are thoroughly tailored to the needs and personal peculiarities of a small group of friends within a single minority group. . . . In some ways the inner city seems the last outpost of the country store. . . . Usually the social relations that take place in these establishments parallel those occurring in the streets. People laugh, argue, insult one another, extend their sympathies, and confide their troubles. Some people spend a good proportion of the day bantering in these business places and then leave without buying anything. In fact, business transactions are often treated as a kind of an afterthought and something of a nuisance. (Suttles, 1968)

Relationships between the sexes

Another area which is influenced by the class to which the protagonists belong is that of male–female relationships. Here also the higher the social class, the greater the ability to abstract, that is, to disregard sexual differences in situations to which they are not relevant.

Let us begin with the lower class. Many men, in this class, are "action seekers":

> For the action-seeker, life is episodic. The rhythm of life is dominated by the adventurous episode, in which heights of activity and feeling are reached through exciting and sometimes riotous behavior. The goal is action, an opportunity for thrills, and for the chance to face and overcome a challenge. It may be sought in a card game, a fight, a sexual interlude, a drinking bout, a gambling session, or in a fast and furious exchange of wisecracks and insults. Whatever the episode, the action-seeker pursues it with a vengence, and lives the rest of his life in quiet—and often sullen—preparation for this climax, in which he is usually said to be "killing time." (Gans, 1962)

In contrast:

> The woman tries to develop a stable routine in the midst of poverty and deprivation; the action-seeking man upsets it. In order to have any male relationships, however, the woman must participate to some extent in his episodic life style. On rare occasions, she may even pursue it herself. Even then, however, she will try to encourage her children to seek a routine way of life. Thus the woman is much closer to working-class culture, at least in her aspirations, although she is not often successful in achieving them. (Gans, 1962)

Given this basic divergence in goals, the relationship between the sexes tends to be mutually predatory and restricted to the search for sexual gratification, including in many cases procreation as a means for ego-enhancement. Men's

> relationships with women are of brief duration, and some men remain single all their lives. . . . In the lower class the segregation of the sexes . . . is complete. (Gans, 1962)

The working class presents a different picture:

> Perhaps the most important—or at least the most visible—difference between the classes is one of family structure. *The working-class subculture* is distinguished by the dominant role of the family circle. Its way of life is based on social relationships amidst relatives. The working class views the world from the family circle. (Gans, 1962)

The male–female relationship is much more stable and affectionate than in the lower class. In spite of that, sex roles are rigidly defined, and companionship outside the traditional role-performance is minimal:

> The typical working-class family is sexually segregated. Husbands and wives exchange love and affection, but they have separate family roles and engage in little of the companionship found in the middle classes. The husband is the breadwinner and the enforcer of child discipline; the wife is the housekeeper and rears the children. Whenever possible, husbands spend their free time with other male companions, women with other women. (Gans, 1967)

In the numerous gatherings of extended families and intimate friends, men usually congregate in one room, women in another (Gans, 1962).

In the lower-middle class family, sex roles are less sharply defined because the husband and wife share a common interest in the raising of their children:

> The lower-middle class family is sexually less segregated than the working-class one. Husbands and wives are closer to being companions, for both sexes have learned to share a few common interests and to participate to some extent in each other's world. Since neither man nor woman is likely to have an intense outside avocation, the home and family are the focal point for mutuality. (Gans, 1967)

The highest degree of abstraction of sex roles may be found in the upper-middle and upper classes. While the common bond among the lower-middle class husbands and wives is the home and family, those of the upper classes share a greater variety of interests:

> Home and family are somewhat less important to this than to the other classes. The upper-middle class family has shed almost all sexual segregation. . . . Interests other than those of the house can also be shared by the spouses, and, conversely, each can have interests that take them away from the home. (Gans, 1967)

This type of male–female relationship is closely connected to the family life and to child rearing practices.

In the lower class, where the male–female relationship is associated chiefly with sexual gratification and with procreation, there exists little of the family life experienced by other classes:

> The lower-class household is usually female-based. The woman who heads it is likely to have a succession of mates who contribute intermittently to its support but take little or no part in rearing the children. In managing the children, the mother (or aunt, or grandmother) is characteristically impulsive: once they have passed babyhood they are likely to be neglected or abused, and at best they never know what to expect next. (Banfield, 1968)

The absence of consistent models on which to base behavior may account for the poor sense of identity often found in lower-class individuals, particularly males.

Although the rearing of the children is also assigned mainly to the mother in the working class, there is a significant difference between the lower and the working classes in this respect. The male in the lower-class family is often a sporadic or an absent figure, while the working class is strongly patriarchal. The authority of the male is supported by the female, and the disciplining of the child is a part of the man's role.

Children in a working-class family are raised in a household in which the adult comes first. They are expected to act in a manner pleasing to adults; the only way in which they can exercise the tastes of childhood is to escape into the peer group of their age, something which the family readily accepts.

> The children's world is their own, and only within it can they really behave like children. Parents are not expected to supervise, guide, or take part in it. In fact parent–child relationships are segregated almost as much as male–female ones. (Gans, 1962)

This method of child rearing can be directly related to the associative collective orientation (as opposed to self-orientation) found in the working class. Since children are treated as miniature adults at home, they must seek identity through close association with their peers.

In contrast to the working class, the lower-middle class family allows children to express themselves, and to act out as children. Since the husband–wife relationship in the lower-middle class is based upon a common interest in the home and family, the lower-middle class family tends to be child centered.

The upper-middle class family is somewhat less child centered, with a stronger emphasis on individualism:

> The upper-middle class is concerned with the development of the child as a unique individual, one who can perform autonomously in all spheres of life valued by the upper-middle class, especially a rewarding professional career. In order to achieve these aims, parents provide direction for the lives of their children, so that while family life is child-centered, it is also adult-directed. (Gans, 1967)

This emphasis on uniqueness (or self-orientation) is more prevalent in the upper-middle class than it is in the lower-middle class, and is found to an even greater extent among upper-class families:

> He wants to express himself (he may carry self-expression to the point of excentricity) and, in principle at least, he favors self-expression by others. (Banfield, 1968)

Of course the method of child rearing found in upper-middle and upper-class families requires the ability to separate or abstract precisely those qualities in each child that are unique.

The associative–abstractive polarity can also be seen in the broader family life of the various social classes. The working class maintains the closest family ties (except for segments of the old upper class), as membership in the peer group is based primarily on kinship:

> For the West Ender, sociability is a routinized gathering of a relatively unchanging group of family members and friends that takes place several times a week. (Gans, 1962)

In the lower-middle class family ties are not so pervasive:

> In America the clanlike extended family is highly valued only in the working class, in some ethnic groups of all classes, and, for other reasons, in the upper class. Lower-middle class people still love and visit their relatives, but if they are too far away to visit, they are not especially missed, for lower-middle class people are able to make friends. (Gans, 1967)

As the upper-middle class places the most emphasis on individual achievement, its members often find it necessary to break family ties in order to achieve:

> Since most upper-middle class people have achieved their present position by their own individual achievement, the relationship with the extended family is even more tenuous than in the lower-middle class. Upper-middle class people are good at making friends, and choose them on the basis of shared interests. (Gans, 1967)

Education

The ways in which the various classes seek identity is reflected in their attitude towards education. The degree to which individuals believe themselves capable of shaping their own futures correlates with the importance they attach to an education. Present-oriented lower-class individuals see little value in an education which prepares them for a future which they cannot visualize. The sense of fatalism found in the lower class is incompatible with the idea of an education, for if an individual believes that he or she has no control over his or her life, an education would be of little or no value and he or she will not respond well to schooling. The Coleman Report (1966) considers the social class of the parents as being the main influence on the performance of children in school.

> Schools bring little influence to bear on a child's achievement that is independent of his background and general social context. (Coleman, 1966)

Since adult-centered working-class families expect their children to act as miniature adults, they see discipline and control as the main function of the school. The person-oriented working-class individual seeks identity by ascription, and does not, therefore, place as much importance as does the middle-class individual on the value of education as a means of achievement. Gans (1962) states that most West Enders favor parochial schools because they identify the parochial school with person-oriented education.

Person-oriented education teaches children rules of behavior appropriate to the adult peer-group society, and stresses discipline. (Gans, 1962)

The working class does possess a stronger sense of the future than does the lower class, and working-class parents do want their children to finish whatever schooling is necessary to obtain a secure and stable job. On the other hand, they are not as confident of their ability to make things happen as are members of the middle and upper classes, and this sense of fatalism does color their attitude towards education.

The working-class individual does not "invest" as heavily in the future, nor in so distant a future, as does the middle-class one. . . . Also, he has less confidence than the middle class in his ability to shape the future and has a stronger sense of being at the mercy of fate, a "power structure" and other uncontrollable forces. . . . As compared to the middle-class individual, he is little disposed toward either self-improvement or self-expression; "getting ahead" or "enlarging one's horizons" have relatively little attraction for him. (Banfield, 1968)

Thus, working-class people prefer an education which stresses control rather than stimulation, as self-expression and self-improvement are incompatible with the mores of the peer-group community.

Middle-class individuals are achievement oriented, and have confidence in their ability to shape the future. An individual who is future oriented will be able to defer gratification for a greater length of time than one who is not, and middle-class individuals consequently place a great deal of emphasis on the value of an education. As lower-middle class persons are naturally more concerned with "getting ahead" than those of the upper-middle class (who have already "arrived"), they tend to emphasize education as a means to attain that goal, while those of the upper-middle class favor an educational system which caters to the unique qualities of each child.

In the lower-middle class, self-improvement is a principal theme of life, whereas in the upper-middle class, self-expression is emphasized. (Banfield, 1968)

These varying attitudes toward education can be illustrated by briefly examining the evolution of the schools in Levittown, New Jersey. Although the population of Levittown at the time of Gans' study consisted of working-, lower-middle, and upper-middle class families, the majority of the population (75%) typified the lower-middle class culture. Therefore, the curriculum in the schools came to reflect this middle ground.

These schools included all the curricular and extracurricular accoutrements one would expect in a modern middle (but not upper middle) class suburb; the education they provided would prepare the students for the same white collar, technical, and subprofessional jobs held by their parents and for the lower-middle class culture that dominated the community. . . . The teachers gave their students individual attention and demanded neither superior intellectual achievement nor oppressive memorizing. (Gans, 1967)

In other words, the schools emphasized neither the strict control ("oppressive memorizing") favored by the working class nor the more demanding approach ("superior intellectual achievement") common in upper-middle class schools.

As it was indicated in the preceding chapter, verbal fluency may be highly prized in the lower and working class as well as in the middle classes. However, it is not the same type of verbal fluency.

The peer-group society trains its members to be sensitive to people, rather than to ideas. Words are used, not as concepts, but to impress people, and argument proceeds by the use of anecdotes rather than by . . . logic. (Gans, 1962)

Such syntagmatic verbal fluency does not fit the goals of the schools to the same extent as fluency in paradigmatic usage. The resulting congruence or lack of congruence between the influences of the school and of the subculture shows in the levels of scholastic achievement.

Conclusions

This chapter shows that it is possible to analyze social stratification in terms of the opposition between the associative and the abstractive cognitive styles—even though, obviously, analyses of stratification in cognitive terms do not account for all the facets of the phenomenon. The import of the analysis in terms of the associative–abstractive polarity can be best grasped by reviewing the meaning of the two poles in terms of the total model as presented in chapter 3.

The associative pole corresponds to the subjective apex of the triangle. The abstractive pole is a synthesis between co-subjectivity and objectivity; as such it represents a point of equilibrium in the transactions between society and the world of the possible: the demands imposed upon the relevant portion of mankind by the physical environment, the state of economic competence, that of political organization, etc.

It may be suggested in consequence that the social class closest to the associative pole is in a state of imbalance with the socioenvironmental reality. Are its members in a state of satisfactory subjective equilibrium with themselves? Observation suggests a negative answer to this question. Contrarily to the even more associative members of primitive cultures, the members of the lower-class subculture are not isolated from the broader society, and the continual impingements of the latter upon them make impossible a satisfactory subjective equilibration.

The working class seems to be living in a healthy balance within its communities—Gemeinschaften forming protected enclaves within the broader American Gesellschaft. However, the equilibrium in question is precarious. It is at the mercy of changing processes in production. Technological and economic changes may require that the working person change occupations; in turn such requirements may demand a flexibility which the working-class person does not possess. The resulting conflicts were described in chapter 3 in terms of the tension between the social definition of identity, at the midpoint between the subjective and the co-subjective apexes, and the possibilities of object-directed action, at the objective apex.

The actual imbalances of the lower class, and the potential imbalances of the working one, lead to upward mobility. No matter how difficult the conditions, at least some individuals move from the lower and working classes towards the upper-middle one.

Let us now look at the other end of the continuum. Upper-middle class individuals—or rather adults having either reached this class or maintained themselves within it—are in a satisfactory state of equilibrium with the sociophysical environment. They are, however, far from the subjective pole, and in consequence, living in a world of strangers, they may suffer from an estrangement from themselves. This is particularly though not exclusively the case in adolescence. Reactions against following the upper-middle class patterns may set in.

A prominent theme of freak culture is the rejection of conventional attitudes toward the importance of financial and occupational success. Career ambitions are seen as a vice leading to the self-repression of the ambitious individual and the oppression of those touched by such strivings. "Self-repression" comes about, in part, through the necessity to conform to society's mainstream, resulting in being controlled from without. In the words of a 24-year-old self-employed fisherman:

"I've gotten away from even desiring a degree right now. And I got tired, I felt like I was always making a sacrifice. Going to school . . . that was, you know, doing this for someone else, doing it for something else, but not for me . . . and I just got tired of doing that."

Freaks are accutely aware of the costs of a successful career. They note, for example, that one must be willing to postpone immediate satisfactions in the interest of long-range goals; that the process of career accomplishment requires that individuals plan their lives, schedule their activities, and adopt a calculating attitude toward the utilization of their resources and other human beings; and that with a career comes the obligation to maintain at least the appearance of conventional morality, acceptable manners, tact, and personability.

Freaks argue that this traditional career orientation requires an impressive amount of impulse-control, the consequence of which, from their point of view, is the smothering of spontaneity and freedom. Ideally, to be free is to leave the future unconstrained, i.e., unplanned, and thereby open to whatever each successive "present moment" offers. (Wieder and Zimmerman, 1974)

Yet alienation from the self is by no means a necessary consequence of the abstractiveness of the upper-middle class subculture. Members of this culture are very heavy consumers of the type of artifacts which were described in chapters 2 and 3 as the products of *individual* associative reactions against the imperatives of the *collective* abstractionism of large and mobile societies: literature, art, the pleasure of going to concerts and to museums, the pleasure of knowing and of acquiring new knowledge; also, perhaps most important of all, the pleasure of being associative within the confines of a rich family life.

Obviously, however, the very tensions postulated as the bases of the model suggest that there is no perfect solution. The very fact that in an upper-middle class marriage in contemporary America the spouse is called upon to be everything—lover, companion, sharer of interests and of responsibilities, co-parent, best friend—imposes a heavy burden on the institution of marriage, which is considered the ultimate, quasi-private Gemeinschaft. Hence, in part, the frequency of divorce.

7

SOCIAL MOVEMENTS AS ASSOCIATIVE REACTIONS

The questions discussed up to this point suggest an evolutionary direction of cultural development: from the associative towards the abstractive, or rather from cultures based on relatively small amounts of information shared on the basis of common and direct experience towards cultures centered around the systematic organization of knowledge permitting the retention of large amounts of information, much of which is obtained from others through socially defined and often specialized channels.

It becomes necessary at this point to introduce another cultural schema, that of often violent social movements which, in many cases, lead to strongly associative behavior, suggesting a change of direction at least on a temporary basis.

The basis for social norms

D. L. Rosenhahn (1972) writes:

Altruism constitutes a paradox for learning theory. By definition altruism is a form of behavior which is engaged at some cost to the actor and without tangible rewards for him. Learning theory, however, implies reinforcement both in the learning and in the maintenance of all behavior. How is then altruistic behavior learned and maintained?

The answer to this question must be sought in the imbedded-

115

ness of the individual in his society *and* in the need for the individual to maintain a considerable degree of constancy in his behavior.

Let us begin with Rosenhahn's second point, which is the less obvious of the two. A good purchase on the question may be found in Piaget's concept of functional assimilation: The subject, placed in a configuration of sensorial inputs differing slightly but not overwhelmingly from previous experience, tests the schemata of action available to him against the new environment. The concept of functional assimilation is fully compatible with that of reinforcement; the reward in this case is the subject's success in testing him- or herself against the environment, and his or her success in structuring transactions with the environment in a manner which makes the latter predictable. Clearly, such predictability calls not only for a knowledge of the environment, but also for a considerable amount of consistency in the behavior of the subject. Such consistency may be derived from behavior learned in situations, in which such relatively near-term rewards as social approval and the pleasure of mastery over a relatively manageable environment are available. Such patterns may become part of the expectations of the subject in regard to him- or herself. The failure to live up to one's expectations may be sufficiently fearsome to make people live up to them—even under adverse circumstances. Once again, the core of the explanation is functional assimilation: the fact that patterns of behavior are usually learned not within the context of their ultimate application, but rather in more attenuated contexts, in which they appear as "pre-exercises," according to Groos (1898, 1901). The behavior of many a military hero began with playing soldiers.

As for the content of behavior learned in this manner, much if not most of it is determined by the needs of the social group, and by the specific manner in which the culture concerned has determined and selected the patterns which make up its expectations in regard to its members.

An example of contrasting norms in two different populations may clarify the point. Comparing the Yoruba and the Hausa, LeVine (1973) writes:

> A most obvious difference had to do with sociability. The Yoruba engaged in a great deal of jovial public conversation with many different persons, often accompanied by laughter and other indications of friendliness. The Hausa, though also sociable, were much more restrained in their expressions of friendly interest. . . . The Yoruba sociologist, Fadipe, wrote:
>
> "The Yoruba is gregarious and sociable. . . . [The] Yoruba is more of an extrovert than an introvert. The self-contained, self-reliant person who can keep his mental and physical suffering to himself so that others may

not express their sympathy for him is regarded as churlish and one to be feared. . . ." (Fadipe, 1970)

In contrast, the Hausa value highly the personal quality called *fara's* . . . which has the connotation of a calm, stoical pleasantness no matter what the stress or provocation, and they admire the quality termed *fillanci* and *filako*, which connote reticence, the denial of one's own needs in public and the ability to endure severe pain without complaint.

These differences in the normative ideals of sociability and sharing one's suffering with others seemed to be widely realized in . . . actual behavior. . . . Physicians and nurses in the local hospital reported that Yoruba women cried out and moaned freely during childbirth, while Hausa women hardly ever made any sound even during difficult deliveries. Here is evidence that conformity with their respective cultural ideals is achieved even during the pain and stress of this universal biological event. This is programmed into personality functioning, determining emotional response to pain.

Here we have two diametrically opposed patterns of behavior, both of which satisfy a number of conditions making possible life within society. In both cases,

1. The behavior of the individual fulfills the expectations of the group and is rewarded by group approval.
2. The behavior of the individual fulfills his or her own expectations in regard to him- or herself.
3. The behavior of the group fulfills the expectations the individual holds in regard to the group, in particular by the group's approval of the type of individual behavior which the subject expects to be approved.

It is the presence of such nexus of mutual expectations which defines pro-social behavior. Can such behavior be properly defined as "altruistic?" Only marginally, in my opinion. What is at stake is not so much the opposition between the interests of the self and those of others, as is an opposition between behavior based exclusively on short range considerations, and behavior determined by longer range views of the self. The fact of being able to describe oneself as "honest" may be more important to the properly socialized individual than might be a material reward obtained through stealing.

Let us consider another example. Kluckhohn and Strodbeck (1962) note that Anglo American children value positively the praising of their performance by teachers and other adult authority figures. In contrast, Navajo children construe such praise negatively. In their culture the individual ought to blend within the group rather than to compete with the other members. Should one interpret the Navajo orientation as being more altruistic or pro-social than is the Anglo American one? Not in my opinion. Competitiveness dominated by the rules of fair play may provide a basis for the organization of society; furthermore there is no clear reason why such a basis would be less satisfactory, from either the pragmatic of the ethical points of view, than is the pattern of noncompetitive cooperation.

The considerations above suggest an interdependence between the individual and the group; the group depends on the individuals' following approved rules of behavior in order to satisfy the community's need for mutual predictability; the individual depends on social approval of the behavior he has learned in the course of socialization for the confirmation of his identity by society. Thus, socially approved behavior is not necessarily behavior in which individuals altruistically sacrifice their own interests for the sake of others; it is rather a behavior in which individuals sacrifice some of their desires for the sake of some other interests.

Yet, a problem remains, and a very major one at that. The comparison between the Yoruba and the Hausa (which could have possibly held in comparing various other national groups) shows two diametrically opposed but equally viable patterns of behavior.

Is then the matter of social norms a purely arbitrary one, a question of the sharing or the lack of sharing of norms, to which the content of the norms is irrelevant? If such is the case, by what mechanism could common codes be developed in cases of mergers of populations into superordinate groupings?

Let us again look at the Yoruba and the Hausa. Both are Nigerians and subject to Nigerian law. The divergent manners in which self-worth is recognized may remain in place only as long as intimate contacts between the two groups are limited. Should the number of such contacts increase—as it probably must—the result must be either friction ("just like a Hausa!" or "just like a Yoruba!") or the development of an attitude of neutrality or even indifference towards the incompatible codes of behavior. The law of the superordinate entity, Nigeria in this case, must take such an attitude of indifference and place itself at a higher level of abstraction. Yet it may be asked what, in such a case, will play the part of the cultural codes of behavior in the coordination of individual identities and of social needs? When neither the Hausa stiff upper lip nor the Yoruba sharing an affect can any longer be described as *the* proper behavior, what can be so described? What sort of guidelines will be provided to individuals, to make them want to act in a manner approved by society, in such a way that identical behaviors will serve the needs of both society and the individual?

Two models of psychosocial homeostasis

Answers to these questions may be sought through analyses based on the evolutionary properties of the model put forward in chapter 3. The first step in the analysis may be the introduction of two models of psychosocial homeostasis, of the manner in which congruence is obtained between pro-personal and pro-social behaviors.

The first model to be discussed was put forward by Hsu (1971). Man and his place within the society and the environment may be pictured in a psychosociogram in which concentric rings represent different modes of knowledge and different subject matters of knowledge:

FIGURE 7:

0	Outer World	
1	Wider Society and Culture	
2	Operative Society and Culture	
3	Intimate Society and Culture	Jen
4	Expressible Conscious	
5	Unexpressed conscious	
6	Preconscious	Freudian
7	Unconscious	

Layers 7 and 6 consist of the "unconscious" and the "pre-conscious" in Freud's formulation. They contain repressed or semi-repressed psychic materials. . . . Layer 5 is termed "unexpressed conscious" because its contents are generally kept to the individual himself. . . .

Layer 4 is termed "expressible conscious" since it contains ideas and feelings which the individual can and does communicate to his fellow human beings. . . . The hallmark of Layer 4 is that its contents can not only be easily communicated to others but also understood and responded to by others without great difficulty. . . .

Layer 3 contains, first, human beings with whom the individual stands in a relation of intimacy. By intimacy I refer to a relationship in which all parties can afford to let their guards down. . . . Layer 3 also contains cultural usages (such as the Hindu's strong sense of caste pollution, the American male's aversion to physical intimacy with another male) and artifacts. . . . The hallmark of Layer 3 is the high degree of affect. That is to say, the individual's relations with humans, animals, artifacts, and cultural rules is this layer is likely to be a matter of *feeling rather than of usefulness.* . . .

By contrast the hallmark of Layer 2 is that it is characterized by role relationships. The individual's Layer 2 is inhabited in the first place by humans to whom he relates according to their *usefulness to him rather than his feeling towards them.* . . . The cultural rules and artifacts in Layer 2 are those with which the individual deals without emotional attachment. Examples are . . . traffic rules [and] . . . courtesy customs. . . .

Of course, for members of different societies the same humans or material substances may be in Layers 2 or 3. For example while spouses are definitely in Layer 3 of most adult Americans, they may only be in Layer 2 of most adult Alorese or Dobuans. . . . Farm land is another example. For most Chinese in traditional China a farm was a man's most important sign of success and security. It not only concerned him but also his relationship with and feelings about his ancestors and his descendents. For this reason, sale of his land was to many a Chinese farmer not unlike being confronted with the funeral of a dear one. He would therefore resort to uneconomic means of holding on to it rather than sell it. Land was definitely part of the traditional Chinese individual's Layer 3. His attitude toward it contrasts sharply with that of the average American, which is to treat ownership of land as one form of investment—like buying shares in a company. Land is, therefore, in the American individual's Layer 2. . . .

Layer 1 consists of human beings, cultural rules, knowledge, and artifacts which are present in the larger society but which may or may not have any connection with the individual. Until very recently Blacks were in this layer for a majority of white Americans. . . .

In Layer 0 are peoples, customs, and artifacts belonging to other societies with which most members of any society have no contact. (Hsu, 1971)

The usual western understanding of "personality" covers everything inside the heavy line separating Layers 3 and 4. Everything inside the line is taken to be the "personality"; everything outside it is the "environment." There may be good reasons for viewing personality in this manner, but there are also good reasons for seeking another concept for the definition of human individuality and identity. To begin with, the contents of an individual subconscious may well be unknown not only to the individual, but also to anyone else. In fact we know much more about the human unconscious in its generality than about the distinctive unconscious of particular individuals. More importantly, restricting personality to the inside of the integumental boundary between Layers 3 and 4 fails to take into account the enormous importance of the intimate environment for the functioning of the individual.

We need a more precise delineation of the individual's relationship with his world of men, gods and things, and to see this relationship not merely in terms of "semantic organization" and "cognitive tasks," but also of the *intensity of affective involvement.*

The first step toward understanding our new formulation is to leave the term personality and to concentrate on the shaded area in . . . [Figure 7], which comprizes Layers 3 and 4, with the shading running slightly into Layers 2 and 5. This shaded area is the central substance of man as a social and cultural being. It is the *human constant*, within which every human individual tends to maintain a satisfactory level of psychic and interpersonal equilibrium, in the same sense that every physical organism tends to maintain a uniform and beneficial stability within and between its parts. We shall term the process in the human constant psychosocial homeostasis. . . .

Borrowing a term from the Chinese, I should like to call the shaded area in the diagram . . . *jen*. This is the Chinese word meaning "man," and if we must have an English equivalent for it we may roughly designate it as *personage*. I suggest the term *jen* advisedly because the Chinese conception of man (also shared by the Japanese but pronounced *jin*) is based on the *individual's transactions with is fellow human beings*. When the Chinese say of so-and-so "t'a pu shih jen" (he is not a *jen*), they do not mean that this person is a human animal. Instead they mean that his behavior in regard to other human beings is not acceptable. . . .

Jen contrasts sharply with the concept of personality. The concept of personality puts the emphasis on what goes on in the individual's psyche including his deep core of complexes and anxieties. The nature of the individual's external behavior are seen as *expressions, reasons or indicators* of these forces. Since the deepest complexes and anxieties are also regarded as the prime movers of the entire psyche, the rearrangement of such complexes and anxieties is seen to hold the key to the solution of the individual's problems. But the concept of *jen* puts the emphasis on interpersonal transactions. It does not concern the individual psyche's deep cores of complexes and anxieties. Instead it sees the nature of the individual's external behavior in terms of *how it fits or fails to fit the interpersonal standards of the society and culture*. (Hsu, 1971)

The relative importance of the shaded and of the white areas for the psychosocial homeostasis of the individual, or of the individual as representative of a culture, depends on the degree of permanence of the inhabitants of Layer 3, and of the coordinate behaviors and thoughts in Layer 4.

Almost every human being in every society begins life with parents (often siblings as well) who are the first inhabitants of his Layer 3. For the Chinese whose culture says his self-esteem and future are tied to his first group, the parents, siblings, and other close relatives in his Layer 3 are its permanent inhabitants. . . . The individual tends to have close relatives nearby, and interact with them most frequently. They are likely to engage most of his attention, and command his respect or respect him depending on his place in the kinship organization. . . . Hence filial piety is the cornerstone of all morality, ancestral land is the basic attachment, and the

individual is enjoined not to be adventurous toward the rest of the world.
(Hsu, 1971)

To use the terminology introduced in chapter 6, this is the picture in so far as the folk man or the Gemeinschaft man is concerned. The situation is quite different in the large Gesellschaft characterized by great social mobility—as in the case of the man attuned to a society of strangers.

> The Westerner also beings his life with parents and siblings. These two are the first inhabitants of his Layer 3. But since his culture says that his self-esteem and future depend on how well he can stand on his own two feet, his parents and siblings are but his Layer 3's temporary occupants. As he grows up he does not invariably leave them or they him, but his relationship with them is a voluntary one, especially after he marries or reaches legal maturity. Consequently his Layer 3 tends to be filled with individuals other than those with whom he began as human being. Since these individuals are non-kin he has to go out to search for them. (Hsu, 1971)

The new inhabitants of Layer 3 are drawn from the outer layers:

> . . . He may have to explore Layers 2 but especially 1 or 0 for new frontiers, other peoples, and other worlds to which he can relate. He needs to convert or incorporate some or all of the inhabitants in these layers into his Layer 3. (Hsu, 1971)

Growing up among the original or natural inhabitants of Layer 3 does not call for the conceptualization of the latter: What correspond to them in the psyche are habits, not concepts. The situation is different in the case of Layers 2, 1, or 0, or even in the case of inhabitants of Layer 3 recruited from the outer layers. Such people are known to ego as conceptualizations of their roles before they are drawn into the intimacy of Layer 3, which in any case happens only to a minority of those encountered. Moreover ego is conscious of the fact that he appears to others first of all as a role which is a part of their conceptualizations of the world. In consequence, he must conceptualize himself, to know in what guise he may appear to others. In consequence excursions into the outer layers of the world imply at least some introspection into Layers 5, 6, and even 7.

The difference between the bases of social homeostasis for members of stable *Gemeinschaften* and for those of broad *Gesellschaften* is in the main that between feedback and conceptualization.

Can conceptualizations, including conceptualizations of right and wrong, provide the reinforcements needed to actuate pro-social behavior? An attempt to answer this question calls for a model of the anatomy of the self and of psychosocial homeostasis different from the one presented in Figure 7.

The behavior of a subject in the face of a given set of circumstances is determined in part by these circumstances and in part by the prior knowledge in the light of which he interprets the cues present in the set. This is the transactional principle as presented in chapter 4. Given different subjects, differences and similarities in their responses to the same environments are determined by the differences and similarities in their prior knowledges. Since such differences (or similarities) in behavior are the data on the basis of which the personalities of the subjects might be described, we will define the *total personality* of an individual as the sum total of the knowledge, conscious or subconscious, which he brings to the oncoming encounters between himself and various aspects of the environment. Taken in this sense, the total personality is the self-as-knower, or the "I" in William James' terms (1890).

Some items within the structure of the total personality deal with the knowledge a person has of him- or herself. The sum and structure of these items will be called the *self-image*. It corresponds to the self-as-known, or the Me. Clearly, the self-image is a part of the total personality:

FIGURE 8:

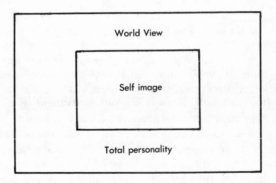

The part of the total personality outside the self-image is the knowledge the self has of the world, or his world view.

Many concepts about man exist within the total personality in conjugated pairs: One member of the pair is part of the world view and the other is a part of the self-image. For example, one member of the pair may be the conceptualization of "a good man," as part of the world view; the other member of the pair is the conceptualization of the self as a good man and is part of the self-image.

The two members of the pair may be in harmony or in disharmony. The subject may view positively a given characteristic within the world view, and find that the characteristic in question either can or cannot be ascribed to his self-image. The first situation is one of cognitive harmony or consonance, the second one amounts to disharmony or dissonance. It may be assumed that harmony is more comfortable than disharmony.

Every concept is an actual or potential schema of action. One of the most important characteristics of cultures in which a great part of the socialization process consists in imparting to the young a theoretical understanding of items they have not yet encountered in the object world is that members of such cultures are frequently on the lookout for situations in which they will have an opportunity to carry out schemata of action previously sketched out in their knowledge. The occurrence of such situations, and the carrying out of the corresponding schemata, amount to functional assimilation.

As it was shown in chapter 4, functional assimilations carry with them their own reinforcements. The successful carrying out of a schema brings with it a confirmation of the world view *and* a confirmation of the self-image; the two are brought into closer harmony, and dissonance is reduced.

The mechanism may be illustrated by a quotation from Geertz (1973):

> Between ethos and world view, between the approved style of life and the assumed structure of reality, there is conceived to be a simple and fundamental congruence such that they complete one another and lend one another meaning. In Java, for example, this view is summed up in a concept one hears continuously invoked, that of *tjotjog*. *Tjotjog* means to fit, as a key does in a lock, as an efficacious medicine does to a disease, as a solution does an arithmetical problem, as a man does with the woman he marries (if he does not, they will divorce). If your opinion agrees with mine we *tjotjog*; if the meaning of my name fits my character (and if it brings me luck), it is said to be *tjotjog*. Tasty food, correct theories, good manners, comfortable surroundings, gratifying outcomes all *tjotjog*. In the broadest and most abstract sense, two items *tjotjog* when their coincidence forms a coherent pattern which gives to each a significance and a value it does not in itself have. . . . In its specificity, *tjotjog* is a peculiarly Javanese idea, but the notion that life takes on its true import when human actions are tuned to cosmic conditions is widespread.

The sort of counterpoint between style of life and fundamental reality which the sacred symbols formulate varies from culture to culture. For the Navaho, an ethic prizing calm deliberateness, untiring persistence, and dignified caution complements an image of nature as tremendously powerful, mechanically regular, and highly dangerous. For the French, a logical legalism is a response to the notion that reality is rationally structured, that first principles are clear, precise and unalterable and so need only to be discerned, memorized, and deductively applied to concrete cases. For the Hindus, a transcendental moral determinism in which one's social and spiritual status in a future incarnation is an automatic outcome of the nature of one's action in the present, is completed by a ritualistic duty-ethic bound to caste. In itself, either side, the normative or the metaphysical, is arbitrary, but taken together they form a Gestalt with a peculiar kind of inevitability; a French ethic in a Navaho world, or a Hindu one on a French world would seem only quixotic, for it would lack the air of naturalness and simple factuality which it has in its own context. It is this air of the factual, of describing, after all, the genuinely reasonable way to live which, given the facts of life, is the primary source of such an ethic's authoritativeness. What all sacred symbols assert is that the good for man is to live realistically; where they differ is in the vision of reality they construct.

Tjotjog is an internalized cultural value. It is also an abstraction. It might be translated as "harmony" or "to harmonize." Taken in this sense, it appears as the metaphorical (and quite usual) sense of "harmony," not in the precisely conceptualized sense it has in musical theory. It is thus somewhat diffuse, and, although definitely an abstraction, it carries many subjective associations. As such it fits with the Javanese culture which is strongly associative as compared with Western cultures—for example with the French notion that reality is rationally structured. The Javanese will say that "south is red," in the sense of existential fit between the two, not, as Westerners might, that it reminds one of red, or that it might be illustrated or symbolized as red. This suggests a type of classification based on subjective harmonies rather than on objective relationships or similarities. This type of classification will be discussed at greater length in the chapter on preliterate cultures, in which an example taken from the Hopi culture will be presented.

Yet even if *tjotjog* carries strong associative connotations, it is an internalized value pairing together notions from the world view and notions pertaining to personal conduct. It parallels the classical Chinese value of no contest with the world. As such it illustrates the model in Figure 8.

Figure 7 is psychosocial homeostasis conceived primarily *in terms of social structure*. The feedback is its essence as derived from close and permanent social relationships. Figure 8 is psychosocial homeostasis conceived primarily *in terms of the internalization of culture*. The model it represents depends less on shared relationships and more on shared abstractions.

There is no necessary opposition between the two models. In most situations of cultural and social stability, the two types of relationships are likely to coexist and to reinforce one another. However, such a harmony between the social and the cultural may not always exist. Social relationships may change without an immediate corresponding transformation of cultural internalizations (Geertz, 1973). This often happens as a result of culture contact. Most of the remainder of this chapter deals with such situations.

There is a point, already brought up above, which must be insisted upon. The looser social relationships are, the more social cohesion must depend on shared cultural internalizations. Immediate feedback is available in closely knit folk societies; in societies of strangers mutual trust must be based on the sharing of values and ideas. The model in Figure 7 applies more easily to societies in which the individual's place in the scheme of things is determined by kinship or by fixed social station. The model in Figure 8 acquires more importance in societies characterized by individual mobility and the definition of identity in terms of roles, that is to say, of abstractions.

Mechanical and organic solidarity; some differences of opinion

Durkheim (1893) suggests that social solidarity in relatively simple and primitive societies is mechanical, in the sense that attitudes and in consequence behaviors are shared; the same things horrify and the same things enthrall all the members of society. There is in this thesis an implication of symmetry, which contrasts with the complementarity upon which is assumed to be based the organic solidarity of complex societies, in which every individual depends for survival on the carrying out by others of the functions they have within the social whole.

There is a degree of contradiction between such an understanding of mechanical and organic solidarities and the suggestions presented in the preceding section. According to the latter, it is the relatively simple and stable communities (Gemeinschaften) which depend on asymmetrical feedback, even though the latter might well be described as mechanical, in the sense of being applied automatically. In contradistinction, it was suggested that more advanced societies (Gesellschaften) base their social solidarity on the sharing of conceptualizations, that is to say on an essentially symmetrical type of relation.

There is an apparent paradox in such a position. Advanced

societies are enormously differentiated from the point of view of the division of social functions or of social labor. In consequence, social relationships within them should be, and unavoidably are, asymmetrical. In contrast, the more primitive communities are poor in functional distinctions. Being relatively undifferentiated from the functional point of view, they should be symmetrical in their attitudes.

Yet even if the functional differentiation in primitive communities is rudimentary, such communities are in fact differentiated, but on another basis—that of kinship and clanship. Social relations in them are based on complex networks of reciprocity. Such networks are particularistic, or rather paleo-particularistic, and unavoidably asymmetrical.

In Tangu, in New Guinea,

> each household has trading or exchange relationships with those households formed by the married men who stand as brothers to the wife, and those in which the wives stand as sisters to the husband. Where the relationship between the spouses of a household can be expressed as brother-sister relationship those households are, or might potentially be, in a trading or exchange relationship. Conversely, where a trading or exchange relationship exists between households, those households are described as standing to each other as brother and sister. (Burridge, 1970)

This particularism, with its attendant separation between intimates and strangers, extends at times beyond the boundaries of kinship. In the vast trading institution of the Kula, in the Melanesian islands northeast of New Guinea, there is no market place in which people can meet in the relatively symmetrical—and conceptualized—functions of traders.

> The exchange of these two classes of *vaygu'a* (valuables), of the arm-shells and the necklaces, constitutes the main act of the Kula. The exchange is not done freely, . . . as opportunity offers, and where the whim leads. It is subject indeed to strict limitations and regulations. One of these refers to the sociology of the exchange, and entails that Kula transactions can be done only between partners. A man who is in the Kula—for not everyone within its district is entitled to carry it on—has only a limited number of persons with whom he deals. This partnership is entered upon in a definite manner, under fulfillment of certain formalities, and it constitutes a life-long partnership. The number of partners a man has varies with his rank and importance. A commoner in the Trobriands would have a few partners only, whereas a chief would number hundreds of them. There is no special social mechanism to limit the partnership of some people and extend that of the others, but a man would naturally know to what number of partners he was entitled by his rank and position. And there would be always the example of his immediate ancestors to guide him. . . .

> Two Kula partners have to *kula* with one another, and exchange other gifts incidentally; they behave as friends, and have a number of mutual duties and obligations, which vary with the distance between their villages and with their reciprocal status. (Malinowski, 1961)

We may compare this, as Weber (1922) did, with the universality and the impersonality of modern trade exchanges, in which the buyer and even to a large extent the selling organization remain largely anonymous. Even the asymmetry between the roles of buyer and seller is in a way negated by the common, and therefore symmetrical, conceptualization each has of the other.

Particularism extends beyond economic and social relationships. Far from being horrified and enthralled by the same things, members of preliterate communities have their particular clan or even individual totems and taboos, or in other words their particular moral obligations.

> In Aurora it is the future mother who imagines that a coconut, the fruit of a bread-tree, or some other object is mysteriously tied to the child, who in a way echoes it. Rivers found the same beliefs in Mota, where many people follow dietary prohibitions because each thinks himself to be an animal or a fruit found or noticed by his mother when she was pregnant.
>
> It happens at times in Lifu that a man specifies before dying the animal—bird or butterfly—in the shape of which he will be reincarnated. The eating or the killing of that animal is forbidden to all his descendents: "It is our ancestor" they say, and they offer it gifts. (Lévi-Strauss, 1962a)

It would appear that social solidarity in associative communities is caused less by the sharing of beliefs than by a network of mutual obligations—an organic solidarity—which give every individual a fixed place in relationship to other members of society.

What, now, is the situation in advanced abstractive societies? Assuredly there is an overwhelming degree of mutual dependence among individuals occupying different niches or playing different roles in regard to the needs of the collectivity. Yet this type of organic dependence may not suffice to insure solidarity. What is needed over and above complementarity of roles is a common understanding or a shared conceptualization of this complementarity. Mutual trust between doctor and patient depends not only on the two needing one another, but also on conceptualizations of disease which the two share. The patient accepts an operation not only because he needs it objectively, nor even because the role charisma of the physician is sufficient to have his ministrations automatically accepted, but also because the patient shares at least the rudiments of the physician's understanding of such items as appendicitis or cancer. Where this type of common understanding is lacking, mistrust is likely to develop.

An example of such mistrust may be found in the movements in opposition to the fluoridation of drinking water which took place in the United States in the middle of the twentieth century. In many places fluoridation was approved by municipal authorities on the recommendation of specialists in dentistry. The population was not consulted, and no significant opposition arose. It may be assumed that the authorities responsible for the decision had a sufficient conceptual understanding of the scientific standing of dentistry to trust the recommendations of its practitioners. On the other hand, the reciprocal relationship between the elected authorities and the voters was sufficiently established to endow the former with an amount of role charisma and the latter with a sufficient habit of responsiveness and trust to make the operation proceed smoothly. However, there were communities in which the question of fluoridation was put to a referendum. Such a referendum amounted to asking for a decision on the part of people, many of whom lacked the conceptual understanding needed for deciding. The result was an outpouring of often hysterical opposition.

Quotations from some of the leaders of the opposition show clearly its associative character:

> According to the "Americanism Bulletin" . . . fluoridation is "a plot of the world planners . . . more dangerous than atomic bombs." It breaks down the "wills of the people." "It is reported that in Russia fluorine was added to the milk given to babies in order to weaken their wills and make them more amenable to dictatorship when they grow up."
> . . . Future defenders of America at West Point and Annapolis are getting a "Russian prescribed dose of fluoride poisoning in their tap water." (Reinmer, 1955)

There is a retired dentist among the active opponents of fluoridation, but in most of his statements he avoids any reference to dentistry, stating instead:

> "I find men like my senator Taft died after drinking this water one year. I find one Supreme Court Justice from Kentucky also buried after drinking the water one year. Many of our Senators and Representatives are gone." (Reinmer, 1955)
> Pro-fluoride people pointed once more to their statistics. When used properly, they said, sodium fluoride affects nothing but children's teeth; And it does them a world of good, e.g., in Newburgh, N.Y., it has cut cavities among children by 30%. The cost would be negligible (about 10¢ a month for each householder). (Fight over Fluoride, 1952)

But

It was plain that the fluoride men were speaking to rising opposition. Seattle audiences had all too obviously been moved by the questionable science of pamphlets that named fluoride as the cause of "arterial and venous hardening, . . . cavities in head bones; premature aging . . . changes of disposition; irritability, apprehension, discontent, undue financial anxiety; loss of memory; satyriasis, nymphomania. (Fight over Fluoride, 1952) In Northampton . . . fluoridation was defeated by a vote of two to one. (Mausner and Mausner, 1955)

At first glance the reason for the anti-fluoridation movements appears to be specific, to wit fluoridation. Yet in reality it is something more; a general destabilization of psychosocial homeostasis, which is no longer assured by direct person-to-person feedback and not yet assured by shared conceptualization. The result is a rejection of the social system.

People were stirred by groups. . . . All of these groups combined and incorporated as a "Liberty Party" and since they were able to defeat the fluoridation program, they have been active in resisting school improvements, attempted to defeat the formation of a hospital district, and [engaged in] the smearing of individuals in the city administration and other political subdivisions. (Mausner and Mausner, 1955)

To consolidate the suggestions presented so far in this chapter: The social solidarity of the group and the psychosocial homeostasis of individuals—and perhaps their sense of self-identity—can be assured by two mechanisms. One of these depends mainly on social interaction, the other on a cultural sharing of values and concepts. In most cases, the two mechanisms operate jointly and reinforce each other. Their importance is unequal in different types of society and culture. The suggestion presented here is that the interaction mechanism is more important in relatively early and/or relatively small communities, or in large but segmented ones, in which interaction within stable cores of people is vigorous; conversely, the conceptual sharing mechanism appears to be of paramount importance in large and mobile societies in which much of social interaction is between strangers or between conceptualized roles, rather than between intimates.

In cultures tending towards a Gesellschaft type of social organization, social mobility has led to a historical weakening of stable human surroundings typical of Gemeinschaften. In consequence the ability of the interaction mechanism has been decreasing. At the same time the amount of shared abstractions has been increasing, in such a way that the second mechanism could (at least theoretically) take up the slack and insure a sufficient level of pro-social behavior and also sufficient opportunities for the self-validation of individuals, on the basis of the use of both mechanisms.

However, in situations in which the development of the system of shared abstractions is insufficient to make up for the weakening of social control and of the corresponding mechanism for developing self-identity, destabilization is likely to occur. The form it may take may be one of individual anomie and criminality. It may also lead to social movements opposed to the society at large and trying to substitute their own culture and morality systems for the standards of the broader society. An example of such a movement may be that of the Kingdoms of Father Divine. This movement was analyzed by Cantril (1963) and will be described in a later section. Other examples involving a considerable degree of cultural pathology may be found in the formation of urban gangs (Thrasher, 1927; Yablonsky, 1970). Complex societies made up of very different cultural groups, such as the colonies or former colonies, are also likely to erupt in violent movements. The schema of such culture contact movements is usually the destruction of the codes of pro-social and self-validating behavior of an indigenous culture under the influence of a colonizing culture which is in many cases too distant from the indigenous culture to be understood and to create a healthy cultural amalgam.

From steady state to revitalization movement

Almost any description of a culture and a society in a state of balance may serve as an example of what may be called a "steady state." Descriptions of preliterate cultures may be particularly striking, both because such cultures tend to remain unchanged for long periods of time in the absence of cultural contact, and because their practices are sufficiently different from "our own" to show that the sharing of values and the feedback leading to psychosocial homeostasis may be established through customs very different from "ours." Particularly clear examples may be derived from the descriptions of systems of exchange aiming at status seeking and self-validation, such as the Kula cycle (Malinowski, 1961). A different example will be selected, for the sake of variety; it deals with an area within the New Hebrides archipelago (Harrison, 1937).

> Pigs are our life and our progress. Without pigs we should only exist. Our pigs are power.

The ownership of pigs is not purely utilitarian. The boars of the local variety have tusks which curve out of the snout if the corresponding upper teeth are removed. They may grow in a circle, penetrate again the lower jawbone, grow through it in another full circle, and, very seldom, reach around for a third time. The growth of the tusk through the bone is extremely painful. The only thing which the pig can eat is a soft, specially prepared mush. At no time can it be left to root for itself, lest it break a tusk and lose all value. For the animal's value is not in the meat. In any case the boars are scrawny, as the pain of the growing tusks prevents proper feeding. What counts is a live animal with magnifically curving tusks.

Young men borrow piglets for bridewealth and for the beginning of a breeding herd. What is borrowed has to be repaid and repaid at interest, not necessarily with the same pigs, but with boars with the length of tusk that would have accrued in the amount of time from borrowing to repayment. The main goal of the householder is to repay his debt and to lend out some of his pigs, so that they can grow their tusks at the borrower's risk. In the meantime the herd grows by reproduction.

Finally the herd reaches the numbers that make the next step permissible. Through a number of prescribed rituals lasting over a year, the man invites the populations of several villages to a great dance. In the course of the ceremonies, the boars are killed and eaten. The man is poor once again—but he is entitled to take a new and honored name.

> Great is the effort of each ascent, its strain and excitement; the result is worth it. For at the end the man will take a new name, a rank, privileges of that rank such as the right to wear a certain feather in his hair, croton in his belt, shell armlet above his elbow, or to make a fence of croton root around his garden. While above all these visible things he will be invisibly higher, away from the earth itself, from the rubbish life. (Harrison, 1937)

What we have in this description is a design for living. This design may appear arbitrary, because its arbitrariness is different from the arbitrariness of "our own" culture, and because it seems to lack the utilitarianism which up to a point rules or seems to rule our own pursuit of wealth and prestige. But it satisfies both models of psychosocial homeostasis and social cohesion presented earlier in this chapter. It clearly revolves around a shared sense of values and, up to a point, of conceptualizations. Every action connected with tradition receives a positive or a negative feedback from the human environment. The system is in equilibrium, in a steady state.

What happens when the culture comes into contact with the more powerful culture of invading colonialism? Obviously enough, the equilibrium is destroyed. The newcomers care little for the accumulation of tusked pigs and for the honor obtained through their sacrifice. And the newcomers cannot be ignored. It isn't only that they possess power; they also own and can dispense goods which the natives cannot help desiring—metal implements, kerosene lamps. Such goods cannot be obtained through the traditional processes of the culture. They can be obtained, albeit with difficulty and in small amounts, by taking up new roles provided or imposed by the invaders—plantation worker, police boy, catechist. None of these are tied to the previously existing social scale. Such rewards as could be obtained varied greatly with the fluctuations of the price of copra, something which depends on world markets and is entirely beyond the understanding of the native population.

> Wages and land costs were extremely low in the New Hebrides. Treatment on the plantations was usually reasonable, by the beginning of this century, though without Government supervision. It was clearly in the planter's interest to keep his natives alive and efficient; if many died, other recruits would not come to work for him. Natives from other and distant islands were always used, so that they could not return home when they were tired of the drudgery; copra-making is pure drudgery. On the plantations the natives were isolated from either Christian or heathen culture, it was a sort of economic interlude, almost a conscription; work for two or three years, so as to get gun, axe and tobacco. (Harrisson, 1937)

The implantation of new values was all pervasive.

> The shirt became the essential symbol of Christianity in the islands. The pastors made an absolute distinction between native and European clothing. A native could not be a Christian in his own clothes; no Christian woman could show her breasts, as every woman had always done before. Trousers and shirts were the entrance marks to church service. Still are.
> Rev. Robertson: "All who wish to attend services must come well clad—the man in shirts and trousers, the women and girls in light print dresses. . . ."
> Rev. Gill expresses the typical impression on first seeing natives "roving about in a state of perfect nudity, they delighted to paint their bodies: as you approached the miserable-looking beings, you could not suppress the emotions of loathing and disgust which involuntarily rose in your mind." (Harrisson, 1937)

All this amounts to a rapid, almost sudden transvaluation of values. The old ways of self-validation become eroded. The new ones are not satisfactory. No matter what their efforts, the natives remain tied to the lower rungs of the social scale.

The net result is an extremely high level of uncertainty, bordering on normlessness and anomie. This often leads to revitalization movements: deliberate attempts at creating a new culture within which identity could become firmly anchored (Wallace, 1956). In Melanesia, such movements typically took the form of cargo cults. Central to many of them was a belief that there existed somewhere in the sphere of the gods a supply of goods of the European type, that such goods were withheld from The People by some European agency, and that an absolute break with the past and the past values would insure the coming of the cargo and a new life of plenty and of honor (Firth, 1955). The belief spreads in the form of a mystical movement, reminiscent of some features of revivalistic religion.

> Then . . . there developed . . . a full blown mystical movement complete with prophet, seizures, promises of immediate delivery of a cargo sent by God and the spirits of the ancestors, and a demand that all present property be destroyed. The . . . prophet . . . was killed by his brothers after no cargo materialized, but not before the main outlines of his revelation and the manifestations of violent trembling ending in loss of control, visual and auditory hallucinations, of planes and ships arriving with a cargo of European goods, and the excited pitching of property into the sea, had been communicated to the people. . . .
>
> Peri (a village) had been prepared for something portentous to happen by vague rummors. . . .
>
> Piloan brought her message to Peri. The message was simply that the cargo had arrived; they had only to make the necessary preparations:
>
> " 'There is a ship with many black men of Tawi on board. It has already anchored. Tawi village is completely filled with cargo. We saw all this when we left. . . . We saw many more ships running beyond the reef. There is one ship for every village. Our ships are on the way. Tawi's has already arrived. These ships are bringing the cargo and everything that belongs to you. Listen, people of Peri, many big ships are coming. All of our people who have died are now coming to us. The cargo has already been landed in Tawi. Why haven't the ships come in here? We are blocked by all the things of the past that we own. All these things of ours are like a reef keeping out the ship. The ships cannot come inside. If you throw away everything, then the ships will come with your cargo. When the ships unload their cargo your village will be so full that you will have no room to walk. Your house will be full.' " (Mead, 1956)

Not all movements follow the same pattern even though commonalities are evident:

> With the end of the war, missionaries on Santo began to be alarmed by the recrudescence of Cargo notions. At first only two small villages were affected, but the movement . . . spread to a large number of villages by 1948, and was openly anti-White. Over a third of the population of some districts in the southern half of the island was affected. The originators of the cult, in central-west Santo, had difficulty in controlling the eastern area.
>
> The leader of the movement, Tsek, advocated the destruction of native-owned European goods as well as the products of indigenous crafts, and refusal to work for the Europeans. Existing huts were to be burnt down

and replaced by communal houses, two in each village, one as sleeping-place for men and one for the women. It was forbidden for families to cohabit at night, and this domestic communism was reinforced by the construction of a large kitchen for each house, where cooking was allowed only in the mornings.

Special steps were taken to emphasize the abandonment of the past: many important taboos were scrapped, clan exogamy and bridewealth abolished. Although the movement embraced many different language groups, a new "language" was now adopted. It was said that it was America who would bring everything the people wanted, and there would be no death. Thus the destruction of property was not merely asceticism; it was an affirmation of faith in a future of plenty. The replacement of the ancestors by the Americans is common in these post-war movements, and reflects the impression made on native consciousness by the plentiful equipment of the U.S. forces.

Although the practice specially insisted upon was the ban upon clothing and ornament, and although dances were also prescribed and cleanliness and purity stressed, this was not in the name of any primitive puritanism. It was rather an emphasis upon purity of heart and freedom of self-expression to such a degree that the sexual act was to take place in public, since there was no shame in it; even irregular liaisons should be open affairs. Husbands should show no jealousy, for this would disturb the state of harmony which the cult was trying to establish. Bridewealth was also abolished and exogamy converted into endogamy within the lineage. . . .

A road several miles in length was built to the sea . . . for the use of the Americans; at the end of it a 'dock' was built to receive the Cargo. (Worsley, 1970)

Some similarities between the movement and the contemporary countercultural attitudes in America, in particular in the areas of communitarianism, openness, and sexual freedom, may be noted in passing. In my opinion they are more than coincidental.

The main point may be the increase in subjectivity and the corresponding decrease in objectivity represented by the cult. True enough, the cultures affected appear strongly subjective and associative as compared with "our" cultures even in their undisturbed state. Yet they are well adapted to their environment. In Dobu, for example, yam magic is accompanied by realistic practices of yam cultivation. In the movements, all is dream; no cargo can come and the destruction of goods and valuables is pure loss.

Some co-subjective elements were undoubtedly present. A new morality was codified and made explicit. The movements often transcended tribal limits and preached the union of the different subdivisions of the native population (Mead, 1956; Worsley, 1970). Avidity for western goods to be obtained by imitating western ways was omnipresent.

The renunciation of old ways was accompanied by the adoption of European practices. The deep concern with European material goods, the root of the Cargo doctrine, is also apparent in the description of the clothes worn by God when He visited one prophet. In another visitation, from an ancestor, his clothing was again detailed; coat, shirt, trousers, hat and "foot." Mission policies also influenced cult practices. Missionaries had carried out "considered suppression" of the ancient rituals. Like the missionaires, the cult leaders enjoined strict Sunday observance, and, in many villages, evening "school," i.e., prayers led by cult leaders, followed by reading aloud from books, and a nine o'clock curfew. "Reading" by wholly illiterate natives was common in this movement; they would hold Bibles in their hands, often trembling and twitching the while. . . .

But if avid for the White man's goods and knowledge, the natives saw the White man himself as the major obstacle between them and their goal. Notions of "Papua for the Papuans" in the early phases, and the prophesied arrival of rifles with which to attain this, aroused great excitement. (Worsley, 1970)

Once again, the elements of a co-subjective codification are present. There is an attempt to substitute a rule-bound Gesellschaft for the traditional Gemeinschaft. But such abstractive co-subjectivity as there is cannot measure up to the magnitude of the task; the ways of the Europeans remain beyond understanding. The strongest feature of the movements is an associative syncretism, with many traits which can be described as Dionysian. The new revitalized culture can be stabilized only through the removal of the initial cause which made revitalization necessary—the presence of the outsiders. In this manner the movements represent attempts at narrowing the overall social and cultural frame of reference.

To what extent can such a narrowing be successful? A complete elimination of culture contact is hardly possible; the desire for the goods of the outsiders remains. The lack of cultural balance is likely to lead to a new ritualism; sharing in such a ritualism can provide a basis, albeit tenuous, for psychosocial homeostasis.

Here is an African image:

"Why do you not choose between Christianity and the cults practiced by your ancestors? That would be clear cut."

"Fetishes cause too much trouble; they divide and weaken us. Anyway, they are things of the past. Only the old chiefs keep them in the hope of some day recovering the authority they have lost through lack of courage. It is the missionaries who have killed our religion. It is important that we make a new one. . . . Every race has its language, its customs, its ways of understanding life. The Catholic religion is not right for us. It forces us to give up all our customs. We no longer know whether we are Bakongo, Basoundi, Balari. . . ."

"Are there no other reasons?"

"No, that's all. We have saviors who can speak for us because they are close to God: Andre Matswa and Simon Kimbangu. They have suffered for the Negroes. Jesus Christ suffered only for the whites. . . ."

From the Congo to the Cape, founders of new churches . . . are heralding the ultimate triumph of Negro saviors over the "pale Christ of the white men. . . ."

When we walked into the chapel, all three of my companions made the sign of the cross. I was amazed at the gesture.

"But what do you mean by making the Catholic sign of the cross?"

. . . Mayela . . . answered.

"We have changed the wording to 'In the name of the Father and of Andre Matswa and of Simon Kimbangu.' " (Balandier, 1969)

There are no relationships of comfortable reciprocity which could join the members of the old culture and the newcomers in a homeostatic community such as the one represented by Figure 7 of the first section of this chapter. And there are too few shared concepts to allow for a stable Gesellschaft uniting the native and the western populations according to the mechanism schematized in Figure 8. There remains only one way out, the separation of the two cultures, to the extent possible.

Nativistic movements

The movements described in the preceding section attempted to create a new culture, centering on a syncretistic combination of foreign ways and foreign goods with such intuitive understanding of these ways as was possible in a preliterate culture oriented towards magic. What could not be obtained in reality was sought in phantasy; and the phantasy in question was naturally representative of the prevalent associative thought patterns of the culture.

Other movements seek the elimination of the alien rather than its absorption. Yet even in such cases the contamination of the native culture by alien influences is such as to make purification impossible. The result is generally a syncretistic amalgam, coupled with a desire for isolation from the information overload due to culture contact.

A study by Krader (1956) of a nativistic movement which took place in 1904 in Western Siberia may be used as an example:

The movement led by Chot Chelpan forms part of the nativistic responses to Western impact which are reported in several parts of the world. The Cargo Cults, the Vailala madness and various wartime movements in New Guinea; the Earth-Lodge cult and the related Ghost Dance cult which swept over native North America during the late nineteenth and early twentieth centuries; the Handsome Lake worship of the early nineteenth century Seneca; all these form part of the general body of nativistic movements. Similar developments have been reported in Africa and South America. Nor is the world of high culture free of them: Linton has mentioned the Celtic revival in Ireland.

The movement in the Altai Mountains at the beginning of the twentieth century should be added to the literature of nativism. It is known as Burkhanism. Like most others, it sought to revive a selected aspect of the past culture, a short-lived empire; like many others, it made a cult of this extrapolated aspect of the bygone way of life. The messianic element is unmistakable. The acculturative impact of western, chiefly Tsarist Russian culture on the Altai Turks is seen in the presence of undoubtedly Christian motifs in the movement, despite the rejection of the West by these Turks. The movement was quasi-religious, quasi-political: the reaction to acculturation and conquest by a dominated group against the conquerors. It was a distinctly revivalistic movement and a mystical one. . . .

The striking element in the Altai nativism . . . is the tremendous complexity of cultural influences. The very empire which the natives sought to revive through means which were at once mystical and politically efficient and rational was not their own, but that of another people, the Mongol Kalmuks, by whom the Altai Turks had been subjugated in the eighteenth century. . . . Various kinds of Christian elements . . . are to be found in the movement, as well as Lamaist influences. The influence of Northern Buddhism was pronounced. The very name of Burkhanism is a mark of this influence, since Burkhan is the Mongol name for Buddha.

The hodgepodge of associations is striking. Elements of various origins are associated and amalgamated into one system. The prescriptions of the system to its faithful determine conduct and make possible the determination of identity: that of true believers. Mystical elements tying the new system to whatever is remembered, in a distorted form, of the distant past of the people concerned come to reinforce this action. The geographical universality of such movements is described by Lanternari (1963), among others. As we shall see in a later section, their historical universality is equally impressive.

Theoretical considerations

Movements such as those described in the two preceding sections can be analyzed in terms of the general model used throughout this study.

The steady state preceding culture contact appears to be close to the subjective apex. There is doubtlessly an element of co-subjectivity present: The collectivity provides the individual with means for the self-validation of his identity. Such means depend on both a shared sense of values and on feedback based on this sharing. There is also an element of objectivity without which the society concerned could not survive. However the striking characteristic is subjective preponderance. The sense of values presiding over such practices as the accumulation of tusked pigs or the Kula cycle is idiosyncratic and arbitrary.

Cultural contact destroys the steady state, mainly by introducing cultural information which cannot be handled by the existing conceptual system, and social contacts which cannot be handled by the existing system of reciprocity. The erosion of the native culture proceeds at all three apexes. The idiosyncrasy of the system of culture-sustaining myths is undermined. So is the co-subjective system tying the individual to society. Even the objective practices insuring material survival become eroded, because they are unable to satisfy the needs newly developed by contact with the goods of the invading culture.

Under the circumstances, two ways out are theoretically possible. The first one is the assimilation of the colonized population to the culture of the colonizer. This could, at least theoretically, solve the problem at the objective apex, teaching the natives a world view validated by science and making possible the production and the acquisition of the goods they desire. It could also, again theoretically, solve the problem at the co-subjective pole. The colonizing society is in the main a Gesellschaft, with explicitly stated rules of behavior applicable to the colonized as well as the colonizer. The identification of the colonized with such rules would provide a solution, if it could be realized. Finally, it could solve the problem at the subjective apex by providing the colonized population with a new sense of personal identity, embedded in a new system of self-validation, and independent of the original Gemeinschaft.

The possibility of assimilation was the more or less conscious premise at the basis of colonization and cultural imperialism. By them, the savages would be transformed into the civilized. What is astonishing is not that assimilationism failed, but rather the extent to which it succeeded.

The reasons for failure are fairly evident. (1) Where cultural distance separating the colonized from the colonizer is great, the amount of information to be assimilated is beyond the limits of the possible. (2) The colonizing culture is not a purely abstractive Gesellschaft; it also has many elements of an associative Gemeinschaft. It is the latter which often come to the fore in culture contact. For example, the wearing of shirts, trousers, and dresses is quite as arbitrary and subjective a practice as is the wearing of nose and ear ornaments. It has no logical connection with the objective traits of the colonizing culture, and with the goods derived from its mastery of the objective environment. It is the latter that the natives desire, and the former which they are offered. They expect that wearing an imitation of western clothing will earn them the love of the western God, and that the latter will provide them with western goods. This does not happen.

Under the circumstances, there remains the other way out—the Movement. Its origin is clearly subjective and associative. Out of bits and pieces of new knowledge and old mental habits, the prophet forges a vision, a new myth. This becomes accepted not only because of the prophet's charisma, but also (as Worsley, 1970, points out) because the followers are predisposed by the anxiety due to information overload towards the acceptance of some sort of explanation.

The content of the prophet's preaching leans toward co-subjectivity and contains elements of abstraction. A new community of the faithful is envisioned and provided with explicit rules of behavior. Many traditional practices and beliefs are abstracted away as no longer relevant. The social frame of reference is often enlarged through the abolition or the weakening of tribal boundaries. The main cultural bond is no longer found in tradition, but rather in the intensely felt common experience of the frustrations of cultural contact.

Yet the movement towards a new and possibly broader co-subjectivity, while striking, is also insufficient. The movement is weak at the objective apex, and in consequence it cannot include the colonizers themselves. In consequence, the society and the culture of the faithful must exclude them, if need be (and if possible) forcibly. The new co-subjectivity creates a new in-group, which must isolate itself from the out-group and from the information overload originating in the out-group.

The long-range success of a policy of cultural isolation is problematic, even if its short-range necessity is hardly questionable. The weakness of the movement at the objective apex makes it difficult to escape forever from the blandishments of the goods of the advanced cultures. Physical and cultural isolation is becoming more and more difficult.

Under the circumstances it may be suggested that the partial isolation created by the movement may provide circumstances for future culture contact characterized by lesser cultural distance than the original one. This, in turn, may lead to cultural synthesis.

Yet the road to such a synthesis is not likely to be smooth. Movements of associative reaction are grounded in myth, and myth, contrary to science, does not easily cross intercultural boundaries.

A quotation from Cassirer (1946) illustrates the inward-looking pattern of myth and the difference between associative and abstractive thinking:

Of all the things in the world myth seems to be the most incoherent and inconsistent. Taken at its face value it appears as a confused web woven out of the most incongruous threads. Can we hope to find any bond that connects the most barbaric rites with the world of Homer—can we trace back to one and the same source the orgiastic cults of savage tribes, the magic practices of the shamans of Asia, the delirious whirl of dancing dervishes with the calmness and speculative depth of the religion of the Upanishads? To describe so widely and entirely incompatible phenomena under the same name and to subsume them under the same concept seems to be highly arbitrary.

The problem appears, however, in a different light when we approach it from a different angle. The . . . [contents] of myth and the ritual acts are of an infinite variety; they are incalculable and unfathomable. But the motives of the mythical thought and mythical imagination are in a sense always the same. . . .

. . . It is a deep and ardent desire of the individuals to identify themselves with the life of the community and the life of nature. This desire is satisfied by . . . religious rites. Here the individuals are melted into one shape—into an indistinguishable whole.

Where such a melting takes place, the problem of individual self-validation is no longer pertinent. Neither is the wide and incomprehensible world beyond the fringes of the participants in ritual. Let us continue the quotation:

If in a savage tribe the men are engaged in warfare or any other dangerous enterprise and the women who have stayed at home try to help them by their ritual dances—this seems to be absurd and unintelligible when judged according to our standards of empirical thought and "causal laws." But it becomes perfectly clear and comprehensible as soon as we read and interpret this act in terms of our social rather than our physical experience. In their war dances the women identify themselves with their husbands. They share their hopes and fears, their risks and dangers. This bond—a bond of "sympathy," not of "causality"—is not enfeebled by the distance that lies between them; on the contrary, it is strengthened. The two sexes form one invisible organism; what is going on in one part of this organism necessarily affects the other part. A great many positive and negative commands, of prescriptions and taboos, are nothing but the expression and the application of this general rule. The rule holds not only for the two sexes, but for all the members of the tribes. When a Dyak village has turned out to hunt in the jungle, those who stay at home may not touch either oil or water with their hands; for if they did so the hunters would all be "butter-fingered" and the prey would slip through their hands. This is not a causal but an emotional bond. What matters here are not the empirical relations between causes and effects, but the intensity and the depth with which human relations are felt. (Cassirer, 1946)

And, clearly, such intense human identification is possible only within a high shared context in-group, particularly where an opposition to the out-group comes to strengthen in-group solidarity.

Millenarian movements in the European Middle Ages and the Renaissance

The history of Europe in the Middle Ages and the Renaissance was punctuated by numerous movements following a general schema very similar to that of the cargo cults and of other nativistic movements. Prophets arose, preaching a millenium of perfect happiness to the elect and total perdition to the unfaithful. The end of the world was often predicted, as was the immediacy of the second coming of Christ. The eschatological tradition, of which such prophecies are a part, reaches far into the Old Testament—and it must not be forgotten that the Hebrews were often subjected to acute culture contact.

In the second century B.C. Palestine passed into the hands of the Syro-Greek dynasty of the Seleucids. The Jews themselves were bitterly divided, for while the worldly upper classes eagerly adopted Greek manners and customs the common people clung all the more resolutely to the faith of their fathers. When the Seleucid monarch Antiochus IV Epiphanes, intervening on behalf of the pro-Greek party, went so far as to forbid all Jewish religious observances, the response was the Maccabean revolt. . . . The Book of Daniel . . . was composed at the height of the revolt. (Cohn, 1968)

The essential schema is as follows:

Already in the Prophetical Books there are passages—some of them dating from the eighth century B.C.—that foretell how, out of an immense cosmic catastrophe, there will arise a Palestine which will be nothing less than a new Eden, Paradise regained. Because of their neglect of Yahweh the Chosen People must indeed be punished by famine and pestilence, war and captivity, they must indeed be subjected to a sifting judgment so severe that it will effect a clean break with the guilty past. . . . The righteous remnant—together, it was held latterly, with the righteous dead now resurrected—will be assembled once more in Palestine and Yahweh will dwell amongst them as ruler and judge. He will reign from a rebuilt Jerusalem, a Zion which has become the spiritual capital of the world and to which all nations flow. It will be a just world, where the poor are protected, and a harmonious and peaceful world, where wild and dangerous beasts have become tame and harmless. The moon will shine as the sun and the sun's light will be increased sevenfold. Deserts and waste lands will become fertile and beautiful. There will be abundance of water and provender for flocks and herds, for men there will be abundance of corn and wine and fish and fruit; men and flocks and herds will multiply exceedingly. Freed from disease and sorrow of every kind, doing no more iniquity but living according to the law of Yahweh now written in their hearts, the Chosen People will live in joy and gladness. (Cohn, 1961)

Western Europe in the Middle Ages was spared conquest by alien and more advanced cultures. But the western family of cultures was vigorously evolving; culture change was the rule rather than the exception. And culture change was not proceeding uniformly; moreover the social change that accompanied it did not always keep pace with it. The cultural and social harmony was often disturbed. Such disturbances destroyed the normal processes of self-validation for parts of the population.

In the Middle Ages the people for whom revolutionary chiliasm had most appeal were neither peasants firmly integrated in their life of village and manor nor artisans firmly integrated in their guilds. The lot of such people might at times be one of poverty and oppression, and at other times be one of relative prosperity and independence; they might revolt or they might accept their situation; but they were not, on the whole, prone to follow some inspired *propheta* in a hectic pursuit of the Millenium. These *prophetae* found their following, rather, where there existed a surplus population, rural or urban, or both. . . . Revolutionary chiliasm drew its strength from the surplus population living on the margin of society—peasants without land or with too little land even for subsistence; journeymen and unskilled workers living under the continuous threat of unemployment; beggars and vagabonds—in fact from that amorphous mass of people who were not simply poor but who could find no assured and recognized place in society at all. These people lacked the material and emotional support afforded by traditional social groups. . . .

Because these people found themselves in such an exposed and defenseless position they were liable to react very sharply to any disruption of the normal, familiar, pattern of life. (Cohn, 1968)

Only a few examples of chiliastic movements can be mentioned (see Cohn, 1968).

The Crusades had stimulated some of the earlier uprisings, and long after their true age was past found an echo in the insurrection of the Pastoureaux, the Shepherds, which may be described as an example.

In 1250 Louis IX of France—Saint Louis—was in Syria, disillusioned by his defeat at the hands of the Saracens, but still hopeful of succors from the west. He appealed by letter to his mother, the regent of France, to the pope and to other princes to come or send men and money to enable him to resume the struggle for the Holy Land. The lay and ecclesiastical powers, however, were differently employed, and, so far as the upper classes

of society were concerned, the crusading spirit was gone. But among the
mass of the people it still existed. (Cheyney, 1936)

We have here a difference between the ways in which two
groups understand the world and determine their own identities. On
the one hand are those with well established positions in society; their
world view has changed and if they do not consider themselves to be
crusaders, they draw on their positions to determine who they are. On
the other side there are those without stable social niches. For them, the
crusading identity, emptied by those who had occupied it in the past,
is free for the taking. The fact that their king, Louis IX, was leading an
unsuccessful crusade, and appealing for help after his defeat at the
hands of the Saracens, may have served as a precipitating cause of a
social movement. Shepherds and rural laborers formed bands wander-
ing and marauding through Northern France, saying that they were
going to the Holy Land. Soon, there appeared among them a charismatic
leader, known as the Master from Hungary, the word "Master" probably
representing an academic degree. Whatever might be, he gave his followers a sense direction, marching through Paris, where he was granted
an audience by the Queen Regent, Blanche de Castille, St. Louis' mother.

But the lack of cohesion of the "crusaders" and their lack of
knowledge of the world in which they lived and suffered, made it impossible to use such successes to obtain the necessary planning and
cohesion. The main feelings of the movement were bewilderment and
anger.

In spite of the religious basis of their mission, the shepherds
abused and attacked the clergy and fought with the students of the
University, which was at that time a part of the organized church. Many
were killed on both sides. After Paris, the "crusaders" continued their
journey southward. Their numbers were constantly increasing, and the
leaders of various bands began wearing bishops' vestments and performing the ceremonies of the Church. In Orleans the shepherds fought
again with the students, burned the houses of the Jews, and mutilated
a statue of the Virgin. By that time they had become outright brigands;
the more stable elements of the population rose against them and massacred them to the last man. The Loire, it was said, was running red
with blood (Cheyney, 1936).

The history of the Anabaptist commune in Münster, in the
1530s, offers a number of suggestive characteristics which justify a description, even at the risk of some redundancy.

Anabaptism was not a homogenous movement and it never was centrally
organized. There existed some forty independent sects of anabaptists,
each grouped around a paracletic leader; and these sects—clandestine,

constantly threatened with extermination, scattered throughout the length and breadth of the German-speaking lands—developed along separate lines which the various leaders set. Nevertheless certain tendencies were common to the movement as a whole. In general the anabaptists attached little importance either to theological observations or to formal religious observances. In place of such practices as church-going they set a meticulous, literal observances of precepts which they thought they found in the New Testament. In place of theology they cultivated the "inner Revelation," the direct inspirations which they believed they received from God—or, more often, which the leader of the group believed he received. Their values were primarily ethical; for them religion was above all a matter of brotherly love. Their communities were modelled on what they supposed to have been the practice of the early Church and were intended to realize the ethical ideal propounded by Christ.

It was their social attitudes that were most characteristic of the Anabaptists. These sectarians tended to be uneasy about private property and to accept community of goods as an ideal. If in most groups little attempt was made to introduce common ownership, Anabaptists certainly took seriously the obligations of charitable dealing and generous mutual aid. On the other hand Anabaptist communities often showed a paranoid exclusiveness. Within each group there was great solidarity; but the attitude to society at large tended to be one of uncompromising rejection. Anabaptists regarded the state as an institution which was necessary only for the unrighteous. They themselves, as true Christians, avoided so far as possible all dealings with it. No Anabaptist would hold an official position in the state, or invoke the authority of the state against another Anabaptist, or take the oath, or take up arms on behalf of the state. The attitude towards private persons who were not Anabaptists was equally aloof; Anabaptists commonly avoided all social intercourse outside their own community. These people regarded themselves as the only Elect and their communities as being alone under the immediate guidance of God: small islands of righteousness in an ocean of iniquity. Even Luther granted that a Roman Catholic could be saved; but for Anabaptists, Lutherans and Catholics alike were worse than Turks, true ministers of Antichrist. The practice of rebaptism, from which Anabaptism received its name, was above all a means of expressing symbolically this voluntary separation from the unredeemed world. But even among the Anabaptists themselves the same obsession with exclusive election prevailed; and the history of the movement is punctuated by schisms. (Cohn, 1968)

The picture appears quite clear in the context of the overall model used in this analysis. The basis of belief is grounded in subjective intuition appearing as a direct understanding of God's ways. The co-subjective ordering of the system of belief—theology in this case—is systematically rejected. As in all the movements described so far, inductive objectivity is absent. The result of the lack of any check on subjectivism and its attendant associationism leads to the narrowing of the social frame of reference. There is no codified body of common belief and common institutions in which a large population could find a common denominator. Anabaptist communities appear as small Gemeinschaften within the larger Gesellschaft and opposed to it.

Another characteristic of subjective associationism will become apparent below. This is the extreme lability of this pattern of thought; lacking systematization it can change its direction in very short order. Humble, benevolent, and puritannical people can change into tyrannical, ostentatious, murderous, and sex-obsessed mobs.

The background of one such transformation, in the city of Münster, was the absence of cohesive government. As in many other places in North-Western Germany, the head of state was a prince-bishop. In many cases the religious function of such bishops was ignored; many were not even ordained. The merchant and artisanal guilds of the cities often opposed governments whose only function appeared to be the collection of taxes. Another source of anarchy was the opposition between Catholics and Lutherans.

The result in Münster in mid-sixteenth century was a political void. This, in practice if not in intention, amounted to freedom of religion. Anabaptist preachers gained the allegiance of a large part of the population, including the cloth merchant Knipperdollinck, very influential among the guilds. The news of these events spread abroad and led to an influx of Anabaptists, including Jan Matthys, of Harlem, a well known preacher, and a recent convert of his Jan Bockelson, of Leyden.

At the beginning of February Bockelson and Knipperdollinck ran through the town calling on the people to repent their sins. This led to outbursts of hysteria, especially among women and even more so among many former nuns who had left their convents and undergone rebaptism. Many claimed to see visions, threw themselves on the ground, screaming and writhing—in the same way as it was described in the Cargo Cults of the South Pacific. Visions of the second coming spread among the Anabaptists and triggered an armed insurrection which forced the town Council to recognize full freedom of religion, thus conferring legal recognition on the Anabaptists. Many Lutherans worried by this development, left town taking their movable belongings with them. A sizable number left their wives behind to guard their houses; this was to have serious repercussions.

The influx of Anabaptist continued, prompted by the belief that the end of the rest of the world was near. Only Münster would remain as a New Jerusalem. Anabaptists gained a majority, both in the total population and in the governing Council.

Freedom of religion was promptly forgotten. Matthys, in order to purify the city, urged the execution of the remaining Catholics and Lutherans. Fearful of reprecussions abroad, Knipperdollinck persuaded him to be content with their banishment. The expulsion was carried out in the most barbarous manner. In the middle of a cold winter night armed bands proceeded with the removal of a population which included the old, the infirm, small children and women who had just given birth. The Anabaptists called them "godless", beat them, and took away all their possessions, including food and clothing. Only those who proclaimed their readiness to be converted were permitted to remain.

The ceremonies of rebaptism took three days; at their end there were no unbelievers in Münster.

In the meantime the prince-bishop set about to recruit an army, with the help of neighboring towns and principalities. He laid siege to Münster, but the Anabaptists defended themself vigorously.

Within the town, Matthys pursued a policy of integral communism. Private possession of money, of gold and of silver was forbidden. Payment for work and all commercial exchanges were carried out by barter.

Another decree of Matthys, whose power had become absolute, called for the destruction of all books, save the Bible. The Anabaptists were thoroughly anti-intellectual and took pride in their lack of book learning. Such an attitude is well in keeping with attempts to escape the macrocosm of bewildering culture change, into the microcosm of a new and simplistic culture made to order for the cognitive development of the cultists.

Towards Easter, Matthys felt that God was commanding him to destroy the besieging army of the prince-bishop. He attempted a sortie at the head of a small but fanatical group of followers. Enthusiasm did not compensate sufficiently the lack of numbers; Matthys and his companions were massacred.

Power devolved on Bockelson, whose youth did not detract sufficiently from his good looks, a gift of spellbinding oratory and considerable shrewdness.

The first step of the new leader was to show that whatever dictates he would promulgate came not from himself but from God. In response to a vision, he ran naked through the streets after which he spent three days in silent meditation. He then proclaimed a constitution which placed him at the head of the state. Included was a totalitarian code of behavior. Even quarrelling was made a capital offense. So was adultery, with the added provision that the only legitimate sexual behavior was marriage between Anabaptists. Relations between an Anabaptist and a misbeliever, and marriage between misbelievers were considered adulterous and called for the death penalty.

The situation was complicated by the fact that women greatly outnumbered men, because many of the exiled Lutherans had left their wives in Münster, and because many former nuns had joined the Anabaptists. Bockelson found a solution in polygamy, buttressed by a law which nullified the marriages between misbelieving emigrants and the wives they had left behind, and another which forbade women below a certain age to remain unmarried. Resistance to polygamy led to an uprising on the part of a small minority; the revolt was crushed and some fifty rebels were executed. Polygamy was put into effect; Bockelson gave the example by marrying some fifteen women.

In the meantime the siege of Münster was proceeding, and so was the defense against it. A major assault by the forces of the prince-bishop was repulsed, after which Bockelson was made king.

As such, he lived splendidly, using all the gold and silver taken in the implementation of communism. Luxury was permitted to him because he was free from any desire for wordly goods and splendors.

But the end was near. The blockade by the troops of the prince-bishop reduced the town to starvation. A final assault overran the defenses. Most of the Anabaptists were massacred; Bockelson, Knipperdollinck and other leaders were tortured before being put to death.

In its original, pacific form, Anabaptism has survived to the present day in such communities as the Mennonites, the Brethren and the Hutterian Brethern, and it has also influenced the Baptists and the Quakers. (Cohn, 1968)

Populations exposed to culture change too complex to be absorbed must seek isolation, either through withdrawal or through the elimination by force of the sources of dissonant information. A striking example can be found outisde of history: in Pirandello's play Henry IV.

China and Brazil

The Tai-ping rebellion which convulsed China from 1851 to 1864 had all the characteristics of a cultist movement of associative reaction (Michael and Chang, 1966; Reclus. 1972).

The rebellion originated in the conjunction of three elements: the general instability of the Chinese culture at the time, following the impact of the West and the trauma of the Opium Wars; the more specific situation of an often oppressed minority, the Hakka; and the personal magnetism of a gifted but unstable individual, Hong Hsieo-ts'uann.

Hong repeatedly failed the examination of access to the mandarinate. He became seriously ill and a prey to hallucinations. He became convinced that he had ascended to Heaven during his delirium. There he saw God the Father, of Whom he had a very concrete image as that of a man with a golden beard, enthroned in glory and surrounded by his family, including a wife and his eldest son, Jesus. The content of Hong's hallucinations was probably due to some exposure to the teaching of missionaries; the physical aspect attributed to God may have originated in an encounter with one of them during a sojourn in Canton. It was revealed to Hong that he was not the son of his natural father, but the son of God and thus the younger brother of Jesus. His mission was to come back to earth to establish an empire of universal peace (T'ai-P'ing) in which there would be complete equality among men, among nations, between the sexes, and between the rich and the poor.

His preaching made converts, at first mainly among the Hakka, but later among the diverse ethnic elements making up southern China. The cultists called themselves at first the Society of Adoration of God, and were tolerated by the authorities. However, they were themselves intolerant, and proceeded with the destruction of what they considered to be idols. This brought about clashes with other elements of the population and with the organs of local administration, in particular the *pen-ti* militia. Clashes led to a full fledged insurrection and to the defeat of the militias and the imperial troops.

As in most movements of this kind, the cultists were possessed by enthusiasm born of earlier despair. The military successes of the T'ai P'ing gave them the mastery of nearly half of China. Britain, worried at what was seen as revolutionary disorder, placed a professional officer, Gordon, at the service of the imperial government. Largely because of his military professionalism, the imperial army gained the upper hand. Its victory led to massacres, as was often the case in similar circumstances.

Ironically, Gordon was later killed while fighting a similar movement, the insurrection of the Mahdi in Sudan.

One of the main theses of the present study is that movements of associative reaction are not isolated phenomena, but rather generic responses to cultural bewilderment. A point in favor of the universality of such movements may be made by bringing in an example from Brazil in the last quarter of the nineteenth century.

The central figure in this episode was one Antonio Maciel, better known as Antonio Conselheiro—Anthony the Counselor. An unbalanced individual, he became a vagabond following marital misfortunes. His ascetic mode of life drew attention and respect among the simple people of the impoverished Brazilian northeast. Little by little he changed from a simple vagabond into an itinerant preacher, in spite of his lack of any connection with the Church in that Catholic country.

As time went by, the prestige and authority of the Counselor grew:

> His entrance into the towns, followed by a silent, contrite multitude bearing aloft images, crucifixes, and holy banners, was a solemn and impressive occasion. All normal occupations came to a standstill, as the population of the surrounding countryside bore down upon the town, where all the stir and movement of a fair prevailed; and for a number of days hereafter, casting the local authorities completely into eclipse, this humble, wandering penitent would give orders and have things all his own way, becoming in effect the only authority in the place.
>
> ... He would mount ... a platform and preach a sermon. Those persons still living who heard him preach tell us that his sermons were barbarous and terrifying, calculated to send chills down the spines of his followers. ...
>
> It was a clownish performance, but dreadful. One has but to imagine a buffoon maddened with a vision of the Apocalypse. (Da Cunha, 1944)

More and more he would announce the coming end of the world. His sermons acquired a political content; he preached against the recently established republican form of government.

Finally the wanderings of the Counselor came to an end. He selected the small town of Canudos to set up his New Jerusalem. Cultists from all over the countryside flocked to the new capital of the elect; lay and ecclesiastical authorities were expelled. It took the Brazilian government four military expeditions to regain control over the area. The cultists fought to the last man.

> Canudos did not surrender. The only case of its kind in history, it held out to the last man. Conquered inch by inch, in the literal meaning of the words, it fell on October 5 (1897), toward dusk—when its last defenders fell, dying, every man of them. There were only four of them left: an old man, two other full-grown men, and a child, facing a furiously raging army of five thousand soldiers. (DaCunha, 1944)

Da Cunha, whose original account in Portuguese appeared in 1902, was apparently unaware of the Münster commune. Neither could he foresee Hitler's last stand in the ruins of Berlin.

Some recent movements

Cantril (1963) analyzed a number of contemporary movements. Central to his analysis is the opposition between the microcosm of the cult and the macrocosm of the broader society. The microcosm is capable of providing its members with a sociocultural balance in which they can establish a satisfactory sense of identity; something which they cannot achieve in the more complex macrocosm. At the same time the microcosm is insufficiently adapted to objective reality to provide by itself the conditions necessary for economic survival; thus its relation to the macrocosm is parasitic, and its duration relatively short (even in the case of Hitler).

A few excerpts set the tone:

> Father Divine's kingdom serves as a prototype of those social movements we know as 'cults'—organized actions, generally rather restricted and temporary, in which the individual zealously devotes himself to some leader or ideal. . . .
> "Father Divine is God."
> Whether whispered, spoken, sung, or shouted hysterically, these words are believed by hundreds, even thousands, of people. They may be heard almost every afternoon or evening at the main kingdom of heaven, which forms part of a crowded street in New York's Harlem. During the past few years the street has been more crowded than ever, for now Father Divine's cars and busses with placards of "Peace," "We thank you, Father," and "Father Divine's peace mission" are lined along the curbing. (Cantril, 1963)

As striking as the isolation of the microcosm is the deliberate rejection of analytic or abstract thought. Isolation and rejection of analysis are two faces of the same coin; analysis is the core of decentration, in Piaget's sense, that is to say of the broadening of the frame of reference.

Analysis and conclusions

Every culture is a particular form of equilibrium between subjective, co-subjective, and objective inputs. Such equilibria are established slowly and maintained for long periods of time by tradition.

Sudden disruptions of the existing balance lead to responses tending in the direction of associative subjectivism. Such subjectivism constitutes the primary response to anxiety, just as, according to Freud, it constitutes the primary system of thought. It can be mobilized rapidly; it calls neither for the slow reflexiveness of co-subjective rationalism, nor for the even slower verification of hypotheses by objectivity.

Yet subjectivity as such does not suffice, except for individuals who manage to isolate themselves from others, usually through pathology. A degree of co-subjective consensus is necessary. Movements of associative reaction establish such co-subjectivity not through the painstaking—and relatively reliable—process of analytic abstraction, but through the participation of the group in a common experience of great emotional intensity. It is such experiences which form the core of what has been called mob psychology. Participating in a common experience makes communication easy and rapid among the participants, particularly where this communication calls for the emotional transmission of a sense of common belonging rather than for the transmission of specific and complex messages. In his description of a lynch mob, Cantril (1963) writes:

> By this time the members of the crowd seemed confident that they would soon have their victim. A feeling of good-natured camaraderie developed. A justice of the peace reported that a man you had never seen before, or one you had seen but never met, would walk up, offer you a cigarette, smile good naturedly, and say in a most agreeable voice, "Well, friend, I believe we're gonna get him pretty soon."

Engaging in a common enterprise, or being subjected to a common experience, reduces the level of uncertainty which strangers feel in respect to one another. This, as noted by Berger and Calabrese (1975), facilitates communication. Under such conditions of eased communication some individuals acquire or display charisma—the ability to influence others in a manner which would appear incomprehensible in more normal circumstances.

The leaders who emerge under conditions of anxiety may display characteristics quite different from those of the influential persons in periods of steady cultural state. Although the case is too extreme to be representative, Cantril's description (1963) of the leader of a lynch mob may be mentioned:

> The acknowledged leader of the mob, Lank Smith, was a man 40 years old who could neither read nor write. He had no particular profession but occasionally did a little cattle trading and "bronc bustin" in rodeos. He drank a great deal and was described by officers as "a rough-and-ready bully." He had been before the courts several times as a bootlegger. With his wife and little daughter, he lived in a shabby part of town near some Negro shanties. He owned no property and belonged to no church. The wife provided most of the family's support by taking in washing. His attitude at the opening of the vault was described as that of a great benefactor—a protector of white woman-hood—doing his duty in a brave and dramatic manner. A few years after the lynching he was killed in a drunken brawl on a South Texas sheep ranch.

Assuredly, not all the leaders of associative reactions are the likes of Lank Smith. Some, perhaps many, possess remarkable intellectual and moral qualities. Yet all seem to have one thing in common; the ability and the willingness to project their subjective visions in an un-inhibited manner.

This ability ties to an essential characteristic of the movement: the rapid development of common attitudes through the participation in a common experience. This leads to an intense feeling of co-subjectivity. But such co-subjectivity, perhaps because of its very intensity, cannot become extensive: The nonparticipants in the experience are necessarily excluded. Moreover, in most cases an essential ingredient of the common experience is an exaltation of an in-group and the rejection of out-groups. For that reason it is only seldom that associative reactions, even if we call them revitalization movements, can achieve the broadening of the social and cultural frame of reference which is necessary to resolve the problems of culture contact and culture change which caused such movements in the first place. The exception may be that of the great religions, which, according to Wallace (1956) originated in revitalization movements. Yet even in the case of the great religions, the result was generally the definition of culture areas which, no matter how extensive, always define cultural boundaries which separate the in-group of believers from the out-groups of believers in something else. Thus those associative reactions which succeed in establishing a new steady state do so only at the cost of the isolation of the group which they shape.

8

POLITICAL IMPLICATIONS

The culture of a population can be defined as the sum total of the meanings shared by that population. Although such a definition is not complete, it is sufficient to suggest that analyses of meaning can be used as partial steps in the analysis of cultures. Such analyses have formed the gist of the present study. The purpose of this chapter is to apply analyses of meaning to the specific problem of the study of political cultures.

It must be noted at the outset that analyses of this type cannot be complete. Political behavior, and behavior in general, is determined by multiple causes. In particular the political culture of a complex population cannot fully determine the actual political actions undertaken by the political unit encompassing such a population. For example, specific information available to the political leaders but not to the population as a whole may exercise a dominant influence in specific situations. Nevertheless, the analysis of political culture (as a part of culture in general) can lead to the understanding of an important factor in the determination of political behavior.

Styles of negotiation and of political rhetoric
(with D. Witmeyer)

The examination of diplomatic negotiations and the styles of persuasive discourse used by the negotiators provide a useful point of entry into the broader question of the analysis of political cultures. We shall begin with differing attitudes towards compromise, as characteristic of co-subjective universalism and objective neo-particularism respectively.

Within the objective neo-particularistic context, individual or national positions are not dictated by an absolute knowledge of an absolute truth, but by opinions and preferences, with the former always being deemed to be affected by the latter. Under such circumstances, stubborn insistence on the entirety of one's stand must be a mark of egoism; tendency towards compromise, on the contrary, is a positive virtue. In a negotiation what one puts forward are one's wishes and not one's principles; in consequence, one expects to abandon a part of them, and one entertains a similar expectation in regard to other parties. Insisting on some measure of compromise becomes almost a matter of principle, since the only alternative is either to demand or to accept unconditional surrender, at least within the context of the object of negotiation. At the Potsdam conference, the Western Allies had to a large extent accepted that Poland would seek a compensation along her western borders for the territories taken over by the Soviet Union in the east. The precise determination of the new frontier between Poland and Germany was, however, a matter of negotiation. The difference of opinion on this point was finally narrowed down to a relatively unimportant strip of territory between the two forks of the Neisse river; the Poles (including non-Communist) insisting on the western one with the backing of the Soviets, while the Americans and the British insisted on the one more to the east. This opposition led to a complete impasse, not because of the intrinsic importance of the territory, which was small, but because the Western Allies, who had given in significantly to reach that point, felt that it was the turn of the Eastern powers to give in, at least symbolically, to preserve the principle of compromise and the possibility of further cooperation. As for Poland, she felt entitled to the territory in question as a matter of principle, since it was a part of the old Polish province of Silesia—the control of which Poland had effectively lost in 1335.

The latter position was well in keeping with the co-subjective universalistic pattern, and its belief that reality is fully accessible to human reason. In such a context, positions are taken on the basis of "what is right," and one's own knowledge of what is right is never questioned. Once such premises are accepted, compromise becomes immoral; error has no rights. It is better to leave the question open, and even to submit temporarily to superior force after having registered a protest, than to accept compromise.

The universalistic inability to accept compromise makes negotiations exceedingly difficult.

Soviet social psychology is characterized by absolutism of thought and political organization, involving centralism, inability to compromise, and

the dominance of ideology over reality. . . . One major stumbling block
in East-West negotiations has been the different interpretation of the concept of compromise. The word and the concept are utterly foreign to the
Russian culture and language. When used at all, "compromise" is used in
a derogatory sense. To the Soviet negotiator, a compromise is not a practical adjustment of principles by partial concession, since principles are
inviolable. Furthermore, there is only one "right" way to proceed, and
Soviet dogma denies the reality of alternative modes of action. Ideological
absolutism does not permit deviation from the established position. . . .

An issue has always to be negotiated as a whole—no concessions, however
minor, are permissible. (Wedge and Muromcew, 1965)

Yet this does not make negotiation completely impossible, even
if it makes it exceedingly difficult. If a question cannot be resolved in
accordance with principle, it can be temporarily shelved, the extent given
to the word "temporarily" depending on circumstances and particularly
on power relationships. Ideological accord may be impossible and ideological struggle must continue, but, pending the verdict of history as
to which principles are correct, coexistence and even detente can be
cultivated. Bartering is possible, not through compromise within a question, but through a quid pro quo of questions resolved versus questions
postponed. "If you give us A, we won't mention B," often with the
mental reservation "until the next opportunity."

This approach . . . fits a characteristic Russian pattern of doing business. . . . Bartering involves a direct exchange of tangible advantages on
a quid pro quo basis, avoiding the necessity of compromise. It is a matter
of balancing-off of values, which do not necessarily involve principles. . . . It
should be noted that the values exchanged need not be of the same quality,
but may lie in quite different realms. (Wedge and Muromcew, 1965)

For example, refraining from exacerbating the Middle East
situation may be traded for technological exchanges and the recognition
of the permanence of the Soviet empire in Eastern Europe.

When a measure of agreement has been reached and

the Soviets do seem to make a concession, they make every attempt to
point out that their basic position has not changed at all and that all the
correct principles have been preserved. . . . The statement [of a delegate]
illustrates this point: "We deem it necessary to stress that the Soviet proposal is in no case a departure from the Soviet Union's fundamental approach to the question." (Wedge and Muromcew, 1965)

With the rejection of compromise goes a style of negotiation which
proceeds from the general to the particular, from principles to consequences, in the universalistic direction of deduction.

Throughout [the negotiations] runs a pattern of absolutistic reasoning and an insistence on approaching . . . problems from the most general and universal position. The Russians constantly demand settlement of general principles first and only then will consider specific instances, the technical and administrative details and the practical issues. There is but one "right" way to solve problems, especially political ones, and that is to agree on principles first, and then proceed to the particulars. Any other way to solve a political problem is inacceptable. (Wedge and Muromcew, 1965)

This attitude may be opposed to the pragmatic and legalistic approach favored by the English-speaking delegations. Non-English-speaking delegates at international conferences are often surprised by the insistence of delegates of countries such as the United States or Britain to have a drafting committee appointed at a very early date of a conference. How is it possible to draft, they wonder, before having at least agreed on the principles which the draft ought to reflect? For the delegates of the English-speaking nations drafting together is the most expeditious way to delimit precisely a possible area of agreement. In international negotiations, drafting together is the equivalent of working together, and working together is a typical method of organizing society within the objectivistic neo-particularistic context. Since in the world of facts not everything can be accomplished, working together, or drafting together, in the surest way to find out how much can be done before strain within the group halts its progress.

The fact that texts negotiated at international conferences are usually of a contractual nature sets the limits of what can be done within the legal area, what can actually be contracted, and what contracts can be effectively enforced. Hence the accusation of "legalism" which is often levelled at English-speaking delegations by spokesmen from the Slavic world. In reality the dominating concept for the English-speakers is one for which governmental jargon has coined the appellation "feasibility" or "area of feasibility": what can actually be done, and what agreements can genuinely be translated into deeds. The direction of such thought is from the study of pertinent facts towards agreement based upon them; this is the direction of induction.

The difference between the two styles of approach was particularly evident in the disarmament negotiations of the late fifties and the early sixties. American delegations invariably included large staffs of experts. Their strategy was to determine first what kind of violations could be scientifically and practically detected at a distance, since it was a foregone conclusion that the Soviets would not accept international inspection on their own territory. Once the determination in question was made and agreed upon, a political agreement outlawing such detectable behavior could be concluded. Any attempt to regulate behavior which could remain hidden was considered a waste of time.

The "open skies" proposal of the Eisenhower administration was an example of this approach—the more armaments there were that could be observed, the more that could be outlawed. In fact, the Soviets brought about a state of affairs which they had assiduously rejected by ushering in the Sputnik era, the effect of which was to broaden the possible scope of disarmament negotiations by making possible observation by satellites.

However, the American approach was strenuously resisted by Soviet delegates, as is shown by the following excerpts:

> Indeed, we cannot seriously and effectively consider other parts and articles of the treaty before reaching agreement in principle on the basic parts of Article I, which defines the general scope of general and complete disarmament. . . . It should be clear to everyone that, before we set about agreeing on procedure, priority and methods of implementing the various disarmament measures, we must settle what we understand by general and complete disarmament. (Wedge and Muromcew, 1965)

It isn't only the priority given to principles, and therefore to generalities, which is indicative of the universalistic pattern of thought. References to "clarity" and "obviousness" likewise point to an attitude in which the clarity of an idea within the mind is a sufficient proof of its correctness.

> We propose that the discussions of technical details should be deferred until such time as we have agreed among ourselves on the fundamental, basic principles that would underlie a final agreement. . . . We do not intend to allow a smokescreen of technical studies to be used as a cover by those who wish to evade a solution of the political question of banning all nuclear tests. (Wedge and Muromcew, 1965)

The lines seem to be clearly drawn: on the one hand the Russians fail to see the relevance of factual feasibility studies to the search for an agreement; on the other the Americans fail to state that they also have a fundamental principle, which is to consider only those questions which can be factually verified. Both sides consider their own pattern to be obvious, not as something to be established, but as a basic premise from which to start in the task of persuasion.

The study of political rhetoric can now be extended to the third apex of the model triangle, that of associative subjectivism.

As was noted, argumentation characterizing the co-subjective universalistic pattern is likely to be dominated by appeals to shared or supposedly shared ideas of great generality or principles, and to proceed on the whole in the direction of deduction. Argumentation dominated by objectivistic neo-particularism is likely to depend on the presentation of specific facts and an inductive search for their significance. Reasoning

characteristic of the third apex, that of associative subjectivism, is likely
to be dominated by appeals to feeling, by careless generalizations lacking
a definitional basis, and by transduction, defined by Werner (1961) as
"the leading over, the transition, from one concrete isolated judgment
to another coordinate, single judgment." It is neither deduction nor
induction, as both of these contain the explicit statement of a general,
abstract judgment, something that is absent from transduction.

The analysis of statements in the Security Council of the United
Nations by representatives of the Soviet Union, the United States, and
the Arab countries, presents interesting results. The meetings to be
analyzed were randomly selected, using whole meetings only, until each
category of speakers was represented by over one hundred paragraphs.
Paragraphs in the minutes of the meetings were selected as the units of
analysis.

Out of 118 paragraphs representing the interventions of the
Soviet delegates 55 were characterized as co-subjective and universalistic,
12 as subjective, 11 as objective; 40 were mixed or uncategorized. Example:

> Some people at this table may perhaps believe that the aggressor has a
> right to keep the territories he has seized and to flout the rights of other
> peoples. But we should ask how it would be appropriate to describe the
> piratical acts of any state which, for instance, seized a part of the territory
> of Argentina or Brazil, Denmark or Canada, and then said that it would
> not withdraw from the territories it had seized until the Governments of
> those countries had complied with the demands of the aggressor and gone
> down on their knees before him. It is this which is the crux of the matter
> at the present time. And we believe that the members of the Security
> Council must approach the solution of this problem with a full sense of
> responsibility and with all seriousness, having full regard to the conse-
> quences which might arise from a failure in this case to observe the most
> important principles of international law and the vital provisions of the
> United Nations Charter. (Mr. Fedorenko, U.S.S.R.)

This passage contains appeals to affect, and therefore some
subjective elements. However, it is characterized mainly by appeals to
rules, laws, codified duties, universal values, which transcend the particular situation at hand. Reality is broadly divided, and elements characterizing the particularity of the situation are omitted. Reasoning moves
deductively from universal principles and broad patterns—in this case
hypothetical—towards the special case at hand. The seizure of another
country's territory can take place only within particular political situations, but the Soviet delegate omits any reference to such particularities.
These are the characteristics of co-subjective universalism.

Let us now turn to the American pattern. Of 102 paragraphs

representing the statements of the United States delegation, 47 were considered to be objective, 25 to be co-subjective, 0 to be subjective; 30 were mixed or uncategorized. Example:

> On 17 May, as the world remembers, President Nasser, citing the supposed danger of an Israel invasion of Syria, requested the withdrawal of the United Nations Emergency Force. And when UNEF vacated Sharm el Sheikh, the United Arab Republic immediately reimposed its blockade of the Gulf of Aqaba, after ten years of free and peaceful navigation of that Gulf. (Mr. Goldberg, U.S.A.)

The paragraph centers around the presentation of an empirically observable fact, directly tied to the situation at hand. Reality tends to be finely divided, and the divisions used are dictated by their relevance to the immediate situation. A sequence of similar presentations is used to build the speaker's case by induction.

Of 258 paragraphs describing the interventions of the delegates of Arab states, 128 were categorized as subjective and associative, 32 as co-subjective and universalistic, and 26 as objective; 71 were mixed or uncategorized. Two examples are given:

> We are very tenacious, we Arabs, and, mind you, the Jews of the area are very tenacious. Otherwise they would not have remained Jews until today. In spite of all the adversities that the people of the area have suffered, we are still tenacious. More tenacious, but may not survive the atom bomb. If anyone of you here lose it, then that is the end of mankind. (Mr. Baroody, Saudi Arabia)

> However, I must say that this tragedy did not come to us as a surprise, since it falls within the criminal, neurotic, Zionist-Nazi complex. It is part of what the Zionists describe as the "final solution of the Arab problem" to deport, expel, expropriate, kill and annihilate. It is another phase of the Israel conquest. (Mr. Tomeh, Syria)

Although its origin cannot be traced with certainty, the association between Zionism and Nazism seems to have originated in the fact that both the Israelis and the Germans in World War II used deep armored penetration as part of their military tactics. Appeals to such a commonality, obviously irrelevant to the political problems at hand, are perfect examples of transduction. Other traits of associative subjectivism are the diffuse character of the statements, the strong we–they dichotomization, boundless emotionalism, and references to tradition (in the Baroody statement).

An exchange between the American and Syrian representatives provides an even clearer example of the opposition between the objective-abstractive and the subjective-associative patterns:

The representative of Syria made a statement in reference to a remark of mine. I will recall the circumstances of this remark. The remark was made in the context of a malicious and false accusation that United States aircraft from carriers had participated in an attack. And I said, with respect to that remark, that people ought to put up evidence that such an accusation was true. There has been no evidence offered. There can be no evidence offered of that because there is no basis for that accusation. That accusation was a false and malicious and scandalous one. That is the remark I made, and I was compelled to make it because of the dangers indicating to anybody involvement on the part of the United States, which has never been the case in this particular situation. (Mr. Goldberg, U.S.A.)

I would not reply to the distinguished representative of the United States were it not for some of the very words that he used in reference to my statement when he said, referring to a previous statement, that it was a malicious, false and scandalous accusation. I confirm categorically that the United States has helped Israel in its invasion of the United Arab Republic and Jordan and is to be held responsible for whatever destruction and killings have taken place in the United Arab Republic and Jordan and are taking place right now in my own country, Syria. If anything is scandalous it is the policy of the United States, which has been shameful for the last twenty years vis-a-vis the Arab world and vis-a-vis the Arab nations. (Mr. Tomeh, Syria)

Ambassador Tomeh's personal comments, which are in violation of every type of diplomatic usage, are beneath contempt, and I would not purport to dignify them with an answer. The remark to which I referred and which I said was utterly false and malicious was the remark that carrier planes from the Sixth Fleet had intervened in this conflict, and I challenge anybody, including the Ambassador, to bring evidence before the Council to this effect. (Mr. Goldberg, U.S.A.)

I shall ignore the venomous attack made personally against me by the representative of the United States. I would merely say this, that it is not enough to belong to a great Power. The United States with one bomb can destroy the whole of Syria. But it is much greater and much stronger to belong to a great cultural and intellectual tradition. And this I am proud of. (Mr. Tomeh, Syria)

In both remarks of the American representative, the emphasis is on a specific accusation, and on the lack of evidence to support the accusation. Thus critical boundaries are firmly placed to delimit the subject of discussion, and to approach it from an empirical point of view. The Syrian representative ignores the specifics of the original accusation and of the denial. Disregarding all critical boundaries, he moves to a more general and more vague category of thought, first accusing the United States of a general responsibility for the war, then further enlarging the frame of reference by attacking the policy of the

United States towards the Arabs for the last twenty years. Finally, he switches from actions or purported actions to ascriptions of identity, characterizing his opponent as merely the representative of a great power, and himself as the representative of a great cultural tradition. The associative lack of a clear perception of the difference between the relevant and the irrelevant seems quite clear in these remarks.

Differences in styles of political persuasion are evidenced not only by the argumentation presented by politicians and diplomats representing different cultures, but also by the responses of members of those cultures to one or another type of approach.

Bronfenbrenner (1964) finds that average Americans respond most readily to argumentation based on facts; in contradistinction average Russians respond better to appeals to emotions and to deductive reasoning.

> At the most general level, perhaps the greatest contrast suggested by the results of the pseudo-experiment was the different power in the two cultures of exposure to facts versus feelings. In general, American respondents were influenced most by being presented with objective evidence about Soviet society; any feelings I may have had on the subject, including antagonistic ones, were best kept in the background. Quite the opposite was true with the Russians; if I wanted to convey something about the American outlook, I had to rely on emotion to carry the message. Communication was most successful when one spoke in the name of ideals and feelings rather than invoking evidence and logic. The lofty principle had to come first; only then could facts be introduced, and even so, preferably as inevitable deductive necessities, rather than as empirically independent observations. (Bronfenbrenner, 1964)

Wedge (1968) arrived at similar results in a study of communication patterns involving Americans on the one side and Brazilian university students on the other. He chose for a topic of conversation the assassination of President Kennedy, a matter on which the plurality of the American opinion has come to accept the culpability of a deranged individual acting alone, while the quasi-unanimity of the Brazilian students believed in a large scale conspiracy theory.

The typically American approach to the investigation

> was to gather, examine, and test the evidence in laborious detail. Having concluded, on the basis of facts, that the assassination was the act of a madman acting alone, we tried to communicate our conclusions. We failed completely with these students, for we expected them to give the same weight to evidence as we did. (Wedge, 1968)

It should be noted that even the American proponents of the conspiracy theory tend to argue their point on the basis of facts or alleged facts: missing frames in a motion picture of the event, a violent movement backwards of the President's body, etc.

> In over seventy instances of extended dialogue with groups and individuals on this subject, I found that efforts to argue from the evidence had no effect. Students would oppose my "facts" with "facts" of their own, often of the most far-fetched nature, but they would also argue logically from their firmly held theories of American society that there *must* have been a conspiracy. (Wedge, 1968)

However

> it was possible to experiment with variations in the presentation of the American viewpoint in actual dialogue with students and to test their reception. It should be noted that no alteration of position was necessary. Two approaches, based on an understanding of what 'makes sense' to Brazilian students, proved to be effective. The first involved confronting the conspiracy theory with another theory—a general theory of assassination motives. It was argued that important figures may assume symbolic value in the eyes of envious and mentally disordered persons and become the objects of their attack. Brazilian students are fascinated with psychological theory, and there was enough evidence of such disturbance in the assassin's personality to back the thesis. The gratifying outcome of several such dialogues was that the students introduced theory and examples from their own national experience. In Brazil, it proved more effective to counter a theory with another theory than with facts.
>
> The second adaptation of presentation to the audience involved the use of emotional association. Instead of discussing the evidence of the Warren Commission we discussed the personality of the Chief Justice. Most Brazilian students associate Chief Justice Warren with social justice, and especially with the popular school desegregation decision. By establishing such acceptable bona fides and then pointing out that the popular and incorruptible Chief Justice had headed the investigation and endorsed its conclusions, the evidence, which had been doubted on its own ground, became more credible.
>
> Americans, in their own society, are suspicious of theory and of authority conveyed by personality. We tend to feel that facts should speak for themselves and that every man should judge the evidence. Since contrasting patterns of reasoning exist in Brazil, it is no wonder that American argument often fails to convey its intended meaning. (Wedge, 1968)

Although no strictly comparable studies are available in regard to the Arab nations, many students of Arabic communication patterns, such as Shouby (1951), Hamady (1960), and Patai (1973) point out the prevalence of such associative-subjective traits as the exaggerated expression of feelings, overassertion, repetition, or substitution of words for actions or for facts.

Examples can easily be adduced to show that both exaggeration and overemphasis intrude even into Arab political statements and discussion. On the eve of the 1948 Israeli War of Independence, Musa Alami, the well-known Palestinian Arab leader, made a tour of the Arab capitals to sound out the leaders with whom he was well acquainted. In Damascus, the President of Syria told him: "I am happy to tell you that our Army and its equipment are of the highest order and well able to deal with a few Jews; and I can tell you in confidence that we even have an atomic bomb. . . . Yes, it was made locally; we fortunately found a very clever fellow, a tinsmith. . . ." In Iraq, the Prime Minister informed him that "all that was needed was a few brooms to drive the Jews into the sea." . . . The common denominator of all these verbal assurances was that they were greatly exaggerated statements as to what the Arabs intended or hoped to do. . . . in reality these statements were not followed by serious or sustained efforts to translate them into action. (Patai, 1973)

Theoretical considerations

In the preceding section parallels were drawn between the Brazilian and the Russian cultures. Yet anyone having observed them, even superficially, must be aware of the deep differences that exist between them. This shows that the analysis of cognitive and semantic styles, which makes up the gist of the present study, deals not with the complete description of culturally determined behavior, but only with one side of it, albeit an extremely important one.

Styles of communication and political attitudes: the subjective orientation

Styles of communication and cognition contribute not only to the modes of political expression, but also to basic political attitudes. Even though it must constantly be emphasized that in the quasi totality of cases, shared meanings reflect the influence of all three apexes of the model triangle; the dominance of one or another mode of thinking leads towards corresponding patterns of behavior, including political behavior.

Communication in the subjective mode is characterized by the sharing of extensive areas of experience among the participants. This suggests either (1) relatively small and homogenous communities, or (2) strongly entrenched traditions, or (3) intense common experiences sweeping through populations which may be numerous.

All three possibilities, but particularly (1) and (2) suggest that the social organization will be that of a Gemeinschaft rather than that of a Gesellschaft. The conditions described under (3) are those that favor the emergence of charismatic leadership. It should be noted that such leadership tends to strengthen the Gemeinschaft characteristics of societies that have reached the Gesellschaft stage of organization. Nazism provides a perfect example. Another one is that of Khomeini's partisans in Iran: assertions, very often of a most far-fetched kind, are made without any felt need for proof or analysis.

As was noted earlier, subjective orientation in meaning and communication emphasizes the distinction between an in-group sharing the common experiences on which mutual understanding is based, and out-groups to which such experiences are alien. The mechanisms by which experience is shared are likely to be those of purely existential historical randomness. Subjective orientation implies the absence of either the co-subjective tendency to define terms broadly and rationally, or the objective tendency towards a determination of terms on the basis of repeatedly observable reality. It follows that what is probably the most important trait of the subjective orientation is irrationality, and in many cases even anti-rationalism.

It may be convenient to examine the possible political consequences of a subjective orientation depending on the size of the populations concerned. Three levels may be conveniently distinguished: (1) groupings smaller than the state, (2) groupings coinciding with the state or with a potential state, and (3) groupings broader than the state.

The subjective orientation: groupings smaller than the state

This is the level of familism or tribalism, which appear as obstacles to nation-building—or rather to state-building. It is also the level of the struggle within a state between dominant ethnic or religious groups and ethnic or religious minorities.

The question of the viability of pluralistic societies can be examined within the context of this level. Briefly, ethnic pluralism can be tolerated if its influence is confined to areas that do not impinge upon the main bases of social and political solidarity. In a country such as the United States this means to a large extent that ethnic particularisms must be confined to such things as culinary preferences and folk traditions remote from the main aspects of political, juridical, and economic life of the country as a whole. Particularism extending into the main areas of common national (or state) actions will not be tolerated for long. It is perfectly acceptable for a judge of Italian descent to eat pasta, but not to follow the philosophy of Roman Law in preference to that of English Common Law.

The subjective orientation: groupings coinciding with the state or with a potential state

This is the area of nationalism. However, as it was shown by Kohn (1944), by Cobban (1970), and by Glenn (1970a), nationalism is a highly ambiguous concept.

Nationalism can be defined in a rather simple manner as the

political attitude of those who place their primary loyalty in the nation-state, rather than in a broader human grouping (mankind), a narrower human grouping (family, region, sub-national ethnic group), a differently conceived human grouping (social class, religion), the individual as such, or an ideology (socialism, democracy, free enterprise). The definition may be extended to those placing their primary loyalty in an ethnic group sufficiently large to become (in the opinion of those described) the basis of a nation-state.

There occurred at various moments in history, but particularly during World War II, phenomena which appear rather strange and illogical in the light of the definition above. In the countries (or nation-states) fighting against Nazi Germany there appeared collaborators or would-be collaborators who either by action or by expressed sympathy sided with an enemy nation-state and against their own. Furthermore, the collaborators or would-be collaborators in question were recruited from among extreme nationalists, that is to say from among the very people who, according to the logic of the definition, should have been adamant in their opposition to the encroachments of a foreign state. In opposition to them, the core of those who remained steadfast in the fight against Nazism was made up largely of liberals and democrats, to the point where one could speak (although with some exaggeration) of a war between an internationale of liberals and cosmopolitans, and an internationale of nationalists. Of the two terms it is only the second one which is or appears to be a contradiction in terms.

Another contradiction of a similar nature can be seen in the postindependence politics of many former colonies, particularly in Africa, in the Middle East and in Sukarno's Indonesia. Here again moderate nationalists use the states they have established as the frameworks of their political thrust. Extreme nationalists seek broader frames of reference: Pan-Africanism, Pan-Arabism or the vaguely defined Bandung community. Of the three, only Pan-Arabism can be described in the classical terms of ethnic nationalism, and even there the definition fits poorly. (Glenn, 1970a)

The subjective orientation: Nation-State?

The core of the contradiction may well be the ambiguity which underlies the concept of nation-state. "Nation" and "state" are concepts of different orders. Placing them together in a hyphenated community suggests that two different social and political processes lead to the same end product—something which may, or may not, be the case. (Glenn, 1970a)

Concept of State

Although the overall topic of this part of the analysis is the influence of the subjective orientation on politics, it will be shown in this section that the concept of "state" is not subjective and associative, but on the contrary that it is abstractive.

Let us begin with "state," by far the clearer and the less ambiguous of the two components. The state is a basic unit of public administration. The conceptual order to which it belongs is that of conceptual rules, of institutions defined by their legal status, and of specific functions carried out in specific manners by specifically appointed officers. . . . In sociological terms, the state is a Gesellschaft: a society governed by explicit rules prescribing and proscribing behavior, and determining mutual obligations.

A particularly important corollary is the way in which the individual appears in the context of the state: as a role (citizen, officer, taxpayer, professional, domiciled, etc.) or at most as a locus of roles, but not as a personality, the wholeness of a human person. In particular, the state is not totalitarian. Inkeles (1954) shows that the characteristic of totalitarianism is not so much its dictatorial absolutism in politics, as its refusal to recognize for every man areas of privacy, beyond the boundaries of any of the roles relevant to the state and specifically defined in the context of the state's own definition.

Once again, the roles of the individual in respect of the state are juridically defined; this gives them, at least up to a point, a contractual character. All those born in the territory governed by a state may be its citizens without the intervention of an explicit contractual instrument; nevertheless citizenship may be terminated by either party (individual or state) in accordance with specific procedures. Moreover, citizenship may be acquired by naturalization, which amounts to an explicit contractual arrangement specifying the obligations and the privileges of both parties—the individual and the public administration definition of the collectivity. (Glenn, 1970a)

The subjective orientation: Concept of Nation

The situation is radically different in the case of "nation" or "nationality." The concept, as commonly used, is germane to the idea of kinship. As such it is immutable—in contradistinction to citizenship, which is germane to the idea of the state. It is also vague, at least in the context of the modern world.

In a changing frame of reference (such as that of the contemporary world) the counterpart of an ideal of immutability is in general vagueness and diffusion. Specific forms of behavior in regard to specific positions in the kinship tree can be prescribed. However, such prescriptions are meaningful (i.e., obeyed) only in primitive or very traditional societies, that is to say under conditions characterized by slowness or absence of change. In more mobile societies, the rigid categories of kinship retain little functional meaning; precise in their verbal definitions, they are nebulous as determinants of behavior. In societies falling somewhere between these two extremes, there is tension between the requirements of a kinship based system of behavior and those of developing contractual or quasi-contractual relationships: nepotism, corruption, or at the opposite pole a tension-ridden rejection of kin are frequent symptoms.

Here again similar remarks can be made in respect to nationality particularly in respect to the vagueness and diffusion of the concept itself, and to incompatibilities between its functional and its declarative aspects. For example, in the American nation-state, "nationality" can be taken in two different senses. One of these makes the concept quasi-identical with that of citizenship, but characteristically more vague, the other refers to a nationality of origin of immigration; in this case it is immutable but has only marginal functional implications. French nationality can be taken only in one sense, congruent with citizenship, embracing German-speaking Alsatians and Celtic-speaking Bretons, but excluding French-speaking Belgians and Swiss. Arabic nationality has only one widely accepted meaning; this time, however, it is one which is antithetical to citizenship, referring to a scientifically questionable but genuinely felt community of ethnic and linguistic appurtenance.

Is there a common denominator between these disparate meanings? The one which may be suggested is an undefinable feeling of belonging together, based on an often apocryphal common ancestry, on often distorted common traditions, and on a usually genuine community of subconsciously felt experience. Where citizenship is a contractually defined role, nationality is a feeling of shared identity.

The lack of definition, the feeling of being anchored in nature, the subconscious basis for solidarity make nationality congruent with the Gemeinschaft form of social organization, one with roots in the past, in a community of behavior the forms of which can seldom be explained but are felt to be right, and also in an avoidance of specific rules elaborated for specific functional purposes. Seen in this light, nation seems to have more in common with the anthropological concept of culture than with the political and juridical one of state.

The last remark suggests that nationality, especially if combined with power, carries at least a suggestion of totalitarianism. In contradistinction to a juridically based state (in which areas covered by law and those not covered by it are reciprocally delimited), culture is all pervasive. There are no state-prescribed ways of cooking noodles, but culture covers cooking and the greeting of friends and everything else. To say that something is illegal is specific; to say that it is un-American is diffuse—and threatening.

The contradistinctions—or oppositions—noted above refer to *forms* of behavior rather than to its *contents*. A law, which is specific and affectively neutral, may proclaim the same things, or have the same content, as a tradition or a custom, which is diffuse and commands affection. Thus a state and a nation may coincide.

However, the opposition between the forms of behavior upon which each is based, the differences between the specific and affectively neutral dimensions of the actions demanded by the state, and the diffuse and affectively charged dimensions of the actions demanded by the nation, or in a slightly different conceptualization, between the abstractive cognitive style of the state and the associative cognitive style of the nation, are sufficiently important to make the coincidence between state and nation far from automatic, and where it exists, to make a tension between the two likely. (Glenn, 1970a)

It is this tension that explains the actions of Nazi collaborators in World War II, even at the cost of a weakening of their state. They preferred an associative identification based on ancestry or tradition to an abstractive and contractual identification which accepted naturalization as a basis of citizenship and ideas borrowed from abroad as legitimate bases of public administration.

The subjective orientation: groupings broader than the state

Major cultural upheavals may result in experiences common to people dispersed over very wide geographical areas. In the nineteenth and twentieth centuries the impact of western cultures on the non-Western world resulted in widespread de-traditionalization and de-culturation. The theme of being suspended between two cultures and at home in neither of them, is extremely widespread in the literature of former colonies or dealing with former colonies.

These voices are worth listening to carefully. The tone may be set by a protest of the late Patrice Lumumba against "the nefarious policy of assimilation and integration which has reduced the Africans to the status of *apatrides*—men without a fatherland."

Or again:

One of our tasks derives from the needs of our peoples to escape assimilation, to become de-Westernized so as to prevent the strangling of our spirit proper to us. This tendency towards de-Westernization, easily observable in our countries, from Madagascar to Haiti, from Timbuctu to Johannisburg, from Nigeria to Kenya, is aimed simultaneously at institutions, hierarchies, the authorities in the field of resources as well as of expression, ethnic references and historical values. Of course, it is not for the sole pleasure of de-Westernization. We are decided to keep the gifts of the West, on the condition of using them according to our genius and to our situations. But we aren't here to present apologies for some ideology or creed. Atheists or believers, Marxists or not, we are not going to concern ourselves with quarrels of ideology or belief which divide the world. We will mention the choices before us only to show to what extent these choices, which we owe to the West, can and must be adapted to the imperatives of our sovereign dignity within independence, and in this manner to confirm their universality. (Aliune Diop, in *Présence Africaine*, 1959)

The following excerpt shows even more clearly the nature of the conflict:

Our presence in Rome, as earlier our choice of the Sorbonne for our meeting place, has a clear meaning: a testimony of gratitude, an expression of respect for this beautiful [Western] culture. . . .

But it is no less true to say: if such are, indeed, our feelings, they do not suffice; they point to only one side of the complex reality of our intellectual lives; they leave in the dark the other half, which, for being the more secret of the two, is not necessarily either the poorer or the less genuine one. . . .

It is that, that unclear and mysterious feeling, which will always mark the difference between our Western colleagues and us: they will never feel the torment and the tearing of which we feel the bite, because they will never need to know the tension which we feel and which comes from our loyalty to our original belonging and to our ties to their culture. . . .

From the Caribbean to the Indian Ocean, from Sao-Paulo to Leopoldville, we have that in common. . . .

This, then, is our tragedy. The tragedy of a consciousness under pressure, subject to a constant pull in two directions. Culturally French, ontologically Malgassy, my personality runs the risk of wasting its strength in this constant struggle, of being broken by the burden of a paradox, of disintegrating under the shock of my ambivalence. (J. Rabemananjara, in *Présence Africaine*, 1959)

Other voices are less moderate:

One mistake which it is difficult to defend, is to attempt a revalorization of cultural activity within the framework of colonial domination. This is why we come to a proposition which seems a paradox and according to which, in a colonized country, the most elementary, the most brutal, the least discriminating nationalism constitutes the most perfervid and the most efficient form of the defense of the national culture. It is opportune, we think, to repeat that there can be no genuine culture other than a national culture. (F. Fanon, in *Présence Africaine*, 1959)

Yet which is this national culture Fanon refers to? Is it one of the many, genuine tribal cultures from which most of the speakers have become estranged? Is it whatever characterizes culturally the various African states about to be born at the time, that is to say in the main the inheritance of the colonial systems of public administration? Or is it Pan-Africanism, or possibly pan-anti-colonialism?

Even though the traditional cultures from which the participants in the experience of partial westernization have become estranged are very different among themselves, de-culturation accompanied by partial acculturation to the West constitute a shared experience for many of the leaders of the Third World. Such a shared experience leads to shared political attitudes, based primarily on resentment against the source of cultural malaise of those concerned. As most cultural reactions, these attitudes are largely associative and anti-abstractive—they produce poets, where technicians are needed. The resentment which they express tends to overtake policies dictated by more pragmatic considerations and to lead to policies based on the dominant anti-western feelings (Glenn et al., 1970). Expressions of such political attitudes dominate the recent history of the United Nations.

The subjective orientation: Nazism

Viereck (1965) and Kohn (1960) see the wellspring of Nazism in romanticism. It may be asked how a political movement, particularly one characterized by unspeakable brutality, can find its origin in a poetic and artistic school, especially one characterized by great tenderness towards man and towards nature. The beginning of an answer may be found in the thesis defended in this study, that styles of communication exercise an often dominant influence on styles of action. Deutsch (1966) derives the concept of peoplehood from the concept of communication:

> The community which permits a common history to be experienced as common, is a community of complementary habits and facilities of communication. It requires, so to speak, equipment for a job. This job consists in the storage, recall, transmission, recombination, and reapplication of relatively wide ranges of information; and the 'equipment' consists in such learned memories, symbols, habits, operating preferences, and facilities as will in fact be sufficiently complementary to permit the performance of these functions. *A larger group of people linked by such complementary habits and facilities of communication* we may call a *people*.

The question is that of the kind of communication and communication networks which romanticism favors and fosters.

The words "classic" and "romantic," we are often told, cannot be defined at all, and even if they could be defined, some would add, we should not be much profited. But this inability or unwillingness to define may itself be only one aspect of a movement that, from Rousseau to Bergson, has sought to discredit the analytical intellect—what Wordsworth calls "the false secondary power by which we multiply distinctions." However, those who are with Socrates rather than with Rousseau and Wordsworth in this matter, will insist on the importance of definition. . . .

The word romantic when traced historically is found to go back to the old French *roman* . . . which . . . came to be applied to tales written in the various vernaculars [—not in Latin, the language of serious thought at the time]. . . . Now with what features of these tales were people most struck? The reply to this question is found in a passage of a fifteenth century Latin manuscript: "From the reading of certain romantics, that is, books of poetry composed in French on military deeds which are for the most part fictitious." Here the term romantic is applied to books that we should still call romantic and for the very same reason, namely, because of the predominance in these books of the element of fiction over reality.

In general a thing is romantic when, as Aristotle would say, it is wonderful rather than probable; in other words, when it violates the normal sequence of cause and effect in favor of adventure. (Babbitt, 1962)

Or, as we might put it, when it subordinates the criterial boundaries of conceptualization to the flow of free association.

Here is the fundamental contrast between the words classic and romantic which meets us at the outset and in some form or other persists in all the uses of the word down to the present day. A thing is romantic when it is strange, unexpected, intense, superlative, extreme, unique, etc. A thing is classical, on the other hand, when it is not unique, but representative of a class. In this sense medical men may speak correctly of a classic case of typhoid fever, or a classic case of hysteria. One is even justified in speaking of a classic example of romanticism. . . .

The type of romanticism referred to in the fifteenth-century manuscript was, it will be observed, the spontaneous product of the popular imagination of the Middle Ages. We may go further and say that the uncultivated human imagination in all places is romantic in the same way. It hungers for the thrilling and the marvelous and is, in short, incurably melodramatic. All students of the past know how, when the popular imagination is free to work on actual historical characters and events, it quickly introduces into these characters and events the themes of universal folk-lore and makes a ruthless sacrifice of reality to the love of melodramatic surprise. (Babbitt, 1962)

Thus the lines are drawn: abstractive reason against associative imagination. It should be noted that these expressions are almost redundant. Reasoning must be abstractive, since it calls at the very least for opposing and comparing, which can be done only on the basis of a determination of what is criterial and what is noise, what is relevant and what is not. Imagination must be associative, since its gist is the appearance of a rich image in the mind, often following the poorest of stimuli. Yet these expressions are not quite redundant. Abstraction is broader than co-subjective reasoning, as it applies also to pragmatic action and to directed, carefully objective observation; association is broader than imagination, since it applies also to the most unimaginative traditionalism.

The last point bears insisting upon. How is it that free imagination may lead to the most rigid conformism? The answer is that truly free imagination is solipsistic—and few people accept standing alone for long. Once the products of imagination come to be shared, under the influence of common emotions combined perhaps with the influence of charismatic leadership, they also become rigid and unchanging, dogma and ritual. Association lacks the mechanisms for analytic examination, for modification, for variation on a theme, for critical testing, once its product is there, the potential faithful can only accept it, or stand alone, away from and opposed to the warmth of human contacts. Early romantics may choose the second possibility—the loneliness of the hero is one facet of romanticism. Later on, lesser souls tend to amalgamate; the other facet is the formation of a herd.

For we must not forget that even though there were always classicists and there were always romantics, romanticism, as classicism had been before it, was more than a question of temperament and more than the sorting of methods according to the fields of endeavor—art or science—which they best fit. It was a large scale movement.

Under classicism, abstractive thought had invaded even the arts. Space in the paintings of the time was static and bounded; the space of romantic painting is swirling and limitless (Canaday, 1960). Thus romanticism repels the invasion of the abstractive from the domain proper to the associative. It does not, however, stop there: It, in turn, invades.

First, it defines a new type of man, with a new sense of values. The gentleman-scholar or the gentleman-philosopher of the Enlightenment passed from the pleasures of the intellect to those of the senses and back; he knew that both are necessary and that a wise man separates one from the other. Instead, the romantic hero dreams, emotes—and suffers. Suffering may have been accepted as, alas, unavoidable by the gentleman of the Enlightenment; it is considered positively necessary by the romantic because he feels that he must make everything in the human experience his own. Here again, we might think back to the positive search for suffering as part of the quest for a vision among the Indians of the Plains; the romantic is a Dionysian. Shakespeare is rediscovered in his native country and discovered on the Continent not, simply, because he is a genius, but because he mixes the sublime and the ridiculous, the emotional and the philosophical. One can find everything in him, including the feeling of the whole.

To sum up: In the classical age, fog—the sometimes hazy inclusion of a whole range of subjective experience in self-identity—was a nuisance; in the romantic age it becomes a symbol, . . .

The subjective orientation: the place of Romanticism in evolution

Babbitt (1962) compares romanticism with Taoism:

Perhaps the closest approach in the past to the movement of which Rousseau is the most important single figure, is the early Taoist movement in China. . . . The phrase which best sums up its general spirit is that of Wordsworth—a "wise passiveness." The unity at which it aims is clearly of the pantheistic variety, the unity that is obtained by breaking down discrimination and affirming the "identity of contradictories," and that encourages a reversion to origins, to the state of nature and the simple life. According to the Taoists the Chinese fell from the simple life into artificiality about the time of the legendary Yellow Emperor, Hoang-ti (27th century B.C.). The individual also should look back to beginnings and seek once more to be like the new-born child, or, according to Chuang-tzeu, like the new-born calf. It is in Chuang-tzeu indeed that the doctrine develops its full naturalistic and primitivistic implications. Few writers in either East or West have set forth more entertainingly what one may term the Bohemian attitude towards life. He heaps ridicule upon Confucius and in the name of spontaneity attacks his doctrine of humanistic imitation. He sings the praises of the unconscious, even when obtained through intoxication, and extols the morality of the beautiful self. He traces the fall of mankind from nature into artifice in a fashion that anticipates very completely both Rousseau's *Discourse on the Arts and the Sciences* and that on the *Origins of Inequality*.

We shall return to Taoism and to its associative character in connection with a brief presentation of the culture of classical China. For the moment, a word on "naturalism" and spontaneity in romanticism may be to the point.

Romanticism's

exaltation of the virtues of the primitive ages is simply a projection into a mythical past of a need that the man of the eighteenth century feels in the present—the need to let himself go. (Babbitt, 1962)

This is true—as far as it goes. It might, however, be pushed a little further: Children's minds are associative. Abstraction implies discipline, and the participation in a far-reaching expansion of abstractive thought requires a lot of it. To reject discipline for the greater freedom of fancy, is to reach for the freedom of childhood. A yearning for an idealized childhood is particularly clear in Rousseau (as is the anxiety of his childhood as it really was). The primitivism which the romantic seeks turns out to be his own.

> This is what he understands by his 'return to nature'. A whole revolution is implied in this reinterpretation of the word "nature." To follow nature in the classical sense is to imitate what is normal and representative of man and so to become decorous. To be natural in the new sense one must begin by getting rid of imitation and decorum. Moreover, for the classicist, nature and reason are synonymous. The primitivist, on the other hand, means by nature the spontaneous play of impulse and temperament, and inasmuch as his liberty is hindered rather than helped by reason, he inclines to look at reason, not as the equivalent but as the opposite of nature. (Babbitt, 1962)

Romanticism and Taoism are not only similar in that they are both associative. Both preach associationism against more abstractive tendencies. Taoism opposed the extremely mild abstractive traits of Confucius, while romanticism opposed the thoroughgoing abstractionism of Descartes and Voltaire. Thus romanticism is not simple associationism, but associationism revisited; we shall see as we go that the difference is fundamental.

The romantic quest for certainty: from hero to herd

From many points of view, Enlightenment marked a beginning. Science and economics took on a scope so much broader than they had in the past that it is possible to speak of qualitative change. Yet in some ways the culmination of the classical era marks an end; its critiques destroyed old systematic Weltanschauungen but provided no systematic new Weltanschauung to replace them. The Enlightenment left its most systematically-minded devotees in a dilemma. It had replaced theological systems by a faith in the intelligibility of nature, and the intelligibility of man as part of nature. But nature is an ambiguous word, particularly when applied to man. It stands for the possibility of discovering sets of abstract laws explaining precisely delimited natural phenomena; and it stands also for the poetic feeling of the whole, that one achieves standing alone among hills and lakes on a spring day.

No one personified this dilemma better than Goethe: in personal life the most classical of gentlemen, in his writings the creator of the romantic hero. "Two souls, alas, dwell in my breast," he wrote in Faust: the soul of abstractive and Apollonian reasonableness, moderation and clarity, and the soul of associative yearning for the undivided whole and of a Dionysian yearning for immediacy.

Because of some of the excesses of classicism, such as the introduction of a plethora of critical boundaries into art where they did not belong, the associative-Dionysian call was also a call for freedom. Within poetry and art, the proper domains of the associative approach, the call for personal freedom, the "why not?" spirit destroying artificial barriers to free association, became also a call for a creative liberation. This led to the first wave of romantic heroes—men richly endowed with the fruits of classical discipline and capable of rejecting this discipline without impoverishment, men who found a feeling of fulfillment (and even of certainty) in the intuitive flashes of the Dionysian way. Such men stood alone and had to stand alone. Their fulfillment, their feeling of inner unity and of unity in understanding, came from the abolition of items already in the mind, but separate and subdivided. And, of course, each man has a unique combination of knowledge and experiences; so that the sudden bringing together of all or many of them—the intuitive flash—is unique and proper to him.

Rare, however, is the man who can stand alone (without regressive deterioration, withdrawal, or suicide). Certainty calls for consensus. In abstractive thought, consensus is always limited to some precise item or items. In associative thought, consensus calls for a community of associations and a community of feeling. Abstractive consensus comes from the sharing of a formal education; associative consensus is more likely to come from a consensus of informal experience, from similarities in past coincidences, rather than from similarities in purposeful elaborations. Abstractive consensus leads scholars to follow disciplines; associative consensus leads alumni to sentimental musings. This is why abstractive thought tends to penetrate across barriers separating national cultures. Associative certainties, on the contrary, are to be sought within "natural" groups, within Gemeinschaften, and even though, in marginal cases, there may exist such a Gemeinschaft group as that of the international set of hedonists or of literati, it is in national cultures that such communities are to be found most often (and even more in the most important cases).

Hence the second wave of romantics: people claiming, openly or otherwise, that their national group, the reference group of their feeling of consensus, had the unique capability to grasp the truth by direct intuition.

This is the sort of feeling we found at the core of nativistic movements. Its importance in romanticism varied from country to country. In Britain and France, where the forces of the Enlightenment were indigenous (the influence of the English on the French *philosphes* was great but well integrated into the national thought), the friction was between different layers of the same culture. The reaction was mild and the second wave of romanticism, the one in which the exaltation of the lone hero is replaced by the exaltation of the herd, did not assume sizable proportions until much later. In Germany and in central and Eastern Europe, the grating between layers was complicated by genuine culture contact. The upper classes and the intellectuals were Frenchified, although in the case of the latter not without inner tensions: To write, one has to use language, and the French of their education was not the language of their childhood and of their subconscious. To escape the French influence of Leipzig, a German city in which there was a predominantly French-speaking court, Goethe had to go to Strasbourg, a part of the Kingdom of France in which there was no princely court and in which the German vernacular flowed freely. The French Revolution came to compound the confusion. The upper classes could understand its ideology, but seldom accepted it, as it was directed against their interests; the lower classes were supposed to benefit from revolutionary ideas, but they could neither understand them, nor reconcile them with the comings and goings of French armies of occupation.

In the face of such ambiguities, the syncretic reaction was bound to be strong. It started as a movement to reject conventionalism for the sake of individual freedom, but later it was led in its search for spontaneous consensus to embrace a folk wisdom imbued with traditionalism.

Let us look at some of the steps in this process:

> Romantic poetry [wrote Friederich Schlegel in 1798] alone is infinite, because it alone is free and recognizes as its only law that a poet's license tolerates no law. (Kohn, 1960)

What we have so far is the statement of an associationism which is basically healthy in the associative context of poetry and of art. However:

> German romanticism began but did not end in poetry. It was an interpretation of life, nature and history, and this philosophic character distinguished it from romanticism in other lands. Disdainful of the rationalism of the XVIIIth Century, it mobilized the fascination of the national, even primitive past to lower the prestige of the principles of 1789. (Kohn, 1960)

Why this rejection of the principles of the French Revolution, of Liberty, Equality, and Fraternity? Because these principles were issued from rationalism and aimed at propagating this rationalism still further, by deeming them to be universally applicable.

In this indirect fashion romanticism came to concern itself with the political and social life and with the state. It did its best to poeticize and romanticize the German concept of the state. It never developed a program for a modern nation-state; however with its great emphasis on the depth of the German mind it led to a consciousness of German uniqueness and to the belief that a nation may be a law unto itself. (Kohn, 1960)

The gist of the conflict may be expressed through the contrast between what is meant by civilization and what many Germans, and in particular the romantics, meant by Kultur. This is brought out clearly by Viereck (1965).

The contrast of Kultur versus civilization is the root, not always consciously, of the "two souls" [about which Goethe wrote]. It has been pointed out how Fichte, in the early 1800s, was perhaps the first to articulate this contrast consciously. (Viereck, 1965)

If western Europe, international in mind and in tendency, looks upon civilization as a system of ways of behavior and spiritual ideas that are humane and susceptible of universal application, the Germans understand by Kultur an intimate union between themselves and the natural forces of the Universe, whose action they alone are capable of apprehending, and as a tribal discipline designed to turn those forces into account. Fichte insisted only the Germans know the method of realizing this intimate union. . . . They, Fichte reminded them, are the "primaeval people" (*Ur-Volk*) who speak the primaeval, aboriginal tongue (*Ur Sprache*) which gives them contact with the forces of Nature. Therefore German minds return more easily than those of other nations to the instincts and concepts of the primitive world from which *"the west," under the joint influences of classical thought and of Christianity* has sought to escape. From Fichte to Hitler . . . the line runs straight. (Steed, 1938, quoted by Viereck, 1965)

It is necessary to clarify some terms. What can be the meaning of "civilization," particularly in the light of the anthropological concept of "culture," in the sense of the totality of the folkways which characterize a population and make that population into an individualized entity, different from other populations and identifiable among them? Within such a context, "civilization" appears to be that part of culture which constitutes "a system of ways of behavior that are humane and susceptible to universal application." Assuredly, "universal" may be an exaggeration as applied to any of the existing civilizations—with the possible exception of western science. Yet even if a claim to universality may be difficult to substantiate, a claim to a broadening of the human frame of reference can certainly be made. Several peoples, each with its distinctive culture (or part of a culture), may belong to the same civilization.

The term "civilization" is strongly evaluative. We tend to oppose "civilized" to "barbarian." It can be easily granted that the opposition in question was often grossly overdone. What was deemed "civilized" was often that which was characteristic of the speaker's in-group; what was deemed "barbarian" was that which characterized the out-groups opposed to it. Yet, in spite of such exaggerations, an evaluative opposition is legitimate. If civilization stands for the broadening of the human frame of reference, it stands also for the abstractive practices which make such a broadening—such a decentration—possible. As stated earlier, this search for abstraction proceeds first through the determination of a logical co-subjectivity, then through a validation (and transformation) of that co-subjectivity by appeals to objectivity. Thus civilization represents the trans-ethnic element of culture, the possibility for the world of coming together in a united society. If, now, we agree that the world is becoming smaller, that it becomes more and more difficult for different peoples to coexist without impinging on one another, we must also agree that the evaluation making the civilized something desirable is a legitimate one.

As for Kultur, as used by the German and other romantics and nationalists, it comes closer to the anthropological concept of culture—again in the sense of that which makes for the distinctness, the individuality, and in each case the collective identity of human groups.

There is, however, a fundamental difference. The concept of culture is nonevaluative. Anthropologists describe cultures, they do not characterize them as good or bad, to be preserved or to be destroyed, to be triumphant or to be subjugated. It is not only the anthropologists, generally outsiders to the cultures they study, who adopt such a relativistic point of view. It is, to a large extent, the cultures themselves. As noted earlier, primitive cultures are never missionary. Their own ways are their own ways; their ways and those of others are mutually irrelevant. Not so in the case of the nationalistic concept of Kultur. It is fiercely evaluative, even while rejecting universality.

Thus the German historian E. Tröltsch writes:

> Whoever believes in the existence of a natural, eternal, and divine Law, I mean in a common and universal basis of humanity, and sees the very existence of humanity in this universal basis, will see in German thought *a queer mixture of mysticism and brutality.* But whoever considers that history is an unceasing creation of living individual forms, which are ordered according to a continually variable law, will see in the western ideas the

product of an *arid rationalism*, a levelling *atomism*—in short a mixture of platitude and pharisaism. (Tröltsch, 1925, quoted in Viereck, 1965)

An essential difference is shown between Kultur—or rather, since this kind of pattern is not exclusively German, between culture as seen from within—and culture in the anthropological sense, which is always culture as seen from without, by a scientist capable of describing it in the universal language of science. The difference is that associative thought, the thought which leads to the acceptance of the popularly given without submitting it to abstractive analysis, is extremely poor in meta-levels. This is why an explanation of a school of thought in terms other than those of the school itself becomes impossible. This is why one either belongs by birthright, or one doesn't belong at all. On the other hand, culture in the anthropological sense presupposes anthropologists, i.e., representatives of a broader civilization in the terms of which every national culture can be described—and circumscribed.

Another point worth insisting upon is that the associationism of romantic nationalism is associationism revisited, not associationism in its pure form. The latter could, and in most cases did, simply ignore the alien. The former came at a time in which such ignorance was impossible. The choice was between civilization and antagonism.

Such, then, are the two poles. To a rational observer, associative nationalism of the type described above appears so strange, so absurd, that (were it not for recent history and also for the history of associative reactions presented in the preceding chapter) it might be taken for something put up, artificial—"they can't really mean it."

The romantic nationalist approaches this choice on the basis that there is no such thing as mankind, and no such thing as a human individual. These are, at best, only misleading mirages. What exists is the nation—or nations, but if the plural is added, so must be the idea of the inequality of ethnic groups, of the superiority of some cultures and of some racial pedigrees over other ones. The better will conquer the weaker.

The conqueror must not absorb the conquered into his state—or at least not on the footing of present or possible equality. Each nation must have only one language. The conquered must not be assimilated, even thought they may be educated by their betters, provided they do so in a manner consistent with the essence and the capabilities of the conquered culture. The greatest crime committed by the French (today it would be the Americans) is that they let foreigners become assimilated to the French culture. Only the avoidance of the development of a culture which can be shared between nationalities, even in part, can guarantee that a state may be *organic*—and only organic nation-states are legitimate. This was the belief of the romantic nationalists at the beginning of the 19th century, this was the belief of Wagner, and finally this was the belief of Hitler. Most states have boundaries determined by history, but this is not good enough for truly organic states; these must integrate the people of the nation's own ethnicity placed by history beyond the fatherland's borders, and subjugate the ethnically alien living within the territory of the organic folk. In Schlegel's words:

> A true nation can tolerate only one language. . . . "It is much more appropriate for the human race to be strictly separated into nations than for several nations to be united as has happened in recent times. . . . Each state is an independent individual, existing for itself; it is unconditionally its own master. . . . governed by its own laws, habits and customs." (quoted by Kohn, 1960)

In terms of this study, the limited co-subjectivity of the ethnic group must eliminate the broader co-subjectivity of an evolution leading to shared abstractions such as the concept of mankind.

A brief reference to Jahn, a romantic nationalist of the nineteenth century, may add to the insight.

> Jahn's credo was that the unconscious force of Volk shapes all history. To describe this force Jahn coined the word "folkdom" (Volkstum), today [1940] one of the most important Nazi words. Folkdom he called "that which the Volk has in common, its inner existence, its movement, its ability to propagate. Because of it, there courses through all the veins of a Volk folkic thinking and feeling, loving and hating, intuition and faith."
>
> Cosmopolitanism Jahn spurned because "humanity appears nowhere by itself pure and simple but only as incarnated by folkdoms." (Viereck, 1965)

We have at this point the atmosphere of a full-fledged movement of associative reaction. The most astonishing element of it is that it took another hundred years before the movement came to full fruition. This may be explained by the ambiguity of the history of Germany in the nineteenth century; the interests of the state and the interests of the nation tended to coincide and to overlap. Bringing the Prussian state out of the chaos of a welter of German principalities satisfied both the yearning for the state and the yearning for the nation. Assuredly, there were conflicts. Bismarck, who was fully aware of the importance of a shared culture for a newly established state, sought to impose cultural uniformity by a policy of at times forced assimilation, directed at the Poles of the eastern provinces and at the Catholics in Western Germany. This was something which Wagner, a pure exponent of the romantic school, considered illegitimate. For him as for Schlegel, Jahn—and Hitler—only identity of ethnic descencence could bring cultural participation. Yet for a long time the community of state and national interests outweighed the difference between the abstractive orientation of the one and the associative orientation of the other. The opposition to the rational development of the state, through urbanization and economic and social progress was submerged, and expressed only by a number of die-hard writers, men like Lagarde, Langebehn, and Moeller van den Bruck, whose attitudes, once again, foreshadowed the coming of Hitler.

> Having abjured religious faith, they could not fall back on the promise of divine deliverance. Having abjured reason, they could not expect a natural human evolution toward the community they sought. The goal, consequently, was a mystique, and the means, though left obscure, suggested violence and coercion. (Stern, 1965)

There is little point in rehashing the characteristics of Hitlerism. One point, however, deserves special consideration. It is the attitude of the Third Reich towards myth, a category of thought representative of associative subjectivism. And the attitude in question is one of exaltation.

> The Old Testament of the Nazi Religion is *Mein Kampf*. . . . The New Testament is the *Myth of the Twentieth Century* by [Rosenberg,] Hitler's Saint Paul and prophet laureate. Outlined in 1917, it was finished in 1925 and first published in 1930. By 1938 *Myth* had run into 142 editions and had sold 713,000 copies. Since Hitler calls it today's greatest philosophical book, it merits . . . our scrutiny as a key to the Nazi mind. . . .
>
> Precisely what myth does Rosenberg mean by this title? The best response to this frequent query is the blurb on the book's cover:
>
> "The myth of the twentieth century is the myth of blood, which under the sign of the swastika unchains the racial world-revolution. It is the awakening of the race soul, which after a long sleep victoriously ends the race chaos."
>
> To understand these slogans we must contrast them with what they replace. "The racial world-revolution:" in contrast with the French and Russian world-revolutions, in contrast with the liberalism of the former and the Marxism of the latter, in contrast with the capitalism of the former and the proletarianism of the latter. In contrast with their economic interpretations of history and in contrast with the church's Christian interpretation of history, the Myth is a racial interpretation of history. History no longer means war of class against class nor of church dogma and dogma, but blood and blood, race and race. (Viereck, 1965)

Class, in the Marxist sense, is abstractive and universalistic. It is a strictly defined concept—difference in regard to the ownership of the means of production constitutes class difference—based on assumptions derived from reality, and which appeared close to reality for a period of time.

The liberalism propagated by the French Revolution aims at a society in which human individuals are to a large extent free to carry out activities of their choice, and to try to assume roles of their choice, including economic and political ones. This, by and large, is the aim of objectivistic neo-particularism.

Thus what *Myth* is purported to replace is, by and large, abstractive. As for "blood" and "race," in the sense used in *Myth*, they are never an object of definition (even an insufficient or inacceptable one) but only of feeling and hint. Thus what is supposed to replace abstractionism is clearly associationism: reflex reactions instead of criterial boundaries.

Myth! What a significant word! Rosenberg is a romantic writing in German; he is not an eighteenth-century rationalist writing in French. Therefore he uses "myth" not sarcastically but piously, not with curled lip but wide-eyed with wonder. His use of "myth" covers far more than a literal English translation could convey. His special use of the word covers something like this: necessary faith, or inspiration, or unifying mass yearning, or folktale truer than truth. . . .

. . . God created man not as an individual nor mankind as a whole, but individual races of men. . . .

A nation is the political expression of the race. Here Rosenberg repeats the Wagnerian contrast of an organic society versus an atomistic society. The chief morality and justification of an organic (living) group body is its being organic (living). Life for Life's sake: Salvation through subjective egoism instead of through obedience to objective universal standards. . . .

Volk nationalism is sharply distinguished from Prussian statism. The mere state, for Hitler, Wagner and Rosenberg is soulless if inorganic (unfolkic). An unfolkic state deserves no loyalty. . . .

When one nation conquers other nations, it must not interbreed with them into one common international state, but must erect a state in which the higher and purer race rules the lower. . . .

. . . No two races have the same soul. Therefore no two races can understand each other; no two speak the same moral, aesthetic, or intellectual language. . . .

Nazism is the revolt against conditioning by environment. Rosenberg denies that environment can give German morals or culture to, say, a Jew or a Slav. Such qualities are determined unalterably before birth. Partly they are determined by physical heredity and partly by a metaphysical race soul. . . .

The first book of *Myth* is entitled "A Conflict of Values". . . . Conflict refers to Aryan versus non-Aryan. "Aryan" is a more inclusive term than "German," and "non-Aryan" is broader than "Jewish." But like Wagner's essay on race in 1881 and like [Houston] Chamberlain, Rosenberg usually treats the Germanic race and the Jews as the only Aryans and non-Aryans worth bothering about in modern times.

Explaining all history's boons and banes as good and bad race, Rosenberg gives us a brand-new history of the whole world. Certainly an unconventional history, based on the infallible intuitions of Rosenberg's somewhat nordic blood instead of mere facts and footnotes. The pages on the origins of man are the most interesting because there Rosenberg's imagination can soar most freely, in regions so remote that no known facts exist to clip its bold wings. Bold certainly is Rosenberg's explanation that the ancient lost continent of Atlantis was the origin of all good things. . . .

"Where today the waves of the Atlantic roar and giant icebergs roam, a flourishing continent once towered, where a creative race reared a great *Kultur* and sent its children as sea-rovers and warriors into the world. . . . streams of Atlanteans on their swan-boats and dragon-boats."

The vision is sheer poetry, possibly good poetry. The swan-boats à la Wagner, the roaming icebergs, the blond godlike children à la Siegfried conquering the globe on their dragon-boats. . . .

The book traces how migrating Atlanteans gave the whole non-Aryan globe its Aryan ruling castes, spreading everywhere their noble blessings—such as war. The book traces the process with the pictorial details of an eye-witness. (Viereck, 1965)

As for more contemporary questions:

The gist of the Führer's myth is that the Führer *is* (incarnates) the Volk, instead of ruling it detachedly like a monarch . . . or representing it like a democrat. (Viereck, 1965)

The subjective orientation: the New Left

It is the prevalent custom to distribute political tendencies along a single dimension, from right to left, placing fascism at the extreme right and communism at the extreme left. Lipset (1960) finds this approach overly simplistic.

Before 1917 extremist political movements were usually thought of as a rightist phenomenon. Those who would eliminate democracy generally sought to restore monarchy or the rule of the aristocrats. After 1917 politicians and scholars alike began to refer to both left and right extremism, i.e. Communism and fascism. In this view, extremists at either end of the political continuum develop into advocates of dictatorship, while the moderates of the center remain the defenders of democracy. This chapter will attempt to show that this is an error—that extremist ideologies and groups can be classified and analyzed in the same terms as democratic groups, i.e. right, left and *center*. The three positions resemble their democratic parallels in both the composition of their social bases and the contents of their appeals. . . .

If we look at the supporters of the three major positions in most democratic countries, we find a fairly logical relationship between ideology and social base. The Socialist left derives its strength from manual workers and the poorer rural strata; the conservative right is backed by the rather well-to-do elements—owners of large industry and farms, the managerial and free professional strata—and those segments of the less privileged groups who have remained involved in traditionalist institutions, particularly the Church. The democratic center is backed by the middle classes, especially small businessmen, white-collar workers, and the anticlerical sections of the professional classes.

The different extremist groups have ideologies which correspond to those of their democratic counterparts. The classic fascist movements have represented the extremism of the center. Fascist ideology, though antiliberal in its glorification of the state, has been similar to liberalism in its opposition to big business, trade unions and the socialist state. It has also resembled liberalism in its distaste for religion and other forms of traditionalism. . . . The social characteristics of Nazi voters in pre-Hitler Germany and Austria resembled those of the liberals much more than they did those of the conservatives.

The suggestion is that a unidimensional classification be replaced by a two-dimensional matrix. One of its axes might be called that of the content of the three main political subdivisions: conservatism favoring the upper classes, compromise favoring the middle classes, or social reform favoring the disadvantaged. This makes up the right, the center, and the left. The other dimension is one of form or temperament: extremism versus moderation. As recent history clearly shows, differences in form are likely to overshadow differences in content. A point to be noted: the subdivision into right, center, and left does not apply to the opposition between (for example) liberalism and fascism; the two belong to different orders of consideration.

A parenthesis is necessary before any further developments in the main line of analysis. It concerns a difference of opinion between the quotation above and the body of this study, and bears on the alleged fascist "glorification of the state." A closer examination of historical developments shows that extremists, including communists as well as fascists, far from glorifying the state did not even recognize its legitimacy *until they managed to take it over*. After that, they subordinate the state to the party: the state is left as a mechanism, the party is the operating force. The state is left to deal with the outer layer of society, the Gesellschaft, the party is an inner core with Gemeinschaft-like characteristics.

Franco's Spain is an exception, in the case of which the state is duly glorified and permitted to retain power. However, Lipset notes that Franco's regime was a conservative dictatorship rather than a fully fascist movement.

The distinction between the content of political goals and the form of political action seems eminently sound. The question is whether the forms of political action can be sufficiently differentiated by a simple dichotomy between consultative government and totalitarianism, or between moderation and extremism. The difficulty with the dichotomy is that it tends to place together fascism of the left, such as Peron's justicialism, and communism. Although the question is debatable, and is dealt with later in this chapter, it may be suggested at this point that the difference between the two ought to be duly recognized. This can be done by distinguishing between an associative and a co-subjective form of totalitarianism, communism being an example of the latter. Fascism, with its doctrinal poverty and its faith in the intuition of charismatic leaders, is an example of the former.

We thus suggest that fascism is the product of an associative reaction affecting mainly the center of the left-right political spectrum. As for the causes of the reaction, they appear to be as much cultural and psychological as political. Laswell (1933) writes:

Insofar as Hitlerism is a desperation reaction of the lower middle classes, it continues a movement which began during the closing years of the nineteenth century. Materially speaking, it is not necessary to assume that the small shopkeepers, teachers, preachers, lawyers, doctors, farmers and craftsmen were worse off at the end than they had been in the middle of the century. Psychologically speaking, however, the lower middle class was increasingly overshadowed by the workers and the upper bourgeoisie, whose unions, cartels and parties took the center of the stage. The psychological impoverishment of the lower middle class precipitated emotional insecurities within the personalities of its members, thus fertilizing the ground for the various movements of mass protest through which the middle classes might revenge themselves.

It might be noted that the exacerbation of the middle-class rooted movements of associative reaction came at a time when upward mobility was becoming more difficult because of cartelization and later because of the depression. The resulting situation was one in which the lower-middle classes not only lacked horizons to reach for, but felt threatened in the places they had conquered for themselves. This is particularly evident in the Poujadist movement in France.

In the election of 1956, much to the surprise of many political observers, the Poujadist movement rose to important proportions. Some saw Poujadism as the latest response of the more authoritarian antirepublican elements on the French right to an opportunity to vote against democracy and the Republic.

In fact, Poujadism, like Nazism in Austria and Germany, was essentially an extremist movement appealing to and based on the same social strata as the movements which support the 'liberal center'. While it is impossible to know whether in power it would have resembled Nazism, its ideology was like that of the Nazis and other middle-class populist movements. Poujadism appealed to the petty bourgeoisie, the artisans, merchants and peasants, inveighing against the dire effects of a modern industrial society on them. It opposed big business, the trusts, the Marxist parties, the trade-unions, department stores and banks, and such state control over business as social security and other welfare state measures which raised the taxes on the little man. But while Poujadism explicitly attacked both the left and the right, it strongly linked itself with revolutionary republican traditions. Appealing to populist sentiments—the idea that the people rather than parties should control the government—Poujade praised the French revolutionaries who did not hesitate "to guillotine a king," and demanded the revival of various revolutionary institutions like the *Estates-General*, to which would be presented lists of grievances submitted by local bodies of citizens in the fashion of 1789. Combined with its attacks on big business, left parties, and unions, were attacks on the Jews and a nationalist defense of colonialism. (Lipset, 1960)

The passage above shows clearly the combination of centrism, fascism, and associationism. For example the call for an Estates-General, presumably elected by the people, in a country in which there already existed a popularly elected parliament, smacks of word magic. So does the opposition between "the parties" and "the people"—as if the earlier named were not the way in which differences of opinion among the people become organized and expressed. Yet this opposition, absurd as it may seem in the light of an abstractive analysis, is revealing of the state of mind of those who make it. Differences of opinion are something which the associative mind cannot handle, and which in consequence it is unwilling to recognize.

Another characteristic particularly evident in Poujadism but present in all fascisms, and possibly in all associative reactions, is the yearning for the simple life, or, more exactly, for life lived according to fully internalized cultural habits and rendered secure against the need for re-evaluation and against the consequences of the complexities which can be resolved only by abstractive reason.

The latter tendency is also strongly in evidence in the New Left, or more properly in the *counterculture* of which the New Left is the political expression. Is such a similarity sufficient to describe the New Left—or the counterculture—as a movement of associative reaction, and at that, one presenting at least a potential kinship with fascism?

First, how much importance should one attach to the term "left" in New Left? No more, it might be suggested, than to the classification of fascism as a movement of the extreme right. The New Left, particularly in the United States, has few connections with the working class, little understanding of the aspirations of working people and no program for improving the condition of the underprivileged. The social base of the New Left, like that of most fascisms (with the main exceptions of the upper-class dominated Franco-ism and the working class dominated Peronism) is solidly middle class.

True enough, it is impossible in the case of the New Left to document a shift of voters from the liberal center towards extremism in the way in which Lipset (1960) did with fascism. However, a fairly similar movement can be observed; the New Left is largely made up of radical children of liberal parents (Keniston, 1968; Decter, 1975).

In trying to determine the significance of such a generational shift, we must first note that it is not unprecedented. Romanticism was an earlier example of a sudden change in the direction of cultural evolution, from abstractive analysis to associative reaction.

As for the causes of the shift, it may be noted first of all that the possibilities of upwards mobility have become distorted in the context of the meritocracy of the postindustrial society. The children of parents who "have arrived" cannot slip easily into the identity of an inherited position. Neither can they find their identity in the challenge of rising above the position attained by their parents, something which is still possible to the offspring of poorer families. What faces the middle class (and particularly the upper-middle class) young is the prospect of having to work hard and long just to regain the position into which they were born. This resembles the labor of Sisyphus, and may be a source of discouragement. Instead of working up to a position for which familiarity has bred contempt, it may be easier to denigrate it.

Let us couple this with another difficulty: that of the search for freedom. To feel free is—largely—to feel that one has a voice, perhaps a dominant one, in the shaping of one's own destiny. This calls for the fulfillment of two conditions: absence of external restraints (or their reduction to a tolerable level) *and* a good understanding of the world around. Let us insist on the second one: to act, one must know how and where; the one who does not know cannot act with the expectation that the outcome will correspond to the intent, ergo he cannot shape his destiny, ergo he cannot feel free.

The end of the eighteenth century (before the onset of romanticism) and the middle of the twentieth (before the onset of the counter-culture) were periods of sudden, almost explosive, removals of external restraints—with which the development of understanding did not keep pace.

The result is a feeling of unfreedom. And, since it is both easier and more natural to accuse others than to examine oneself, the feeling is attributed to the hypocrisy of a "system" which "pretends" to have removed the external restraints, while "in reality" loading "its victims" with chains all the more heavy because they are invisible, hidden. (Glenn, 1969)

The most important factor in the alienation of many in the young generation, and probably also in the lack of understanding noted above, is a characteristic inherent in the modern, mobile society: the fact that man appears less and less often, and in fewer and fewer eyes, as a whole person, rather than as a depersonalized role or at best as a collection of such roles. Within such a context, it is difficult for the individual to develop a firm feeling of self identity. Following Mead's terms (1934), it is difficult for ego to assume the role of the generalized other, since others see him only in some of his many different roles; in consequence the attitude of others in regard to ego is constantly shifting. Zijderveld (1970) expresses this characteristic of contemporary social environment:

> Modern society is essentially an abstract society which is increasingly unable to provide man with a clear awareness of his identity and a concrete experience of meaning, reality and freedom. This abstract nature of society is caused primarily by its *pluralism*, i.e. by the segmentation of its institutional structure. Compared to tribal societies and their overreaching kinship systems, or to medieval society with its uniform, namely Christian, structure of meaning, modern society appears to be chaotically pluralistic. As a result of this pluralism, society has lost . . . much of its existential concreteness. . . . On the level of interpersonal relationships the abstract nature of contemporary society is illustrated by the fact that a large number of the personal face-to-face relations of premodern society have been replaced by the relations of official functionaries who practice the roles of their social positions.
>
> Many social channels of communication have broken down.
>
> The abstract nature of modern society is sufficiently illustrated by such modern cultural expressions as abstract painting and sculpture and electronic music. (Zijderveld, 1970)

The same thing, of course, may be said about contemporary science. Neither are understandable to the layman, and both produce the anxiety associated with an unknown the presence of which cannot be escaped. True enough, the medieval serf was probably quite as incapable of understanding the subtleties of scholasticism as the average modern man is incapable of understanding Pollock or Einstein. But the medieval peasant was never told that he had the right—indeed, the duty—to make up his own mind. The scholars of his time inhabited a different world, and the reciprocal social positions of all were fixed and immutable. Yet even then social feedback occasionally proved defective, and the Middle Ages were punctuated by explosive associative reactions (as we have seen in the preceding chapter).

In the face of the fragmentation of roles, there takes place a fragmentation of identity. The contemporary man becomes a "double man" (Zijderveld, 1970): on the one hand a series of roles each of which is validated independently of the others, and on the other hand, the private man who seeks a feeling of being a unified personality by validation at the hands of a small group, or—at the risk of pathology—within his own mind.

Under the circumstances, the attraction of reducing the human context to a necessarily small primary group becomes very strong. This, again, is the search for the Gemeinschaft which we have noted previously.

One of the ways in which such a restriction of the human frame of reference can be achieved is by "dropping out" of the society at large. This is the essence of the nonpolitical or pre-political stage of the counterculture. Hippies, of course, are nonpolitical or even anti-political. Yet this is not out of a lack of conviction; they are passionately convinced that the society and the culture are wholly wrong and must be replaced by a consciously developed counterculture, even though what the latter might be is vague in both their ideas and their behavior.

It may be interesting to note that despite the hippies' usual passivity, Yablonsky (1968) could use to describe them a quotation from Hoffer, meant originally for more cohesive and more active movements:

> A rising mass movement attracts and holds a following not by its doctrine and promises but by the refuge it offers from the anxieties, barrenness, and meaninglessness of an individual existence. It cures the poignantly frustrated not by conferring on them an absolute truth or by remedying the difficulties and abuses which made their lives miserable, but by freeing them from their ineffectual selves—and it does this by enfolding and absorbing them into a closely knit and exultant corporate whole. (Hoffer, 1951)

Again there is the search for the Gemeinschaft. As in romanticism, this search is conscious and programmatic. The point of the movement is not to remedy specific shortcomings of society, but rather to eliminate the very nature of an abstractive culture.

> It is not easy to question the thoroughly sensible, thoroughly well intentioned, but nevertheless reductive humanism with which the technocracy surrounds itself without seeming to speak a dead and discredited language. Especially so if one admits—as I do . . . —that it may lie within the capability of the technocracy to utilize its industrial prowess, its social engineering, its sheer affluence, and its well-developed diversionary tactics, to reduce, in ways that most people will find perfectly acceptable, all the tensions born from disorganization, privation, and injustice which currently unsettle our lives. . . . The technocracy is not simply a power structure wielding vast material influence; it is the expression of a grand cultural

imperative, a veritable mystique that is deeply endorsed by the populace. It is therefore a capacious sponge able to soak up prodigious quantities of discontent and agitation, often well before they look as anything but amusing eccentricities or uncalled-for aberrations. The question therefore arises: "If the technocracy in its grand procession through history is indeed pursuing to the satisfaction of so many such universally ratified values as The Quest for Truth, The Conquest of Nature, The Abundant Society, The Creative Leisure, The Well-Adjusted Life, why not settle back and enjoy the trip?"

The answer is, I guess, that I find myself unable to see anything at the end of the road we are following with such self-assured momentum but Samuel Beckett's two sad tramps forever waiting under that wilted tree for their lives to begin. (Roszak, 1969)

The way out is to replace the abstractive domination of culture, of which technocracy is a byproduct, by faith in the nonintellective functions of the mind, the ability to mythologize, and the type of knowledge known as gnosis (Roszak, 1969, 1973).

What, now, is this gnostic knowledge that is to be trusted? It is the feeling of certainty which can be derived from personal or borrowed intuition:

During their many ages of development, the civilizations of Occident and Orient have both explored various ways to escape from routinization and its inherent coercion. Among several, the "road inward" has always been most prominent. . . .

Many techniques have been designed to enable man to follow the "road inward"—from religious mysticism to the artificial trip of psychedelia. Like Hellenistic man, many a modern individual thirsts for the meaning that overrationalized abstract society denies him. He is in search of charismatic experiences and believes that these can be found in his "deepest" subjectivity. Incidentally, as always in the history of the Occident, it is at this point that truth and redemption are sought from the Orient: *ex oriente lux.* . . .

Thus floating on emotions and impressions only, man will need ever newer and stronger stimuli. Without the restrictions of institutional norms and values, i.e. without some form of institutional asceticism, human emotions are in danger of running empty. Ever stronger shocks must be invented. In a rather hysterical mood, man will begin to follow each fad that presents itself as extraordinary, or, in native language, "far out". . . .

These then are the Gnosticists in our society. They are not protesting against war or social injustices—unless such protests bring thrills and emotional shocks. They withdraw from reality into one or another form of subjective nirvana. . . .

As Gilles Quispel, H.Ch. Puech and other specialists in the field of gnosticism have said, *the gnostics of all ages search for God (i.e. for utter reality, meaning, and freedom) in the depth of their own souls.* Whatever one can attribute to the gnostic religion, this subjectivism seems to be its essential feature. Since it naturally rejects all limits and traditional parameters which to a certain degree always curb the operations of man's subjectivity, gnosticism stays open to all kinds of syncretism: in ever different configurations, gnosticism has always displayed a peculiar mixture of the exotic, the strange and the alien with the subjective and emotional. It is an emotional revolt against an objective and rational world. Fundamentally, gnosticism is a romantic and erotic Weltanschauung, and a world religion. (Zijderveld, 1970; Quispel, 1952)

The question is now whether subjectivistic protest must necessarily evolve in the direction of a fascist type of totalitarianism.

A first answer is that it may not evolve at all. Like romanticism before it, it may not enter the political arena, but remain restricted to a type of literary, artistic, and personal attitude, only marginally connected with politics. Yet where it does move into the political sphere, it seems to have fascism as the only possible outcome.

The first and most basic point is the subjectivism of the movement; there is no mechanism other than abstraction or force for reconciling personal intuitions. Where the movement seeks to go beyond the establishment of semi-isolated communes and to modify society at large by associative political action, violence is bound to erupt. In fact, the proneness to violence of the politicized elements of the counterculture has been amply demonstrated.

A second point is the totalitarianism of the movement:

This brings us to another aspect of the Gnosticist type of protest. . . . I call it *romantic absolutism*. The Gnosticist is in search for *utter* reality, *total* meaning, and *absolute* freedom. Every compromise is rejected. The modern Gnosticist longs for the absolute and the final, just like his Romantic brother in the nineteenth century. (Zijderveld, 1970)

Totalitarianism and intuition go hand in hand:

I have used the term "mystique" to represent the combination of elements which make the totalitarian's distinctive approach to social organization. . . . A word about the general term "mystique" is in order here. The term is used to express that the totalitarian . . . is convinced that he has *directly* perceived some immanent law of social development. This law is seen as relatively overriding, and its implications as bound eventually to be manifested. Consequently, the totalitarian's knowledge of the law is seen by him as dictating necessary action on his part, and as guaranteeing the "correctness" of that action. (Inkeles, 1954)

It is to that mystique—and not to the state, as it is often assumed—that total loyalty is due. An example of what this entails may be the occupation of Grand Central station by the yippies, who sat down in large groups at the doors leading to the commuter trains, in order to prevent commuters from reaching their destination and thus carrying out a way of life of which the yippies disapproved. Such a willingness to invade private lives, and in fact such a failure to distinguish between the private and the public is a hallmark of totalitarianism.

A third point is the antinomianism of the counterculture (Bell, 1973). Members of the movement are so completely convinced of their own intrinsic goodness that they feel themselves to be above moral law; they are also so completely convinced of the evil of their opponents that they feel that the latter do not deserve the protection of moral law.

> The mystique dictates their morality, indeed it stands above ordinary human morality and places its adherent outside the demands normally to be made of a man and a leader. Hence the totalitarian may be cynical about and manipulate "law," "loyalty," "truth," "honesty," and so on. For as long as he manipulates these in the service of the mystique, his action is beyond question—it is law, truth, honesty, loyalty, unto itself. (Inkeles, 1954)

Once again, the argument that the movement is anarchist in its tendency, and that it rejects the state, and that in consequence it cannot lead to totalitarianism, simply does not hold water. It is out of the anarchism of Sorel that many of the seminal ideas of fascism emerged: the priority of will over reason and the necessity of myth (Horowitz, 1968; Gregor, 1969). As for the state,

> the totalitarian sees the state as predominantly an instrument of another purpose, a mere vessel to which he gives content. It is precisely this which makes him so great a threat to established institutions and freedom—that he has no real respect for the state as such, for the state as an institution with legitimacy and purpose in and of itself. Paradoxically, it is rather the non-totalitarian who accepts the state as sufficient unto its own purpose of governing, of allocating authority, and of regulating relations among men. The characteristic of the totalitarian is that he sees the state as an institution with no right to existence in itself, but rather as a mere tool serving the attainment of some higher goal which is above the state. It is essentially the imperatives of this higher law which spell the doom of "the rule of law." (Inkeles, 1954)

The co-subjective orientation: communism

A quotation of Professor Norman Cohn, appearing at the end of the preceding chapter, suggests that both communism and fascism may be considered as examples of chiliastic movements, such as the medieval ones he has analyzed, and which were labelled movements of associative reaction in this study. Strong arguments may be advanced to support such an identification. For example, one may point out the enormous role played by charisma in both contexts—the cult of personality. One may also look at the almost total immersion of the party member within the party, in such a way that the party becomes for its member a primary group or a Gemeinschaft. In both cases this Gemeinschaft, or more properly its inner core, monopolizes political life and rules the broader Gesellschaft within which it is embedded. Gregor (1969) points out that in actual practice the results of communism in power are closer to the ideology of fascism than to the ideology of Marx and even Lenin.

> Leon Trotsky . . . maintained that "Stalinism and Fascism, in spite of a deep difference in social foundations, are symmetrical phenomena. In many of their features, they show a deadly similarity."
>
> Those similarities include a commitment to national development and/or reconstruction under a highly centralized and authoritarian party elite, a restoration of the authority of the state, an effective program of class and category collaboration within the confines of a national economic plan, exclusive and systematic training of the youth of the nation in conformity with a secular ideology characterized by a relatively specific constellation of exclusive social and political beliefs, a unitary party monopoly of the means of coercion and communication, and leadership by charismatic or pseudocharismatic leaders charged with enormous responsibilities and endowed with prodigious powers. In all cases the totalitarian state assumes pedagogical, enterprisory, and tutelary functions unknown in traditional parliamentary regimes. (Gregor, 1969)

Yet the similarities should not make us neglect the differences. The first of these is the much greater ability of communism to postpone gratification, something which is alien to the associative mentality. While communism carries with it the conviction that the "inexorable laws of history" are bound to insure its universal triumph, it is capable of understanding that the conditions for such a triumph may "not yet" be ripe, and that attempts at hastening historical evolution may amount to dangerous "adventurism." This patience is something of which fascism, particularly in its Nazi variety, was incapable.

A second difference is that while fascist loyalty is to an individual and to his intuitions, communist loyalty is to a codified body of beliefs. This difference is not always apparent: one may think of Stalin and even more of Mao; in both cases loyalty seems to be directed more towards the "thought of the leader" than towards a coherent body of doctrine, capable of standing alone as pure dogma independent of personality. Yet different examples can also be adduced; for example, faithful adherence to an interpretation of Marxism-Leninism long after Marx and Lenin have disappeared from the world scene.

Such a reliance on specifically stated dogma, rather than on the often implicit and changeable intuitions of a leader (what is the precise meaning of Mobutism?) has a number of consequences.

The problem of succession, which fascist regimes have not' generally been able to handle, is one which communism has been able to handle fairly smoothly. Assuredly, the presence of charisma still counts, but to a large extent the charisma is no longer tied to an individual but to a role—it appears as what Weber has called Amt-Charisma. This is a sign of bureaucratization, and a movement in the direction of abstraction.

Another important point is that communism has a much greater capacity for cross-cultural penetration than does fascism. Assuredly, the ability of fascism (or nationalism in general) to penetrate cultural barriers is not as low as it might have been expected. This was already touched upon at the beginning of this chapter. A common dislike for abstractive patterns of thought and behavior led to the gathering of various fascist collaborators around Hitler. A similar dislike presides over the anti-western coalition of third world countries which dominates the United Nations at the time of this writing. On the other hand, communism never achieved the monolithic aspect which might have been expected on the basis of loyalty to a common dogma. Yet the difference remains clear, even if it is not absolute. It is easier for, let us say, a Frenchman, to be an outright communist, than to be an outright Nazi.

These differences, as well as the doctrinaire character of communism, suggest that the latter is an example of a co-subjective rather than of an associative approach. Once again, the difference is not absolute, as the ideal types used for analysis never actually develop in reality. But the leaning-over of communism in the direction of co-subjectivity constitutes a dominant, and possibly the principal characteristic upon which to base an analysis.

The foundation of co-subjectivity is the sharing of well defined concepts. These concepts are deemed to be universal, since concepts correspond to the definitions of classes and to words identifying classes. A network of such concepts, with their definitions, provides a basis for deductive reasoning—and the basic tool of universalistic co-subjectivity is reason. From the political point of view, this implies that the basic aim of government is to bring the country into conformity with a reasoned system of ideas, or an ideology.

The universalist out of power or coming into power is likely to conceive this ideology as a program to be implemented. The universalist already in power is likely to consider the arrangement he has authored as the only good one, and to resist any change. Out of power, he is likely to be a revolutionary; in power, he is likely to be a conservative.

In either case, his central preoccupation is likely to be the imposition of ideas upon reality: what the mind perceives clearly is true and ought to work.

Examples of this attitude were presented in chapter 2 in reference not to Marx, but to an earlier thinker in whom the tendency appears in a purer state, Plato.

Some preliminary explanations are in order. Plato's theory of ideas is considered as idealistic; reality is knowable through the exercise of pure reason, and any admixture of information coming from the senses is likely to bring nothing but confusion (a statement of this position in the *Phaedo* was quoted earlier). Marx and his followers consider themselves materialists. Yet to what extent should their claim be accepted? Materialism can be looked upon from two points of view: that of its content, and that of its method. From the point of view of its content, it is the affirmation that reality is material, and not spiritual or mental—whatever such words may mean. From the point of view of its method, materialism should take an approach diametrically opposed to Platonicism, and put faith in empirical observations. This, however, is something which Marxists and Leninists never do. Marx's predictions have been disproved by actual observable historical evolution. At their core there were the pauperization theses, according to which the disparity between an ever diminishing number of the rich and an ever increasing number of the poor would go on increasing in industrialized countries; the middle classes would simply disappear, and the poverty of industrial workers would become ever more absolute. In reality exactly the opposite took place; between Marx's days and our own the rewards of capital greatly decreased, the welfare of industrial workers greatly increased, and the middle classes came to include an ever increasing proportion of the population. Yet this did not lead to any revision of the basic theses of Marxism; these continue to be propounded through the same logical arguments as a hundred years earlier. Empirical observation, the necessary process of a true materialism, simply has no place in Marxism.

At the time of Lenin's exile in western Europe, the Austrian physicist and philosopher Ernst Mach put forward an epistemology based on radical though somewhat naive empiricism, in which the basis of all knowledge would be the act of perception.

Lenin protested: "Materialism generally recognizes the objectively real being (matter) as existing independently of mind, sensation, experience, etc.". . . .

Surely . . . matter existed before man. There were trees, rocks, seas, beasts, and so forth before a living person was there to perceive them. . . .

"Historical materialism recognizes social being as existing independently of the social consciousness of humanity." They are not one, he contended, they are independent, therefore plural. "You cannot eliminate even one basic assumption, one substantial part of this philosophy of Marxism, it is as it were a solid block of steel," Lenin, the doctrinaire, stated, "without abandoning objective truth, without falling into the arms of bourgeois-reactionary falsehood." He called the Machist effort to unite matter and consciousness "conciliatory quackery." The Machists, he wrote, "are all wretchedly pulpy, a contemptible party of *middle-roaders* in philosophy, in every question confusing the materialist and idealist points of view." They claim to rise above materialism and idealism, "while *in fact* all these gentle-men continuously deviate toward idealism, and lead an incessant struggle against materialism." The expression "graduated flunkeys of theism," Lenin charged, "best befits Mach, Avenarius and their school." (Fischer, 1964)*

Whatever be the merit of these arguments, one thing is certain: They are purely metaphysical, and thus fit with Plato's method and not with the type of materialistic inquiry which is exemplified by science.

In conclusion, there seems to be good justification in tying the phenomenon of communism—or Marxism-Leninism—with the cultural type first and most clearly represented by Plato. It might be mentioned that the placing in parallel of Plato and Marx is by no means original with this author; it was done earlier by Popper (1962).

Elites and abstractions

Whatever be the content and the purpose of political dogma-tism, the result is in most cases the separation of the polity into an elite and "the masses." Formal reasoning is something at which some people are good, while other people are not. In Soviet parlance *propaganda* is the demonstration by reason of the truth of the dogma: the tool of propaganda is dialectical reason and the goal is the indoctrination of the elite. Communication with the masses is not carried out by reasoned presentations beyond their intellectual capacities, but through "*agita-tion*," a technique in which repetition replaces reasoning and appeals to feelings replace appeals to understanding.

According to Lenin a spontaneous awakening of revolutionary consciousness in the proletarian masses was unlikely; guidance would have to be provided by a vanguard, an elite of party members. Even though Lenin often voiced his mistrust of intellectuals, and hoped that most of the guiding elite would be drawn from the ranks of manual

---

*The quotations are from Lenin's *Materialism and Empirio-Criticism*.

workers (something which seldom was the case in reality), the criterion for admittance in the governing vanguard was one of awareness, understanding, and doctrinal purity—precisely the kind of criterion by which an idealistic philosopher might be evaluated.

The guiding role of the elite is often willingly accepted by the majority. An excerpt from a conversation with a Russian "man in the street" may be used as an example:

> "But why," I persisted, "do you believe the Party leaders will find the correct answer?"
> "Because they understand and apply the laws of historical evolution."
> "And why do you think they have a greater claim to such understanding than other people?"
> "*Im vidnyeye*," he replied, using a common Russian phrase that means roughly "because they see things more clearly." (Mehnert, 1962)

The co-subjective orientation: on elections

The communists and communist-oriented members of the armed forces in Portugal have tried to bring about "direct popular democracy" by rejecting and ignoring the results of the elections to the Constituent Assembly. From the point of view of the western cultures, their attitude appears hypocritical. From the point of view of co-subjective universalism it is simply logical, and in fact the only logically possible stance.

The logical justification of holding elections is not only the attempt to balance various divergent interests. It is mainly an expression of intellectual humility, the admission that no one really knows what is best for the commonwealth. Under such conditions of fairly uniformly distributed ignorance, it makes sense to seek out the opinion of the majority, since, after all, no one has the monopoly of truth.

The situation is entirely different in the context of a belief that truth can be reached, and in particular that it can be reached by the proper application of a doctrine based on reason. From the universalistic point of view, a democracy whose organs of decision operate through the majority vote of representatives themselves elected by majority vote, is unadulterated nonsense. If reason can tell you what is right, what should be done, what is the reality around you and how problems should be solved, then counting noses or opinions makes no sense at all; the only thing to do is to learn how to reason well. If the majority opposes what one knows is reasonable and right, it can be only out of a preference for particular interests to the general good, or else out of ignorance and delusion. One wouldn't think of voting on the solution of a mathematical problem. The basic tenet of universalistic politics—or religious theology—is that reasoned knowledge in these fields is quite as dependable as in mathematics. It is such an attitude that is often expressed by the Soviet use of qualifiers such as "correct" and "incorrect" in regard to political questions. Within such a frame of reference, the only meaning which can be logically and honestly given to the word "democracy" is that of a government for the people by those who know best.

Such, then, is the relationship between the ruling class of guardians of truth and the mass of the people. It might be noted that

the concept of the Party as the ruling class was introduced by Lenin, who said in August 1917: "Russia used to be ruled by 150,000 landowners. Why should not 240,000 Bolsheviks do the same job?" (Tucker, 1963)

The co-subjective orientation: words and deeds

In the universalistic approach reason—or words—comes first, action second. This may mean that action may come later, as the implementation of a program, or that it may become neglected.

The emphasis upon words, ideals, and elegance of expression has been condemned by some Latin American critics. One of the causes of instability in political life, as they see it, is the tendency to feel that the job is finished when written expression has been given to ideals, through the composing of constitutions, party declarations, and statutes, while systematic, determined efforts to translate the verbalized ideals into reality often are wanting. (Gillin, 1960)

Or again:

Like many other things in Venezuela, democracy is something new as an experience though it is old as an ideal. Arturo Uslar Pietri, a respected historian and novelist who is today a leader of one of the nation's political parties, the Frente Nacional Democratico, a centrist group, has written: "The high-minded, steadfast enthusaism for the republican ideal is one of the determining factors of Venezuelan history; it is, in some respects, analogous with the tenacious and resolute search for the city of El Dorado during the sixteenth century. The Venezuelan seeks the City of Justice as his forerunners sought the City of Gold, with the same dedication, the same indestructible hope, and the same splendid determination." And, Uslar Pietri might have added, with the same impracticality and the same fated lack of success. The City of Gold and the City of Justice are both mirages. While searching for them, the Venezuelan has always neglected the real world around him and shirked the job of making it, if not perfect, at least a little better. He has never learned the art of reasonable compromise or found a working mean between unrestricted liberty and total subjection, between extravagant wealth and abject poverty. It is now nearly a hundred and fifty years since Simón Bolivar inspired the South American colonies to break away from Spanish rule and proclaimed his own country a republic. During that time, Venezuela had twenty-four constitutions, each document being more noble than its predecessor but no more effectual, and it has had more than a hundred revolutions. (Taper, 1965)

It might be useful to present an example typifying the same tendency in another culture, in this case less a national culture than a common cultural trait shared by intellectuals in developing countries:

In a conversation between an American and an Algerian about the situation in the two countries, the American mentioned that one of the most negative and difficult aspects of contemporary America is the race question, an area within which Americans have not been able so far to translate the ideals proclaimed by an immense majority into practices followed by all. He then asked the Algerian whether any comparable problems existed in Algeria (the time was 1962). The Algerian answered in the negative, saying that in his country no distinction whatsoever existed between citizens of different ethnic origins or religious preferences. It so happened that a few days earlier, newspapers had carried stories of ethnic strife in Algeria in which two members of a minority group had been killed by a mob. This was mentioned by the American. "This is entirely unimportant," answered the Algerian, "it was done by ignorant people who do not understand the ideals of our revolution and our government."

The important point is to avoid disturbing the intellectual order of things, rather than to deal with what happens to creatures of flesh and blood outside the officially sanctioned order.

More generally speaking, Marxism, as the most contemporary of the great systems of dogma deemed applicable to the entire range of social, economic and political affairs, is bound to appeal to intellectuals whose language it speaks. This is particularly true in the case of young intellectuals from countries in the process of modernization. Marxism provides them with an all-embracing doctrine supplying answers to questions that traditional cultures do not answer, and that modern neoparticularism answers in a nonsystematic way difficult to master.

The objective orientation

This orientation, which may be also called nominalistic or neoparticularistic, is derived from the need to subordinate the universality of meaning to the diversity of objective situations (Pribram, 1945). The diversity of human goals, coupled with the diversity of circumstances under which such goals can be sought, leads to pragmatic attitudes in which reason is considered only as a tool for making hypotheses, the value of which can be established only by the test of action.

Probably the purest example of the objective orientation can be found in the free enterprise system, and also in the *ad hoc* legislation by which this system was modified when it did not perform satisfactorily (particularly in the United States). In fact the expression 'ad hoc' can be considered a leitmotiv of the objective orientation—together with "crossing bridges when one comes to them" and "muddling through."

One of the consequences of the corresponding state of culture is decentralization. No solution is considered as having universal validity; problems should be solved on the basis of the particular circumstances that define them. In the place of the single bureaucracy characteristic of the co-subjective approach, the objective approach favors numerous mutually competing bureaucracies. In place of an annointed elite of "guardians of truth," it favors a multiplicity of types of experts.

Rather than trying to determine "the just price" of things (as did Catholic philosophy in the Middle Ages) or the right program of production (as does socialistic dogmatism), objective neo-particularism tends to depend on the market place. A theory of the advantages of competitiveness is derived from the practice of competition. Later, systems of checks and balances may be developed to preserve at least a degree of openness to competition and a multiplicity of foci of decision making.

Objective orientation: Democracy

In the earlier sections of this chapter, fascism was placed at the subjective apex, and communism at the co-subjective apex. Placing democracy at the objective apex would complete the symmetry. Yet the situation is not quite that simple. An objective orientation may indeed be at the origin of democracy; but, as we will see shortly, it does not provide by itself the conditions sufficient for the equalitarianism of political rights which has become the central attribute of democracy in contemporary thinking.

A point to bear in mind is that all three requirements of meaning are operative at all times (or almost all), but not to the same extent. Their interplay is often a synthesis, a form of behavior (political or other) which can be explained by neither of the apexes taken in isolation. This, as we will see further below, is the case of democracy as we know it.

A form of democracy may be compatible with a subjective orientation, as long as the polities concerned are small and culturally uniform. In such contexts discussion as to the course of action to follow may be opened to the entire population (or, more often, to the entire male population). The aim of the discussion is to divine the right portents dictated by tradition or by the supernatural; discussion proceeds by allusions and hints until a consensus emerges. Such a consensus is seldom based on pragmatic considerations; rather, it constitutes a diagnosis of the nature of the total situation. Once the sense of the community is voiced, total endorsement is required from all; opposition is construed as impious. There is no question of a majority temporarily in power and a minority retaining full rights to public respect. Examples may be found in the functioning of village councils in South and Southeast Asia (Geertz, 1965). It is, of course questionable whether a participatory regime based on the principle of unanimity rather than majority should be called democracy.

Whatever the answer to this question, democracy and a subjective orientation appear to be at loggerheads in more complex societies. A subjective polity may be based on shared and *often subconscious* common experiences, forming the basis of a Rousseau'ist type of general will. Outsiders are excluded—whether they be ethnic minorities even if legally endowed with full citizenship, or natives considered as renegades because they have espoused different patterns of thought. Shared feelings may form the basis of a majority within existing practice, giving an appearance of democracy, but once such a majority is in power, it seeks to become a unanimity by excluding those who do not belong: Nazism and Fascism are examples.

Likewise, democracy is antithetical to co-subjectivity. The point of view of the latter is that *the right* answers to all questions can be derived from the application of the proper doctrine. As it was mentioned earlier, within such a frame of reference weighing individual preferences is both silly and unethical. What needs to be done is convincing the deviants by a proper application of dialectical reasoning.

Democracy (at least in the modern and western sense of the word) finds its source in objectivism. Since reason can serve only to establish hypotheses and the resolution of conflicting points of view can be obtained only *ex post facto* by experience, it is reasonable to let the different interested parties to exercise their influence on the form of action that will be tried out first (Pribram, 1945).

Thus objective orientation provides the necessary basis for democracy. However, this basis is not sufficient. The degree of influence of the participants varies. The principle of equal and universal suffrage amounts usually to a denial of objective conditions and can be introduced only through co-subjective rationalism (or perhaps dogmatism). Interestingly enough, the countries that were the first to move in the direction of what evolved into modern democracy were also among the last to institute universal and equalitarian suffrage. In Britain, alumni of some of the universities had the privilege of voting twice up to 1946, in Switzerland women are still largely excluded, and in the United States most blacks could not vote in many states until 1965. In contradistinction, many countries which espoused democracy through imitation, introduced equalitarian suffrage much sooner.

Thus democracy as we know it appears to be a synthesis between an objectivistic thesis and a co-subjective antithesis.

It is not, of course, fully devoid of subjectivistic elements. Living in a democratic society is an experience, and those who have shared it tend to adopt the subjective point of view that all that is democratic is holy, and all that is not democratic is evil. This is primarily true in the United States (excluding to a large extent the Old South which had few foreign born persons) as democracy often is the only experience common to citizens of various ethnic stocks. However, subjectivistic tendencies are relatively weak in democracies. One of the consequences of this weakness of subjectivistic elements in democracy is the relative lack of cohesiveness of democracies in the international arena, particularly as compared with the political cohesiveness often displayed by countries dominated by common co-subjective doctrines or by common subjective feelings. Once again, the attitudes exhibited in the United Nations are an example: Any motion voicing the subjectivity of anti-western resentment can count on solid support, while the western democracies are not united.

Political parties

The terminology surrounding political partisanship is fairly similar in countries with very different cultures. However the reality beneath similar pronouncements is likely to be very different from situation to situation, and to reflect the overall logic of the culture.

In predominantly subjectivistic cultures (including the Old South of the United States) belonging to a party is often more an affirmation of self-identity within the group than the utilization of a channel for specific political action. As a matter of fact the entire approach to partisanship is diffuse, associative, and all-inclusive, rather than specific, abstractive, and limited to definable political questions. Parties are often based on ethnic or class belonging (in which case membership means being *truly and faithfully* an ethnic, a worker, or an aristocrat), on family tradition, or on loyalty to a charismatic leader. The tendency to single party polities is strong; belonging to a party is an expression of faith, within a context in which only the faithful are to be trusted.

In polities with a strong co-subjective orientation, parties are considered as channels for promoting specific ideologies. From the point of view of their number, this means either a multiplicity of parties (as many as there are ideological nuances) or a single party (once triumphant, the party which embodies the truth in its own eyes suppresses those who promote what it considers to be error).

In polities with a strong objective orientation, parties are considered as frameworks for the working out of alliances among those willing to trade favors in order to gain some specific goals. The number of parties tends toward two umbrella organizations, often bringing together people with diverging opinions but with temporarily converging interests.

International alliances

Subjectively oriented polities see alliances in the image of friendship, in which friend helps friend regardless of the circumstances in which aid is required. Neutrality or indifference are considered as treacherous, again regardless of the particular content.

Objectively oriented polities consider alliances as contracts; these must be honored regardless of affective considerations, but nothing beyond contractual obligations is required from the allies.

Examples of misunderstandings due to such divergent interpretations can be found in the present state of Greek-American and Turkish-American relations. Both Greece and Turkey felt that their alliances with the United States entitled them to friendly support in the dispute over Cyprus; the United States viewed the disputeas falling outside the contract of a defensive alliance against the Soviet Union, as a nuisance which might interfere with Turkey's and Greece's ability to fulfill their contractual obligations in NATO. Attempts at a hands off policy on the part of the United States led to a deterioration of relations with both countries. America is perceived as a false friend—worse than an enemy—in both Greece and Turkey.

As for polities with a co-subjective orientation, alliances are viewed as expressions of the natural solidarity of those who share the same principles. As such they are deemed to be permanent and unlimited in their content. Attempts at limiting the scope of mutual obligations are likely to be considered as betrayals. Alliances with nonparticipants in the ideology are viewed as temporary accommodations, at most.

Aggression

This is not the place to attempt an exhaustive analysis of the complex problem of aggression in international life. However, even a cursory analysis shows that the type of cultural analysis used in this book may contribute insights into the problem.

For the purpose of analysis, we shall subdivide aggression in international life into three categories:

1. Political aggression,
2. Economic aggression, and
3. Cultural aggression.

Political aggression may be defined as an attempt on the part of one country to gain advantage over another country by political or military means. Attempts on the part of one country to gain a position of leadership over other countries will be included under this heading, even if the effect of such leadership leads, not to endangering or diminishing the country or countries placed in a position of followers, but to the enhancing of their well-being and security.

Economic aggression may be defined as an attempt to transform the economy of another country by a variety of means, including capital investment, trade, or technical assistance. Again, such a definition covers not only situations in which one country "exploits" another, but also situations in which the economic transformation realized under the leadership of a donor country leads to increased *economic* well-being in a recipient country.

Cultural aggression may be defined as attempts on the part of a donor country to transform the culture of a recipient country. Such attempts may be deliberate, as was often the case in colonial empires, and as is the case in missionary efforts and in technical assistance programs. They may also be involuntary; the wealth and the personal freedom so evident in the lives of people in the more developed countries have for byproduct a degree of cultural subversion in less developed countries, the inhabitants of which are attracted to the cultural ways of the West without necessarily understanding them. This is what Lerner (1958) has called the revolution of rising expectations—or, as it often appears, the revolution of rising frustrations.

Let us look at the type of behavior which can be expected from cultures dominated by the patterns of each of the three apexes of the model.

Countries with cultures following mainly the objective pattern may have been aggressive politically, but are not likely to follow aggressive policies in the second half of the twentieth century. War doesn't pay, and neither does political tension falling short of war. States having an objective appreciation of these facts are much more likely to be defensive than aggressive in the international arena.

The policies of the United States since World War II appear to partly contradict the statement above. It was implied earlier, and it will be explicitly stated in a later chapter, that the culture of the United States is in the main objective, neo-particularistic, and nominalistic. Yet American foreign policies often appeared as aggressive in the terms of the very broad definition given above. The United States has tried to lead other countries, often with a considerable amount of arm-twisting. The fact that the direction in which the U.S. led or tried to lead is that of the defense of peace through collective security mitigates the aggressive epithet, but it does not eliminate it totally. Witness the tragedy of Viet Nam, where American policy attempted to induce the Vietnamese to defend a democracy which neither existed nor could possibly be developed given the cultural background of the country.

The fact is that even though American behavior at home tends to be dominated by an objectivistic pattern, American behavior abroad often exhibits messianic qualities which fit better the co-subjective, universalistic pattern. This has been exhibited in missionary efforts, and at the level of national policy, particularly under Woodrow Wilson and John Foster Dulles, by attempts at imposing on the world a universal formula based on experiences which had worked well at home: self-determination, democracy, and a parliament of nations. We shall return to this anomaly in a later chapter; we can only note it at this stage of the analysis. A point not to be omitted is that even the aggressive aspects of American policies had a defensive posture as ultimate goal, and that, by and large, objectively oriented cultures are unlikely to pursue aggressive foreign policies in an age in which the pay-off of such policies is likely to be negative.

The situation is different in regard to economic aggression. Objective orientation leads in general to good economic development. In consequence, members of objectively oriented cultures are likely to exhibit a good grasp of the possibilities of the market place and to seize opportunities which are neglected by people with other cultural approaches, often including the inhabitants of the geographical areas in which the opportunities are located. Once again, the resulting enterprises need not be exploitative. Even the former colonies seem to have profited more from the colonial relationships than did the colonizing countries—at least in the economic sphere. This is suggested by the heavy burden of foreign aid of a country like France, which has to a large extent succeeded in maintaining her economic relations with her former colonies. It is also suggested by the surge of prosperity in the

Netherlands after economic relationships with its supposedly profitable colonies had been severed.

However, even profitable economic partnerships have cultural consequences. Investment of foreign capital may not be exploitative—and in fact it very seldom is exploitative—but it imposes changes of behavior on local capital and local labor. For example, local capital may have to seek increased efficiency because of foreign competition, and local labor may find that it has to pay for the higher wages it receives by a complete change in life style.

This means that economic change induced from abroad, no matter how profitable, represents a cultural aggression. Economic contacts between developed and underdeveloped countries amount to a cultural aggression on the part of the former, no matter how great may be the benefits derived by the recipient countries, or even their stated desire for economic aid and modernization. In requesting such aid, the developing countries seldom realize that a cultural revolution necessarily goes with it; in most cases they want the fruits of economic modernity without the cultural changes which make the harvesting of those fruits possible.

There remains the question of purely cultural aggression. Objectively oriented polities are culturally aggressive, often without realizing it. As it was already suggested above, the way of life they represent and the objective knowledge they have tend to seduce the participants or more traditional societies. The very wealth of material goods suggests to the people who do not have them that they should change, that they should become culturally similar to the rich, in order to be as rich as they are. At the same time, objectively oriented cultures seldom provide a blueprint, a comprehensive analysis, of what the poor must do in order to become less poor. Technical aid usually amounts to specific advice the background of which is neither understood nor systematically presented. The same weakness in communication appears in the advertising that business uses primarily to influence the home audience of the society in which it operates. Such advertising cannot limit its influence to the home audience; even if it is not aiming at influencing new markets abroad, it penetrates across cultural boundaries and presents to members of other cultures images of a desirable life, without providing information as to the manner in which such a life can be achieved. The resulting cultural aggression comes to be resented in spite of, or perhaps because of, its limited character. The populations that it disturbs do not understand that it is limited to the cultural area, and tend to assume that the aggression of which they feel themselves to be the object is either political or economically exploitative.

There is very little that the governments of objectively oriented polities can do about the situation. Cultural aggression is carried out by the very fact of existence of societies the ways of which appear desirable—or partly desirable—to others (Glenn et al., 1970).

Co-subjectively oriented cultures tend to be aggressive both politically and culturally. The economic aspects of aggression hardly need to be discussed separately, as in most cases co-subjective, universalistically oriented cultures tend to hold a tight political rein on economic activities (this was largely true even in the case of mercantilism) and to subordinate economic efforts to political goals.

The double aspect of universalistic aggression as both political and cultural stems from the organization of the culture aròund one or another explicitly defined doctrine. People governed by this pattern

> believe . . . that they must tell people from other cultures what is right and true, for their own good. Since universal orientation means an official ideology, the state becomes involved in the missionary effort; this applies to the Christianity of the Crusades as well as to Communism today. (Glenn et al., 1970)

The co-subjectivistic pervasiveness of the state and its participation in the definition of a universal truth makes it possible for the state to manipulate and if needed to dampen both its political and its cultural aggression. This distinguishes it from the democratic or potentially democratic objectively and neo-particularistically oriented states, in the case of which much of the cultural aggression is carried out by private individuals and private organizations independently of the state. A co-subjectively oriented state has the mechanisms lacking in an objectively oriented state for decreasing the intensity of its cultural aggressiveness if such aggressiveness becomes counterproductive from its point of view.

In addition, the very generality of co-subjective universalistic doctrines makes them attractive to people in search of new cultural certainties. We have already noted the tendency of intellectuals in hitherto associative traditionalistic cultures to prefer co-subjective universalism to the objective lack of dogmatism, and the concommitent complexity of objectivistic positions. This preference for co-subjective universalism may be due to an often desperate search for new certainties, and may determine one of the strongest of the appeals of communism.

> The very elaborateness and explicitness of the code is an element in the appeal of Communism. It opens the way for becoming "something very definite" which is quite attractive to individuals confused and uncertain about their own identities. (Almond, 1954)

Under the conditions of culture contact prevailing in this century, subjectivistic-associative polities are likely to be nonaggressive in the cultural and economic domains. In these areas, they are the weak and likely to be the victims rather than the perpetrators of aggression.

The situation is quite different in the political arena. Polities in the course of change feel threatened. While the threat to them may be cultural rather than political, the resistence to the threat is likely to center around frankly political components of action, often in the form of paranoid accusations of exploitation and political aggression directed against the more culturally evolved states. The mechanism determining a political counteraggression against cultural aggression is likely to be a projection of the often paranoid feelings of anxiety created by cultural aggression, and which find no outlets other than in political action. Once again the political aggressiveness of many of the Third World countries in the United Nations may serve as illustrations.*

These remarks point to what may be the main political problem of this century. Cultural misunderstandings are likely to poison the political atmosphere as long as many cultures remain associative and subjective, and thus incapable of looking at problems from points of view other than that of their own affectivity. However, any attempt at speeding up their cultural evolution in the direction of the development of an objectivity capable of recognizing that cooperation may be more fruitful than conflict, would in itself constitute an aggravated cultural aggression, and thus lead to political counteraggressions more dangerous even than is the present state of tension. We may remember that to a large extent Hitler was the response to an attempt coming largely from the outside to change the German culture under the Weimar Republic.

Conclusions

The newly independent countries in the twentieth century are almost all ruled by single party regimes and/or by military dictatorships. This situation is not difficult to explain. The politicians who presided over the gaining of independence had in most cases one of two bases of political strength. They were either the spokesmen of tribal groupings or the representatives of anti-colonialist movements transcending the geographical limits of the states or potential states in which they operated. In both cases they were, at least to a point, subversive in respect

---

*This study was prepared before Iran's taking of American hostages in late 1979. The events of the "Iranian crisis" provided a clear example of cultural aggressiveness on the part of the Americans and of political agressiveness on the part of the Iranians.

to the states inherited from the apparatus of public administration set up by the former colonial power. The cultural contradiction between the country to be governed and those aspiring to governing it deprived the latter of any firm constituency. However, there was one organization which was co-extensive with the state and which needed no constituency: the armed forces. In many or perhaps in most cases the latter took over from politicians whose cultural preoccupation was either with a unit smaller than the state (the tribe) or broader than the state (the ideology of anti-colonialism) (Glenn, 1970a).

What is certain is that the democratic type of political organization favored by the former colonial powers and often in the early phase of independence by the former colonies, did not take in most cases. The reasons for the failure of democracy are in the main cultural—as are the reasons for the success of democracy as the dominant political form in the western countries. This justifies the adding of cultural analysis to the other investigative tools of political science.

9

PRELITERATE CULTURES

The next few chapters will attempt to bring into focus the cognitive characteristics of a number of types of culture. The first type to be taken up will be that of "primitive" or preliterate cultures.

Are there pre-logical cultures?

The question which unavoidably comes up for discussion is that of the controversy, surrounding Lévy-Bruhl's unfortunate use of the concept of "pre-logical" thought (1910). Is there such a thing as a pre-logical mentality, or, complementarily, a logical mentality opposed to it?

This question was answered in the affirmative in the preceding chapters. In all of these contexts it was shown that there existed associative ad abstractive patterns of approach. At the same time, most of the examples given suggested that the two patterns coexisted in the same cultures. Under the circumstances, the question should be rephrased. Are there any cultures which are entirely associative and pre-logical, and other cultures which are entirely abstractive and logical?

The second part of the question was also answered in the earlier chapters, this time in the negative. Examples of associative, "pre-logical" thought were found in the most advanced cultures, and this in two ways—in the form of movements or pockets of associative reaction, and in that of the omnipresence and the necessity of affectivity and artistic creativity.

There remains the first part of the question. This can be answered, at least hypothetically, in three different manners:

211

1. Logical or abstractive thought is totally lacking in some cultures, which in consequence deserve to be considered as truly primitive.
2. There exists a developmental continuum consisting in a relative decrease in the proportion of associative approaches and a relative increase in abstractive approaches; various cultures are distributed along this continuum.
3. There is no difference in patterns of thought between preliterate and advanced cultures.

The point of view that will be defended in this chapter is the middle one. Associative and abstractive thought, or better subjectivity, co-subjectivity, and objectivity are present in all cultures, but their reciprocal distribution varies from case to case, and is characteristic of the culture concerned.

A hypothesis on the dynamics of evolution

Let us begin with two examples of transductive reasoning, as described by Piaget (1962):

"Daddy's getting hot water, so he's going to shave."

"I haven't had my nap, so it isn't afternoon."

Transduction is an associative and a pre-logical type of mental operation. It does not have the rigor of systematic deduction or of systematic induction. It ties together, or associates, two particular events, without showing that the tie is legitimate because of the existence of a superordinate universal concept. For example, the first transduction can be faulted because it does not take the form of a syllogism, such as: "Daddy gets hot water if and only if he is going to shave; he is getting hot water, therefore he is going to shave."

Yet even if the childish statement can be faulted, it does make sense; in all probability Daddy has been seen frequently getting hot water before shaving and seldom under other circumstances. As for the syllogism itself, it can also be faulted, if not at the co-subjective apex at least at the objective one; hot water may be used for other purposes than shaving, even by Daddy. Furthermore, the syllogistic form of reasoning is seldom used, even by adults in advanced cultures. What takes its place is the presence in the mind of adults of concepts such as "hot water," with its different uses, and "shaving," with the different manners in which it can be carried out. It thus appears that childish transduction can be faulted mainly because it is based on a limited field of experience. Within the narrow confines of this experience, both of her transductive conclusions are likely to hold.

The question, then, is one of the extent of the subject's experience and one of the degree of codification of this experience into clear and unequivocal concepts, delimited by criterial boundaries. From the developmental point of view this suggests differentiation between cultures capable of dealing with rich and complex environments through the use of extensive structures of concepts, and cultures dealing with relatively narrow environments capable of coping, in many cases, by using associative complexes tied together by transductions.

Several examples of transductive, associative thinking among preliterates were noted earlier. In one case, when a man was pulled out of his canoe by a crocodile, the members of his village attributed his death to witchcraft on the part of his companions and of a man who had a hut on a nearby shore. This is an obvious example of a transduction based on simple spatial and temporal association; the concept of the inherent danger presented by crocodiles is missing.

It may be suggested that the danger presented by crocodiles in the environment of the people concerned was not critical, or that the experience of death by crocodile was relatively rare. On the other hand, the sharing of the belief in witchcraft was likely to provide a strong basis for social cohesion. The co-subjective value of this belief was probably more important than a possibly minor objective dysfunction due to a poor analysis of the feeding habits of crocodiles.

Such situations are likely to reverse as the amount of experience available in the culture increases (possibly as a result of some culture contact), and as there appear in the culture specialized body of scientists or codifiers of concepts. At that point the search for a definition of the concept of "crocodile" is likely to accomplish something which occasional mishaps failed to do, namely to describe them as potentially dangerous carnivores.

Yet any new state of balance between man, society, and environment should not be expected to be perfect. Many of our concepts turn out sooner or later to be complexes in Vygotsky's terminology (1962), i.e., to contain inner contradictions which make reasonings based upon them little better than transductions. The concept of "length," which is perfectly clear to the average western adult, is shown by Einsteinian physics to be quite equivocal within a certain range of experience, that of bodies moving at high velocity in respect to one another.

Thus the differences between the circumstances under which associative patterns of tought may appear in the usage of one or another culture can be assumed to be an expression of the total amount of information available in the culture. This does not mean that there is no qualitative difference between associative and abstractive reasoning. Rather, it means that whether one or another type of reasoning will be used is likely to depend on the degree of familiarity that the culture has with the problems at hand.

Primitive classifications

Lévy-Bruhl (1910, 1922) held that the thought of preliterate peoples was governed by a "law of participation" which tied together in a mystical manner all the elements of experience and made it impossible for the primitives to perform the basic logical operation which can be stated as "if this is X, it cannot be non-X" (1910, 1922).

Lévi-Strauss (1962a, b) showed that this inability to distinguish between categories does not exist in fact. Preliterate cultures are replete with classifications, often based on a very keen observation of nature.

However, the classifications of preliterate cultures are often organized in such a manner that they appear to someone familiar with more scientific approaches as expressing irrelevant fantasies. For example, the Hopi divide their environment into the main categories of North-East, North-West, South-East, South-West, the zenith, and the nadir. Each of these subsumes a color (yellow for NW, blue and green for SW), an animal (mountain lion for NW, bear for SW), a bird (oriole for NW, bluebird for SW), a tree (Douglas fir for NW, white pine for SW), a shrub (green rabbit-brush for NW, sage for SW), a flower (mariposa lily for NW, delphinium for SW), a species of corn (yellow for NW, blue for SW), and a variety of beans (green for NW, butter for SW). It seems that a classification of this sort contains two elements: a keen observation of the environment which leads to the ability of distinguishing even among closely related species, and a preoccupation of a different kind with ritualistic and social subdivisions.

This double preoccupation is nowhere clearer than in the phenomenon of totemism. The most obvious characteristic of totemism is the association of a human grouping with a natural phenomenon, in general an animal species.

> The Trumai (a tribe of Northern Brazil) say that they are water animals. The Bororo (a neighboring tribe) take pride in being red macaws. This does not merely mean that after their death they become macaws, nor that macaws are metamorphosed Bororos, and should be treated as such. It means something quite different. "The Bororo," says Mr. von den Steinen, who didn't want to believe it but who had to give in before their formal affirmations, "the Bororo state coldly that they *really are* macaws, exactly as if a caterpillar were saying that it is a butterfly." It is not a name they give themselves, it is not a kinship they proclaim. What they want to express is an identity of essence. That they should be at the same time the human

beings they are, and also birds with red feathers, is incomprehensible to Mr. von den Steinen. But . . . all totemic cultures have collective representations of this type, implying a similar identity between the individuals belonging to a totem group and the totem of the group. (Lévy-Bruhl, 1910)

Does this mean that primitives cannot distinguish between themselves and animals? By no means; what we have here are *statements* of identity, and in all probability *feelings* of identity. But there is *no identity in behavior* and relatively few facts which would indicate that belief in identity actually affects the behavior of man in his transactions with nature. True enough, the eponym species is in general taboo; it is neither hunted nor eaten, except at times in special ceremonies reminiscent of ritual cannibalism and human sacrifice. But the Bororos neither attempt to fly nor to mate with pretty macaws, for example. Such an identity-with-non-identity is an example of the autonomy of levels of integration (Glenn, 1973). There is identity at the level of naming, and at the level of social integration which, together with symbolic systems such as speech, are dominated more by subject-to-subject than by subject-to-object relationships. There is no identity at the level of action within and upon nature.

However, there still remains the question of *why*. It can be answered if one looks at it in a manner suggested in chapter 3; namely that the central action is that of naming for the sake of co-subjective uniformity and solidarity, and not that of describing for utilitarian purposes.

The centrality of naming is consistent with a remark made by Bergson and quoted by Lévi-Strauss (1962b):

At the same time as the nature of the animal becomes concentrated in one single attribute, one could say that its individuality becomes dissolved in the species. To recognize a man consists in distinguishing him from other men; to recognize an animal means ordinarily to visualize the species to which it belongs. . . . Notwithstanding that an animal is concrete and an individual, it appears essentially as an attribute, essentially also a species.

Differences between species are easy not only to perceive, but also to visualize. On the other hand one may know clearly enough that human individuals differ among themselves, but one has still to *name* this difference. This is even more important in the case of human groups such as clans or sections. Associating clan difference with differences between animal species amounts to visualizing and naming the first one. It amounts also to abstracting, for what is visualized in the animal is the species, an abstraction of a higher order than the individual. But it amounts to abstracting the easy way, without going beyond the level of perceptual schemes.

> Nothing can be derived from the fact that a clan should be such or such an animal; much can be learned, however, from the fact that two clans belonging to the same tribe must necessarily be two different animals. . . . Thus when members of two clans state that they are two different animal species, *it is duality and not animality that they express.* (Lévi-Strauss, 1962b)

To make a long story short, in many parts of the world too distant among themselves to explain the phenomenon by cultural diffusion, two or more species are selected in such a way that they have one characteristic in common and one (or more) by which they clearly differ. They may be the hawk and the crow, one of which hunts while the other scavenges; the white and the black cockatoo; the bat and the woodpecker, both of which live in tree hollows. What such combinations of similarity and opposition—association and abstraction—express is not similarities and oppositions of men's actions having the animals for objects, nor even (at least in most cases, for there are exceptions) similarities or purported similarities between the characteristics of human groups and animal species. What they express are simply *a structure* of similarity and opposition, association and abstraction: in most cases between exogamous moieties of the tribe, and in the case of the last example, between men and women (Lévi-Strauss, 1962b).

Totemic similarities and oppositions are usually tied to mythical tales.

> One Western Australian version describes Falcon and Crow, the first named being the maternal uncle of the second, and thus his potential father-in-law, because of the preferential marriage with the mother's brother's daughter. The father-in-law, whether real or potential, is entitled to gifts of food from his nephew and son-in-law, and so Falcon orders Crow to catch a wallaby for him. After a successful hunt, Crow gives in to temptation: he eats his prey and pretends having caught nothing. But the uncle refuses to believe him, and questions him about his prominent belly: the reason is, says Crow, that he ate *nyssa* gum to assuage the pangs of his hunger. Still incredulous, Falcon tickles his nephew until the latter throws up meat. As punishment, he pushes the guilty party into the fire, and keeps him there until his eyes become red and its feathers black; pain draws from Crow its characteristic cry. Falcon then decrees that from now on Crow will no longer hunt for itself, but be forced to steal game from others. Such is, since then, the state of affairs. (Lévi-Strauss, 1962b, based on Radcliffe-Brown, 1952)

What is the significance of this story, and of hundreds like it?

First, that the minds of those who tell it are not prepared to present in abstract terms the combination of solidarity and competitiveness which makes up much of the life of society, or of similarity and dissimilarity which make up the structure of any description of nature. Instead of direct statements they use the imagery of myth which consists in cross-level associations, such as the association of a human grouping and an animal species. Second, that the genesis of telling is not the simple one of observation of nature──→objective description, but the more involved one of observation──→dream or fantasy──→myth. The earlier scheme corresponds to the rather naive concept of knowledge as correspondence. The latter one shows the sequence of experience──→association──→abstraction──→new experience made possible by the appearance of new conceptual structures.

Totemic animals should not be looked upon as being in the main

> dreaded, admired or desired creatures: one can see beneath their sensed reality notions and relations conceived by speculative thought from the data of observation. At this point it becomes possible to understand that natural species are not selected [as totems] because they are good to eat, but because they are easy to think about. (Lévi-Strauss, 1962b)

Let us look at these phenomena from an evolutionary point of view. The point of departure, early mythical thought, is a complex cluster of associations, with a structure and purpose that often escape the conscious understanding of those whose lives are largely governed by it. The point of arrival—the analyses by Radcliffe-Brown and by Lévi-Strauss, which are a part of "our" culture even if they are about preliterate cultures—are abstract statements about social structure. Thus the direction from association to abstraction seems indeed to be there. In societies such as "our own" the terms used to describe social structure are seldom totemlike; in most cases they are abstract concepts such as class, nationality, or profession. These terms are such as to apply to a range of situations going far beyond the particularity of one culture. In contradistinction, the fact that the process of myth formation may be the same in distant communities could be discovered only through painstaking analysis. The myths as immediately apprehended, particularly by those who believe in them, are culture specific. The nature of the change from the point of departure to the point of arrival is consistent with the thesis that the need for evolution derives from the appearance of societies too complex to be described in terms of myth. The appearance of such societies leads to a broadening of the frame of reference, both in terms of what needs to be made clear to make it possible for the society to function, and in terms of the cultural and linguistic styles of the statements involved.

The "tinkerer" metaphor

In describing the differences between the world views of pre-literate cultures and the scientific outlook which forms an important part of advanced cultures, Lévi-Strauss (1962a) compared the earlier named to the creations of a *bricoleur*, term which is often translated as jack-of-all-trades even though tinkerer comes closer to the meaning of the French original.

A tinkerer, in his description, is a man who makes things in his garage, using materials which he finds here and there according to the chance events of life. Such elements are incorporated into the product in a manner which shows much ingenuity but which leads to a degree of incongruence in the finished product. Contemporary science may be compared to the work of a professional engineer and placed in contradistinction with the tinkering of the preliterates. The main characteristic of the creations of a professional is that he uses only materials specifically selected for the task at hand, and that he rejects materials that are found by chance, and which may fail to fit the characteristics of the end product and may be obtained in quantities that may not fit his production schedules. The end products of a tinkerer's genius are always somewhat particularized, because he depends for their creation on the chance elements of experience. The end products of a man of science are at least potentially capable of generalization or even universalization, because he depends more on method than on improvisation.

The distinction is not an absolute one. Even the scientist has to face the limitations of the knowledge characterizing his or her culture. But the scientist always tries—or deals with others who try—to expand the existing knowledge and to systematize an ever increasing amount of knowledge. On the contrary, the tinkerer is limited by the size of the existing corpus of cultural lore, which can be transcended only through chance produced associations. Thus the difference, even if not absolute, is nevertheless real.

In the terminology of this book, the metaphor suggests that the knowledge of the preliterates is replete with mythical complexes, which would appear as derived from chance associations to people whose thought is based upon a body of knowledge that is more structured and derived from a broader range of experience. This may lead to the conclusion that primitive knowledge is in need of pruning through abstraction as well as of expanding through the efforts of specialized, professional researchers.

This does not mean in any way that preliterates are incapable of abstraction, while members of advanced cultures find abstractions an easy and natural task. Radin (1953) holds that all cultures have their men of action, satisfied with the existing state of knowledge and likely to grasp the chance events in which this knowledge can be put to use, and their men of thought, always trying to clarify and to expand knowledge. The earlier named are by far the more numerous. In the case of small populations, as that of most preliterate tribal cultures, the men of thought may be too few to reach a critical mass which would permit the setting up of a social body the function of which would be to codify and to expand knowledge. In the great literate civilizations, which usually have much larger and more mobile populations, the critical mass may be reached. This may lead to the establishment of specialized institutions such as universities or think tanks in which the thinkers of the civilization react among themselves, systematizing and expanding knowledge.

In the case of cultures such as the contemporary advanced ones, even men of action act in a manner which *appears* to be more abstractive than that of the preliterates and even of preliterate men of thought, because the process of socialization in such cultures includes the teaching of bodies of conceptual structures developed by the men of thought.

The findings of ethno-science

Most of the observations presented so far in regard to the behavior of preliterate peoples were based on direct observation. Such observations can now be supplemented by controlled experiments.

Lerner (1958) reports that illiterate members of traditional cultures lack the ability to reason hypothetically. When asked what he would do if he were the President of Turkey, a Turkish sheepherder was terrified and insisted that such a thing was impossible and even unthinkable. In contrast, a Turkish university student asked the same question gave an answer rich in suppositions. Obviously, the student was more abstractive than the sheepherder since he was able to distance himself from his actual status and to assume hypothetically the role of another man.

Cole et al. (1971) investigated the question of whether the inability to reason hypothetically (also reported by Werner, 1961) held for all preliterate cultures. Their findings appear at first glance to suffer from contradictions.

First, the researchers named above found spontaneous examples in which hypothetical reasoning was used among the Kpelle of Liberia, the largely preliterate society they were studying. One such case was a divorce proceeding, in which the paramount chief was acting as judge to determine who, the husband or the wife, was the guilty party—an important matter, since the placing of the blame determines whether the bridewealth should or should not be returned. In this particular case, the woman accuses her husband of having failed to make a garden and build a house for her. The husband defends himself by stating that she had left him. The wife's defense is that she had to return to her family because her father had died. However, she stayed away from her husband for a year and a half, which is excessive according to custom. In consequence, the judge found against her. What follows is a brief excerpt of his statement of the verdict:

> If a woman spends a year and a half away, can the man stay there and start a farm for her? Who will scratch it? And, in addition to that, who will he make the farm for? (Cole et al., 1971)

There is clear evidence of hypothetical reasoning in this and other excerpts.

Other findings, however, point in a different direction:

> EXPERIMENTER: Spider and black deer always eat together. Spider is eating. Is black dear eating?
> SUBJECT: But I was not there. How can I answer such a question?
> EXPERIMENTER: Can't you answer it? Even if you were not there, you can answer it.
> SUBJECT: Ask the question again for me to hear.
> EXPERIMENTER: (repeats the question).
> SUBJECT: Oh, oh, black deer was eating.
> EXPERIMENTER: Black deer was eating?
> SUBJECT: Yes.
> EXPERIMENTER: What is your reason for saying that black deer was eating?
> SUBJECT: The reason is that black deer always walks about all day eating green leaves in the bush. When it rests for a while it gets up again and goes to eat. (Cole et al., 1971)

In this case the ability to abstract the hypothetical premises of the problem from everyday experience appears to be lacking.

The situation is similarly complex in other experiments. Piaget and Inhelder (1969) report that young children find it difficult to put themselves in the place of someone else. Young children asked to describe complex shapes in such a way as to enable a listener to recognize them fail to grasp what the other person needs to know in order to complete the task. For example, a young child may describe a design by saying that it looks like his mother's hat, without realizing that such a comparison may be meaningless for the other person. Older children in "our" cultures come to understand that idiosyncratic descriptions may not lead to communication, and describe the shapes in a public rather than a private manner.

Cole and Scribner (1974) describe an experiment in which adult rice farmers belonging to a preliterate culture were tested for ability to describe objects in a way understandable to others.

> Two men are seated at a table. The men are Kpelle rice farmers from central Liberia. Every year since they were small boys they have gone into the jungle to clear patches of land where upland rice is grown. They know the forest and its vegetation well; they work there almost every day; it gives them food, building materials, tools, and medicines.
>
> On the table in front of them are 10 pairs of sticks (pieces of wood of different kinds) divided into two piles, each pile having one member of every pair. One pile is in front of each man.
>
> A barrier is then placed between the two so that they can neither see each other nor each other's sticks. The experimenter, who is sitting where both men can see him, picks a stick from the speaker's pile and lays it on the table at the speaker's left. The speaker is told to describe the stick so that his partner (the listener) can pick its mate out of his pile.
>
> After hearing the description, the listener tries to select the appropriate stick from his pile. . . . The procedure is continued until all 10 sticks have been described by the speaker and laid in a row in front of him, and the listener has tried to duplicate these activities.

In general the subjects fail to provide adequate descriptions. A representative example is given below, listing on the left a possible description of the items and on the right the actual responses of the subject:

thickest straight wood	one of the sticks
medium straight wood	not a large one
hook	one of the sticks
forked stick	one of the sticks
thin curved bamboo	piece of bamboo
thin curved wood	one stick
thin straight bamboo	one piece of bamboo
long fat bamboo	one of the bamboo
short thorny	one of the thorny
long thorny	one of the thorny sticks
	(Cole and Scribner, 1974)

The results are not much better in a second trial, after the subjects had both seen the results of their interaction and participated with the experimenter in a discussion of the errors committed.

It seems that, to the extent of the representativeness of the subjects, preliterate adults are incapable of the decentration necessary to communicate to others things that are not a part of common experience; they remain egocentric past childhood.

Although this interpretation may seem plausible when applied to children 4, 5, or even 7 years old, is it reasonable to claim that the average Kpelle adult is no more developed cognitively than a Genevan first grader, or that Kpelle speech patterns are inadequate for purposes of communication?

Our doubts about the reasonableness of this interpretation are quickly reinforced as soon as we step outside of the experimental situation—at just about the time when our two subjects have talked us into buying them a bottle of beer! Our own, real-life, non laboratory observations and the more controlled observations of many anthropologists attest to the fact that there are no *generalized* problems of communications among traditional people. (Cole and Scribner, 1974)

Under the circumstances, how can such contradictory observations be brought together?

A number of anthropologists writing about the learning processes of nonliterate peoples have remarked on the fact that learning and teaching are almost always an integral part of ongoing activity such as hunting or a round of household chores. Children are said to be learning by observing.

Observational learning is usually contrasted with learning that is acquired primarily through the medium of language. Mead points out, for example, that in traditional societies adults rarely formulate a particular practice in words or rules; instead they demonstrate what is to be done. Fortes observes that traditional children (he worked with the Tale people of Ghana) were rarely heard to ask *why* questions. He concludes that such questions are rare because so much of the child's learning occurs in real-life situations where the meaning is intrinsic to the context.

If these anthropological observations and speculations are correct, we might hypthesize two cognitive consequences of a reliance on learning by observation. First, we might expect to find that people who have a lot of practice in learning by observation will be good at it—they will learn quickly if given the chance to learn by observing. Second, the same people ought to experience special difficulties if they are asked to teach or to learn something when the teacher and student are not engaged in a common, on-going activity. (Cole and Scribner, 1974)

Or, it might be added, when they have to teach or learn something principally through the medium of language used to express conceptualization.

First, the apparent lack of the necessary verbal skills in the experiment above does not mean that the ability to speak is poorly developed. Very much to the contrary, eloquence is highly prized and highly developed in many if not most preliterate cultures. However, language is used less in its referential function than in its social function. This was noted by Malinowski (1923):

> Language, in its primitive function, to be regarded as a *mode of action*, rather than as a *countersign of thought*. Analysis of a complex speech-situation among savages. The essential primitive uses of speech: speech-in-action, ritual handling of words, the narrative, "phatic communion" (speech in social intercourse).

In other words, speech is valued more for its real or supposed efficiency than for its descriptive ability.

Second, those who learn by observation are necessarily more limited in their world view than those who learn mainly through the medium of language. The amount of knowledge that can be learned through direct experience during one lifetime, even if a part of the experience is derived from the teaching by others, is necessarily lesser than the amount of knowledge which can be communicated by speech and by books. In addition, knowledge acquired through personal, non-controlled experience is more associative than is the knowledge transmitted by books, since the latter forces the student to abstract his personal life from his role as a reader.

Some generalizations can be made on the basis of the research presented in this section.

Members of preliterate societies are capable of hypothetical reasoning and of an indirect as well as of a direct approach to communication. However, the circumstances in which such abilities were observed were those of their daily life. They perform less well in an experimental context, in which the subject is supposed to place a criterial boundary between his or her overall experience and the instructions given by the experimenter. This appears particularly clearly in the problem of the spider and the black deer. This means that preliterate cultures are more associative and less abstractive than are "our" cultures, in which the ability to distinguish between task-irrelevant and task-relevant inputs is taught in school.

Other experiments, particularly those of Luria (1976) and his co-workers confirm the interpretation above:

> The experiments used were sorting tasks, and the subjects were illiterate peasants from the Soviet Western Asia. The experiments were introduced to the subject through an example. The images of the following array were presented to the subjects: *shirt–boots–skullcap–mouse*. The first three were shown to have a characteristic in common, which the last one did not share; thus *mouse* could be eliminated from the

array. Following this exercise, the subjects were given the array *hammer–saw–log–hatchet*. The subjects stated that all four objects shared a similarity, and none of them could be eliminated from the array:

> They all fit here! The saw has to saw the log, the hammer has to hammer it, and the hatchet has to chop it. And if you want to chop the log up really good, you need the hammer. You can't take any of these things away. There isn't any you don't need! (Luria, 1976)

Even when the experimenter mentioned that three of the objects could be described by one word, tools, which did not fit the fourth one, the subjects insisted on keeping all objects in the array. What is the use of a hammer, a saw, and a hatchet, if there is no log to work upon?

Thus the subjects rejected an abstractive classification capable of defining paradigmatic structures which can be used in sorting a great many objects, in favor of an associative–syntagmatic one fitting better their own concrete experience. The situation was different with subjects who had some formal schooling; the latter understood classifications based on the lexical structure of language.

Comparison between two experiments

In an experiment dealing with American subjects, Milgram (1965) found a disposition to ignore moral and ethical positions in situations where behavior was initiated and in part supervised by an authoritative person. Subjects were told that they were playing a game in which the first player to make his move could count on winning, if the move he made would be one that would also entail subjecting his opponent to a severe and painful electric shock. A large percentage of subjects made the move in question, even though it involved acting out an unethically selfish attitude on their part.

It would be absurd to claim that the subjects in question, who constituted a representative sample of the American population, totally lacked moral sense. However, another explanation can be suggested, particularly as a contrast with the attitude of Kpelle farmers as described in the preceding section.

Americans, like most of the populations of industrialized countries, are used to assuming a variety of roles. Placed in the laboratory environment, they were ready to assume still another role, and they considered the responsibility for ethical conduct as being versed in the experimenter; in this fashion they felt obligated to carry out the experimental task, without regard for what appeared to be task-irrelevant considerations.

By contrast the Kpelle and Asian illiterates are not used to assuming roles different from the 'ones to which they are accustomed: Hence their inability to act in an unaccustomed experimental situation.

Clearly, this comparison points out the abstractive attitude of Americans, who were ready to set aside their daily preoccupations to assume the role of subjects. Likewise it points out the associative character of the Kpelle and of the Asian illiterates who were incapable of setting aside their usual identity, based on empirical experience.

Social structure

One of the most striking features of preliterate social organization—at least when compared with "our" societies—is the poverty of or the lack of functional differentiation. To a large extent, the division of social labor has not yet taken place. This does not mean that there is no role differentiation; much to the contrary, such differentiation is very rich, but it is based on the position of the person in the kinship or clanship structure, rather than on task structre.

One of the correlates of this state of affairs is the particularization of human obligations. Abstractions such as "the duty of any person under a specifically defined set of circumstances" are lacking. In their stead there are specific obligations of one individual towards another one, the relationship between the two being defined on their reciprocal positions within the kinship structure, nephew and maternal uncle, for example.

In keeping with this, codes of ethics or tenets of religious belief are not considered as having a universal or even a broad application. They bind particular individuals within a particular community in a specified manner, and do not apply to outsiders. An outsider has neither rights nor obligations. The nature of the insiders' beliefs about the world is deemed of no interest to the outsider whose beliefs are in turn of no interest to the insiders. There are no trans-cultural laws, either in the sense of descriptions of the universe or in the sense of prescriptions for human behavior.

The enforcement of codes is either automatic or left to public opinion. The absence of laws applying to "any" person implies the absence of specific bodies for the enforcement of law. When serious conflicts arise, conciliation may be sought. Those presiding over a search for conciliation may be wise old men whose position in society suggests a rudimentary form of functional structuration—again insisting on the word rudimentary. Such is, for example, the case among the Nuer of the upper Nile. Conciliation, where it takes place, tries to resolve in the best possible manner an unpleasant situation; in doing so it takes into account elements of reality such as the reciprocal power positions of the clans concerned, which "our" judiciary, preoccupied as it is with precisely stated abstract statutes or accumulations of precedents, would consider irrelevant (at least in the ideal).

Responsibility for torts—including murder, which would not be placed under such a heading in universalistic jurisprudence—is considered to be collective rather than individual; if a serious transgression is the work of one man, in general all the members of his clan are considered responsible.

A comparison between individual definition in a preliterate and in an industrial society suggests that the patterns of the former are rigid but identity enhancing. An individual is what he is in the kinship and clanship structure, and the pattern of social interaction is in general such as to keep him in his place, constantly reminding him of what he is. By contrast, the patterns of industrial and postindustrial societies are flexible and identity-corroding: The individual is largely left to his own devices in the search for a social niche; his transactions with others take place often on a stranger-to-stranger basis. This question was discussed in chapter 6.

This does not mean that no flexibility at all can be found in preliterate societies, nor that the identity-defining system of any culture is without flaws.

An example of flexibility can be found in the position of homosexual men among the Indians of the American plains. A man with homosexual tendencies would claim that he had a vision in which double-woman had appeared to him. This justified his taking on the role of a transvestite or *berdache*.

As for identity-eroding practices, an example may be found in a practice of the Cherokees which is also found elsewhere. Upon marrying, a young man would move into the family and clan of his wife, and for most purposes act as a member of her clan. There was, however, one set of circumstances under which he would revert to his clan of origin. This was revenge for an act of a member of another clan, who had harmed a member of the young man's clan of origin. If the transgression was murder, blood revenge was required. In keeping with the general rule of collective responsibility, the life which should be taken was not necessarily that of the murderer, but of a person belonging to his clan. If the guilty party belonged to the clan of the young man's wife, the life he should take was that of the most easily available member of her clan. This in general would not be the murderer himself, who would often protect himself by hiding in a place of worship in which the taking of a life is forbidden. The probability is high that it would be the young man's own children, who were considered as belonging to his wife's clan, because of the general rule of matrilineal descent. Whatever the resolution of the problem, it is certain that the situation must have been emotionally stressful for the young man concerned, and thus identity-eroding (Gearing, 1962).

The earliest functional group to become separated from the bulk of society is in many cases that of priests or shamans. Although the calling of shamanism is in general the product of a particular personality structure, in many cases shamanism tends to become hereditary. An example may be found among the Buryats of central Asia:

> The shaman is an ecstatic, a soul-projector, a spirit-master; he has special powers over and special relations to the extra-mundane sphere. These powers he obtains through a special gift, having undergone a specific kind of experience of self-abnegation and vision-quest. Accompanying the sha-man-cult are a number of rites and myths relating to the worship of rocks, high places and peculiar features of the landscape; of fire and the hearth. The shaman is often a transvestite who may be of either sex, a highly nervous person, one subject to nervous disorders; his powers, when they are not disposed to harm mankind are sought in the cure of (psychoso-matic) illness. (Krader, 1954)

Although the profession of shamanism is tied to a given personality structure, shamanism tends to become hereditary:

> Although any Buryat can become a shaman if the call descends on him, yet he would find himself unable to compete with other shamans who had a descent line from shamans and a series of shaman ancestors. These ancestral shamans mediate for their client and help him. The hereditary shamans are helped in another way, for they begin to learn their business from infancy on. . . .
>
>   The Buryat shaman is an anomalous person . . . for while he is a psychologically unstable individual, nevertheless his social position has been stabilized as an occupational group and as a descent line. (Krader, 1954)

Blacksmiths tend likewise to become a separate group, with some caste-like characteristics, not only among the central Asian peoples, but also in Western Africa.

> Another special occupational group beside the shaman, one also formed in lineages, and in whose descent a mystical power inheres is the smith. There are a special group of mythical beings called the Smiths. . . , and the practitioners of the craft on earth are descended from one of them. (Krader, 1954)

In Africa, smiths are often dreaded because of the special spirit world to which they have access.

What these remarks seem to indicate is that the early steps in the division of labor are not carried in an abstract and purely utilitarian fashion. Myth and magic, the access to special parts of the spirit world, are associated with differences in product and occupation. This associative tying together of what would appear mutually irrelevant in "our" cultures may be illustrated once more by the practices of west African gold miners:

The search for gold leads to an all-out mobilization of powers: anything that works is good. One might say that the role of experimental knowledge is limited. Examination of soil, rocks and vegetation does not seem to go very far. Still, I am told that the lode of Manitoro was discovered through the presence of a downy-leafed shrub, the *soh wanie*, which serves as an indicator. . . . But it is better to enter in communication with the sovereign divinities of the metal. Dreams are consulted, and if they show fire or red monkeys running toward a certain spot, the miners begin a series of soundings there. The old men consult cola nuts, which answer yes or no and tell where to search. However, it is the magical and religious apparatus disseminated by Islam which seems the most popular. The marabouts consult the Koran as well as Oriental traditions; they conduct the prospecting by preparing collections of suras which will be washed on the spot, or magic squares which ensure success; finally, they provide the protection of animal sacrifices. . . .

For the Sudanese, gold is the least natural of the products offered by nature. God created it and entrusted it to the care of genies whose complicity and consent must be obtained. It remains a dangerous product, subject to a law of ambivalence which divides it into "living gold" and "dead gold." Living gold cannot be attained by men; it is concealed and possesses the power of lightning and fire; it is manifested in the violence of landslides, the splitting of rock and vitrified land. Dead gold has been partly neutralized by the effect of sacrifices; it is regarded as the part temporarily conceded to man. Nevertheless it remains dangerous and its sudden disappearance or appearance in too great quantity arouses anxiety, requiring the setting up of protective devices. . . .

. . . An unexpected stroke of luck may cause the danger to reappear. At the Doko deposit Ngolo, a relative of the head of the mine, has just extracted a nugget weighing over 1,000 grams, which sparkles in spite of its matrix. The news circulates, work ceases in all pits, the miners become restless and grumble. . . . General consternation. There are only two solutions: put the nugget back in the ground, or neutralize it. The head of the mine hurriedly consults the council of elders, but he has already decided not to relinquish such a beautiful piece. He orders emergency measures: all men will abandon work until order is restored. The nugget, fascinating and dangerous, is displayed in the center of the mine, creating around it a large no man's land. Ngolo wanders among his companions, stupefied by such a severe shock. Hastily the head musters his policemen, armed with guns, and arranges them in an alarming and picturesque firing squad; at his order all fire together toward the nugget to dispel the *ginné* responsible for such a dangerous generosity. (Balandier, 1969)

Conclusions

The examples given in the body of this chapter present only a summary picture of preliterate cultures; much more can be found in the literature. If one considers the traits described above, and if one expands one's view of preliterate cultures by studying the literature, one is bound to come to the conclusion that preliterate cultures are narrower in the scope of situations with which they can cope, more associative and more subjective than are "our" cultures. However, this means neither that primitives are incapable of abstractive "logical" thought, nor that such thought comes naturally to members of "our" cultures. It means rather that the cultures which have expanded their scope to very broad areas of experience, have in the course of this expansion developed numerous groupings and matrices of concepts, providing ready-made abstractions for the use of the participants in the corresponding societies.

Chapters 7 and 8 have shown that members of "modern" cultures do not always avail themselves of the conceptualizations available to them, and do revert to more archaic patterns of thought and behavior. They seek to recapture some of the characteristics which preliterate cultures offer to their members. Even though they unavoidably fail in their attempts, because the societies to which they belong must face up to very broad ranges of circumstances, their desire to obtain a rebirth of the primitive should prompt the question of what it is that is so attractive in preliterate cultures. The answer which might be suggested is that the strength of primitive cultures lies in their relative constancy, and in their ability to enhance the individual's sense of belonging and identity.

As for their weaknesses, they derive primarily from an attachment to beliefs based on myth, that is to say on narrow conceptions of the world and of mankind.

10

EAST AND WEST

Eastern cultures differ among themselves in many ways. Under the circumstances a simple opposition between East and West seems to make little sense. Yet it has been extensively analyzed in literature, for example by Northrop (1953) and Suzuki (1960), excerpts of whose works will be pesented in this chapter. If the opposition can be made meaningful, it is not because eastern cultures have much in common, but rather because the western family of cultures is unique in certain aspects, and because these aspects can be contrasted with their absence, or rather with their subordination in the East.

The contrast can be put in a nutshell. The philosophers of the basic eastern cultures concerned themselves primarily with the wisdom by which human life could be regulated—or, in the language of this study, with the establishment of co-subjective codes which could be accepted in relatively unchanging ways by generations of their followers. The scientists of the western cultures concerned themselves with the reality of nature. This led western scientists to statements of an objective nature, which were invariably proven to be in need of revisions. The attempts at correcting errors led to the restructuring of belief, and ultimately to research and to science. In the process, the knowledge of nature became an instrumentality of action. This led to an image of the relationship of nature and man which is radically different from that of most eastern cultures. Where the latter see man as a part of nature, one who should seek to reach an accommodation with the rest of it, western cultures see man as a subject whose object is nature; as such he tries to utilize and dominate the nonhuman world.

The concentration on co-subjectivity, or the codification of human behavior, can lead to great cultural stability. Cultural stability over long periods of history is indeed a characteristic of the great civilizations of the East. Some might even call this stability stagnation, and contrast it with the unceasing inventiveness of the West. The matter is to some extent one of personal prference; stability means a permanence which one approves of, stagnation is permanence of which one is contemptuous. Likewise, instability is change which one condemns, and inventiveness is change one praises. Yet there is in this contrast something more than simple preference. Taking nature as the object of his action, western man was led to examine the world of things from varying points of view. This gave him a wealth of insights and enriched his culture to the point where it was bound to become an invader of the cultures of others. It had so much more to offer than did cultures governed by tradition. It is only after the fact that it became apparent that many of the offerings of western cultures were poisoned fruit for those who tried to emulate the ways of the West without understanding them. This question was addressed in the two preceding chapters.

What concerns us at this point is not so much the opposition between the artifacts of western technology and western art, as opposed to the often splendid but much less varied artifacts of the arts and crafts of the East—even though this question is obviously important. It is rather the difference in the patterns of thought and of expression.

A quotation from Northrop may be used as an opening.

> The Easterner . . . uses bits of linguistic symbolism . . . often purely ideographic in character, to point toward a component in the nature of things which only immediate experience and continued contemplation can convey . . . as Lin Youtang points out, although Oriental symbolism results in especially good poetry, it cannot compare with the language of the West in producing excellent prose. (Northrop, 1953)

The contemplative attitude of the Easterner reaches deep. Poetry is a syntagmatic involvement of the subject with the object. Prose tends towards the paradigmatic, that is, to a way of thinking in which the involvement of subject with object is limited to a defined point of view.

We can now move on to Suzuki.

> Many able thinkers of the West, each from his specific point of view, have dealt with this timeworn topic, "East and West," but so far as I know there have been comparatively few Far Eastern writers who have expressed their views as Easterners. This fact has led me to choose this subject. . . .
>
> Basho (1644–1694), a great Japanese poet . . . once composed a seventeen-syllable poem known as *haiku* or *hokku*. It runs, when translated into English, something like this:
>
> > When I look carefully
> > I see the *nazuna* blooming

by the hedge!
yoku mireba
Nazuna hana saku
Kakine kana.

It is likely that Basho was walking along a country road when he noticed something rather neglected by the hedge. He then approached closer, took a good look at it, and found it was no less than a wild plant, rather insignificant and generally unnoticed by passers-by. This is a plain fact described in the poem. . . .

. . . Basho was a nature poet, as most of the Oriental poets are. They love nature so much that they feel every pulse beating through the veins of nature. Most Westerners are apt to alienate themselves from nature. They think that man and nature have nothing in common except in some desirable aspects, and that nature exists only to be utilized by man. But to Eastern people nature is very close. This feeling for nature was stirred when Basho discovered an inconspicuous, almost negligible plant blooming by the old dilapidated hedge along the remote country road. . . .

This is East. Let me see now what the West has to offer in a similar situation. I select Tennyson. He may not be a typical Western poet to be singled out for comparisons with the Far Eastern poet. But his short poem here quoted has something very closely related to Basho's. The verse is as follows:

Flower in the crannied walls,
I pluck you out of the crannies;—
Hold you here, root and all, in my hand,
Little flower—but if I could understand
What you are, root and all, and all in all,
I should know what God and man is.

There are two points I like to notice in these lines:

(1) Tennysons's plucking the flower and holding it in his hand, "root and all," and looking at it, perhaps intently. It is very likely he had a feeling somewhat akin to that of Basho who discovered a *nazuna* flower by the roadside hedge. But the difference between the two poets is: Basho does not pluck the flower. He just looks at it. He is absorbed in thought. He feels something in his mind, but he does not express it.

As to Tennyson, he is active and analytical. He first plucks the flower from where it grows. He separates it from the ground where it belongs. Quite differently from the Oriental poet, he doesn't leave the flower alone. He must tear it away from the crannied wall, "root and all," which means that the plant must die. He does not, apparently, care for its destiny; his curiosity must be satisfied. As some medical scientists do, he would vivisect the flower. Basho does not even touch the *nazuna*, he just looks at it, he "carefully" looks at it—that is all he does. He is altogether inactive, a good contrast to Tennyson's dynamism.

I would like to notice this point specifically here. . . . The East is silent, while the West is eloquent. But the silence of the East does not mean just to be dumb and remain wordless and speechless. Silence is in many cases as eloquent as being wordy. The west likes verbalism. . . .

(2) What does Tennyson do next? Looking at the plucked flower, which is in all probability beginning to wither, he proposes the question within himself, "Do I understand you?" Basho is not inquisitive at all. He feels the mystery as revealed in this humble *nazuna*—the mystery that goes deep into the source of all existence. He is intoxicated with this feeling. . . .

Contrary to this, Tennyson goes on with his intellectualization. "*If* . . . I could understand you, I should know what God and man is." His appeal to understanding is characteristically Western. Basho accepts, Tennyson resists. Tennyson's individuality stands away from the flower, from "God and man." He does not identify himself with either God or nature. He is always apart from them. His understanding is what people nowadays call "scientifically objective." Basho is thoroughly subjective. . . . Basho stands by this "absolute subjectivity" in which Basho sees the *nazuna* and the *nazuna* sees Basho. Here is no empathy, or sympathy, or identification for this matter. . . .

In Tennyson, as far as I can see, there is in the first place no depth of feeling; he is all intellect, typical of Western mentality. He is an advocate of the Logos doctrine. He must say something, he must abstract or intellectualize on his concrete experience. He must come out of the domain of feeling into that of the intellect and must subject living and feeling to a series of analyses to give satisfaction to the Western spirit of inquisitiveness.

I have selected these two poets, Basho and Tennyson, as indicative of two basic approaches to reality. (Suzuki, 1960)

What runs through the quotations and the remarks above is a clear realization that the West is abstractive, at least as contrasted with the East, and that the East is associative, at least as contrasted with the West. At the same time, however, we must remember that eastern cultures have reached high levels of abstraction, and these historically earlier than comparative achievements of the West. For example, a quotation of Confucius was used in chapter 2 to exemplify the need for an abstractive codification of language in the course of the passage from the community (Gemeinschaft) type of social organization to a society (Gesellschaft) ideal type. Even more to the point is the invention of the arithmetical zero, which is due to the development of the Indian culture and which was transmitted to the West by the Arabic culture, which can also be credited with the discovery of algebra.

Could it be that the cultures of the East experienced counter-currents which revivified associative thinking and brought it into a state of stable compromise with abstractive trends? This is a problem to be examined in the sections to follow.

China

A famous passage from Confucius was quoted in chapter 2. It is repeated here, in more detail, to facilitate reading.

> Tradition considers Confucius to be the inventor of traditional logic. The basis for this is a passage from the *Luen yu*: "Tseu-lu said (to Confucius): 'The lord of Wei intends to place government in your hands. What do you consider as the first thing to be done?' 'The main thing is to correct the use of titles...,' answered the Master. And he added: 'If the titles... are not correct, words cannot be conform to truth; if words do not conform to truth, the affairs (of State) have no success; if these affairs have no success, neither rites nor music flourish; if rites and music do not flourish, punishment cannot be fair; if punishments are not fair, people do not know how to act. Thus the Wise Man..., when he specifies designations, makes always certain that words can conform to them, and, when he uses them in his speech, he makes certain that they can be realized in action. That the Wise Man commit no error in his words, that is sufficient." Thus good order depends entirely upon the correctness of language. (Granet, 1950)

The aim expressed in this passage is clear: to overcome the ambiguities created by the random promiscuity of association when the area of experience of a culture becomes enlarged and diversified. Criterial boundaries must be introduced; words must be used in conformity with their definitions. This represents a movement toward abstraction. The question is how far it goes—and it does not go very far. It is not the entire conceptual sphere, or even the entire language which is to be reformed and codified; it is mainly the titles by which the hierarchy of men is to be addressed, and also what is needed in ritual. Confucius did not undertake the search for "the true nature and essence of all things," as did Socrates and Plato; he was satisfied with stating what were the wise ways of behavior. He did not seek clarity in pure thought, at the risk of defying tradition, but rather in the purity of a tradition which had been compromised by latter accretions. The moderation of Confucianism led to an acceptance much broader than could be claimed by any of the Greek philosophers. At the same time the very breadth of this acceptance meant a weakness in the contrapuntal disputatiousness out of which new ideas tend to emerge.

This does not mean that disputatiousness was altogether absent. An absolutism somewhat reminiscent of the Platonic turn of mind can be found in Mo Tseu, and also at a later date in the *Fa Chia*, the School of Law.

A few lines about Mo Tseu may be illustrative. His main concept is that of Universal Love, which he opposes to the principle of the Confucians, according to which people are to be loved on a decreasing scale, beginning with parents, who were to be loved a great deal, and ending with remote persons ... who were to be loved much less. Such a principle, said Mo Tseu, was the cause of all the wars and dissensions which were then rending China. If men loved citizens of other states as much as they loved their parents, they would not consent to "slay, destroy ... cities, upset ... shrines." The whole trouble comes from having one moral standard in dealing with "what is near" and another in dealing with "what is far." (Waley, 1939)

It seems clear that what is put forward is a universal idea. The thought appears very modern, as do the difficulties which beset it. The absolute, be it love or anything else, is more easily felt than defined operationally.

Like the Confucians, Mo Tseu believed in the Righteous War, in which a good king, at the command of Heaven, punishes a bad one, and he even condemns the chivalrous etiquette of warfare upheld by the Confucians, on the grounds that it handicaps the virtuous in their stern task: "Suppose there is a country that is being persecuted and oppressed by its rulers, and a Sage ruler in order to rid the world of this pest, raises an army and sets to punish the evildoers. If, when he has won a victory, he conforms to the doctrine of the Confucians, he will issue an order to his troops saying: 'Fugitives are not to be pursued, an enemy who has lost his helmet is not to be shot at ...' if this is done, the violent and disorderly will escape with their lives and the world will not be rid of this pest." (Waley, 1939)

Error has no rights—and the thought that the righteous might be the losers is not taken into consideration. Early universalistic thought, of the type which comes the closest to the co-subjective apex of the triangle of meaning, emphasizes criterial boundaries to the extent of seeing everything in blacks and whites, of ignoring the greyness not only of compromise, but also of most situations encountered in reality. The same pattern which will make science possible, begins by making fanaticism necessary.

The Mohists were an organized body, under the strict control of a leader known as the Grand Master, who enforced absolute obedience to an exacting code of honour and self-sacrifice ... "Wearing coarse hair cloth and rough clogs, they rested neither by day nor by night from the hardship that it was their aim to impose upon themselves, holding that those who were incapable of enduring such a life were not worthy to be called followers of Mo." (Waley, 1939)

Yet it is not the absolutists of abstraction who provided Confucius with his greatest challenge. This was done by Lao Tseu and the Taoists, who may be described as the proponents of a deliberate associationism based on the rejection of all definitions. The following passage of the Tao Te Ching sets the tone:

> When people all know the beautiful as "beautiful"
> there appears the "ugly."
> When people all know the good as "good"
> there appears the "evil."

Wisdom consists not in separating contraries—or polar opposites—but rather in realizing their intimate union:

> Something and nothing are mutually generative; the difficult and the easy are mutually complementary; the long and the short are mutually relative; the front and the rear are mutually accompanying. (Chang Tung-sen, 1959)

The logic behind such thought has been called by Chang Tung-sen (1959) a "logic of correlative duality" as opposed to the two-valued logic and the Aristotelian law of the excluded third, of the either . . . or . . . which forms the basis of abstractive thought.

Tao, the road, is the road to the feeling of the whole; it is also a knowledge which is whole and indivisible.

> Taoists oppose the word *tao* to other terms (*chu, fa*) which mean "formulae, methods, rules" and suggest the procedures of specialized technicians. Notwithstanding this, they hold that the total knowledge of the tao can lead to success in astronomy or in physics. (Granet, 1950)

In spite of the claim of applicability to specific questions, the knowledge of the tao cannot be defined; it can only be felt, or at most hinted at. It is made up of two aspects, *yin* and *yang*, which may be opposed one to the other, but which cannot be separated one from the other. The closest which one may come to an intellectual understanding of these terms is that *yin* suggests the mood of shadowy places and is also a female principle, while *yang* suggests the mood of sunshine and also the male principle.

It would probably be an exaggeration to say that the Taoist masters understood that a large and relatively mobile society would need the unifying definitions which they rejected. But it is quite clear that they envisaged the ideal human organization as a highly segmented society—in Durkheim's terms (1933)—made up of practically autonomous villages, living in separation one from the other, and rejecting any functional definitions which would organize and bind together such small and autonomous communities.

> The Taoists objected to machinery. There are of course many grounds upon which labour-saving devices may be condemned. The common mod-

ern objection is that they cause unemployment; but religious leaders (Gandhi, for example) reject them on the ground that they have a degrading effect on those who use them. The Taoist objection was of the latter kind. . . .

"We must then 'bind the finger' of the technicians, 'smash their arcs and plumb-lines, throw away their compasses and squares'. Only then will men rely on their inborn skill, on the 'Great Skill that looks like clumsiness.' "

. . . There are passages in the *Chuang Tzu* and other Taoist books where the ideal State is depicted, the sort of community in which the Taoist would like to find himself. There are no books; the people have no use for any form of record save knotted ropes. "They relish the simplest sorts of food, have no desire for fine clothing, take pleasure in their rustic tasks, are content to remain in their homes. The next village is so close that one could hear the cocks crowing in it, the dogs barking, but the people would grow old without ever having been there." (Waley, 1939)

This, of course, is a formulation which is bound to lead to a segmented society. The presence of a Confucian mandarinate moderated this tendency, but didn't oppose it. The main rituals it prescribed were tied to ancestor worship; in consequence, even if the forms of ritual may have been shared in the population, the goals of these rituals differed from family to family, since each of them had ancestors of its own.

The cohesiveness of the Chinese clan or lineage has been noted by both Weber and Hsu. Weber (1951) notes that

the belief in spirits bound the sib members . . . together.

According to Hsu,

The principal effect of the Chinese pattern on the individual is cohesiveness or a centripetal tendency among fellow men. Since the individual's first social group is the family, the centripetal outlook of the Chinese can be expected to lead him into a desire to remain within the family and, outside it, to keep within the boundaries of its immediate and direct extension—the clan—and not stray much farther beyond. (Hsu, 1963)

The attachment of the Chinese to their human surroundings is further fostered by the lack in the religion of China of the concept of a transcendent Godhead to which the individual might have direct bonds. On the contrary, that which is worshipped is immanent—as it was in the religions of Egypt and Mesopotamia, and more generally in all religions untouched by Semitic monotheism or the Hindu concept of the Atman. The immanent rapport of the Chinese sage with the subject matter of his reflection made it impossible, in Weber's view, for the Chinese to know genuine prophecy aiming at a unified cosmology.

This contrasts sharply with the Puritan ethic which amounts to an objectification of man's duties as a creature of God. The religious duty toward the hidden and supra-mundane God caused the Puritan to appraise all human relations—including those naturally closest in life—as mere means and expression of a mentality reaching beyond the organic relations of life. The religious duty of the pious Chinese, in contrast, enjoined him to develop himself within the organically given personal relations. (Weber, 1951)

It may be useful at this point to go back to the two models of psychosocial homeostasis presented at the beginning of chapter 7: The contrast between them seems to be the contrast presented by Weber between the Puritan—or more generally the Occidental—and the Chinese ethical orientations.

Let us return to the main line of exposition. As we have seen, abstractive absolutism reminiscent of the main currents of early western thought can be found in Chinese cultural theory. However, it has gained little lasting influence. For all practical purposes, the culture of China until recent times can be considered as the polarity and the synthesis between Confucianism and Taoism:

There is a touch of the Confucian and the Taoist in every Chinese. A Confucian is a voracious do-gooder who wants politicians moral, sons filial and widows chaste. A Taoist is a vagabond who, laughing at man's folly, sneaks off to a bamboo grove or a misty lake to be a part of it. A Chinese is consciously Confucian and subconsciously a Taoist. He is Confucian when enjoying fortune and success, and a Taoist in the face of adversity; a Confucian in public and a Taoist when alone. Confucianism without Taoism would make him a stuffed shirt. Taoism without Confucianism would make him a beatnik. (Chu, 1963)

Confucianism and Taoism have at least one very important characteristic in common; both stress the *process* at the expense of the *product*—how a life should be lived rather than the ultimate goal of life. In this they differ from the main intellectual currents of the West (at least up to the close of the 18th century and probably beyond), which stress the attainment of an ultimate and absolute truth, placing varying degrees of stress on the method through which truth can be reached.

This comparison between China and the West leads to an apparent paradox. China stresses the dynamics of the process, and yet its cultural history is to a large extent one of long-enduring stability. The West stresses the statics of the ultimate product, and yet its cultural history is one of restless change.

The paradox is more apparent than real. A process governed and rendered almost uniform by the prescriptions of tradition leads to a state of equilibrium between subject and object—or rather between the co-subjects sharing in the process and the objects of their endeavors.

This is on the whole the case of China. On the other hand, the search for the product is stabilizing only if the product can be achieved. In the case of the West the transcendental goals were those of religious perfection introduced by the Hebrews, and of cognitive perfection imagined by the Greeks and exemplified by some passages of Plato quoted earlier in this study. Both of these proved to be elusive. It is only after Kant, after the advent of operationalism as a philosophy of science (Einstein and Bridgman, quoted earlier), and even more after a perhaps exaggerated acceptance of cultural relativism, that it was realized that the knowledge of things-in-themselves and of virtue-in-itself could never be reached. In the meanwhile the perpetually unsatisfactory search for the ultimate goal led to the trying out of different methods, and the suggestion of various solutions to the insoluble problem. This led to cultural turmoil—and to cultural creativity.

As noted above, there exists an important area of similarity between Confucianism and Taoism. There exists also an important difference. Confucianism is pervaded by modesty; one might say that it is conscious of its own limitations and even more of human limitations. Such is not the case with Taoism. As all thoroughly associative movements or ways of thinking, it sees no definite limit to what it can bring about. The Taoist sage may be contented with the simplest of lives, possibly with being an anachorete. But Taoism itself does not admit any limitations. The total intuition, once grasped, may be directed at any goal. The perfect knowledge of astronomy and the perfect knowledge of physics were mentioned as examples.

From the popular point of view this means that the search for the perfection of the Tao was often used as a cover for magical and divinatory practices. More importantly, it was also a reservoir of enthusiasm and of faith for periods of trouble. Neither the T'ai P'ing, nor the Boxer rebellions were Confucian.

Babbitt (1962) was one of the first to draw parallels between Taoism and romanticism. Both were associative movements, rejecting specific knowledge and moderation in favor of intuition and boundless dedication.

> Perhaps the closest approach in the past to the movement of which Rousseau is the most important single figure is the early Taoist movement in China. Taoism, especially in its popular aspects, became later something very different, and what I say is meant to apply above all to the period from about 550 to 200 B.C. . . . The Tao Te Ching of Lao Tzu is a somewhat enigmatical document of only a few thousand words, but plainly primitivistic in its general trend. The phrase that best sums up its general spirit is that of Wordsworth—a "wise passiveness." The unity at which it aims is clearly of the pantheistic variety, the unity that is obtained by

breaking down discrimination and affirming the "identity of contradictories," and that encourages a reversion to the origins, to the state of nature and the simple life. (Babbitt, 1962)

The opposition between the tradition of moderate abstractiveness, Confucianism, and the unbounded associativism, Taoism, may help in understanding some of the convulsions of postrevolutionary China. To the cautious and goal conscious prudence of the Party bureaucracy is opposed the rejection of all limitations characterizing the radicals around Mao Tse-tung.

A first episode is that of the Great Leap forward. Will and enthusiasm were to accomplish immediately what had taken so long to the West, including the Soviet Union—instant industrialization. The question of whether the pig iron produced in backyard furnaces was technically utilizable in the manufacture of steel was simply not asked, and this is only one example. The Cultural Revolution, which followed the failure of the Great Leap, offers examples of the associative approach in an even purer state. Lifton (1968) describes the motivation behind the actions of Mao and of his closest associates as a desire for "Revolutionary Immortality." The total devotion of the way of life which belonged to the revolutionary period at a time when Communism was opposed by an entrenched regime, must not be allowed to disappear from the face of the world. It must be renewed and revived among the young, even if a genuine enemy is lacking. Such a genuine enemy must be found—and the place to look for him is the moderating pseudo-Confucian tendency which is unavoidably that of all bureaucracies and even of all governing bodies. The young are mobilized by charisma—but they do not know what it is that they are mobilized for. There remains to find what they are mobilized against: first, their teachers, who by the necessity of their profession insist on results rather than on a frame of mind; second, all that carries on the habits and the thoughts of the "old" culture; finally, against one another—where there is no specific dominant pattern of guidance, clashes between the intutions of self-appointed leaders are bound to occur (Ken Ling, 1972). In the end, the cultural revolution collapses, when it is apparent that the various operations of making a living can no longer be subordinated to frenzy. But it had its moment of glory. Lifton compares a rally of the Red Guards around Mao to the documentary on the 1934 Congress of the National Socialist Party around Hitler. The title of the documentary is singularly apt: *The Triumph of the Will*. For the clash is genuinely one between two opposed tendencies of the human mind: knowing and willing, abstraction (even as mild as that of Confucius), and association.

What next? The first cultural revolution has collapsed, leaving bureaucracy in command. By 1975 the "gang of four" had identified a new enemy: Confucius. In western eyes this makes little sense. Why inveigh against a philosopher long dead? However, if one takes Confucius as the symbol or maybe even the author of one cultural tendency, then the attacks upon him from the tenants of the opposed tendency become fully meaningful.

There is little doubt about the Taoist affinity of the cultural revolution; its core was the rejection of the social value of specialized knowledge. Schools were closed, and students were dispersed throughout the countryside to regain a purely natural manner of thought and behavior, opposed to the "cunning hearts" of technicians influenced by western science.

Japan

A question which one cannot ignore when dealing with the Japanese culture is that of the ability to emulate and often to surpass the technological achievement of the West, while at the same time retaining many traits which may be described either as Eastern or as specifically Japanese, including a group-centeredness as opposed to the individual-centeredness which is often considered to be the main basis of the western spirit of inquiry, from which technology is derived.

We will attempt to find an answer to this question by turning once again to the culture of China, which has for centuries greatly influenced that of Japan.

The first concept which must be analyzed is that of *situation centered* ethic attributed by many writers to the cultures of China and of Japan and contrasted with the *individual-centeredness* of the western family of cultures.

> The situation-centered world is characterized by ties which permanently unite closely related human beings in the family and clan. Within this basic human constellation the individual is conditioned to seek mutual dependence. That is to say, he is dependent upon other human beings as much as others are dependent upon him, and he is therefore fully aware of his obligation to make repayment, however much delayed, to his benefactors. The central core of Chinese ethics is filial piety, which defines the complex of duties, obligations, and attitudes on the part of children (sons) toward their fathers and mothers. Why do sons owe filial piety to their parents? Because of their "indebtedness" to the elders who brought them forth and who reared them to maturity. Since the kinship structure, no matter how widely extended, is built on expanded consanguine and affinal relation-

ships represented in the parent-child triad, all members in it are either in the receiving or the giving end of a human network of mutual dependence.

The individual enmeshed in such a human network is likely to view the world in a complacent and compartmentalized way; complacent because he has a secure and inalienable place in his human group, and compartmentalized because he is conditioned to perceive the external world in terms of what is within the group and what is outside it. For what is within his group and what is outside have drastically different meanings for him. As he generalizes from this basic assumption, there are quite different truths for different situations throughout his life's experiences. Principles which are correct for one set of circumstances may not be appropriate for another at all, but the principles in each case are equally comparable.

The good situation-centered Chinese, in fact, tends to have multiple standards. The prisoner's standards are not his jailer's, and the man's are not the woman's. Because he enjoys within his primary kinship group a security, continuity, and permanence that he cannot find outside it, the situation-centered Chinese has a greater feeling of certainty about life than does an average individual in many other societies and therefore is more likely to be complacent. Since double or multiple standards of morality and conduct are normal, they present the individual with no inner conflict. The individual feels no resentment against conforming and no compunction about behaving differently under contrasting sets of circumstances. He may be taught charity as a personal virtue, to improve his fate and that of his ancestors and descendants, but he will have no necessary compulsion or desire to champion the cause of the oppressed as a whole or to overthrow the privileged position of all oppressors. The primary guide for his behavior is his place, the place of his primary group in the accepted scheme of things, and the knowledge of how to better that place; but he will have little sense of the justice or injustice of intergroup relations as a whole or any desire to change them. Consequently the Chinese society through history has tended to be remarkably static, for it lacked *internal* impetus to change. (Hsu, 1963)

In contrast:

The individual-centered world is characterized by temporary ties among closely related human beings. Having no permanent base in family and clan, the individual's orientation towards life and environment is self-reliance. That is to say, he is conditioned to think for himself, to make his own decisions, and to carve out his future by his own hands and in his own potentialities. (Hsu, 1963)

Such direction as is available in the individual-centered world comes less from the primary group than in the case of the situation-centered world. In its place there are general or abstract rules of propriety; the individual is given a choice of possible goals, but the quantity of such goals is restricted by an agreed upon definition of what is good and what is bad.

Where does Japan fit in this comparison between China and the West? Many researchers, including Benedict (1946) suggest that Japan is even more situation-centered than is China. In the classical Japanese culture all generalizable definitions of good and bad, ethical and nonethical are lacking. What takes their place is a precise definition of all possible situations and an equally precise definition of the proper way of dealing with them.

> The Japanese view of life is just what their formulas of chu and ko and giri and jin and human feelings say it is. They see the "whole duty of man" as if it were parceled out into separate provinces on a map. In their phrase, one's life consists of "the circle of chu" and "the circle of ko," and "the circle of giri" and "the circle of jin" and "the circle of human feelings" and many more. Each circle has its special detailed code and a man judges his fellows, not by ascribing to them integrated personalities, but by saying of them that "they do not know ko" or "they do not know giri." Instead of accusing a man of being unjust, as an American would, they specify the circle of behavior he has not lived up to. Instead of accusing a man of being selfish or unkind, the Japanese specify the particular province within which he violated the code. They do not invoke a categorical imperative or a golden rule. Approved behavior is relative to the circle within which it appears. When a man acts "for ko," he is acting in one way; when he acts "merely for giri" or "in the circle of jin," he is acting—so Westerners would judge—in quite different character. The codes, even for each "circle," are set up in such a way that, when conditions change within it, the most different behavior may be properly called for. Giri to one's lord demanded utmost loyalty until the lord insulted his retainer; afterward no treachery was too great. Until August 1945, chu demanded of the Japanese people that they fight to the last man against the enemy. When the Emperor changed the requirements of chu by broadcasting Japan's capitulation, the Japanese outdid themselves in expressing their cooperation with the victors. (Benedict, 1946)

This compartmentalization of life into different roles and different ethics, each ethical code being determined by the role, explains much of Japanese behavior during the Second World War. Allied prisoners of war were often treated with unspeakable brutality. In the Japanese mind, such treatment was fully justified by the behavior of the prisoners, who refused to act in accordance with the code applicable to those who let themselves be captured by an enemy. The British and the Americans felt themselves to be soldiers, even after their capture. In the eyes of their Japanese captors such behavior amounts to intolerable provocation. Soldiers are one thing and prisoners another one. For a prisoner to act as a soldier is an unbearable departure from the code governing the appropriate circle.

The situation was quite different in the symmetrical situation. Japanese soldiers behaved with almost incredible bravery to avoid capture; they often preferred suicide to being made prisoners. However, when captured, for example after having lost consciousness because of the explosion or a grenade, they behaved with total meekness and accepted anything their captors required from them, often going so far as to point out camouflaged Japanese positions to Allied artillery observers and air liaison officers. They felt that their very identity had changed; they were no longer soldiers but prisoners, and had to behave in accordance with their new situation with the same dedication they exhibited in regard to the previous one.

I remember a Japanese couple I had met in Tokyo. They were dressed in the western manner, and when we strolled together the wife walked at her husband's side, together with myself as their guest. I visited the same couple in the countryside. This time they were dressed in traditional kimonos; when we went for a stroll, the wife let her husband and me take the lead, and took her position three paces behind her husband.

The descriptions above were based on observations made by Americans and directed at the Japanese society and culture. It may be interesting to bring in the observations on the United States made by visitors from Europe and particularly from Eastern Europe. They often attribute to Americans characteristics very similar to the ones attributed by Americans to the Japanese. In particular they found that Americans acted in a manner determined by circumstances rather than by their integrated personalities.

At one time after the 1956 elections, a group of French representatives of the labor movement asked an American labor leader what would be the attitude of the American unions in regard to President Eisenhower. They were quite shocked when their American interlocutor stated that the unions had opposed Eisenhower in the election, but now that he had been elected they would recognize this fact and work with the Eisenhower administration, and in particular with its Secretary of Labor, in the customary way. The Frenchmen asked whether this did not constitute a violation of the principles of the labor union movement. The American replied that there were times when one should rise above principle.

The malapropism of the American unionist is of secondary importance, except perhaps as an example of the careless manner in which speakers of English treat their language. What is important is the reasoning it reveals. This might be put forward as three hypotheses.

(1) The basic principle of democracy is to accept the position of the majority. If this is the case, the American's expression means that the true principle is that of respect for democracy, while loyalty to ideological—i.e., theoretical—positions held before the elections are of secondary importance. (2) The basic mechanism of democracy consists in preserving interpersonal collaboration, even at the cost of not being able to bring action in conformity with strongly held policy preferences. Or, (3) the results of the elections constitute a new reality, and it is wise to take this new reality into account, even at the cost of previous or present preferences.

All three of these interpretations—which are by no means incompatible among themselves—suggest a greater reliance on situational elements and on situational logic than does the position of the Frenchmen, which might be summed up as loyalty to a set of voiced political ideas, even at the cost of pragmatic advantages which might have resulted from an acceptance of working within the situation and within the regime resulting from the elections.

One can see at this point certain parallels between the neo-particularism of the Americans and the paleo-particularism of the Japanese. Both result in emphasis on role rather than on an identity integrated on the basis of strongly held and mutually consistent ideas.

A parenthesis must be opened at this juncture. How do we know that it is possible to obtain a system of ideas which we would know to be internally consistent? We know, since the demonstration of the Gödel theorem which states that the internal consistency of a system of propositions can never be demonstrated within the system, that such internal consistency can never be proven. It follows that the essence of a universalistic culture is defined by attempts at proving the logically nonprovable, while the essence of an objectivistic culture consists in attempts to prove internal consistency by a recourse to observation. As for associative-subjective cultures, they seek harmony rather than consistency, and the locus of the search for harmony is tradition.

We can now return to the main point of the discussion. It was suggested earlier that the separation of various roles from the total personality was both a consequence of, and a condition for the development of a "modern" society, strongly influenced by the economic market place and capable of developing mass-production economies.

A subdivision of social identity into a locus of largely autonomous roles is characteristic of both the Japanese and of the modern middle-class cultures in the West. The background and the ultimate consequences of such a subdivision may be different in the two cases, but the similarity between them is one of the possible factors which led to the remarkably quick assimilation by the Japanese of the technology and the commerce of the West. All that was needed was to add one more "circle" to the earlier "circles" governing the behavior of the individual. This time, the circle was one of the behaviors appropriate to the role of a modern technocrat or businessman.

Yet it would be a mistake to assume that such a convergence means that the cultural and social patterns are merely a repetition of the patterns characterizing the West, with some local color added.

Probably the most succinct manner in which deep differences between Japan and the West and also between Japan and China can be presented is through the use of Nakane's concepts of *attribute* and *frame* (1970).

> Groups may be identified by applying . . . two criteria: one is based on a common *attribute* . . .

for example, a description of a quality or an area of competence defining an individual's role, such as engineer, printer, farmer, or physician,

> the other on a situational position in a given *frame*. . . . *Frame* may be a locality, an institution or a particular relationship which binds a set of individuals into one group.

Examples may be households, universities, parts of the civil service, or industrial corporations.

An individual's position is defined in most cultures by the intersection of his relevant attribute and of the main frame where he belongs. In the West, including the United States, the attribute forms the most important part of personal identification (except where the frame is the household or the nuclear family). In Japan, the most important part of the identification is the frame, even in a context very distant from the family.

> The ready tendency of the Japanese to stress situational position in a particular frame, rather than a universal attribute, can be seen in the following example: when a Japanese "faces the outside" (confronts another person) and affixes some position to himself socially he is likely to give precedence to institution over kind of an occupation. Rather than saying "I am a type-setter" or "I am a filing clerk," he is likely to say "I am from B Publishing Group," or "I belong to S Company." Much depends on context, of course, but where a choice exists, he will use this latter form. (Nakane, 1970)

The difference can be emphasized by the relative weakness of family ties in Japanese society, as contrasted with the strength of household ties—a distinction which is only dimly perceived in most cultures.

The business enterprise, no matter how large, is usually seen in the image of a household. Employment is generally for life regardless of economic fluctuations. Complementarily, the tendency of a man to seek more advantageous employment elsewhere is condemned and interpreted as a lack of loyalty and trustworthiness.

Relationships within the company are shaped by the overriding importance of the frame, and the complementary weakness of the attribute. Communication does not flow horizontally, among equals possessing the same attribute, but vertically, between superordinate and subordinate.

The strength of the vertical bonds should not suggest that a sort of equalitarianism prevails in Japanese society. On the contrary, consciousness of rank is one of the main characteristics of Japanese society. Social relationships within the group are at the same time pervasive and nonsymmetrical; this, we may note, is a characteristic of the community or Gemeinschaft type of social organization; it is also strongly reminiscent of feudal bonds.

> In Japan once rank is established on the basis of seniority, it is applied to all circumstances, and to a great extent controls social life and individual activity. Seniority and merit are the principal criteria for the establishment of a social order; every society employs these criteria, although the weight given to each may differ according to social circumstances. In the West merit is given considerable importance, while in Japan the balance goes the other way. . . .
>
> Without consciousness of ranking, life could not be carried on smoothly in Japan, for rank is the social norm on which Japanese life is based. In a traditional Japanese house the arrangement of a room manifests this gradation of rank and clearly prescribes the ranking differences which are to be observed by those who use it. The highest seat is always at the centre backed by the *tokonoma* (alcove), where a painted scroll is hung and flowers are arranged; the lowest seat is near the entrance to the room. This arrangement never allows two or more individuals to be placed as equals. Whatever the nature of the gathering, those present will eventually establish a satisfactory order among themselves, after each of them has shown the necessary preliminaries of the etiquette of self-effacement. . . .
>
> Since ranking order appears so regularly in such essential aspects of daily life, the Japanese cannot help but be made extremely conscious of it. In fact, this consciousness is so strong that official rank is easily extended into private life. A superior in one's place of work is always one's superior wherever he is met, at a restaurant, at home, in the street. When wives meet, they, too, will behave towards each other in accordance with the ranks of their husbands. (Nakane, 1970)

The overall picture is that of a number of tightly woven communities or Gemeinschaften, arranged vertically, side by side, rather than horizontally, one on top of another.

Moreover, the structure of the Gemeinschaften coincides with the table of organization of economic enterprises. In consequence, economic efficiency does not require the society of strangers that was described earlier as one of the conditions for the development of economic modernity.

This state of affairs is illustrated by the manner in which new members of the group are indoctrinated into the existing structure. An introductory training program into a banking enterprise, for example, would center in most of the western countries around a detailed exposition of the company's business and inner structure. In Japan it is more likely to include such things as a long hike undertaken collectively by a group of recent recruits, common meditation in a Zen monastery, and a common visit to the well-preserved quarters of the World War II Kamikaze pilots, who had sacrificed their individual lives to the needs of the community.

A number of Japanese sociologists consider the organization of communities around the enterprise as providing an ideal model of social equilibrium, capable of satisfying both the needs of personal subjectivity and those of an efficient objectivity, capable of ensuring the material and the spiritual needs of the members at the same time.

I do not quite share this optimism.

There are many indications that role diffusion exists in Japan as it does in other industrialized societies, even though its impact may be lessened by the organization of the productive apparatus along the lines of parallel communities. An even more important point is that Japan has discarded the isolation which had hitherto made it possible to minimize the problems created by contact with other cultures. In the face of such a double threat to the existing cultural status quo, many Japanese and particularly the young and intellectual Japanese are seeking a more integrated world view, which might serve as a basis for a more stable and especially a more comprehensive definition of self identity.

At first glance, the problems faced by young Japanese and young Americans appear to be in diametrical opposition.

> Young Japanese focus upon differentiating the self from engulfing traditional groups, while young Americans, in possession of a differentiated but chaotic self, look to the creation of new groups to which they can be anchored—but in both cases there is a simultaneous quest for meaningful self-process and community. (Lifton, 1971)

This can be put in slightly different terms: that there is in both cases a vigorous even though often inefficient search for a satisfactory world view.

In postwar Japan, especially among young people, it is good to be "dry" (or *durai*) rather than "wet" (or *wetto*). This means—in the original youth language, as expanded by the mass media—to be direct, logical, to the point, pragmatic, casual, self-interested, rather than polite, evasive, sentimental, nostalgic, dedicated to romantic causes, or bound by obligation in human relations; to break out of the world of cherry blossoms, haiku, and moon-viewing into a modern era of bright sunlight, jazz and Hemingway. (Lifton, 1971)

Given this definition, "dryness" appears to be almost co-extensive with abstraction, and "wetness" with associative subjectivity.

Concerning images of the wet and the dry, these could be explored . . . to reveal pulls and tensions accompanying accelerated historical change anywhere. "Wetness" could be seen to include a whole constellation of familiar and reassuring emotions derived from one's personal and cultural past—"soft" feelings associated with mother and family, with the geographical and psychological simplicities reminiscent of childhood, nostalgic expressions of sadness and gaiety and of aesthetic and sensual pleasure. Wetness, then, epitomizes the earliest sense of connection to the point of merging with one's original sources of nurture—the "potato love" that Saul Bellow speaks of, safe and unchanging, but also (at certain moments) stifling and even suffocating. "Dryness," on the other hand, suggests that which is new and critical in tone; emotions that are 'hard' in their rejection of past niceties and indirections, and in their insistence upon selfhood based upon a new aesthetic and a new sensuality, divested of the encumbrances of traditional cultural learning. The dry vision of liberation from the past and of self-discovery risks the loss of the safe haven of wetness—of connection and tender nurturance—even to the point, at its most extreme, of severing the bonds of identification required by all groups in all societies. (Lifton, 1971)

A Japanese student in an American university, when asked to define the meanings of "wetness" and "dryness" for the benefit of the class, answered that "wetness" means to be nationalistic, and "dryness" as being not so nationalistic. Her definition points out the tie of wetness to tradition and to the associative nexus which accompanies all traditions, and dryness to the rejection of tradition, together with the rigorous logic that comes to replace traditions at times when the latter are no longer sufficient to define self-identity. This points out that it would be a mistake to associate wetness with tenderness: Among Japanese youth, those who preach wetness rather than merely succumbing to it, have provided as many "right wing" political assassins and terrorists as those associated with the logic of dryness have provided "left wing" killers seeking to reach political objectives through terror.

Nakamura (1960) analyzes traditional Japanese culture as lacking in the development of logic, and even of exhibiting anti-logical trends. Yet:

> Young Japanese repeatedly assert their desire to be logical, objective, scientific, to be in every way tough-minded. They stress their urge to *wari-kiru*—a verb which means "to divide" but which now conveys the sense of cutting through a problem, giving a clear-cut and logical explanation. (Lifton, 1971)

The struggle between associative subjectivity and abstractive objectivity may often lead to their synthesis at the third apex of the model, that of co-subjective idealism. Young middle-class Japanese

> have an unusually strong response to the totality of a situation, and both their immediate and enduring judgments depend greatly on the extent to which purity and beauty are perceived. I believe that one of the reasons of the attraction of Marxism as an overall doctrinal system is its capacity to evoke this sense of aesthetic totality, of the universal "fit" and feeling of truth. At the same time, Marxism readily lends itself to the equally necessary stress upon "scientific logic" and tough-minded analysis. (Lifton, 1971)

The last point calls for additional analysis. Postwar Japan can be put forward as the prime example of the lack of fit between Marxist economic and even sociological theory and such objectivity as we are capable of achieving. The economy grows at rates incomparably higher than those of any Marxist or proto-Marxist society, and the alienation which we have been analyzing applies so far to a fairly small minority of the population. Yet some alienation can easily be found. Among the middle and upper-middle classes it takes the aspect of a search for a unifying world view, with Marxism always available to fill the conceptual void. Among the lower-middle and working classes it appears as a multiplication of new religions. A particularly important case is that of the Soka Gakkai, derived from the Nishiren sect of Buddhism, and sponsoring a political party, the Komeito. As in the case of many of the groupings which appear in times of cultural instability, what is striking in the Soka Gakkai is the almost fanatical commitment of the members, and the almost complete lack of a doctrine. Once again the human ability to will appears to be almost triumphant, while the faculty of understanding is almost absent.

To sum up, the cultural synthesis carried out by the Japanese has been almost incredibly successful. Yet past successes should not lead to the automatic expectation of smooth progress. Signs of dangerous cultural dislocations are easy to detect.

India

Nakamura (1960) underlines the particularism and the predominantly concrete character of Chinese and Japanese thought. In contradistinction, he stresses the universalism and the tendency to abstraction of the thought of the high culture of India.

> That Indians were skillful in abstract speculation can be seen in their skillful expression of the ideas of numbers. A great number of infinitesimal numbers often appears in religious books and literary works. This reveals their rich imagination and analysis. The Arabic numerals of today had been invented by the Indians, and the Arabians only transmitted them into European countries. The manner of writing by numbering order and the idea of the zero were both invented by Indians. (Nakamura, 1960)

It would appear that from this extremely important point of view the culture of India came closer to the cultures of the West than to those of the Sinic East. At the same time, however, the cultures of India have failed to develop science as a discipline of the human mind. Even more to the point, their culture shows much of the stability of the other cultures of the East, and little of the progressive development of the cultures of the West.

A very basic reason for the different evolutions of India on the one hand and of the Greco-Hebrew West on the other can be seen in the different interpretation of universal ideas as they appear in the Platonic tradition and in the living Indian thought.

Let us begin with a similarity. For both Plato and the major Indian thinkers the particularity and the extreme differentiation which are observed by the senses are less perfect than the ideas which can be reached through the mind, and which remain unchanged through the changes in the superficial world. For the philosophy which began with the Greek masters and in particular with Socrates and Plato, the unchanging reality is in the true essences which correspond—roughly speaking—to the words of the language. Thus, in the words of the Phaedo which were quoted earlier, the power of reason apprehends true or abstract reality of a concept such as "equality" in the perfect absolute, behind the merely approximate equality of "wood with wood or stone with stone." Such an approach is bound to state as truth descriptions of the world which are later found to be merely hypothetical; this, little by little, leads to the experimental verifications of abstract statements derived from experiential inputs—in short, it leads to science.

The position of the Indian thinker is different.

> The first issue that the Hindu thinker raises here is: What is the end or the ultimate goal of life? Through one birth or several, whatever man has

come to be has an origin. Why should he have been born at all? Now the Hindu believes that man is born and exists in accordance with the wish of God (*Iśvara*) of the Universal Principle, of the Primal Cause; and that he is to that extent separated, as it were from it. And from birth to birth, all the struggles he goes through and the means that he employs, are the means to go back to the source of his existence. We are born to fulfill the wish of God. All sparks that radiate from Him most naturally desire to return to the original source. The whole problem seems to be reduced to this, that the whole universe is a process, first of evolution—of the many evolving out of the One; and then of involution—the Many trying their best to return to the origin from which they came. (Radhakrishnan, 1962)

It follows that anything that is differentiated cannot be permanent, and that anything which is permanent may not be differentiated. This leads to a high valuation of an unknowable absolute, and the devaluation of anything knowable. It is only a slight exaggeration to say that anything that can be known is not worth knowing.

Yet it cannot be completely ignored. Rules of conduct must be stated. A move in that direction can be seen in the conception of human life which prescribes that the individual divide his life into four stages: *brahmacarva*, the period of training; *gārhstya*, the period of work for the world as a householder; *vānaprasthya*, the period for the loosening of social bonds; and *samnyāsa*, or the period of renunciation, leading in some cases to the expectation of freedom—freedom being understood not in the usual American sense of freedom *to* pursue one's wishes, but rather in the sense of freedom *from* wishing or desiring anything.

These general principles form an empty structure which still needs to be filled. What is it that a householder should do in order to work for the world? What should the period of training lead to?

The answer can be found in the theory of reincarnation, and in the practice of caste. The cycle of evolution and involution does not take place in one lifetime. It takes several reincarnations. The individual—human or animal—who acts righteously is reborn in a higher status position; this gives him more opportunities for right action, up to the point of his return to the One and the disappearance of the individualized self.

What, now, is right action? Even less than with the Chinese and the Japanese is it something that can be reduced to clear principles with a universal application. The righteous course of action depends on the individual's status in life—from god-like to animal or even vegetal. If it is human, it depends on caste—and castes are numbered in the hundreds, each of which obeys a dharma and an ethic of its own.

There was no universally valid ethic, but only a strict status compartmentalization of private and social ethic, disregarding the few absolute and general ritualistic prohibitions (particularly the killing of cows). This was of great moment. The doctrine of *karma* deduced from the principle of compensation for previous deeds in the world, not only explained the caste organization but the rank order of divine, human and animal beings of all degrees. Hence it provided the coexistence of different ethical codes for different status groups which not only differed widely but were often in sharp conflict. This presented no problem. In principle there could be a vocational *dharma* for prostitutes, robbers and thieves as well as for Brahmans and kings. (Weber, 1951)

Quite obviously, a society governed by such a culture had to be segmented. The framework of human action was the caste, and up to a point, the structure of castes within the village. Tradition—and in particular local tradition—was enough to tell people how to live. A few examples from the lives in the traditional sectors of society may be to the point.

Here in Tanjore, a man owning even one acre of land calls himself a "*mirasdar*." He will never go to the field and work with his hands, a group of *mirasdars* explain to me in fluent English. . . . "this is a land of gentlemen farmers."

More paddy (rice) is cultivated here than in any other district of the State. Irrigated lands, which are extensive, grow two consecutive crops of it. . . .

. . . No landowner works for himself. Usually he prefers to give his land out for cultivation on *waram*, that is share-cropping; or he employs landless labourers. (Nair, 1962)

Nair interviewed a population at the social level opposed to the standing of the mirasdar: the untouchables who actually till the soil. They were asked whether they would like to be given land of their own, and if so, how much.

"You would like to have land of your own, wouldn't you?"

"Yes." Many heads nod.

"Then how much?"

Samu is the first to speak. He is an old man. He has never possessed any land. There are five members in his family. But he wants only one and one-third acres. He is precise. Even from that, he says after some mental calculation he would be prepared to share 50 percent with the *mirasdar*. . . . And finally, it is the same story with another young hopeful. . . . There are nine in the family, and at present they are cultivating .3 acres. Yet he asks only for three acres on 60/40 basis.

"Are you sure you would not like to have more?" I asked again incredulously.

"Yes," they are sure, quite sure.

The sun is setting on a roseate rice-girdled horizon. Mental horizons are apparently similarly circumscribed. (Nair, 1962)

It is not that change is excluded. But it takes the form of sudden jumps rather than of a smooth development. The acquisition of literacy leads often to changes in behavior amounting to something like a change of caste, or the acquisition of a new dharma.

Cultivation, or in fact any kind of manual work in the rural context, is considered totally incompatible with education.

As a school teacher in Burbhum district put it: "Only education makes men of us. But education and cultivation can never be combined. The two must be kept separate. How can a boy who has been to school do the hard labour which cultivation requires?" (Nair, 1962)

Looking at the overall picture of Hinduism, one tends to find in it a grand design made of the ideal of renunciation and complicated at various nodal points by the specific prescriptions of the various dharmas which, indeed, may go very far from renunciation: The Marharabathara teaches us the dharma of the *kshtria,* the princely-warrior caste, is very far from renunciation and on the contrary demands warlike acquisitiveness of those who belong to it. The logic of the grand design is that renunciation be the conduct of brahmins, those who from incarnation to incarnation have come the closest to losing themselves in the eternal and formless ātman. However, most of the holy men, the *sadhus* from whom miracles are expected, are low caste; the manner in which they could attain the supreme renunciation of holiness without going through the avatars of the specific recommendations of successive reincarnations is never properly explained. This is what might be called the minor design of Hinduism, and the connection between the minor and the major designs is never made unequivocally clear.

It might be suggested that contrarily to the Sinic civilizations, which seek pragmatic objectivity, often at the cost of theoretical co-subjectivity, the Hinduistic civilizations—and also their Buddhist influence on the Sinic civilizations—seek to reach absolute abstraction in one single bond. Under such circumstances, ratiocination becomes not the guide to knowledge, as it is in the Occident, but rather its obverse. Wisdom consists in the turning back on tangible particulars, rather than in their analysis.

There is nevertheless a point worth insisting upon. The civilizations of China and Japan always impressed the cultures of the West with their artifacts. The civilization of India—and also that of Tibet—impressed them mainly by their ideas, and especially by the idea of renunciation.

Arabia

A considerable number of analyses of the Arab character has been published over the last few years. Most of them agree on common themes. The two which are probably the keenest in analytic insight are Hamady's *Temperament and Character of the Arabs* (1960) and Patai's *The Arab Mind* (1973). A quotation from Patai shows the essence of the problem:

> In attempting to recognize correlations between various aspects of the Arab personality, it is helpful to examine the discrepancy that exists among the Arabs among the three planes of existence that can be distinguished in each individual and group. All of us engage constantly in action. Our actions express our intentions, but, at the same time, are influenced by external factors, such as the control the social and physical environment has over us. The world of action and activity is the first plane of our existence. The second is that of verbal utterance. We often express verbally intentions that we cannot carry out because of external impediments. In this respect, verbal expression corresponds more closely to intentions than actions. But even in words we do not express all of our intentions. We refrain from uttering certain things because of the realities of the environment in which we live. The third plane is that of the intentions themselves, that is, of the thoughts we entertain, the wishes we have, the ideas we believe in, and so on. The world of the mind, as this plane can be called, is the one most independent of the limiting influences of the environment. Yet, while thoughts cannot be censored, thought is to a considerable degree related to reality. A normal person will not entertain thoughts which are in overt conflict with reality. He may engage in "wishful thinking," or even "day dreaming," but he will always be aware of the difference between such idle thoughts and reality.
>
> As to the control of the reality factor over ideas and words, there are unquestionably significant differences between individuals and groups. In a pragmatically oriented community, the modal personality is strongly influenced by reality and his verbal expression even more so. At the other end of the scale we find societies where reality does not exercise a strong degree of influence on thinking and speech. Western peoples stand at one end of the scale, the Arabs near the other end. In the Arab world, thought and verbal expression can be relatively uncorrelated with what the circumstances actually allow.
>
> Y. Harkabi found that among the Arabs both thought processes and verbal utterances enjoy a high degree of autonomy. Thoughts, wishes and their oral expressions develop in freedom from the control of reality. Since the thought processes are generally hidden from the eye, it is in particular the discrepancy between the verbal utterance and the acts that is apparent. The verbal utterance, which develops such mental functions as feelings, aspirations, wishes and thoughts, is quite divorced from the level of action.

Harkabi goes on to show that numerous observers are themselves aware of the discrepancy between Arab wishes, desires, imaginings and the words expressing them, and the reality to which their action must conform. While a certain discrepancy between ideology and verbal formulation on the one hand and actions on the other is a general human phenomenon, among the Arabs the difference is considerable, although even here there is no absolute break between the ideal and reality.

Related observations were made some years earlier by Morroe Berger who speaks about "the Arab's infatuation with ideal forms" to which he clings "emotionally even while he knows they are contradicted by reality." While a "distinction between ideal and real exists in other societies too," in them there is a greater awareness "of the gap between the two, and the ideal is more consciously held up as a basis upon which to *judge* the real." The Arabs, on the other hand, "confuse the two, professing to believe against reality that the ideal is carried out in conduct and is identical with practice. . . ." One modern manifestation of this tendency is the Arabs' love of adopting a plan which "can be a perfect thing, like a work of Arab calligraphic art," with "emphasis upon appearance and not meaning," and without considering their capacity to carry out such a plan. "There is also the feeling that one need not go beyond the plan, for the ideal picture is sufficient, and is in any case esthetically far more pleasing than the uncertainty and disorderliness of reality." (Patai, 1973)

Divergence between facts, to the extent to which we are capable of knowing them, and words or ideas, to the extent to which we are truly capable of separating them from our beliefs and the image we have of reality, can be called by brutally contrasting terms. It can be called mendaciousness or lying, and it can be called poetic freedom and even poetic sensitivity. The two are not always as easy to separate as it might seem. Examples of one shading into the other can be found in all cultures; it is perhaps a mark of the Arabic culture that such examples are easier to find in it.

Let us begin with the concept of "face," remembering that its somewhat childish overtones are likely to fade away when we come to think of a cognate concept: honor. Both of these assume an enormous importance in the Arabic culture.

There is a considerable difference between the intensity with which the concept of "face" affects the thinking and the conduct of people in the West and in the Arab world. In simplest terms one can say that in the Arab world "face" is a much more powerful consideration in weighing one's acts and words than it is in the West. The difference is so great as to amount to one in kind. Hence a more detailed discussion of *wajh* and its working in the Arab psyche is helpful here. Let us begin with an illustration.

On Monday, June 5, 1967, in the early morning hours, the Israeli air force destroyed practically all the combat planes of the U.A.R. [United Arab Republic] with negligible losses to itself. At about 9 A.M. Marshal Abdel Hakim Amer, commander of the Egyptian forces in Cairo, sent a coded message to General Abdel Moneim Riad, the Egyptian officer in command of the Arab forces on the Jordanian front. The message, according to the account given by King Hussein of Jordan, read as follows:

1. Israeli planes have started to bomb air bases of the U.A.R. and approximately 75% of the enemy's aircraft have been destroyed or put out of action.
2. The counterattack by the Egyptian air force was underway over Israel. In Sinai, U.A.R. troops have engaged the enemy and taken the offensive on the ground.
3. As a result, Marshal Amer has ordered Commander-in-Chief of the Jordanian front (i.e., General Riad) to open a new front and to launch offensive operations, according to the plan outlined the day before.

A few hours later, in a second message, Marshal Amer informed the Jordanian front

> that the Israeli air offensive was continuing. But at the same time, he insisted that the Egyptians had put 75% of the Israeli out of action. The same message said that the U.A.R. bombers had destroyed the Israeli bases in a counterattack, and that the ground forces of the Egyptian army had penetrated Israel by way of the Negev.

King Hussein concludes his account of Marshal Amer's messages with an understatement that bears the stamp of Harrow and Sandhurst rather than the impassioned eloquence of his Hashemite ancestors: "These reports—fantastic to say the least—had much to do with our confusion and false interpretation of the situation."

It is not often that one encounters such a telling example of both the overriding imperative of saving one's face and the price it can exact. While nobody can tell what would have happened had the Egyptians frankly and without procrastination notified Jordan that on the morning of June 5, 1967, they had suffered a serious setback, it is almost certain that Jordan would either have refrained from entering the fight or could have extricated itself from it with fewer losses. But both peoples and their leaders are, as a rule, the prisoners of their cultural values. Given the traditional Arab value of "face," it was impossible for the Egyptian military leadership to act differently. Before having a closer look at *wajh* and the hold it exercises on the Arab mentality, let us first conclude the story of the Egyptian-Jordanian communication in the Six-Day War of 1967, since it allows some additional insight into this tyrannical hold of the *wajh*.

On the same fateful day of June 5, Nasser phoned King Hussein and told him the same story: "Israel bombed our air bases. We answered by bombing hers. We are launching a general offensive in the Negev."

Next morning, when the damage done by the Israeli air attack could no longer be kept a secret, Nasser in a telephone conversation with King Hussein suggested that a communique be issued by the Jordanians, as well as by the Syrians, to the effect that American and British aircraft were collaborating with Israel and attacking Egypt from their aircraft carriers. This at the time seemed a perfect plan to save face. It was no longer little Israel that had dealt the blow to Egypt, but the great powers, the United States and Great Britain, to whose combined strength it was not shameful to have succumbed. Yet in the very same telephone conversation in which he suggested this face-saving device to King Hussein, President Nasser could not resist the temptation to save his own (that is, Egypt's) *vis-a-vis* Hussein, and said:

> We will fight with everything we have. We fought on all fronts, all night. If we had a few problems at the beginning, so what? We'll come out of it all right. God is on our side. . . . We dispatched our planes against Israel today. Our planes have been bombing the Israeli airports since early morning.

A few hours later, at 12:30 P.M., King Hussein sent a personal telegram in which he informed the Egyptian President in simple and matter-of-fact language (we are again reminded of the King's British education) that the situation on the Jordanian front was desperate. This frank admission of defeat by Hussein finally broke the hold *wajh* had on Nasser, and he was able in his reply (which he sent after a delay of eleven hours, at 11:15 P.M.) to admit that he, too, had been defeated. His long cable speaks of a situation that demands "courage beyond human capacity," and of the necessity to "face up to our responsibilities without fear of consequences." Then Nasser ties the admission of his own defeat to that of Hussein: "We are fully aware of your difficult situation as at this very moment our front is crumbling too." Finally, he is able to come to the point: "Yesterday, our enemy's air force inflicted a mortal blow on us. Since then our land army has been stripped of all air support and forced to withstand the power of superior forces." Thereafter, Nasser continues to talk about matters quite extraneous to the issue at hand: "When the history books are written, your courage and tenacity will be remembered. They will not forget the heroic Jordanian people who went straight into battle without hesitation, and with no consideration other than honor and duty." After suggesting that the Jordanians evacuate the West Bank, and expressing the hope that the Security Council will order a cease-fire, Nasser remarks philosophically, "The histories of nations are full of reverses, victories and defeats. . . ." and that "It is Allah's will—and maybe something good will come out of it. We trust in Allah and he will not desert us. Perhaps, thanks to him, the days ahead will bring us victory." Then after repeating the compliment already paid to the courage and heroism of Hussein and the Jordanian people, Nasser closes his telegram with the traditional blessing: "Peace be with you and may Allah bless you." In reproducing the full text of Nasser's telegram, Hussein caustically commented in a footnote "the Jordanians had to wait 48 hours to learn what had really happened in Egypt at the start of the conflict which determined the war's outcome." (Patai, 1973)

Once again the incident selected as an example of the overall cultural attitude, as well as this attitude itself, appear hardly understandable within the context of the utilitarian theory of language, and of symbolic behavior in general, which is held more or less consciously by most of the participants in "our" cultures. This theory considers symbolic usage, and particularly language, as something secondary and ancillary. The "purpose" of language is to communicate information about a "reality" independent of the symbolic system as such, but which it may be convenient to explain linguistically—or by symbols such as drawings—for all sorts of pragmatic reasons.

As indicated earlier, and also in Glenn (1973), this theory is not acceptable. What we have instead are more or less autonomous functions in mutual tension and cooperation: (1) The need to prolong into areas of subject-domination operations which either cannot or cannot yet be carried out in reality. The "cannot yet" stands for the fact that the impossibility of realistic operationalization may not be due to the appearance of obstacles to the present realization of an operation which had been successfully carried out in the past, but rather to the fact that the individual exercises his schemata of action under circumstances under which he is only partially competent: We have in mind Groos' pre-exercise or Piaget's functional assimilation. (2) The need to forge social cohesiveness. And (3) referential communication. It is only the last named which fits the utilitarian theory, even though it is far from being the dominant form of expression, and even though it is usually a late-comer in the evolution of communicative usage.

Once again, all languages are capable of fulfilling all three of the needs—but not to the same extent.

We may ask at this point what might be the attitudes of the Arabs towards their language, and how this language is most often used socially, that is to say in the context of *parole* rather than in that of *langue*.

The high praise of Arabic by the early medieval Muslim and Christian authors is echoed to this day in the opinion the Arabs have of the value of their language. Throughout the vast Arabic language area, people hold with relative uniformity that Arabic is superior to other languages because it is beautiful and has a strong appeal, especially for the recitation of classical poetry and for formal or semi-formal oratory. . . . Jabra even talks of the 'mystique' of the Arabic language. (Patai, 1973)

The most common stylistic features through which Arabic achieves its quasi-poetic eloquence are exaggeration, overassertion, and repetition.

The Arabic need for emphasis leads to many misunderstandings, particularly when coupled with the English speakers' tendency toward understatement. For example, when an Arab accepts an invitation to a visit in a tone which is tepid and unassertive, his statement should be interpreted as a refusal. An outright refusal would be rude; as for a failure to show up, it is a secondary matter, since only God has the power to determine events, and in this case He has decided in his wisdom to make the putative guest otherwise engaged. Likewise a refusal lacking in emphasis may be interpreted as merely a ploy aiming at a more emphatic repetition of the invitation. Arabic is not a language of monosyllables.

> The Arab people possess a rich storehouse of oral literature, consisting of folk stories and legends, poetry and songs, riddles, sayings and proverbs. Poetry is today, as it was thirteen hundred years ago, a part of everyday living. People improvise it by way of a pastime or quote it as a means of communication. Versification is indulged by people in all walks of life, including the illiterate, who usually know a certain number of famous verses and recite them on every occasion. (Hamady, 1960)

> Arabic literature and language seem to overemphasize the significance of words as such and to pay less attention to their meaning. An aspect of this situation is the Arab's delight at playing with words. Various words are used for the same meanings. There are numerous repetitions of the same ideas in different words. There are also abrupt transitions. The tendency to fit the thought to the word or to the combination of words rather than the word to the thought is a result of the psychological replacement of thought by words, which become the substitutes of thought and not its representatives. (Shouby, 1951)

Such are the very genuine splendors of Arabic. They all enhance the poetic use of language, or at least a quasi-poetry in prose. What about the expression of thought which must be precise, which cannot be brought to the grasp of the mind by the vagueness and the concrete imagery of poetic similes and metaphors?

North African diplomats, thoroughly schooled in Arabic as well as in French and genuinely bilingual, often use Arabic for public speeches but almost invariably prefer French for diplomatic negotiations in which juridical precision is necessary and the expression of feelings is often set aside.

Let us place these findings within the overall theoretical assumptions of this study.

Social solidarity is based partly or even mainly on the sharing of a symbolic system; such sharing must bear not only on the purely descriptive characteristics of the symbolic system, but also on its semantic values. One can say that social solidarity is firm and deviance is low when and only when the subjects concerned react identically to the same symbolic stimuli. As was suggested earlier, this applies also to complex societies the solidarity of which is organic rather than mechanical (In

Durkheim's terms), since the asymmetrical relations through which different roles are tied (physician-patient, for example) can operate only where there is a considerable sharing of the conceptualized definition of the roles involved. (What is a physician? Why should I let him govern some important part of my behavior? When should I consult him?) Such sharing of concepts reintroduces a considerable amount of symmetry into complex societies. It is this symmetry which makes it possible for different subjects to act in a manner consonant with the organization of the broader society. The origin of such a body of common understanding should be sought in common experience.

Two basic strategies can lead to the development of commonality of experience:

(1) *The abstractive way.* Concepts are endowed with ever more precise definitions. Their meaning increases in generality at the objective apex: The area of applicability of scientific laws and of the concepts through which they are expressed is simply enormous. At the same time the scope of precisely defined concepts becomes narrower at the subjective pole. The riches of personal life and personal imagination cannot be described with scientific precision. Concepts sufficiently precise to become understood in an invariant manner by large populations are by the same token incapable of expressing personal thoughts and personal feelings.

(2) *The associative way.* In the normal course of events, associative patterns may be expected to apply within relatively small communities, in which people are "naturally" exposed to the same experiences and acquire the same habits. Again, let us repeat that the populations in question are likely to be small, because large human groups are likely to be exposed to a variety of experiences, and this exposure is likely to lead to a development of diverse points of view.

There are, however, two ways in which large societies can develop a considerable degree of social and political coherence without following the abstractive road.

1. The maintenance of identical or similar traditions in segmented societies.
2. The sharing of an overwhelming, usually charismatic experience by a large population. Examples of the mechanisms by which such experiences can be attained are easy to come by. Feelings of community can be induced within groups by common listening to music or to poetry, to the voice of a great leader, or simply to repetitive propaganda on the radio or television.

Everything said above about Arabic linguistic usage suggests that the most important role of speech within the culture is to provide the participants with a mechanism for the sharing of affect. Since the linguistic usage described shuns the fixity and stability of abstractive conceptualizations, and since it pays relatively little attention to the correlation of what is said with what is objectively observable, it should be expected that the human groupings derived from the sharing of common reactions to predominantly symbolic experience will be easily changeable: The friend of today may be the enemy of tomorrow and again the friend of the day after.

Human relations are seldom neutral. What is expected in person-to-person relationship is not the American meshing of roles which is at the same time efficient, pleasurable and superficial, but rather the total commitment of the persons concerned. Feelings are strong, even if they are not stable, and they are expressed in strong terms, even if the terms in question correspond only to an ephemeral truth.

> The Arab loyalty is evoked only in personal relationships, that is only where he acts in a "subject-to-subject" or an "I-to-thou" context. Anything outside his kin and the near circle of his friends represents to him an "object" and a "they." With the feeling of responsibility awakened only in personal relationships, . . . the Arab is not used to being impartial in assigning jobs or distributing help. To take care first of one's own people, irrespective of merit or order of priority, is his duty; it means fulfilling a part of his elementary role. (Hamady, 1960)

Outside the group,

> individualism is expressed by a keen sense of self-esteem. . . . Pride is one of the main elements on which Arab individualism rests, since it is sheer being which is primarily respected. . . . The Arab is very touchy and his self-esteem is easily bruised. It is hard for him to be objective about himself or to accept calmly someone else's criticism of him. (Hamady, 1960)

The social organization that correlates with such cultural traits may be represented by a series of circles each of which has an individual for the center. What is proper, indeed what is ethically imperative, is to side with the members of the circle with the shortest radius—usually the family—against those with whom there exists a slightly more distant relationship, even though one may have been allied with such people against a still more distant group and expects to be again allied with them at some future time. This tendency, which can be easily documented by considering the mutual political relations between Arab states, and also by the relationships of the Arab states with the non-Arabic world, is expressed by proverbs such as, "I and my brothers against my cousin; I and my cousins against the world."

Such a labile organization of social bonds does not mean any tepidity in the feelings of the moment: Within a given constellation of circumstances, the friend of the moment is all good, and the enemy of the moment is all bad.

> Semites had no half-tones in their register of vision. They were a people of primary colours, or rather of black and white, who saw the world always in contour. . . . This people was black and white not only in vision, but by inmost furnishing: black and white not only in clarity but in opposition. Their thoughts were at ease only in extremes. They inhabited superlatives by choice. (Lawrence, 1940)

The overall picture is that of an overwhelmingly subjective and associative culture. It is impossible in such a context not to bring up the commanding position of the Arabic culture during its golden age, from approximately the seventh to the thirteenth centuries. This was the time when the Arabs excelled Europe in the development of abstractions, both in the creations of pure thought and in the organization of social life. After that came a period of stagnation. While practically all the literature on the matter, Arabic as well as foreign, agrees on the fact of stagnation, the reason for it remains in the realm of hypotheses. Within such a context, one more hypothesis can be offered, albeit very briefly.

The Arabic conquest of a great part of the Mediterranean basin was a great deed of a small population. Since this population had become the elite of the new imperium, it exercised a great deal of attraction on the native majority. This resulted in the Arabization of many of the conquered. At the same time, the conquerors relaxed their usual standards of endogamous patrilinear tribes, thus opening the possibility of a stirring and a mixing of populations and of cultures. People of different origins and traditions acceded to the Arabic culture and the Arabic language, bringing with them a considerable amount of cultural baggage, parts of which the Arabs absorbed in their turn. The result was a hybrid vigor which often leads to cultural innovation and inventiveness, as long as the cultures in contact are not so different among themselves as to make amalgamation impossible. This was the time when algebra was invented (or discovered) in Egypt. It was also the time when Arabic and Arabized scholars commented on the great works of Greek philosophy, including in particular Aristotle, whose thought became known to the West through the intermediary of Arabic scholars.

The situation changed as the populations became more stable, particularly after the Turkish conquest of the greater part of the Arab world. Populations of diverse origins were permitted to coexist—but not to mingle. Each non-Moslem group was organized around its own religious authorities, and granted considerable autonomy as long as it kept in its place and paid taxes. As for the Arabic Moslems, they returned into an organization dominated by autonomous tribes. All in all, the society became segmented, and the contact between the segments reduced to a minimum. Cultural stagnation is one of the characteristics of such segmented societies.

Shame and guilt

The cultures described in this chapter tend to rely more on shame than on guilt as an instrument of social control—even though this applies somewhat less to India than to the other cultures mentioned. Although shame and guilt tend to fuse one into the other, as most polar opposites do, the differences between the two taken as ideal concepts can be clearly described.

First of all, guilt presupposes a specific transgression on the part of the guilty party. We are, of course, familiar with the concept of free-floating guilt, in which the subject feels guilty without being conscious of the specific action or abstention from action by which guilt feelings are caused. Such guilt without identification is in general explained as the residue of a repression, which led to the elimination from the conscious mind of the "evil" action or thought because of which remorse is being felt. It does not suggest the absence of such an action or thought.

This characteristic of guilt strongly contrasts with the conceptualization of shame. A person may be ashamed, or "put to shame" without being guilty of any transgression. A naked person realizing that his or her privacy has been violated and that she or he is under the observation of a peeping Tom is likely to feel shame (at least in some cultures, even though not in Japan where the causes of shame do not include nudity). Yet such a person has not violated any part of the juridical or ethical system of his culture. On the contrary, it is the other person, the peeping Tom, who is guilty of a transgression, which in many cultures is punishable by law. Why, then, the feeling of shame on the part of the victim? The same phenomenon occurs even more strongly in the case of rape. Victims of rape may be the perfectly innocent objects of a crime; nevertheless they often suffer from a crushing feeling of shame. They often describe themselves as feeling dirty. If, now, we take a person who is actually dirty without circumstantial justification, we find the same feeling of shame; this time, however, it is easy to see that the failure to wash up is a transgression. Thus the difference between shame and guilt is not necessarily that between innocence and culpability.

What then is the difference? Lynd (1970) suggests that the feeling of shame comes from being uncovered or stripped of the attributes of the role or roles defining the person in the eyes of society under normal circumstances. Thus shame is a denial of a person's feeling of identity; moreover, the denial in question causes shame only or mainly if it is public and not private.

The difference between the private and the public is essential. Guilt—or sin—is carried by the transgressor even if no one has witnessed the guilty action. This is the essence of the ethical concept of conscience. A proverb from a culture which depends more on shame than on guilt (in this case the Arabic one) illustrates the difference: "A sin concealed is two-thirds forgiven."

Guilt is also private in another sense. At least in the ideal, guilt is personal and cannot be attributed to noncorporate groups; for example, the family of the perpetrator is not considered guilty, at least in the western family of cultures. Shame, on the other hand, affects an entire social group. For example, sexual misbehavior on the part of a woman shames her "menfolk" (primarily the husband in the case of some Romance language countries, and the father and brothers in the Arabic culture).

There is a feeling of definiteness and clarity in guilt: a specific person is guilty of a particular action. There is no such definiteness in the case of shame. The situation from which the feeling of shame derives need not be one in which specific misconduct is attributed to the person shamed; moreover shame may be borne not only by the persons directly involved, but also by their kin, or by a grouping defined in some other manner to which the shamed individuals belong. Clearly, then, shame is associative and guilt abstractive.

The degree to which a culture uses one or the other of these means of social control—and no culture known presents an absolutely pure case of one or the other—is one of the indications of the place of that culture on the associative–abstractive continuum.

Some similarities

There are considerable similarities between the ways in which Beduins are described by urban Arabs, all Arabs by non-Arabs, Corsicans by continental Frenchmen, Sicilians by other Italians, Andalusians by other Spaniards, all Spaniards and Latin Americans by English-speaking peoples, village Greeks by Athenians, and even Scottish Highlanders by Scottish Lowlanders. All such descriptions insist on the inflated importance of honor, both the strictly individual and that attributed to the group.

> The Arab is ruled by a strange pride which he calls *sharaf* and which he values almost above life itself. Scold an Arab or call him ugly names, and he is ready to knife you. His temper explodes to the limit when his honor has been attacked. (Hamady, 1960)

Honorable behavior includes the obligation of hospitality pushed to the extreme, often beyond what the host can afford, and to which he feels obligated even in regard to strangers. When meals are served to the guests, the host often refrains from eating with them, but ostensibly serves them, and eats later, with the servants.

> It is rare to visit an Arab village without being impressed by the courtesy and the hospitality which is extended to you, and which bewilders and embarrasses you when you both know and see the background against which it is offered. The children may cry "backsheesh" on the roads, but the fellah would be deeply insulted if you tried to pay him, however obliquely, for giving to you, not as an Englishman, or a European, or as anything but a visitor, the very best that he can offer. . . . You would have it whether you wanted it or not, and whether you arrived in bare feet or a Rolls Royce. . . .
>
> In hospitality, as in everything else, the Arab carries his virtues to fantastic extremes. (Hamady, 1960)

Another trait shared by most of the cultures presented at the beginning of this section—with the conspicuous exception of the Scots—is an extreme double standard in sexual matters.

It may be noted that all the cultures mentioned in this section, with the exception of the most central one, that of the Arabs, are made of people who are participants but not always full participants in a broader culture. They find themselves in an intermediate position in regard to some of the identity-defining processes described earlier in this study. They are no longer fully defined by kinship, since the broader culture has largely abandoned kinship in favor of role as the main identifying characteristic, and they are not yet defined by a combination of roles, since their subculture has not yet reached the stage which was called that of "a society of strangers" in an earlier chapter.

The description above does not apply to the Arabic culture in general, even though it does apply to the Beduin culture, which many settled or even urbanized Arabs consider as an ideal to be emulated. As for the Arabic culture in general it did move beyond the kinship stage during its period of greatness, after which it turned its back on the abstractive process and returned to an exaltation of tradition and to loyalty to the endogamous patrilineages as principal source of identity.

Epithets such as "intermediate" or "transitional" may be applied to such cultural constellations, as long as one sets aside the implication of ephemerality which they contain. Otherwise, honor and sensitivity about such an implication may be explained as a compensation or overcompensation for the anxiety the individual feels about his own identity:

> The Arab is characterized by an inflated personality. He shows overt self-confidence, challenges and menaces everyone. . . . He promises more than he can give or do; he relates fantastic stories about himself and his family, and asserts himself by boasting, without feeling any shame. (Hamady, 1960)

Within the context of such verbal inflation, such a total acceptance or total rejection of other persons, it is not surprising that the Arabs should mistrust any information couched in factual terms and accept only expressions of feeling. They lack the tools of abstraction by which to evaluate the verisimilitude of statements of fact, but are past masters at judging the sincerity and the depth of expressions of friendship. An important American official and an equally important official of one of the Arabic countries were discussing American aid in an atmosphere of great cordiality. At one moment the American informed his counterpart of the amounts of expected American aid. The Arab became frigid and uneasy; though the amounts were favorable, the very fact of dealing with precise figures disconcerted him and made him feel distrustful. Sensing this, the American official simply reaffirmed that he was acting as a friend. This brought back a feeling of mutual trust; the conversation had been returned to a familiar terrain.

It must be emphasized that the above does not apply only to Arabs. All cultures can be described according to their relative orientation towards people (subjective), orientation towards ideas (co-subjective), and orientation towards action (objective).

"Individual" orientation and "action" orientation

Several authors, and in particular Stewart (1971), describe the American culture as being "individual" oriented. At first glance, this would come closer to the "person" orientation as described in the preceding section, rather than to the "action" orientation, which was assigned as an American characteristic. The contradiction is more apparent than real.

The word "individual" may be taken in two different manners. On one hand, "individual" may stand for the total person, including the nexus of social attachments—family, religion, ethnic group, etc.—which everyone carries to a greater or lesser extent. On the other hand, insistence on the rights and the freedom of the individual may mean the favoring of the free play of individual efforts, by which the subject seeks to reach his or her individual goal. It is in this second sense that the American culture is individual oriented; such an interpretation of the individual orientation as the freedom for each person to pursue the course of action from which will result his self-identification is clearly equivalent to "action" orientation.

To take the individual as a total person can not only be defined as "person" orientation, but as involving the human matrices of the individuals concerned.

> The existence of . . . clear distinctions between ingroup and outgroup makes the Greeks appear to be extremely suspicious when they first meet strangers. The newcomer has to be classified and until this happens he remains in limbo. If he is classified in the outgroup, all kinds of competitive and unfair play are 'par for the course'. If he is classified in the ingroup, all kinds of help are likely to come his way.
>
> Thus the self-concept of normal achieving Greek adolescents is characterized by dependency on others and by questions concerning their own effectiveness. At the same time the ideal of the hero . . . requires achievement, fame and immortality. Furthermore, the social status of the Greek woman is very low unless and until she is the mother of an achiever. Thus there are great pressures on mothers to "push" their sons to achieve. As a result most Greek mothers are prone to make unrealistic efforts to increase their sons' self-esteem. Greek mothers tend to tell their children that they expect them to become important and to consider them unique. This leads to a facade of self-confidence which could increase exaggerated inner insecurity and lower the self-esteem. (Triandis et al., 1972)

The picture above is in sharp contrast with the American action-oriented insistence on self-reliance. Self-reliance is esteemed even in the context of quite pedestrian and ordinary achievements.

Probably no example shows more clearly the difference between person orientation and action (or task orientation) than the relationships between American employers and their Greek employees.

> As an example, some Americans complained, in interviews with Triandis, that they get little cooperation from their Greek maids and other servants. On the other hand, some other Americans were enthusiastic about the cooperation, honesty and devotion of their servants. What seemed to be the difference between these two kinds of American was whether they included the servants in their "extended family" or simply treated them as belonging to "another group." When the servant was made part of the family, the *philotimo* principle required sacrifice to help the family. Under such circumstances stealing never occurred, but when the family was in the servants "outgroup" stealing was quite likely. (Triandis et al., 1972)

The immersion of Arabs in their human matrices, generally the family, is much stronger than in the case of the Greeks. Within the family

it may be said that the Arab has not attained full individuation as a person. (Hamady, 1960)

On the material side,

in urban areas, private property is common. Yet, even here members of the immediate family, in particular brothers, keep their property joint. (Hamady, 1960)

This is only an indication of a situation in which the individual still

lacks complete formation of his personality with respect to his emancipation from home, [and] has yet to be weaned from his family, [of which] he still is a nondifferentiated part. (Hamady, 1960)

Conclusions

The cultures presented in this chapter differ in many aspects. Yet the pressure upon them of the highly abstractive cultures of the western family has for effect to emphasize one characteristic which they seem to have in common as opposed to the abstractivity of the western cultures, namely that they appear strongly associative because of the contrast.

Another characteristic that nonwestern cultures have in common and which they share with some strata of the western cultures is a common co-subjective and universalistic attitude prevalent among many of the modernizing elements within them, particularly the western-educated youth.

This is clearly indicated by Szalay's comparison between Korean and American students (Szalay et al., 1971). The following anecdote illustrates the kind of mis-communication which can arise when the co-subjective universalism of modernizing youth comes into contact with the neo-particularistic objectivism of the more advanced elements of western cultures.

A group of American university professors had just returned from India where they had been teaching under the Fullbright exchange program. A conference was arranged with a group of professors about to leave for India on a similar assignment. The returning scholars said that one of the greatest difficulties they had to face was gaining the respect of their students. Indian students seem to expect that intellectually respectable scholars should have a dogmatic position on all pertinent questions, which they must be ready to defend these positions in discussions with the class. The American teachers felt that this approach went against what they conceived to be academic honesty, which required from them first of all a presentation of the data, and only later the development of theoretical hypotheses compatible with the data.

After some discussion, a suggestion was presented to the group on their way to India: that they state as a dogmatic principle that one should always approach the field of study with an open mind, free of any dogmatic preconceptions, so as to make it possible to judge the data impartially and to be guided by them in the elaboration of any theoretical synthesis. Reports of the group which used this approach showed that it was often successful in establishing the proper attitude of mutual respect between teachers and students.

The approach recommended often strikes American audiences as being a slightly dishonest ploy. It is nothing of the kind, but simply a dogmatic presentation of an empiricist position. The point is that the Indian students accepted such a dogmatic presentation, while they had rejected the simple presentation of facts and conclusions reached in particular cases by the application of the universal principle.

Such a search for a dogma is characteristic of many modernizing thinkers in nonwestern cultures. An extremely interesting example of this pattern of thought can be found in an interview of a Palestinian intellectual, F. Kaddoui, which appeared in *Newsweek* (Chesnoff, 1976).

> K.: . . . The final settlement as far as we are concerned is a secular, democratic state of Palestine.
> Ch.: This clearly implies no right for Israel to exist. Why should the Israelis accept that?
> K.: With time they will have to accept this. In the meantime, the first right to exist is Palestinian. We exist because we are dispersed across the world without an entity of our own. Israel is a Jewish Zionist state. This means that there is no tolerance on our part for Israel because there is an ideological conflict. They have a racist, theocratic ideology. We have our open, democratic ideology.
> Ch.: Is there any open, democratic society in the Arab world today comparable to the one you want to establish?
> K.: Any Arab state is more democratic than Israel *by definition* [italics added].
> Ch.: Saudi Arabia, for example?
> K.: Even Saudi Arabia. . . . If we are to maintain peace, it will have to be in a Palestine where Jews, Muslims and Christians live together.

The most striking part of the exchange is the expression "by definition." This is an expression used mainly in mathematics, in order to define and render manageable to the mind entities such as points without dimensionality and lines and planes without thickness, even though none such were ever observed in reality. Physical reality, however, is not what mathematics deals with, even though it can be applied to the study of reality by abstracting the relevant characteristics of the object. For example, an expression such as $5 = 5$ is mathematically true. On the other hand an expression such as 5 apples $=$ 5 apples is not a mathematical statement at all: counting is mathematically defined, but apples are not. The truth or falsity of this expression can be determined only by inspection: Good apples and rotten ones are not the same things even if they bear the same names. Statements based on definitions are co-subjective, in the sense that they determine a common manner of thinking. But the thinking in question is likely to lead to cultural regression if it is not checked against objective reality.

What now is the objective reality in this case? Israel has a multiparty system in which power is won or lost by elections; those Arabs who chose to remain in Israel have the right to vote and have elected representatives in the legislative body. On the other hand, Saudi Arabia is an absolute monarchy, and the establishment of the secular state according to the program of the Palestine Liberation Organization is to be accompanied by the expulsion from Palestine of all those who settled in it "after the Zionist invasion," a date which is generally interpreted as that of the Balfour declaration in 1917.

What we have in this case is an attempt at a co-subjective and logical organization of purely subjective feelings. This can be partly successful, as shown by the acceptance by the General Assembly of the United Nations of the "definition" of Zionism as racism. It cannot be fully successful, because it cannot be accepted either by those who are its victims, or by those whose patterns of thought take into account objective reality rather than arbitrary definitions.

Yet even if full success must elude those who disregard the objectivistic apex and try to base their communication on syntheses between subjectivity and co-subjectivity, the degree of their success may be quite considerable. In particular an approach such as Marxism, replete with definitions and deductions from subjectivity and co-subjectivity, may take hold of the minds of people whose cultures are in the process of rapid transformation more easily than does the basically—and purposefully—disorganized approach of the empirical and pragmatic method which doubts definitive systems of explanations. It is such doubt that underlies democracy and makes it unattractive to peoples whose certainties were shattered by culture contact and who search feverishly for new certainties to replace those they have lost.

It may be useful at this point to bring in an example concerning the Soviet Union.

In the late fifties and early sixties there appeared in the Western press descriptions of the increasing social inequality and stratification in the Soviet Union. The descriptions in question were precisely that: descriptions based on observation of the different patterns of life in Russia, based on such items as earning power, access to privileged stores, housing, social interaction, etc. The Soviet journal *The New Times* characterized the reports in question as totally false. In doing so, it did not mention anything observable, but stated that (1) everyone knew that social stratification is due to private ownership of the means of production; (2) the tools of production cannot be privately owned in the Soviet Union; and therefore (3) stratification could not possibly take place.

What matters in this case is not so much the truth or falsehood of the accounts in the western press. It is rather the manner of arguing against them. Both in this case and in those noted earlier, the criterion of truth appears to be the one trusted by Plato and later by Descartes: What is true is that which appears clearly and distinctly to the mind—not that which is confirmed by observation or by experimental testing of hypotheses.

From the point of view of the model, these examples suggest indeed that the cultural evolution of belief proceeds from subjectivity towards co-subjectivity, and only later from co-subjective theorizing to the abstractive objectivity of the scientific method.

11

THE WAYS OF THE WEST

THE TWO SOURCES OF WESTERN CULTURE

Seemingly explosive development can be found in the history of all of world's great civilizations. What characterises the West is that it never found the quietude into which other civilizations settled after reaching more or less permanent states of balance. This may be because both of the main sources of what was to become the West, Hebrew and Greek thought, replaced a monistic approach to experience in which the feelings, the dreams, the knowledge, and the work of life mingled in a single stream in which the subjective and the objective were fused together, with a dualism in which thought or hypothesis was opposed to proof or disproof through action. The development of this dualism was not abrupt and automatic; it evolved little by little from obscure roots. The entire process was somewhat ironical. Contemporary thought in the philosophy of science, the philosophy of art, and the psychology of cognition suggests that the separation of subject and object was and is erroneous. Nevertheless, it was precisely this error that was at the origin of the extraordinary creativity of the developing West.

Let us begin with the Hebrew break with earlier and more universal patterns:

> When we read in Psalm XIX that "the heavens declare the glory of God; and the firmament showeth his handiwork," we hear a voice which mocks the beliefs of the Egyptians and Babylonians. The heavens, which were for the psalmist but a witness of God's greatness, were to the Mesopotamians the very majesty of godhead, the highest ruler, Anu. To the Egyptians the heavens signified the mystery of the divine mother through whom man was reborn. In Egypt and Mesopotamia the divine was comprehended as immanent: the gods were in nature. The Egyptians saw in the sun all

273

that man may know of the Creator; the Mesopotamians viewed the sun as the god Shamash, the guarantor of justice. But to the psalmist the sun was God's devoted servant who 'is as a bridegroom coming out of his chamber, and rejoiceth as a strong man to run a race'. The God of the psalmists and the prophets was not in nature. He transcended nature—and transcended, likewise, the realm of mythopoeic thought. It would seem that the Hebrews, no less than the Greeks, broke with the mode of speculation which had prevailed up to their time.

The mainspring of the acts, thoughts and feelings of early man was the conviction that the divine was immanent in nature, and nature intimately connected with society. . . . In the significant moments of life, early man was confronted not by an inanimate, impersonal nature—not by an "It"—but by a "Thou". . . . Such a relationship involved not only man's intellect but the whole of his being—his feeling and his will, no less than his thought. Hence early man would have rejected the detachment of a purely intellectual attitude towards nature, had he been able to conceive it, as inadequate to his experience. . . .

Transcendence implies abstraction: the concept of God and thought about God become freed from the changeable associations of immanence. Permanence is discovered, and with it the desire to seek the invariant under the vagaries of concreteness.

With infinite *moral* courage the Hebrews worshipped an absolute God. . . . In transcending the Near Eastern myths of immanent godhead, they created . . . the new myth of the will of God. It remained for the Greeks, with their peculiar *intellectual* courage, to discover a form of speculative thought in which myth was entirely overcome.

In the sixth century B.C. the Greeks, in their great cities . . . were in touch with all the leading centres of the civilized world; Egypt and Phoenicia; Lydia, Persia and Babylon. There can be no doubt that this contact played some part in the meteoric development of Greek culture. . . .

The Ionian philosophers gave their attention to the problem of origins; but for them it assumed an entirely new character. The origin, the Αρχη means "origin" not as "beginning," but as "sustaining principle" or "first cause."

This change of viewpoint is breathtaking. It transfers the problem of man in nature from the realm of faith and poetic intuition to the intellectual sphere. A critical appraisal of each theory, and hence a continuous inquiry into the nature of reality, became possible. . . .

Yet the doctrines of the early Greek philosophers are not couched in the language of attached systematic reflection. Their sayings sound rather like inspired oracles. . . . The Ionians moved in a curious borderland. They forefelt the possibility of establishing an intelligible coherence in the phenomenal world; yet they were still under the spell of an undissolved relationship between man and nature. . . . Thales, for instance, said that water was the αρχη, the first principle or cause of all things, but he also said: "All things are full of gods. The magnet is alive for it has the power of moving iron. (Frankfort et al., 1964)

The proximity of the early philosophers to myth, and the enormous distance which they succeeded in placing between myth and their thoughts can be shown by another example. The Pythagoreans defined the mathematical concept of the plane. They also had a rule, which they applied with the utmost rigor in their confraternity, that every member, upon arising, had to smooth the sheets of his bed so that no imprint of the sleeper's body would remain seen or felt. This practice is probably tied to a quasi-universal superstition which we have mentioned earlier in connection with Frazer's analyses of magic. To leave an imprint or a severed part of one's body (such as hair or nail-clippings) in such a way that an enemy can act upon them, for example by cutting them with some sharp instrument, is to place oneself in his power. Such a rule was probably used by the Pythagoreans to define an abstraction which could overcome and eliminate the superstition; the rest is geometry and science. It is also, and obviously, abstraction.

Another qualitative jump takes place with Socrates and Plato. It is not only that they (or at least Plato) profess that reality is made up of universal ideas rather than of some ideas such as those of water or of air. It is mainly that they propose a universal epistemological principle, which appears in the passage from the Phaedo quoted earlier: that the search for knowledge should be carried out by reason alone, rejecting as far as it is possible any inputs from sensorial experience. This establishes a criterion of truth, which will be presented here in its Cartesian rather than Platonic formulation: That is true which the mind can conceive clearly and distinctly (Descartes, 1934).

Once again, the main importance of such a precept is that it is controversial. Once the statement is made—but only then—it becomes possible to respond to it, for example by defending the thesis that the only way to learn truth is to rely on rigorous observation or on empirical tests of hypotheses by pragmatic action.

No such statements were possible before a formulation of a radical idealism-universalism. Primitive empiricism, or paleo-particularism is a habit, not a doctrine. It has no clear criteria for distinguishing the experience originating in observation from the experience originating in dream. It lacks such concepts as "everything is . . ." or "the only way to secure reliable knowledge is. . . ." It lacks such concepts mainly because it doesn't need them; truths differ from individual to individual, or from folklore to folklore. We have already mentioned the fact that the religions of the primitives, of the Chinese, the Indians, and the Japanese were never missionary (with the brief exception of the reign of Asoka, India's Buddhist philosopher-emperor, in the third century B.C.). In contrast, the most successful application of the radical idealist precept to trust rigorous reasoning, mathematics, is also at least potentially the most universally acceptable system of thought.

A historical note may be added to the examination of the relative anteriority of idealism and empiricism, mainly because the latter tends to appear to many people in "our" cultures as the self-evident truth. Aristotle recognized induction, which leads us from experience to the determination of the true and necessary universals. Nevertheless, the core of his teaching is deductive logic, that is to say the reasoned manipulation of concepts. Aristotle was, of course, a former student of Plato, whom he followed by the span of a generation.

The first thoroughgoing critique of universalistic idealism was the medieval quarrel of the universals, which took place in the twelfth and thirteenth centuries. Platonic realists, such as William of Champeaux, held that universal ideas represented genuine reality (which is why these idealists called themselves realists, a name which they have retained in the history of philosophy). Their opponents, the nominalists, held that it was particular things, which could be sensed, seen or touched, that were real; universals were mere names, or at most concepts. Roscelinus, Abélard, and William of Occam are representative of this group, over fifteen hundred years after Plato. Probably the first codification of empiricism was Locke's *An Essay on Human Understanding*, which appeared in 1690. A more basic statement of abstractive rationalism, Descartes' *Discourse on Method,* had appeared half a century earlier.

The polar opposition between these two works may be used to set the tone for an analysis of the cultural differences within the western family of cultures: It is the polarity between universalistic co-subjectivity and neo-particularistic objectivity.

Two apexes, a median point, and their filiation

A first point to be reiterated is that no culture represents any part of the model in its purity. All of the cognitive characteristics of the pure model are represented in every culture, but (as it was stated earlier) in different proportions and different arrangements.

Second, the three submodels selected for description in this chapter exhibit a much higher degree of abstractive thought than did many of the cultures mentioned earlier. Yet each of them retains perforce a significant amount of associative attitudes.

As mentioned earlier, universalistic co-subjectivity is the earliest abstractive type of cultural organization to emerge from the associative matrix. This emergence is due to an intellectual critique of associative belief. Here again Plato may be used as an example. More generally, the transformation in the direction of abstractive, universalistic co-subjectivity may be viewed as a cultural revolution:

> The immediate sign of a revolutionary change in his [man's] mentality is the great names which have come down from that period [from about 800 to about 200 B.C.] Almost all the well-known names before it are the names of kings and conqueroros, and of their gods. Now we hear of great individuals of a very different kind: Zaroaster, Buddha, Confucius and Lao-tse; Amos, Jeremiah, and Isaiah; Homer, Thales, Solon, Aeschylus, Socrates, Plato, and a hundred other Greeks. Together they represent the most extraordinary creative era in man's history between the rise of civilization and the rise of modern science. The era made a mark on every great society thereafter, and provided standards by which we judge all previous societies. (Muller, 1961)

The common denominator of all these intellectual movements is that they were characterized not by discovery but by reform and a critique of all that came immediately before them.

> The advance represented by such loftier spirituality is plainer because it signified as well a growth of rationality. Thought was much freer, more conscious, and more critical. Above all, it was no longer governed by myth. . . . The founders all defied universal, timeless tradition, when they did not—like Buddha—attack point-blank the tyranny of the reigning superstition. (Muller, 1961)

Interestically enough, a good appreciation of the scope of this reform or rather of the need for it, may be derived from another discipline, psychology, in a quotation from the work of Vygotsky (1962):

> In genuine concept formation, it is equally important to unite and to separate: Synthesis must be compared with analysis. Complex thinking cannot do both. Its very essence is overabundance, overproduction of connections and weakness in abstraction.

Association leads to accumulation; in vigorous and well-developed associative cultures this accumulation was reaching chaotic proportions. Then reform came. In Anaxagoras words "all things were in chaos when Mind arose and made order." Yet no matter how well the abstractive–universalistic critique operates on the legacy of associationism, the latter is never completely eliminated. It isn't only that there remain the less-educated layers of society, on whom abstraction has little hold. It is also that the critique bears on public notions, thus not only ignoring but even freeing the entire area of personal feelings and even of community formation, as long as the communities in question abide by the dictates of society and do not come into competition with it.

It was already indicated in the chapter on political implications that Eastern Europe on the one hand and the Iberic countries on the other may be used as examples of universlistic co-subjectivism. We shall return to this question (presenting it with some reservations) in the next section. In the meanwhile we will turn to some of the broad characteristics of abstractive neo-particularism.

Abstractive neo-particularism derives from the critique of a critique. It does not seek to organize and generalize the raw material of the accumulation of associative culture. Instead, it seeks to criticize the universals of the verbal, symbolic, and conceptualized structure of co-subjectivity. It does not do so for trivial reasons. Only where the universal concept interferes with unavoidably particularized action (which this very concept may have suggested in the first place) does the critique of universals takes place. And, once more, this critique does not aim at the rejection of universals, but only at their subordination to objective operations, in such a way that they serve as hypotheses of which action provides a verification, a disproof, or a need for refinement and adjustment.

The criticism of those universals that suggest action, often means a neglect of those that do not. The mind of the neo-particularist is not systematic, except in areas which concern directly his schemata of action. The Anglo Saxons (from which most of the examples of neo-particularism will be drawn) were until recently, and to a large extent still are, the only countries to resist the introduction of the metric system; even though, *taken as a system* it is infinitely more convenient than the British system, which is why it is used in the science departments of American universities. On the other side, however, a tailor or even a specialized engineer does not deal with whole systems, but only with practical measurements. In his context the meter is neither better nor worse than the foot; he might as well stick to the one to which he and his customers are used.

The behavioral distance between the universalistic and the neo-particularistic or nominalistic apexes is sufficiently great to justify the schematic description of an approach which would fall between these two apexes, as compromise or possibly as synthesis. This schema of behavior will be called relational.*; the gist of relationality being sus-

---

*The word "relational" is used here in an entirely different meaning from the one it has in the work of R. A. Cohen, who gives to "relational" a meaning very similar to the one given here to "associative." The use of "relational" in some of my previous publications has prevented me from reconciling my vocabulary with Cohen's.

tained attempts at reconciling the indications of theory and those of practice, at limiting action to what can be rationally explained, and more generally at establishing relations between universals and particulars.

The culture which comes the closest to the relational ideal is the French one. Other European cultures may be distributed along the line between the co-subjective and the objective apexes, without forgetting that no matter what degree of abstraction is achieved by a culture, associative subjectivity always retains a considerable hold on the minds and behaviors of people.

Some aspects of the Russian culture

A number of examples of the Soviet belief in the existence of only one solution to the problems of life, and at that of an absolutely true solution derived from doctrinal rather than observational considerations were presented in the chapter on the political implications of the model. It is useful at this point to present similar conclusions drawn from another source.

The Bolshevik concept of the Party Line sums up the doctrine that the policy making group knows the "correct" course to take. Krupskaya, Lenin's widow, said at the 14th Party Congress in 1925:

"For us, Marxists, truth is that which corresponds to reality. Vladimir Il'ich (Lenin) said: The teachings of Marx are immovable because they are true, and our congress should concern itself with searching for and finding the correct line. It is impossible to reassure ourselves with the fact that the majority is always right. In the history of our party there were congresses in which the majority was not right. . . . The majority should not get drunk with the idea that it is the majority, but should disinterestedly search for a true decision. If it will be true it will put our party on the right path."

The line, as understood by the policy-making group, represents absolute Truth; therefore, while temporary retreat before a strong enemy may be necessary and in fact dictated by the Line itself, true compromise—in the Western sense—is not comprehensible to the Bolshevik leadership. As one American negotiator reported in an unpublished memorandum:

During negotiations they feel that appeals to public opinion are just a bluff. If American public opinion is contrary to what they want to do, our government or some hidden body, a 'capitalist Politbureau' must be manipulating it. We think of compromise as a natural way to get on with the job, but to them 'compromise' is usually coupled with the adjective 'rotten'. They are puzzled by our emphasis on the desirability of compromise. They think we can be pushed around when we propose compromises prematurely, i.e. before they have fully tested the firmness of our position. When we or the British advance a series of compromises, we confuse them by changing our position so often."

The Anglo-American idea of political compromise is based on the expectation of there being at least two sides to a question, so that a workable compromise represents a position somewhere between or among a series of positions each of which is sincerely believed and stoutly defended. But the Bolshevik idea of the Line is more accurately represented by the figure of a lens which is correctly focused; there is only one correct focus for any given situation, and this is not seen as arrived at by finding some midpoint between lens readings which are too open and those which are too closed; rather, all settings except the correct focus are seen as deviations from the single correct position. (Mead, 1966)

Correctness is more easily reached in thought and words than it is in action; action must confront the stubbornness of the environment. In consequence the belief in there being fully determined and absolutely correct solutions to the problems of life, rather than mere approximations and compromises, leads to placing the main emphasis on words rather than on actions. From the point of view of the model, this means emphasis on the co-subjective apex, the one at which full agreement and full conformity are the easiest to reach, through disregard for both the particularity of subjective behavior and the imperfection of human knowledge in respect to the world of objective reality.

Such a primacy of the verbal over the real is a characteristic not only of communism, but of the Russian culture as such. The following excerpt was written under the Tsarist regime, in the first half of the nineteenth century:

Peter the Great promised [Russia an outlet on the sea]; he opened to her the Gulf of Finland without perceiving that a sea necessarily closed eight months out of the year is not the same thing as other seas. But *labels are everything for the Russians* [italics added]. (Custine, 1951)

More generally, the history of Russia has followed a revolutionary rhythm well in keeping with co-subjective universalism. In such a rhythm periods during which the government seeks to prevent any change alternate with periods of total reconstruction. The latter often take the form of revolutions from above; the changes are brought about by the country's rulers. This applies to revolutionary tsars, such as Ivan the Dread or Peter the Great, as well as to Lenin and Stalin. The Bolsheviks seized power through the appeal of the promises of peace and of distribution of land among the peasants; once in power they collectivized the land through a revolution from above, against the resistance of much of the peasantry.

The concept of revolutionary tsardom calls for some illustrations. We can begin with Ivan the Dread's entail, *oprichnina*, a state within the state, which Ivan could bring into total subservience.

The new system he [Ivan or John] set up was madness, but the madness of a genius. He had failed to find support in men of the middle class. He would now walk out of the whole system as it stood, leaving it in existence but taking with him all the resources of power. Let the boyars go on with the ordinary work of administration; he appointed two of them of whom he had no reason to be afraid. But outside the normal State, as a kind of personal possession, or, if you like, as a kind of supreme police control, lay the *Oprichnina*, the Apart, the Peculium—the word was derived from the term used to describe a wife's or a widow's portion. Here John was supreme and unquestioned; the *Oprichniki* swore an oath that allowed neither God nor man to come before his commands. "Set apart" were to be any domains that John might care to claim; they amount in the end to about half of the realm; Moscow itself was divided between the two. In this reshuffling of all property, John astutely took for the *Oprichnina* those regions, especially in the North and centre, which still preserved nominal principalities of their own and rights of local jurisdiction. The *Oprichnina* had its own special court, its ministerial offices, its own army, its own special police—at first one thousand and later six thousand in number. The *Oprichnik* police rode on black horses and were clad in black, carrying a dog's head at their saddle-bow and a broom as the emblem that they were to clear the land of robbery. The *Zemshchina* (the other half of the country) was later mocked by John with a separate sovereign, and his choice fell upon a Tartar prince who had accepted Christianity, to whom John made a mock obeisance and gave the title of Prince of All Russia, contenting himself with the modest title of Prince of Moscow. John returned for a time to the armed suburb which he now established for himself in Moscow, but later lived in the Alexandrovskoe monastery, alternating between orgies of license and repentances half mocking and half sincere, in which, dressed as a monk, he would take part in Church services, read to his riotous company about the virtues of temperance as preface to a night of feasting and drunkenness, now delighting in torturing prisoners, now beating his head against the church floor in contrition, now praying for his thousands of victims—"whose names, O Lord, Thou Thyself knowest." (Pares, 1937)

The reforms of Peter the Great had none of the madness of Ivan; they were practical in their approach to reality. But his revolution from above was no less total and even more comprehensive. It penetrated every nook and cranny of social life, establishing a new centralized bureaucratic structure, prescribing compulsory education for the sons of the gentry, and forbidding the gentry to wear beards.

In future birth was to count for absolutely nothing, rank was to be given according to efficiency, and rank alone was to determine a man's status in society. All officers became gentry. Peter completed the formation of a huge and motley service-class of various origins swamping the remains of the old nobility. . . . State service was compulsory for all. A table of ranks was drawn up in three parallel columns representing respectively the military, the civil and the court services, in which grades corresponded throughout. Those in the first eight grades automatically became gentry. Peter had his hands on the children of the gentry from the age of ten, when their names had to be reported; and the adult gentry had to present themselves for periodical reviews. The punishment for absence was the loss·of all civil rights; defaulters could not invoke government protection against robbery.

The gentry were required not only to serve but also to train themselves for service. (Pares, 1937)

Immediate needs were subordinated to eternal perfection even under tsars lacking the strong personalities of Ivan or of Peter.

In Russia at that time everything was sacrificed to the future; they were building monuments, magnificent to excess, for the following generations. The constructors of so many superb public buildings, without feeling the need of luxury for themselves, were content with the role of scouts of civilization, far ahead of the unknown potentates for whom they were proud to build the city, while expecting that their successors would come to inhabit and embellish it. Certainly there is grandeur of soul in this solicitude of a chief and his people for the power and even for the vanity of generations yet to be born. The confidence of living men in the glory of their remotest descendents holds something noble and original. It is a disinterested and poetic sentiment far above the ordinary respect of·men and nations for their forefathers. (Custine, 1951)

In circumstances under which a more objective frame of mind would lead to the abandonment of the theory or the mental vision, Russians often stage ritual events which have the appearance of conformity with the mental expectation.

In Tsarist Russia there were attempts to give an appearance of reality and solidity to matters of dubious truth, as in the great insistence on written confessions as early as the seventeenth century or in the Potemkin villages specially set up to satisfy the demands of Catherine the Great for speedy development of the newly acquired province of Novorussiya.

These earlier customs of theatrical enactment of that which was desired by those in power or by their subordinates have become very marked characteristics of the Soviet regime. In Bolshevik doctrine, what the leadership decides shall be done is what History has already ordained is going to happen (although it is also what needs the utmost effort to make it happen). Hence, any gap between what is ordered and what occurs is proportionally less bearable. Although Bolshevik doctrine also includes stern exhortations to sobriety and recognition of facts as "stubborn things,"

and although romantic overoptimism is one of the condemned characteristics of the Left, nevertheless a great quantity of falsification and theatrical
enactments of the ardently desired or deeply feared do occur.

The acceptance of falsification shows itself in the sort of reports which
are passed through channels in a bureaucracy reporting overfulfillment
of a plan, when the overfulfillment of, for example, the readiness of the
machines in a Machine Tractor Station is of such a nature that half of the
tractors may break down within a week. The Machine Tractor Station will,
however, already have celebrated its overfulfillment and the appropriate
higher levels will have been able to include its success in the report of their
successes. Although bureaucratic conditions are particularly favorable to
the tendency to believe what is most comfortable to believe, this particular
type of belief goes to special lengths in the Soviet Union. As so many
reports are concerned with real events—the amount of grain harvested,
the number of trucks turned out by a factory—false reporting has very
real repercussions in actuality and so can be branded as sabotage, the
possibility of such repercussions hardly discourages the practice of inaccurate reporting.

The falsification takes many forms, even within a single factory. One
informant described his wife's experience: she worked in a silk artel which
listed itself as a whole as overfulfilling the plan by 110 percent, when
actually the plan had been only 65 percent fulfilled. Within this artel, his
wife's unit had actually overfulfilled by 250 percent, but this was only
credited as 121 percent since over 120 percent warranted a premium.
Such attempts to establish groups in which the weak can lean on the strong,
as when one kholkhoz borrows from another, are very frequently reported.
(Mead, 1966)

The Iberic and the Slavic cultures contrast and more simply
differ from many points of view. However a deductive pattern characteristic of co-subjective universalism is present in both these families
of cultures. Some of the consequences of this attitude can be brought
out by comparing the establishment of cities in the Spanish and the
English colonies in America. Recourse to large-scale planning may be
due not only to human preferences, but also to the nature of the circumstances. Not only Petrograd and Brazilia, but also Washington and
Canberra were built along the principle of plan first, city later.

Yet differences between the Iberic and the English ways out-
weigh similarities. In the Spanish lands, the *cabildo* gave legitimacy to
the claims of the band of *conquistadores* who established it by tying their
enterprise to the system of the crown; this discouraged and weakened
rival claimants. In the English colonies, the township's status had nothing
in common with that of the boroughs of the Realm; it was a local creation
aiming at providing local services.

In Latin America,

the basic instrument of royal authority was the *cabildo* or city council. The Spaniards, true to the Roman tradition, had long exalted the city (more accurately the city-state, with a considerable area dominated by the municipal center); Spanish America followed the same tradition, magnifying the city to a degree unfamiliar to those of English heritage. This difference is described by Bernard Moses: "In the English colonies of America, the town grew to meet the needs of the inhabitants of the country but in the Spanish colonies, the population of the country grew to meet the needs of the town." It was therefore consonant with Spanish tradition that Columbus, after landing upon Hispaniola, should lay out the ill-fated settlement of Navidad; that Balboa should found Darien; that Cortez should establish Veracruz; that Pizarro should celebrate victory by erecting the City of the Kings—Lima; and that Valdivia, while still threatened by the Araucanians, should organize the city of Santiago. (Herring, 1961)

In all those cases, the cities were established and magistrates appointed before any settlement existed, by soldiers on the march.

Then we gave [Cortez] the very fullest powers in the presence of the King's notary, Diego de Godoy. . . . We at once set to work to found and settle a town, which was called the Villa Rica de la Vera Cruz because we arrived on Thursday of the Last Supper and landed on Holy Friday of the Cross. . . . As soon as the town was founded we appointed *alcaldes* and *regidores*. (Diaz del Castillo, 1956)

With all that, no houses were built and the expedition moved on shortly. When the city of Veracruz finally became a reality, it was some years later and at some distance from the place of founding. Truly the universal—the city-at-law—came before the thing.

It might be useful to present North American usage by way of contrast. In Indiana,

Wherever one pioneer settled, others followed. In this manner "neighborhoods" and "communities" were established. Solon Robinson, one of the earlier pioneers in Lake County where he settled in 1834, described as follows . . . the recent history of that establishment: ". . . in 1833 a white family settled near the river mouth . . . and opened an inn. In the spring of 1834, another family came and put another inn along the trail. In the summer of 1834, most of the county was surveyed and the pioneers began to record their claims. Four or five families settled in the fall. One of the men started to build a mill. . . .

"The first school was opened by widow Holton at her home. There were three pupils.

"In the spring of 1836, a post office was opened at the request of the inhabitants; the county was divided into three townships, and each selected a justice of the peace. . . ."

Every common activity, whether economic (mill, sawmill, smithy, store), religious (church), cultural (school) or administrative (courthouse) usually became a center of polarization within the diffuse entity of the county, and, as a rule, the nucleus of a village. (d'Haucourt, 1961)

Even today, Silver Spring, the second largest urban community in the state of Maryland, is not incorporated and has no municipal identity of its own. Clearly (to the extent to which these examples are representative) what comes first in English America is the thing; the universal comes later, if at all.

The Latin American tendency toward substituting words for actions has been noted in the chapter on the political implications of the model. Similar tendencies are noted in regard to Russians.

We can give an internally consistent, although limited, account of the traditional Russian character structure, which developed individuals prone to extreme swings in mood from exhilaration to depression, hating confinement and authority, and yet feeling that strong external authority was necessary to keep their own violent impulses in check. In this traditional character, thought and action were so interchangeable that there was a tendency for all effort to dissipate itself in talk or in symbolic behavior. While there was a strong emphasis on the need for certain kinds of control—by government, by parents and teachers—this control was seen as imposed from without; lacking it, the individual would revert to an original impulsive and uncontrolled state. Those forms of behavior which involve self-control rather than endurance, measurement rather than unstinting giving or taking, or calculation rather than immediate response to a situation were extremely undeveloped. The distinction between the individual and the group and between the self and others were also less emphasized than in the West. (Mead, 1966)

The character structure described above is primarily that of the traditional Russian rather than that of "the new Soviet man." From the point of view of the model, it falls somewhere between the subjective and the co-subjective apexes, with few of the skills called for in the handling of more objective problems. Subjectivism, however, is frowned upon by Soviet leadership. The passage to follow shows how Soviet education instills a sense of responsibility—and also of conformity:

Now let us look more closely at this teacher-mediated monitoring process. In the beginning, we are told, the first grade teacher attempts to focus the attention of children on the achievements of the group; that is, she accentuates the positive. But gradually, "It becomes necessary to take account of negative facts which interfere with the activity of the class." As an example we are given the instance of a child, who despite warnings, continues to arrive in class a few minutes after the bell has rung. The teacher decides that the time has come to invoke the group process in correcting such behavior. Accordingly, the next time that Serezha is late, she stops him at the door and turns to the class with this question: "Children, is it helpful or not helpful to us to have Serezha come in late?" The answers are quick in coming. "It interferes." "He ought to come on time." "Well," says the teacher, "How can we help Serezha with this problem?" There are many suggestions: get together to buy him a watch, exile him from the classroom, send him to the director's office, or even exile him from the school. But apparently these proposals are either inappropriate or too extreme. The teacher, our text tells us, "helps the children to *find the right answer*" [italics added]. She asks for a volunteer to stop by and pick Serezha up on the way to school. Many children offer to help in this mission. (Bronfenbrenner, 1970)

The socialization process, one example of which was summarized above, may lead to rigidity and even compulsiveness. It is nevertheless far from being without its good points, especially if one bears in mind that the personality structure it is destined to modify has many anarchistic traits, or, in another order of ideas, that the freedom prematurely introduced in the American system may amount to adult neglect of the children's psychological needs.

However, the italicized sentence in the description stands out as an example of the cultural differences between the U.S.S.R. and the U.S. The phrase suggests that there exists *one right solution* to the problems outlined.

Before exploring the implications of this phrase in other fields of endeavor, it may be useful to describe another facet of the relationship between children and adults. In the Soviet Union, if a child temporarily separated from parents or guardians is caught misbehaving, *any adult*, even a total stranger, feels that it is his or her right and duty to admonish the child. The acceptance of such a practice shows a widespread agreement as to what is good and what is bad in children's actions, and more generally in the code of ethics.

Let us return to the question of *one true solution*. A few years ago a conference on housing sponsored by the Economic and Social Council of the United Nations gathered at the headquarters of this organization. As is often the case in conferences of this type, the major powers sent as representatives their experts in the field concerned. The minor Third World nations lacked experts in the field of the conference and also the money to hire any. In consequence, they were represented by relatively junior diplomats, drawn from the offices of their permanent representatives in the U.N. Shortly after the beginning of the conference, the U.S.S.R. and the U.S. found themselves at loggerheads. The Soviet expert suggested that *the right way* to cope with housing shortages was to increase the use of prestressed concrete. The American delegate agreed that there were cases in which this approach would be useful, but at the same time he argued that there was no unique right solution, but that the particular characteristics of each situation had to be taken into account before deciding on the solution which would appear the most promising in each case.

The attitudes of the Third World diplomats were in general extremely interesting, even though somewhat marginal to the question under consideration at this moment. The majority of these delegates considered the Soviet point of view as being friendly towards them, and the American point of view as being inimical. One of those concerned stated the question in the following terms: "The Russians want us to adopt the solution which has worked for them; this means that they consider us as brothers. The Americans say that what they do themselves may not be applicable to us; this means that they look at us with contempt." The orientation expressed by such statements is clearly subjective. Positions deriving from technical and economic considerations are mistaken for declarations of human feelings; the difference between relevant and irrelevant is not perceived.

Let us return to the contrasts between the co-subjective universalism of Russians and the objective neo-particularism of Americans. In meetings between Americans who do not belong to the diplomatic profession and Soviet Russians, the former often ask how the existence of a single party regime can be reconciled with a desire for freedom. The usual answer Russians give to this query is "why have more than one party, if that party is right?"

Another incident goes further into the analysis of underlying attitudes. One of the persons involved was a Pole, a member of the Communist Party who had travelled extensively in the United States within the context of one of the official exchange of persons programs. The other participant was an American in whose car the conversation took place, in the course of a sightseeing tour of Washington. After expressing several flattering opinions concerning the United States, the Pole said that frankness compelled him to condemn American commercial radio, the programs of which are in bad taste, decadent, and likely to prevent people from acquiring an ear for the great musical masterpieces mankind had produced. The American, instead of replying, turned on his car radio; what was heard was a beautiful rendition of a relatively seldom heard classical composition.

The Pole asked how did the American know that this kind of music would be played at that time. The American answered that he did not know it specifically, but that the station to which he was tuned played classical music twenty-four hours a day. The conversation continued for a few minutes about programming, with the visitor expressing his admiration and stating that the Polish radio did not offer a correspondingly highbrow fare. Then the Pole asked: "Who listens to this station?" After the usual whoever wants to, the American remembered the recently published content of a survey, and said that the listeners of this station on an average made more money and were more educated than the cross section of the American public. "You see," said the Pole, "you do nothing for the people. Those who are educated and have a properly developed musical sense are given the possibility to listen to this marvellous music, but you let the plain people wallow in the decadent and the ugly. How can you expect that they will acquire more cultured tastes, unless you force them to listen at least part of the day to classical music?"

In order to understand the cultural gap exemplified by this anecdote one should avoid a rush to judgment. There are circumstances under which Americans act exactly in accord with the Polish visitor's suggestion. A first example might be a class in music appreciation—although such classes are not generally a part of required curricula and can be avoided by those who want no part of them. The situation is different in regard to arithmetic: In classes of arithmetic it becomes compulsory for the young students to accept and to learn publicly defined truths rather than personal preferences—$3 \times 3 = 9$ and not 10.

More generally speaking, society imposes its beliefs in those areas in which it is convinced that it is right, and leaves to democratic choice those areas of human thought in which it has not firmed up a doctrine.

The important point is that the scope of what is considered amenable to public reason rather than to private taste differs greatly from culture to culture. East Europeans may consider as determinate and determined not only musicology but also politics. Americans consider mathematics determinate (without, in general being aware of the limitations of mathematical axiomatic systems) but seldom accept an extension of this area of determinacy, even to areas such as economics.

I remember a conversation with several members of the Polish Embassy on board of the Presidential yacht, the Sequoia. The subject was Viet Nam. Speaking with a friendly earnestness, my interlocutors insisted that it was "historically unavoidable" that the North would triumph and the South collapse. When asked what they meant by "historical necessity" these very intelligent and sophisticated men reverted to rather elementary Marxism, surplus value, exploitation, and all. I was by and large in agreement with their conclusions, but not with their reasoning. In my opinion what made the strength of North Viet Nam and of its Southern partisans was not opposition to capitalism, and even less the desire of national independence in the manner in which Americans conceive it, that is to say in an atmosphere relatively free of censorship. What these people rejected, in my opinion, was continued culture contact with the West, i.e., the continuous input of ideas and of goods, not understood in their own light, but disturbing such certainties as were accepted by this time. The greatest attraction of communism for them was its ability to impose censorship. Behind the walls of censorship new cultural certainties could be elaborated without the constant threat of information overload. I could not even begin to voice such considerations to my interlocutors, and all I could see was that events—fortuitously but undeniably—were strengthening their faith in "the identity of thinking and of being" (Pribram, 1945), in other words in the same pattern to which we owe the wars of religion, among others.

The reference to the wars of religion is trite, but it should not be omitted at the risk of missing a deep preoccupation with morality which one finds among many Russians and other East Europeans. This is true at least as long as one speaks with relatively privileged intellectuals—one can also meet many people in whom the constant practice of petty graft has destroyed all moralistic attitudes ("Give me three bottles of vodka and I will find a new tire for your car").

Party dogma should be merely a means for an end. But it is not limited to such a role. A leader of one of the factions of the Italian Socialist Party said that he and his political friends must hurry to break the structure of Italian capitalism before the rising standard of living of the workers robs them of their political following. Obviously (though the example is dated and not applicable to Italy as of this writing), his party's program was not conceived only as a means to improve the welfare of the "working class"; over and above that it sought to achieve "dignity for the working man"—by which he meant an organization of society by which the values of labor, humility, and intellectualism would be exalted, and those of luxury, idleness, and success due to chance or to strictly personal initiative would be despised. Likewise, Soviet visitors to the United States, in spite of their professed materialism, often say in the face of American workers' prosperity, that "the standard of living isn't everything."

What is it, then, that should count? The answer was given by a Polish visitor, who said that what he saw in America made him despair of humanity. He noted the high standard of living and he recognized that the sharing of wealth was much more equalitarian than in the Soviet Bloc countries, but he deplored that "speculation," in particular on Wall Street, could bring "unearned wealth" to some people. This he considered immoral. "Must immorality be the price for a high standard of living?" asked he.

Those examples show that the aim of universalistic co-subjective reasoning is not merely to use reason as a tool for a specific purpose, but rather to assure the congruence of *shared* belief with reality; if reasoned belief fails to conform to reality, reality must be made to conform to reason. Otherwise, if reasoning were to be periodically and partially modified to better fit reality, the cherished feeling of certainty based on universal agreement would be eroded. (It might be worthwhile to report that the Polish gentleman mentioned above became partly reconciled to Wall Street after it was explained to him that those who make money on the exchange do so by performing the socially useful function of transferring capital from industries whose prospects are poor, to industries whose prospects are better because their products are more needed, and when, furthermore, the mechanism was presented to him in mathematical terms. What was mathematical couldn't be wholly bad, he seemed to think—even though he still had great doubts about the wisdom of letting the demand of mere customers decide which product was more and which one less needed by the economy.)

Similar assumptions seem to govern the functioning of jurisprudence. The gist of the universalistic style is placing full trust in the feeling of certainty with which certain ideas are grasped by the mind. Within such a context what is right and what wrong can be easily perceived; laws may be brief and succinct, because the seeming vagueness of words does not detract from the clarity of ideas. Guilt or innocence can likewise be determined intellectually; detailed evidence of perceptually obtained knowledge is secondary and not considered very reliable. The worst offences are not those against men—mere particulars—but those against ideas. An action against a human victim is to be considered primarily as an indication of the degree of moral depravity of the criminal, and it is the degree of depravity rather than the nature of the specific act which should determine punishment. Preventive justice is acceptable: If moral certainty exists on the part of the judge as to the moral depravity of the accused, preventive action may save a potential victim, and even more, the exposure of society to a source of infection.

Let us look at some cases.

The first one—very typical in Stalin's days—is that of a certain Pole arrested by Soviet authorities in the part of Poland which was taken over by the Soviets in 1939. He was condemned to four years at hard labor for "tendency to commit espionage" without having ever been brought before the court or given a possibility to defend himself. His crime was proven to the court's satisfaction by his old Polish passport, which bore entries proving that the man had travelled outside Poland prior to the war.

This case may appear completely arbitrary, in the light of western legal thought, in the sense of being illogical and bound by no rule, even of reasoning. In the first place no commission of any crime is even

alleged, only a "tendency." Moreover, the court obviously had no jurisdiction. Finally, even if foreign travel did prove an affinity to espionage,
the aggrieved party should have been the prewar Polish government,
towards which the Soviets felt little friendship.

Yet if one looks at the situation in the manner suggested by the
model, not in the light of the legal concept of crime, but rather in the
light of the more archaic concept of sin, than the case no longer appears
illogical (even though one is still bound to find its disposition unjust).
A sin is a sin even in the absence of any overt act of commission; a
wrong thought or a wrong attitude is enough. There is no limitation of
jurisdiction in cases involving attitudes, since a man carries his attitudes
with him. As for the attitude itself, freely undertaken travel abroad does
indeed indicate an interest in things foreign, possibly even in open-
mindedness and "cosmopolitanism": attitudes distasteful to any group
claiming to have the monopoly of truth. Moreover, there was no reason
for bringing the prisoner before his judges, since they could arrive at
a verdict by the means which universalism considers to be the best, that
is to say by clear reasoning.

Had this prisoner not been liberated by the Churchill–Stalin
agreement which freed most of the Poles in Soviet concentration camps
to make it possible for them to fight the Nazis, the serving of his sentence
would not have meant that "he had paid his debt to society," and that
closure had been obtained. He would still have been forbidden to live
within one hundred kilometers of any capital of a Soviet Republic or
any other of the principal cities, and he would never have been given
any but the most menial jobs. A sinful attitude is a sinful attitude, and
the burden of proof is on the sinner before he is pronounced worthy
of returning to paradise.

It should be noted that it is the whole man who is being punished, not a specific act. And what the man is punished for in failing to
embody the idea of what a man should be. In the case of Brodsky, the
poet, the presiding judge based the court's decision on the fact that, to
her, he was "obviously anti-social."

> Soviet law cannot be understood unless it is recognized that the whole
> Soviet society itself is conceived as a single great family, a gigantic school,
> a church, a labor union, a business enterprise. The state stands as its head,
> as the parent, the teacher, the priest, the chairman, the director. As the
> state, it acts officially through the legal system, but its purpose in so acting
> is to make the citizens into obedient children, good students, ardent be-
> lievers, hard workers, successful managers. (Berman, 1963)

Approximately one out of five defectors or escapees to the
democratic West seeks to return or at least expresses the wish to return.

Approximately the same percentage of East Germans having escaped to the West seek to go back to Communist Germany. The motivation behind the attempts to go back may be summarized by the statement of one of them, a young woman who had reached the United States, where she had rich relatives who provided her with all the creature comforts. Nevertheless she stated that "in the U.S. there is nothing for the soul"—no constant appeals to sacrifice the self to a cause greater than a human individual.

The domination of the idea over the man or the act extends into the manner in which reality is grasped by the courts.

In the Soviet press there regularly appear articles exposing various forms of corruption. . . . [Most cases are characterized by such an] excellent organization of corruption through bribery, intimidation, mutual amnesty and counterattack against critics [that] it remains somewhat of a mystery how these scandals come to be known to the top level and so be exposed in *Pravda* and *Izvestia*. The process of investigation is never revealed. This is no doubt in part related to Stalinist secrecy about intelligence departments procedures. But it also seems to express more deep-lying feelings about knowing and guilt.

The articles express a double attitude about the concealment of the crimes they describe. On the one hand, it would seem as though these crimes could be concealed indefinitely. On the other hand, there are recurrent vague statements that everything eventually comes to light. . . . The suppression of the process by which [crimes] become known, together with the vague warning that everything must come to light, produces the illusion of omniscience at the top level. . . .

Aside from the utility of maintaining that the leadership is omniscient, there would seem to be a deep-lying Russian belief that true knowledge is omniscience. Empirical ways of thinking, which stress the detailed steps through which something happens and the detailed clues by which it is found out, have had less time to take hold in Russia than in the West. The ideal of knowledge remains much more an immediate and complete core of events, of the soul of another person. This is related to the great stress on motives rather than on means. One sees that in older Russian literature, such as *The Brothers Karamazov*. There is no crime investigation in the Western sense of assembling clues and reconstructing how the crime was committed. Ivan, once he confronts his own guilty motives, understands everything. The omnipotence of motives is implicitly assumed. In the Moscow trials, there was no reference to how the crimes of the defendents were detected. Material clues adduced to substantiate alleged acts were minimal. (Contrast the prominence of the typewriter, the pumpkin, etc. in the Hiss trial). The emphasis on motives and goals was greater than on means, with the double implication that once the bad motive exists, the most extreme acts inevitably follow, and that where there have been bad acts there must have been bad motives behind them.

In the stories about the crooks, another aspect that contributes to the impression of omniscience at the top is the reproduction of private conversations. The stories are written in literary style, replete with dialogue—the writer relates, and the reader can listen in on the conversations of these crooks among themselves. Fictional writing, which these stories approximate in style even while purporting to be news reports assumes the viewpoint of omniscience. But presumably from the Russian point of view omniscience is not only a literary convention but a credible attribute of the authorities. (Wolfenstein, 1953)

A few vignettes may add to the understanding of the often contrasting attitudes and behaviors of East Europeans on the one side and of Americans on the other.

The commoner types of lenses are preground and a prescription is filled quickly. The Russian chooses his frame . . . and the clerk puts in the prescribed lenses. . . .

I asked Dr. Sandler whether the benefits of the eyeglasses might not be somewhat diminished by the possible errors made by a drugstore clerk in mounting the lenses and fitting the frames to the wearer.

She expressed surprise. "Oh no," she assured me, "the clerks are trained for their jobs. Besides," she added in a typical pronouncement of inexorable Russian logic, "the prescription clearly states the measurement between the centers of the lenses and the distance from the eyes to the lenses."

Having watched clerks lean over the counter to fit a frame to a standing customer's head, I felt somewhat less confidence in the efficacy of Soviet drugstore spectacles. (Mehnert, 1962)

In an international meteorological conference, the American delegate proposed that a certain code group be omitted from one of the regular radio transmissions of weather observation; the group in question he said, was theoretically desirable; unfortunately, as it dealt with relatively rare phenomena, operators tended to omit it frequently, which caused confusion. The Soviet delegate opposed the proposal; it was agreed that the group was desirable, and that it was up to the stations to follow regulations. When asked—later on, at cocktails—whether Soviet stations really did observe the international regulation calling for the code group, he answered that, unfortunately, most of the time they didn't, which caused untold confusion. The situation was obviously the same in the Soviet Union as in the United States. Americans, however, took the position that a theory which could not be practically implemented should be modified, while their Russian counterparts considered it preferable to maintain the theoretically superior regulation, regardless of factual shortcomings.

The universalist mind takes it for granted that something

clearly conceived must have a counterpart in reality. Words such as "the best" are taken as if they described not subjective preferences but objective reality:

A Yugoslav visitor in the United States was shocked by the "economic waste" represented by advertising and by the diversity of models of automobiles. In his opinion a nationwide committee of engineers should determine *the best* model of automobile which could be built under existing technological conditions in each major category of utilization; the model in question would be the only one to be manufactured; if necessary, quotas might be assigned to every manufacturer.

American traits

Stewart states that the individual is the quantum of the American culture; much is done to create conditions under which the individual is free to seek what he desires, by whatever means he finds useful and lawful (Stewart, 1971). The same theme is heard from other sources. An African, a wise ambassador of his country in Washington, said once: "The source of the greatest misunderstandings between Americans and Africans is the positive value attached by the Americans to individualism, and the negative value attached to it by Africans. To you, individualism means freedom, and you value it positively; to us, Africans, individualism means loneliness, and we value it negatively."

Yet at the same time, many of the cultures which have reached from subjective associationism towards abstractive co-subjectivity consider Americans to be a nation of joiners and of conformists.

Many of the visitors who come to this country under the auspices of one of the exchange of persons programs come into contact with local organizations, made up of volunteers, largely free of the dictates of the Government in Washington, and devoting their freely given time to make it easier for the visitor to observe the local scene. The visitors are almost always astounded at having something which in their eyes is a governmental function performed by a private organization. They are still further astonished when they find that the volunteers they meet often have divergent opinions, both among themselves and with the State Department in Washington. Yet the volunteers can work together in spite of their differences. Moreover, in addition to these differences, they also exhibit many examples of conformity. They tend to dress in similar manners, address one another uniformly by their first names and avoid in their conversation any of the controversial matters on which the visitors know that they do not agree among themselves.

Clearly, the visitors from largely universalistic cultures and the neo-particularistic Americans have different understandings of individuality and of conformity.

The universalist considers himself individualistic within the context of *being*. He is an individual because no one else is exactly what he is. For him, the importance of being overrides the problems of doing.

The neo-particularist understands that in most cases his personal goals can best be reached through cooperation with others. Hence the conformism of Americans: following the etiquette of the group (first name communication, avoidance of premature controversies) is the best way to find out which persons are likely to cooperate in the pursuit of his own needs and desires. This is the individualism of *doing*. Its core is not being different but being self-reliant. The pursuit of self-reliance requires the ability to avoid disputes which are of secondary importance in the pursuit of a person's goals.

Attitudes in regard to friendship have much in common with the definition of individuality. Examples of the difference between American ways and those of many other countries can be observed in the attitudes of foreigners visiting America. Short term visitors—those who limit their visit to a few weeks or those at the beginning of their stay—are in general charmed and even astonished by the friendliness, the hospitality, and the willingness to help displayed by Americans. Those who stay longer, though not long enough to become fully accultured, tend to change their opinion. In addition to the normal and general homesickness, they suffer from a loneliness due to what they perceive in the American character as a refusal to enter into deep commitments, a basic indifference to the feelings and even the fate of others, a refusal to let their friends penetrate their private sphere of feelings, and even a degree of hypocrisy.

Such changes of attitude on the part of the visitors may be easily accounted for in terms of differences in the understanding of friendship in the cultures concerned. In many cultures friendships develop slowly. A person has but few friends, with whom he or she is joined by the deepest intimacy. A friend, above all, is a friend for all seasons and for all occasions. Only such true and intimate friends extend to one another the helpfulness which an American may show even to casual acquaintances: the intimacy implied by the use of the familiar pronoun and the first name, and the trust which makes friends fully confide in one another. Friends must see one another often; a lapse of a few days must be accounted for by an explanation. Mutual invasions of privacy are considered as strengthening the fabric of friendship. Differences in opinion are debated at length, particularly among Russians and Iberians; the tone adopted may be disputatious and grating, but this in no way interferes with the continuation of friendship.

The situation is entirely different within American contexts. Most Americans have many friends and many occupations. As a result, a considerable amount of time may elapse between encounters with some friends; this is not generally interpreted as a cooling of the relation. Mutual invasions of privacy are seldom tolerated; disputatiousness and an insistence that each of the friends accept one another's opinions are even less tolerated. If a difference of opinion on any given topic develops, the corresponding subject matter is dropped and left out of subsequent conversations.

This does not mean that Americans never fight for their beliefs. However, such fights generally take place within the context of business, of decisions to be made, and of courses of action to be selected. This excludes disputatiousness from invading social occasions and friendly meetings. The purpose of such exclusion is to bring pleasure to the participants, something that is more likely to be obtained if differences are placed outside the pale of possible subjects of conversation.

One of the consequences of this broad approach to friendliness is that friendships become almost as specialized as do job positions. For Americans there are friends for games, friends for mutual support in the more serious phases of life, friends for partying, friends for talking politics, and neighbors. These positions in respect to ego are generally filled by different people.

As a result, the visiting foreigner, in whose culture the extent of friendliness received at the first meeting would imply a promise of an intimate relationship, generally becomes just one among many friends, and at that, one characterized by the specialized niche of interest in the exotic. Long periods of time may elapse between successive meetings, leading someone not fully accultured to America to the belief that either he or she is personally disliked, or that Americans are deliberately cold and distant. In reality, if the visitor remains in the United States, the only possible solution to this malaise is to broaden the circle of friends, so as not to be too dependent upon any one person or group of people. In other words this amounts to acquiring the ability of living in what was called earlier a society of strangers: a society that is the product of modernization, of extreme division of social labor, and of a high degree of social mobility.

Political and administrative practices of Americans stem from attitudes very similar to those described as guiding patterns of social behavior. The main role of government is not seen as the development and implementation of a broad ideology—not even that of democracy, since it is assumed that democracy is "already there." Instead, the government is seen as an umpire whose task is to resolve or to contain frictions between individuals and groups, and as an implementor of specific programs of common interest. Hence an *ad hoc* character given to many if not most governmental or quasi-governmental bodies.

Agencies, for example the federal regulatory bodies, are established as the need for them arises, not according to an overall planned table of organization. There is a Tennessee Valley authority but no agencies of a comparable nature for the basins of other rivers. The territories of agencies dealing with other facets of public administration are not coextensive.

Similar remarks can be made in regard to Great Britain. Wales is an entity, but there are no administrative bodies which express its separate identity. Scotland has no local parliament, but has a Bank of Scotland, and a legal system of its own, based on Justinian's code, and not on English Common Law. However, the precedents of English Law apply in the United States, two hundred years after independence. Northern Ireland sends members to the British parliament in London, but also has a parliament of its own in Belfast.

The overall political character of universalistic regimens is "from up to down." The political character of neo-particularistic societies is "from down to up."

> It is incontestably true that the love and the habits of republican government in the United States were engendered in the townships and the provincial assemblies. In a small State, like that of Connecticut for example, where cutting a canal or laying down a road is a momentous political question, where the State has no army to pay and no wars to carry on and where much wealth and much honor cannot be bestowed upon the chief citizens, no form of government can be more natural and more appropriate than a Republic. But it is the same republican spirit, it is these manners and customs of a free people, which are engendered and nurtured in the different States, to be afterward applied to the country at large. (Tocqueville, 1845)

It was mentioned earlier that the rhythm of change in universalistic cultures is revolutionary. The existing is deemed to embody perfection; when its weaknesses become too flagrantly obvious, a revolution sets up a new perfection. In contrast, the rhythm of evolution in neo-particularistic and objectivistic cultures is evolutionary. Perfection is not believed in; the existing system can always be improved upon, and a desire to do so arises either when some of its weaknesses have been repeatedly demonstrated, or when an ambitious individual sees an opportunity for inventing a better mousetrap. The central idea of neo-particularism in regard to change is that of crossing bridges when one comes to them. Change is accepted easily, if the need for it is demonstrated, and if it is limited to the particular set of circumstances, the particular case for which the demonstration has been made. Theoretical extrapolations are frowned upon. The expression *Gleichsanschaltuung*—lining up, making identical, like soldiers on parade—which was used by the Nazis to describe many of their goals and which Tucker (1963) uses to explain the guiding motives of Stalinism is alien to the neo-particularistic mentality. Thus changes, including radical ones, are made in respect to particular problems rather than to the social organization in general. Such changes may be revolutionary in their accumulation, but the revolution in question is hardly perceptible as each individual change is made within its own context, and at its own time and place. The picture presented is one of evolution, not revolution.

The greatest revolution of the English-speaking world is probably the industrial revolution, or rather the industrial revolutions, including Henry Ford, automation, and the computer. Even in the political and socioeconomic fields evolutionary reforms such as the New Deal and the semi-official Keynesianism of the postwar period in the United States transformed society without truly inflaming imaginations. Latin American visitors in the United States often say with some contempt that there is no *mystique* in North America. It is perhaps this lack of a mystical tendency that leads to an overall facility in accepting and promoting change, accompanied by difficulty in describing it. In neo-particularistic cultures, revolution may be truly permanent, but it is seldom admitted.

Very similar observations can be made in the field of jurisprudence. The universalistic, co-subjective type places full faith in the feeling of certainty on the part of the judges, whether the latter are the representatives of a crowned autocrat, of the Church, or of the "dictatorship of the proletariat." The relational type, of which France is perhaps the main example, likewise places full faith in human understanding but it does not treat the matter lightly. It depends on tightly written codes, assumed to be capable of forseeing all possible contingencies.

The gist of objectivistic neo-particularism is the acting out of the belief that generalized reason can only approximate reality, but can never grasp it fully. Only the examination of particular facts can be fully relied upon. It follows that the statute, where it exists, indicates mainly the intent of the legislator, as words written in advance of the facts cannot do much more; the precedents contained in precise descriptions of particular cases and of the disposition of them by the courts constitutes the main basis of judgement. At the same time, the system of common law is very abstractive; one of the main duties of the court is to determine what is and what is not relevant. One can go so far as to suggest that the heart of the system is not so much in the definition of the illicit and the calibration of punishment as in the rigor of the definition of admissible evidence.

One of the consequences of this state of affairs is that a modification of what is known, or of what can be scientifically established, implies a modification of the juridical system, without any necessity for legislative action. For example, in 1897, in the case of the *U.S.* v. *Knight Company*, the Supreme Court ruled that the Sherman Act could not be invoked in cases involving a de facto monopoly of manufacturing a product, even though it could be invoked in cases of a monopoly in the trading of a product. This was because the Interstate Commerce Clause of the Constitution, on which the Sherman Antitrust Act is based, gave the Federal Government the power to regulate commerce between the states, but not to regulate manufacturing within a State. In 1937, the effects of this verdict were reversed by the Supreme Court in the case of the *Jones & Loughlin Co.* v. *N.L.R.B.*, which did not even involve the Sherman Act directly. In this case the Court found (1) that the framers of the Constitution intended for the Federal Government to have the power to regulate commerce between the States, and (2) that under the present technological and economic conditions, which the authors of the Constitution could not have foreseen, it was illusory to try regulating trade without regulating manufacturing.

The same subordination of the letter of the statute and of earlier precedent to newly uncovered facts characterized the *Brown* v. *Board of Education* case, which led to the desegregation of schools. In this case the Court's finding that separate schools could not be equal was based on an increased understanding of human behavior, derived from the progress of psychology and sociology.

Similar considerations are called for in the analysis of the educational system. Let us take France as a counterpoint. In the French system the curriculum follows the directions determined by a central body. The Ministry of Education, controls not only the elementary and the secondary schools, but also the universities. The national territory is divided into a number of "academies" centered around a university, the rector of which is also the educational director of the entire region, exercising authority on all the public and elementary schools in the region.

The elementary and secondary curricula are designed in a manner that will give to the student a modicum knowledge of the world. Not only are both geometry and algebra required of all secondary students, but history and geography are taught in a way that will allow the student at least a glimpse into the development of the civilizations of Egypt and Mesopotamia, of Greece and Rome, and of the Western world from the Middle Ages to the date of the teaching. Similarly, the teaching of geography is supposed to acquaint the student with the entire world—even though, obviously enough, such an acquaintance can be no better than superficial.

In contrast, the American system is decentralized from the point of view of its administration. This does not lead to the diversity that might be expected. Strong, nationally established, though officially private groupings, such as the National Education Association, prose-lytize in favor of what may be termed educational theories or even fads. These are accepted by principals and by teachers from all the parts of the United States, leading to a considerable amount of similarity between school districts.

However the curriculum is so structured as to allow the students a considerable amount of autonomy. Geometry can be taken in lieu of algebra, or vice versa. History and geography are taught in separate units covering some period or some area. While students will seldom gain an overview of the history or the geography of the world, they may be called upon to undertake projects in which they will become ac-quainted with a modicum of research methodology, something which French students' will often reach only at the graduate level.

Nor does the difference disappear after the end of formal studies. Americans consider education as something one pursues all one's life, while the French tie it to specific periods of childhood and youth.

> While Americans view education as a continuing process aimed at provid-ing the individual with the necessary knowledge as he comes to face various contingencies of life, the French view it first of all as a system of knowledge which is necessary to the individual regardless of the particular contin-gencies which he may expect. In consequence the French subdivide their education into comprehensive chunks; upon acquiring a solid general education a man "comes of age" and is deemed prepared for life without needing to continue to study: from then on it is the experience of life which will provide him with wisdom.
>
> The very notion of "educational" which appeared in the title of many of the exchange of persons programs was negatively received by most French participants. Invitations to attend lectures and orientation classes were received with irritation, because of a subconscious feeling on the part of the adult visitors of being relegated to an age group which they deemed to have transcended. (d'Haucourt, 1958)

The excerpts to follow are taken from the account of travel in the United States of a French journalist, J. M. Domenach. They are quite illuminating in respect to the cultural values of the describer as well as to those of the society he describes.

There is, in Russia, a ruling ideology, which fashions the economic and the political realities; there are, in France or in Italy, ideologies confronting one another. Nothing of the sort in the United States. . . . One of the things which are the most disconcerting for a foreigner is the lack of something he could understand within American politics. The Frenchman naturally seeks to find a right and a left. . . . However, at a different level, that of particular problems and of local business, political life is vigorous: the real political questions, in the United States, concern urban renewal, the incorporation of new suburbs, school administration. . . .

From one point of view, this is tragic: no overall planning, no overall conceptualization. . . . From another point of view, it is hopeful: through patience, good will, social spirit, solutions are found. . . .

No matter how obsolescent and imperfect, ideologies provide at least a translation of reality. But how can the world problem be understood by a citizen whose political activity . . . is limited to the consideration of a school bond issue. . . ?

For the American, politics is not a specific kind of mediation and of action: it is a number of interventions, always particularized, always circumstantial, which are not tied among themselves by any . . . consistency. . . . It is up to every individual to make his happiness by himself; it so happens that the piling up of individual fates raises, here and there, common problems which must be arbitrated by the people: this is the implicit credo of Americans. . . .

Americans, who build wonderful one family houses, have not undertaken anything which resembles a city, in the sense given to this word by the peoples of the Mediterranean. . . .

Clubs, groupings, associations . . . are poor substitutes for the absence of a collective vision, of a social structure. . . .

Most Americans do not feel personally involved in what they believe or in what they think. They have opinions, but seldom convictions. I often met students and professors to whom I presented ideas openly critical of the American system; I was listened to carefully and asked questions frequently, but I was not contradicted and no one failed to compliment me at the closing for a 'very fine meeting'. At first I felt uncomfortable in facing what I took to be concerted politeness. But no, they were really satisfied, first of all because they always like to be together, and also because they were touched by my frankness; they did not see any need in refuting ideas which they did not suspect me to take any more seriously than they took their own. (Domenach, 1960)

Two incidents and one reference may be added by way of a postscript. The incidents involved a visit by two European cost analysis groups to the Harvard School of Business Administration in the days of the Marshall Plan. One group was French, the other German; yet the questions they asked the American experts were almost identical: "What are your principles of cost accounting?" The answers of the Americans were also identical in both cases: "What do you mean by 'principles of cost accounting'? Tell me what your problems are and I will try to show you how I would go about solving them."

Another reference might be to the McClelland (1964) study of the patterns of socialization in the United States and in Germany. The results showed that German boys are taught a code of principles of the right behavior, which they then have to apply to the situations in which life places them. In contrast, American boys are seldom placed in the face of a clearly stated code; socialization in their case is based on the experience of life in society, which they acquire early in life by interaction with peer groups and with other significant groups or individuals. Even the parents subordinate both the role of exponent of the code and, up to a point, of figures of authority. They try instead to use the family as a living example of what is required by life within groups.

All three cases, as many of the ones mentioned earlier, show that the usual method of abstractive neo-particularism, of which the American culture offers many examples, approaches problems inductively. In contrast, the examples drawn from continental Europe and from Latin America show a preference for a deductive approach.

France

Many continental European cultures seek a compromise between the generalities of the universalistic approach and the particularism characteristic of the American and the English ways of living. The first goal in such a context is the development of "idées générales," as the French call them, that is to say, of universals insuring the participation in a common world view and facilitating verbal communication between the members of the culture. A second goal is to make certain that the universals in question fit reality as it is known, through the verification of general ideas in particular examples. Such a verification has also another purpose: that of permitting a personalized development of the individual, in such a way as to make him somewhat unique and different from others, while remaining at the same time a member of the common matrix.

The entire process calls for clear descriptions of the relations between the universal and the particular. The understanding of such relations leads to the development of an inner logic within the mind. This inner logic—"être logique avec soi même"—is considered more important and valuable than any specific content of opinion. A culture which fits particularly well such an ideal of balance is the French one.

I have designated this cultural type as "relational," because of the importance in it of clear relational concepts.*

> To an observer who studies school life in Peyrane over a period of time it is apparent that children learn much that is not explicitly in the curriculum. From the attitude of the teachers, from the way school work is presented, from the textbooks, the children learn to make basic assumptions concerning the nature of reality and their relationship to it. These assumptions are not mentioned in the directives of the Department of Education. . . . If the teachers are conscious of them, they never discuss them directly in class. Yet the assumptions are so important that they will determine to a large extent the frame of mind and the manner in which a child will approach the problems with which he is confronted throughout his life. (Wylie, 1964)

As much could have been said about any school in any country. Culture is transmitted by the old generation to the new one not only by explicit statements but also by the implication of the older generation's often subconscious patterns of behavior. However, let us note once more, in passing, that there is a Department or a Ministry of Education which determines the curriculum for the school in Peyrane and for all the other schools in France, something which the U.S. Department of Education cannot do.

What, now, are the implicit assumptions governing the world view taught in the French schools?

> In teaching morals, grammar, arithmetic, and science the teacher always follows the same method. She first introduces a principle or rule that each pupil is supposed to memorize so thoroughly that it can be repeated on any occasion without the slightest faltering. Then a concrete illustration or problem is presented and studied or solved in the light of the principle. More problems and examples are given until the children can recognize the abstract principle implicit in the concrete circumstances and the set of circumstances implicit in the principle. When this relationship is sufficiently established in the minds of the children, the teacher moves on to another principle and set of related facts.
>
> The principle itself is not questioned and is hardly discussed. Children are not encouraged to formulate principles independently on the basis of an examination of concrete cases. They are given the impression that the principles exist autonomously. They are always there: immutable and constant. One can learn only to recognize them, and accept them. The same is true of concrete facts and circumstances. They exist, real and unalterable. Nothing can be done to change them. One has only to recognize

---

*This nomenclature must be distinguished from that of A. Cohen, and J. Kagan, H. A. Moss and I. E. Sigel who use "relational" in a way similar to that of "associative" in the present text.

them and accept them. The solution of any problem lies in one's ability to recognize abstract principles and concrete facts and to establish the relationship between them.

Another basic assumption is seen most clearly in the way history, civics, geography, and literature are studied, but it is important in all subjects. In learning history the children are first presented with a general framework which they are asked to memorize. Studying history consists partially in filling this framework, that is, in learning how the facts of history fit into the framework. An isolated fact is unimportant in itself. It assumes importance only when one recognizes its relationship to other facts and above all its relationship to the whole framework. In learning geography, a child first studies his own country-side, then the surrounding region, then France, then the world. Heavy stress is placed on the relationship of each geographical unit to a larger whole. In the study of morals and civics the children learn the proper relationship and reciprocal obligations of the individual to the family, to the community, to France, and to humanity.

This emphasis on the relation of the part to the whole is also seen in the . . . study of literature. . . . No attempt is made to understand or to appreciate the text which is presented to the class until it has been thoroughly dissected and analyzed. It is broken down into its logical divisions, and the author's purpose in each division is explained. Difficult or obscure words or expressions are explained. Only when each of the component parts of a passage is understood and when the relationship of each part to the whole is made clear is the passage put together and appraised as a unit.

Thus a child comes to believe that every fact, every phenomenon, every individual is an integral part of a larger unit. As in a jigsaw puzzle each part has its own clearly defined and proper position. They make sense only if their proper relationship is recognized. (Wylie, 1964)

The Americans and the English tend to see individuality and even creativity as self-reliance. The creative individual is given to lonely efforts; but if a group is necessary to overcome a problem, the creative, self-reliant individual is seen as the one who assumes a role of leadership. The results of creative efforts may appear in any field of endeavor; what counts is the feeling that some deed would not have been accomplished, or that something would not have been made if it were not for the creative person. The attitude of the French in the face of creativity and originality gives another impression. First of all, the areas in which creativity is exercised are not viewed as more or less equal among themselves. Life, whether of the mind or of the body, is seen in terms of strict hierarchies. In a civilization in which artisanship has lost none of its quality and its prestige, an artist is always placed higher than an artisan. Second, what is created is respected only if it is seen as developing and

enriching the entire body of civilization—that is to say, if it can be placed
with the required precision in a cultural analysis or an anthology.

What is done for the child and what the child must do is phrased as
necessary fo the child's present and, more especially, future well-being.
Indeed an important aspect of teaching is making what is taught *personal*
to the one who is learning. Thus, the child is told constantly that he should
behave in a certain way for his own sake (*pour soi-meme*). And as part of
its formal education, the child is taught how to use models in a "personal"
or "original" way. Describing how this is done in French composition
lessons in a Lycée, a woman says:

"For instance, if we were studying La Bruyère, after we had had *dictée*
(dictation) and had analyzed passages very carefully and had memorized
them, wee would be told to go home and write a composition—perhaps
the portrait of one of our classmates—in the style of La Bruyère portraits.
We did this with many different kinds of writers. . . ."

Or, as another informant explained, the students would be given the
outline of an idea in a paragraph, which they would then be expected to
expand into an essay in a given style. This gave each student "real scope
for originality." In this sense of having assimilated what had been taught,
people say that "the French hate conformity . . . detest uniformity," and
so on, and can assert with confidence, as one young woman did, that "in
our old civilization everyone feels that, no matter how he acts, he acts in
a French way. . . ."

Implicit in such statements is the belief that individuality consists in the
development of new variations on accepted designs. And so, in order to
become an individual, the child must learn the design, must make it his
own. In this sense standards are not, in the first instance, personal but
exist in the external world and are learned by approximation; once assimilated, they provide the means for and the measure of individual self-
expression. Congruent with this is the expectation that the most complex
and personally stated idea is communicable if it can be related logically to
the traditional and the known. . . .

The ability to make selective use of the traditional in a personal way—or,
alternatively, to become an innovator through the use of models other
than the traditional ones—is the desired outcome of education. During
the earlier stages of learning, the child does not yet have the capacity for
a personal style as it has not yet assimilated the standards on which a
personal style is based, or in contradistinction to which one may be worked
out. (Métraux and Mead, 1954)

The emphasis in all these passages is on the realization that
neither universals nor particulars may be neglected. A common core of
universal concepts is taught as a paradigm, then the forms of the paradigm are brought out, and possible variations of the forms are studied.
The final objective may be a modification of the paradigm, in a manner
characteristic of the individual learner.

Such a philosophy may be contrasted with American usage in which students are considered as people who will be called upon to solve the particular problems of life. Some problems are very general, such as the problem of "getting along"; other ones are likely to be of the student's own choosing. In consequence, once a minimum of basic subjects is learned, free choice and early specialization are encouraged. Education in America is never considered completed; if new problems come up, new studies will be called for. On the other hand, very little knowledge is considered necessary for those who encounter few problems. Here again the American and the French approaches can be contrasted.

Differences of approach extend even into professional education. French medical doctors are often superior diagnosticians; they carry in their heads the precise identification of a huge number of syndromes and often can identify the category of illness into which a patient falls more rapidly and with greater precision than the majority of their American colleagues. However, they are less efficient in those situations where the individual peculiarities of the case obscure the characteristics of the illness. In such cases the inductive and problem centered approach of American medicine through a battery of laboratory tests generally proves to be superior.

The contrasts between these two approaches correspond to the differences between the legal systems. For the French the core of the law is a painstakingly thorough classification covering every possible contingency—or at least attempting to do so. For the Americans the core is the accumulated experience of precedents and case studies, with an ever present possibility of breaking new ground.

A similar contrast can be found in almost every area of life. English and American painting and poetry have had more than their share of innovators. One may think of Turner's revolutionary explosion of light and color. But the development of artistic and intellectual life in Britain and America witnessed few of the battles which characterized the change from one school to another in France. Among the English-speaking nations innovations are viewed as particular events, which may or may not interest the public. In France the advent of a new taste is taken as a new interpretation of beauty, to which the generality of intellectual life must be adjusted. Hence the battles between the classicists and the romantics, or between the official academic painting and that of the impressionists. Both of these (and many others) drew in important segments of the public, and their reverberations reached even political life.

On the whole, the American system of education aims at preparing students through a core of methodology to the solving of problems which cannot be foreseen, and to occupying positions which may not even exist, or be describable with any precision, at the same time as the learning is taking place. In contrast, one of the side effects of the French presentation of the world and of the *summa* of all knowledge in a systematic fashion, is the determination of the social position which the student will occupy by virtue of his education. One of the mechanisms which determine this place is a profusion of competitive examinations. In addition to universities, France has a considerable variety of *grandes ecoles,* "great schools," which accept students on the basis of competitive examinations; graduation from one of these schools insures that the graduate will occupy a privileged position in society. Even the universities, which are open to all those having satisfied an extremely difficult examination at the conclusion of secondary studies, have mechanisms for determining the proper position of their graduates in the French meritocracy. For example, the prestige, the earning power, and more generally the opportunities offered to medical doctors depend on their entitlement to adding to their main title of doctor, titles such as *ancien externe* or *ancien interne,* obtained by competitive examination preceding graduation, or of *chef de clinique* or *médecin des hopitaux* for which they compete once provided with a medical degree. Recruitment for the better careers in the civil service is likewise by competitive examinations. Success determines not only purely professional positions, but also the place a person occupies in society.

> The image of the circle, with its implications of closure, is one that is used by the French to describe social groups to which they belong. [*Milieu* refers to the broad social context; *cercle* to the structure of a group.] *Cercle* is, for instance, commonly part of the names of clubs. . . . It is also used in a generally descriptive way. So, in speaking of his father's position, a man says: "After he finished the *Ecole Normale Supérieure . . .* he immediately entered the class or *cercle* which in France is called *les universitaires.*" It is a class of people very much apart from the rest of the population and very self-contained. . . . Or comparing French and American experiences, a [French] woman says: "There are many circles in France, but these are completely closed groups. In America there are clubs whose sole purpose is to permit strangers to make acquaintanceships. That simply doesn't exist in France. There one participates in a group simply because one belongs to it, as, for example, I belong to the university group, to another group of the family, and equally to a . . . religious group. The people of these different groups do not mix at all. . . ." Thus, the adult through his different associations belongs to various "circles," each of which . . . both closes in its members and keeps strangers out. (Métraux and Mead, 1954)

The description of the school system, and even more that of the atmosphere surrounding teaching, shows the importance given by the French to the sharing of a detailed and extensive system of beliefs about the world. But, contrarily to the Russian situation, the system does not aim at subjugating the individual. Its goal is to provide individuals with a shared system of orientation, so that they can find and occupy a preserve within which they will be at the same time safe and free.

The definition of protected preserves is physical as well as behavioral.

> The arrangement of French dwellings conveys something of the distance between the world without and the world within. . . . One need only to recall houses in provincial France where a high wall, enclosing the garden or the court or the plot of land around the house, shuts out too-curious neighbors or passers-by; where a bell on a garden gate rings, perhaps automatically, to announce each person. . . . Or one may visualize the urban apartment building where the incomer must first pass the sharp scrutiny of the *concierge*. . . . Designs of nineteenth-century luxury apartments in Paris provide another image of . . . privacy. . . . Here each apartment occupies an entire floor of a building which also, on the first two floors, houses a business establishment, and, in the attics, has rooms for servants and poor tenants. The close proximity of these unrelated worlds implies the detachment of each from the other. The specific image alters from one type of house, from one region of France, to another. Common to them is the sense of the boundary set, the protection against possible intrusion. (Métraux and Mead, 1954)

Safety requires protective barriers; freedom requires the possibility of exploring a field. The French are past masters at devices which warn the strangers from their preserves, without making anyone feel that his freedom is being limited.

> The highly elaborated *formules de politesse* are an elegant way of maintaining proper distance between individuals. By comparison with the American's desire for quick intimacy, for promptly reaching a first-name basis, there is a general appreciation in France of the reserved person. The mark of a person *bien elevé*, raised with a proper sense of right conduct, is *la reserve*. A rule that governs personal distances in France is *"il faut garder ses distances."* It is generally believed that a person is likely to suffer if, *par manque de reserve*, he exposes himself to the will and way of others. (Lerner, 1956)

Yet if Americans generally find Frenchmen over-polite, at times they find them downright rude. Frenchmen consider it proper at times to attack the opinions of others in a manner which leads to a level of verbal violence entirely inacceptable to Americans. In 1963, during a visit to the United States, Madame Nhu delivered a series of scathing attacks on American policies; the American press reacted with a sense of shock. The feelings of outrage expressed by the American press astounded a number of Frenchmen visiting Washington at the time; in their view the level of vehemence reached by Madame Nhu was fully permissible and even normal in political controversies. This apparent contradiction can be explained by the fact that for the French attacks directed at opinions generally do not imply attacks upon individuals. There are *formules de politesse* which make it possible to affirm at the same time full respect for an individual and total contempt for the world view—supposedly fully disembodied—to which that individual subscribes. *Il faut savoir distinguer*—one must know how to distinguish the one from the other.

The freedom to discuss and explore ideas implies faith in the creativity of such a process; reason creates, as in universalism. But whatever is created in this manner must not become finalized without thorough and prudent testing. Until this is done the individual—the particular—must be protected.

> The French desire for an environment arranged in a stable fashion, with familiar routines defined by recognizable limits, manifests itself also on questions of public consequence. Typical expressions of distaste for innovation are *"Pas de surprise!"* and *"Pas d'aventure!"* People reared in a tradition which values adventure often fail to notice this systematic French distrust of whatever is new and strange. Yet it underlies a variety of otherwise inexplicable phenomena. (Lerner, 1956)

The problems of essence and existence

> The sociopsychological approach to modernization treats it mainly as a process of change in ways of perceiving, expressing and valuing. The modern is defined as a mode of individual functioning, a set of dispositions to act in certain ways. It is, in other words, an "ethos" in the sense in which Max Weber spoke of "the spirit of capitalism." As Robert Bellah expressed it, the modern should be seen not "as a form of political or economic system, but as a spiritual phenomenon or a kind of mentality." As such it is much less tied to a particular time or place than is a definition of modernity in terms of institutional arrangements. If modernity is defined as a state of mind, the same condition might have existed in Elizabethan England, in Periclean Greece, or in Tokugawa Japan. (Inkeles and Smith, 1974)

All the major nations we can consider modernized are either part of the European tradition or have extensively borrowed from this tradition. As for the core of this tradition, it can be defined as a willingness to abstract, both from the raw data of experience, and the results of earlier abstractions.

The main result of abstraction is the developing of groupings of conceptualizations based on considering the phenomena of the environment from a series of different points of view. What is obtained by the bringing into consciousness of the points of view governing the elaboration of such groupings are the essences which we can use as predicates for ordering and structuring the phenomena of experience.

The definition of essences brings with it the problem of existence. What is reality? Is it the phenomena which we witness but cannot clearly describe, or the predicates in terms of which we describe the world in which we live, but which we do not personally experience? This is a problem which abstraction creates, even while solving the problem of sharing personal experiences with others.

In philosophy, this problem is known as the quarrel between universalism and nominalism (or neo-particularism). What this chapter has tried to show is that the problem—or the quarrel—is not limited to differences of opinion between professional philosophers, but that it can serve as a way to analyze differences between cultures, particularly those of the West.

12

CONCLUSIONS

Models

The model used in this book as presented in chapter 3 has proved useful in suggesting areas of cultural conflict and perhaps certain directions of cultural evolution.

Other models could have perhaps accomplished the same things. R. A. Cohen (1971) has put forward a model consisting in a four field matrix based on two dimensions: the relational (associative in our terms)–analytic (abstractive) and the field-dependent–field-independent. Likewise, Glenn and Wedge used a four field matrix based on the associative–abstractive and the universalistic–particularistic dimensions (Glenn et al., 1970). Glenn (1966) suggested a 125 matrix derived from three dimensions: the associative–abstractive, the universalistic–particularistic, and the Apollonian–Dionysian (or ritualistic–mystical). The difficulty with matrixes is that the axes tend to load upon one another. In addition, the picture they present tends to be static rather than dynamic. This makes them more suitable for classifying the cultural aspects of well-defined populations rather than for seeking directions of cultural change.

The primary purpose in using the triangular model has been to obtain a set of concepts applicable in the analysis of social structures, of cultures and subcultures, of individual minds, and of situational contexts, including those resulting from culture contact. Its main basis is the position that the processing of ever increasing amounts of information calls for the development of hierarchical structures with ever increasing levels of abstraction.

For example, the brain damaged patients studied by Goldstein (1963) could not face situations containing any "disorder"; i.e., they could process only very limited amounts of information. The preliterates studied by Cole, et al. (1971), Cole and Scribner (1974), and Luria (1976) could not assume roles independent of their everyday experience; i.e., they lacked the abstract concepts capable of guiding the mind in other than usual situations. The Chinese analyzed by Hsu (1963, 1971) derived their psychosocial equilibrium from human contacts generally limited to primary groups. By contrast, many westerners are capable of at least a degree of equilibrium in a world of strangers; i.e., they possess conceptual structures capable of dealing with relatively large inputs of information.

The basic method for deriving the model from existing data was a hypothetical one:

1. If a Set A of processes presides over the manner in which a society and a culture are organized, the pattern of organization would be A'; and
2. If a culture and a society are organized in a way describable as A', the thought processes of the most influential or the modal members of the culture are A.

Clearly, (2) is only a possible but not a necessary derivation from (1). This is a weakness of the model; however, it is a weakness it shares with almost all of science.

Another weakness is that the phrase "the most influential members of the culture" is ambiguous. Different people may be influential in different areas of organization, and also under differing sets of circumstances. Thus we may expect that no single description of a culture in terms of the model will remain applicable under all situations. For example, the present culture of the United States may be viewed in summary as being objectivistic, pragmatic, and neo-particularistic. However, American foreign policy since Wilson seems to be dominated by universalistic and co-subjective tendencies—the belief that universal panaceas may be found in self-determination, a parliament of nations, and a western, individualistic understanding of human rights. The lack of fit between such beliefs and the present situation suggests that all the three components of the triangle are present everywhere and all the time; what differs are cultural attitudes in specific situations.

Although the purpose of the model was to help in analyses of intercultural communication and miscommunication, the conceptualizations undertaken for such a purpose called for hypotheses amounting to basic postulates in anthropology, psychology, and sociology. The effect of these postulates was the transformation of the analysis from its limited purposes to a general theory of action.

As such it differs from an earlier statement of a theory of action (Parsons and Shils, 1951) by greater parsimony, and, more to the point, by a dynamic rather than a static formulation. The apexes (and even the sides) or the model triangle, are seen as loci of conflict as well as of harmony. An overall direction of development is postulated; it leads from a preponderance of associations reflecting the randomness of individual and cultural experience, towards abstractions presiding over the structuration and universalization of information. From the point of view of the graphics of the model, development is represented by an increase in the size of the triangle, from a relatively simple structure of shared experience, to a complex organization derived from the differing experiences of members of the same society and culture.

It was also shown that a development of this type is likely to be interrupted at times by movements in the opposite direction—towards more associationism, calling for attempts at decreasing the flow of information and making possible a simplification of conceptual structures, generally for rather limited periods of historical time.

In addition to such collective movements, the model suggests cultural and individual compensations for the movement towards abstraction, by the definition of strongly associative thoughts and artifacts with limited applicability. The antithesis between science and art may be considered an example of such compensation. So can the opposition between public roles and private dreams be considered.

Another point is the vexed question of the existence or the lack of it of parallelism between phylogenetic and ontogenetic developments. Positing the need to cope with increasing amounts of information as the principal motor of evolution, we can suggest such a parallelism without suggesting invidious comparisons. At the same time, a limit to parallelism is implied by the fact that the child and the "primitive" move towards different equilibria due to the differences between the cultures and the environments with which each will have to cope.

Ethics and abstraction

A number of psychologists working in the area of ethical development, in particular Piaget (1966), Kohlberg (1969), and Loevinger (1962), have tied the development of moral behavior to the development of abstract thought and its use in the structuration of the ego. The following presentation of Kohlberg (1971) shows clearly that the passage from relatively early stages of ethical understanding to fuller understandings of moral principles parallels the development of the mind (personal and cultural) from associative to abstractive dominance:

I. Preconventional level. At this level the child is responsive to cultural rules and labels of good and bad, right or wrong, but interprets these labels in terms of either the physical or the hedonistic consequences of action (punishment, reward, exchange of favors), or in terms of the physical powers of those who enunciate the rules and labels. The level is divided into the following two stages:

Stage 1: the punishment and obedience orientation. The physical consequences of action determine its goodness or badness regardless of human meaning or value of these consequences. Avoidance of punishment and unquestioning deference to power are valued in their own right, not in respect to an underlying moral order supported by punishment and authority (the latter being Stage 4).

Stage 2: the instrument relativist orientation. Right action consists of that which instrumentally satisfies one's own needs and occasionally the needs of others. Human relations are viewed in terms like those of the market place. Elements of fairness, or reciprocity, and of equal sharing are present, but they are always interpreted in a physical, pragmatic way. Reciprocity is a matter of "you scratch my back and I'll scratch yours," not of loyalty, gratitude or justice.

II. Conventional level. At this level, maintaining the expectations of the individual's family, group or nation is perceived as valuable in its own right, regardless of immediate and obvious consequences. The attitude is not only one of *conformity* to personal expectations and social order, but of loyalty to it, of actively *maintaining*, supporting and justifying the order, and identifying with the persons or group involved in it. At this level there are the following two stages:

Stage 3: the interpersonal concordance or "good boy–nice girl" orientation. Good behavior is that which pleases or helps others and is approved by them. There is much conformity to stereotypical images of what is the majority or "natural" behavior. Behavior is frequently judged by intention—"he means well" becomes important for the first time. One earns approval by being "nice."

Stage 4: the "law and order" orientation. There is orientation toward authority, fixed rules, and the maintenance of the social order. Right behavior consists of doing one's duty, showing respect for authority, and maintaining the given order for its own sake.

III. Postconventional, autonomous, or principled level. At this level, there is a clear effort to define moral values and principles which have validity and application apart from the authority of groups or persons holding these principles, and apart from the individual's own identification with these groups. This level also has two stages:

Stage 5: the social contract, legalistic orientation. Generally with utilitarian overtones, right action tends to be defined in terms of general individual rights and standards which have been critically examined and agreed upon by the whole society. There is a clear awareness of the relativism of personal values and opinions and a corresponding emphasis upon procedural rules for reaching consensus. Aside from what is constitutionally and democratically agreed upon, the right is a matter of personal "values" and "opinions." The result is an emphasis upon the "legal point of view" but also an emphasis upon the possibility of changing the law in terms of rational considerations of social utility (rather than freezing them in terms of Stage 4, "law and order"). Outside the legal realm, free agreement and contract is the binding element of obligation. This is the "official" morality of the American government and constitution.

Stage 6: the universal ethical principle orientation. Right is defined by the decision of conscience in accord with self-chosen *ethical principles* appealing to logical comprehensiveness, universality, and consistency. These principles are abstract and ethical (the Golden Rule, the categorical imperative); they are not concrete moral rules like the Ten Commandments. At heart, these are universal principles of *justice*, of the *reciprocity* and *equality* of human rights, and of respect for the dignity of human beings as *individual persons*.

Here, as in the questions explored earlier, the movement towards higher levels of abstraction makes it possible to face increasing numbers of problems: greater numbers of individuals, of practices, of new situations, and of accelerating change. Not all the individuals in any culture reach the higher stages, and many cultures do not reach these stages at all.

The problem of pro-social behavior

One of the most striking conclusions than can be derived from this study deals with the comparison between the two models of psychosocial equilibrium presented in chapter 8. The first of the two models (Hsu, 1971), may be called the Gemeinschaft system of balance. Social control and self-validation are assured by the informal but constant intercourse between the individual and primary groups. The second model may be called the Gesellschaft system. Social control and self-validation depend upon the internalization by the individual of a structure of abstractions capable of describing society and of dictating to the individual a system of behavior consonant with such a description.

In actuality it is only seldom that either of the models will fully describe the pro-social and the self-validating influences leading to the mutual adaptation of the collectivity and the individual. In most actual cases both enter into consideration; moreover, in most situations each of them is likely to reinforce the other.

Of the two models, the Gemeinschaft orientation is clearly the more associative and the Gesellschaft orientation the more abstractive. In consequence, cultural evolution is likely to lead to a progressive decrease of the importance of the Gemeinschaft model and the progressive increase in importance of the Gesellschaft model. Even a cursory analysis of the West shows that such, indeed, is the case.

As long as the congruence and the combination of the two types of equilibrium is sufficient to determine the actions of most individuals, the society may be expected to remain in balance. However, the present conditions in many countries, conspicuously including the United States, are such that the obvious weakening of community (Gemeinschaft) ties has not been sufficiently compensated by the strengthening of societal (Gesellschaft) abstractions. The result is widespread anomie and criminality, and the possible appearance of strong associative reactions.

Another point to be mentioned in the present context is that the abstractions offered by various brands of totalitarianism, including Marxism, are simpler than those offered by the complex democracies of the Western world. Thus, even if they are incapable of explaining the complexity of the present economic, social, and political situations, they are easier to understand and thus provide at least an appearance of psychosocial balance to peoples suffering from widespread anomie due to culture contact. It can be said in consequence that an upsurge of totalitarianism is to be expected.

Differences within society

Cultural uniformity in societies having reached high levels of abstraction may be more apparent than real. Well established legal and ethical duties and obligations may derive from the thought of a cultural leadership, accepted by less elaborated subcultures on the basis of obedience dictated by the greater prestige or the greater power of the leadership. Changes in environment—particularly in cultural environment—may lead the more sophisticated members of a society to an increased level of abstraction. Such a development may erode or destroy communication between leadership and followship. The latter is likely to use its newly won independence from the former to advance rules of behavior reflecting their own level of sophistication, that is to say expressing more associative and narrower world views.

Some examples may be found in the post-World War II Turkish politics. When multiparty voting was introduced by Inonu, the majority espoused clerical and anti-democratic attitudes aiming at weakening the modernizing reforms of Ataturk. It took an army coup to restore the "spirit of democracy!" The present situation in Iran is very similar, except for the fact that a "pro-democratic" or a "pro-modernizing" coup has not taken place.

Ethical Implications

The recognition of the cognitive autonomy of cultures implies a relativistic approach to questions of ethics. However, ethical cultural relativism can stand only in the context of cultural independence and the lack of contact between cultures with different moral standards. This, obviously, is not the case nowadays. While it is possible to favor situations in which culture contact is minimized through the raising of barriers to intercultural communication, it is only possible to hope that such barriers will attenuate contact to the level at which constant grating and the conflicts deriving from it are held to a manageable level. Otherwise, contact increasing with time appears unavoidable.

Absence of conflict within the context of culture contact implies a coincidence between the moral imperatives of the cultures concerned. The search for such an identity of views about the basic premises of acceptable social behavior implies in the last analysis the development of a common world culture. However, strong pressures in the direction of cultural similarity are likely to constitute cultural aggression and to precipitate the very conflicts which the achievement of cultural similarity and of a common ethical code are designed to prevent (Glenn et al., 1970). The form likely to be taken by conflicts due to clashes between cultures or subcultures are criminality and civil strife in the case of subcultures within the same population, and war in the case of conflicting national cultures.

Yet if the resolution of cultural-ethical conflicts is difficult, it is nevertheless possible in the long range. This is proven by the fact that most if not all of the ethically well-balanced societies have originated historically in mutually clashing cultures, and in the resolution of the conflict among them through the process of abstraction leading to the development of common ethical codes.

The last remark suggests an answer to the difficult question of individual ethical imperatives in the face of culture conflict. This answer is, in brief, that the overriding ethical imperative amounts to siding with the more abstractive culture in the face of conflict (Glenn, 1970).

This does not mean that an associative and quasi-automatic internalization of ethical standards is not necessary to guide the individual behavior. It simply means that the more abstractive of the cultures involved is more likely to provide conceptualizations capable of guiding behaviors acceptable to both or all of the populations in conflict. This, of course, is not automatically assured; the cultures involved, even the more abstractive ones, may be lacking the abstractions necessary to insure harmony. An example can be found in the extremely associative attitudes found in the more abstractive of the cultures concerned in the context of colonialism. Even where the most educated classes of the colonial power are ready to accept the similarly educated groups of the indigenous populations, the lower classes of the colonizers—the so-called "petits blancs" in the French sphere of influence—reject with contempt all of the indigenous population. What may be necessary in the face of such conflicts is the development and the assimilation of abstractions of a higher order than those existing in either culture.

It is likely, however, that evolution in the direction of such abstractions is likely to have for point of departure the existing thought of the more abstractive cultures. This, in fact, is what led to the independence of the former colonies: The abstraction adopted was the concept of self-determination, which, just as colonialism itself, had originated in the West.

What needs to be recognized at this time are the limitations of this concept: All that self-determination is likely to accomplish is to buy time through the erection of temporary and incomplete barriers to culture contact. The utilization of the time thus earned in order to obtain a more permanent solution to the existing conflicts may call for the internalization of still more abstract concepts, such as the full acceptance of the principle of a common humanity embracing all. This, again, is likely to come from the West, but it is unlikely to come soon.

REFERENCES

Adorno, T. W., Frenkel-Brunswick, E., Levinson, D. J., & Sanford, R.N. *The authoritarian personality.* New York: Harper & Row, Pub., 1950.

Albert, E. M. Rhetoric; Logic; Poetics. In Burundi, Culture patterning of speech behavior, *American Anthropologist,* 1964, *66,* No. 6, Pt. 2, 35-54.

Allport, G. W. *The nature of prejudice.* Cambridge, Mass.: Addison-Wesley, 1954.

Almond, G. *The appeals of communism.* Princeton: Princeton University Press, 1954.

Babbitt, I. *Rousseau and romanticism.* Cleveland: World Publishing Company, 1962.

Balandier, Georges. *Ambiguous Africa,* translated by Helen Weaver, Pantheon Books, a division of Random House. 1966.

Bally, C. *Cours de linguistique Francaise et de linguistique generale.* Bern, Switzerland: Francke, 1944.

Banfield, E. C. *The unheavenly city.* Boston: Little, Brown, 1968.

Bartlett, F. C. *Remembering.* London: Cambridge University Press, 1932.

Bateson, G., Jackson, D. D., Haley, J., & Weakland, J. Toward a theory of schizophrenia. *Behavioral Science,* 1956, *1,* 251-264.

Bell, D. *The coming of post-industrial society.* New York: Basic Books, 1973.

Benedict, R. *Patterns of culture.* Boston: Houghton Mifflin, 1934.

Benedict, R. *The chrysanthemum and the sword.* Boston: Houghton Mifflin, 1946.

Berger, C. R., & Calabrese, R. J. Some explorations in initial interaction and beyond: Toward a developmental theory of interpersonal communication. *Human Communication Research,* 1974, *1,* 99-112.

Berman, H. T. *Justice in the U.S.S.R.* Cambridge: Harvard University Press, 1963.

Bernstein, B. Elaborated and restricted codes. *American Anthropologist,* 1964, *66,* No. 6, Pt. 2, 55-69. (a)

Bernstein, B. Social class and linguistic development. In A. H. Halsey, J. Floud, and C. A. Anderson, Eds., *Education, Economy and Society.* Glencoe, Ill.: Free Press, 1964. (b)

Bernstein, B. A socioloinguistic approach to socialization: With some reference to educability. In F. Williams, Ed., *Language and poverty.* Chicago: Markham, 1970.

Bever, T., Fodor, J., & Garrett, M. A formal limitation of associationism. In T. Dixon & D. Horton, *Verbal behavior and general behavior theory.* Englewood Cliffs, N.J.: Prentice-Hall, 1968.

Bridgman, P. W. *The logic of modern physics.* New York: Macmillan, 1949.

Bronfenbrenner, U. Allowing for Soviet perceptions. In R. Fisher, Ed., *International conflict and behavioral science.* New York: Basic Books, 1964.

Bronfenbrenner, U. *Two worlds of childhood, U.S. and U.S.S.R.* New York: Russell Sage Foundation, 1970.

Brown, R. W., & Lenneberg, E. H. A study in language and cognition. *Journal of Abnormal and Social Psychology,* 1954, *44,* 454-462.

Brunner, J. S. Le Processus de preparation a la perception. In J. S. Bruner, F. Bresson, A. Morf, and J. Piaget, *Logique et perception.* Paris: Presses Universitaires de France, 1958.

Bruner, J. S., Goodnow, J. J., & Austin, C. A. *A study of thinking.* New York: John Wiley, 1956.

Burridge, K. *Mambu.* New York: Harper & Row, Pub., 1970.

Canaday, J. *Metropolitan seminars in art.* New York: Metropolitan Museum, 1960.

Cantril, H. *The "why" of man's experience.* New York: Macmillan, 1950.

Cantril, H. *The psychology of social movements.* New York: John Wiley, 1963.

Cassirer, E., *The myth of the state*. New Haven: Yale University Press, 1946.
Chang Tung-sen. A Chinese philosopher's theory of knowledge. In S. I. Hayakawa, Ed., *Our language and our world*. New York: Harper & Bros., 1959.
Chesnoff, R. Z. As the PLO sees it. *Newsweek*, January 5, 1976, *88*.
Cheyney, E. P. *The dawn of a new era*. New York: Harper & Row, Pub., 1936.
Chomsky, N. *Aspects of the theory of syntax*. Cambridge: M.I.T. Press, 1965.
Chu, V. *Ta ta, tan tan*. New York: W. W. Norton & Co., Inc., 1963.
Cleaver, E. *Soul on Ice*, McGraw-Hill, 1968.
Cobban, A. *The nation state and national self-determination*. New York: Thomas Y. Crowell, 1970.
Cohen, R. A. Conceptual styles, culture conflict and nonverbal tests of intelligence. *American Anthropologist*, 1969, *71*, 828-856.
Cohen, R. A. Influence of conceptual role sets on measures of learning ability. In C. L. Brace, G. R. Gamble, & J. T. Bond, Eds., *Special Issue of the American Anthropologist on Race and Intelligence*, 1971, Anthropological Studies No. 8, pp.
Cohn, N. *The pursuit of the millenium*, New York: Oxford University Press, 1968.
Cole, M., & Scribner, S. *Culture and thought*. New York: John Wiley, 1974.
Cole, M., Gay, J., Glick, J. A., & Sharp, D. W. *The cultural context of learning and thinking*. New York: Basic Books, 1971.
Coleman, J. S. *Equality of educational opportunity*. Washington, D.C.: U.S. Government Printing Office, 1966.
Condon, J. C., & Yousef, F. S. *An introduction to intercultural communication*. Indianapolis: Bobbs-Merrill, 1974.
Da Cunha, E. *Rebellion in the backlands*. Chicago: University of Chicago Press, 1944.
Davis, A., & Dollard, J. *Children of bondage*. Washington, D.C.: American Council on Education, 1940.
de Beauvoir, S. Adieu to America. In M. McGiffert, *The character of Americans*. Homewood, Ill.: Dorsey Press, 1964.
de Custine, A. L. L. *Journey for our time*. Chicago: H. Regnery, 1951.
Decter, M. *Liberal parents, radical children*. New York: Basic Books, 1975.
Deese, J. *The structure of associations in language and thought*. Baltimore: Johns Hopkins Press, 1965.
d'Haucourt, G. De quelques difficultiés dues aux différences de cultures rencontreés dans les missions d'assistance technique. *Proceedings of the 5th International Congress of the Anthropological Sciences*. Washington, D.C.: American Anthropological Association, 1958, pp.
de Haucourt, G. *La Vie agricole et rurale dans l'Etat d'Idndiana a l'epoque pionnière*. Paris: Mouton, 1961.
Descartes, R. *Discours de la méthode*. Paris: Larousse, 1934.
Deutsch, K. W. *Nationalism and social communication*. Cambridge, Mass.: M.I.T. Press, 1966.
Deutsch, M., Katz, I., & Jensen, A. R. Eds. *Social class, race, and psychological development*. New York: Holt, Rinehart & Winston, 1968.
Diaz del Castillo, B. *The discovery and conquest of Mexico*. New York: Farrar, Straus, & Cudahy, 1956.
Domenach, J. M. Le Módele Américain. *Esprit*, Paris, 1960, pp.
Drake, S. C., & Cayton, H. R. *Black metropolis*. New York: Harper & Row, Pub., 1962.
Durkheim, E. *De la division du travail social*. Paris: F. Alcan, 1893.
Durkheim, E. *The division of labor in society*. New York: Macmillan, 1933.
Duvall, E. M. Conceptions of parenthood. *American Journal of Sociology*, 1946, *52*, 193-203.
Eliade, M. *Myth and reality*. New York: Harper & Row, Pub., 1963.
Erickson, F. D. F'get you honky! In A. L. Smith, Ed., *Language, communication and rhetoric in Black America*. New York: Harper & Row, Pub., 1963.
Ervin, S. Changes with age in the verbal determinants of word associations. *American Journal of Psychology*, 1960, *74*, 361-372.
Fadipe, N. A. *The sociology of the Yoruba*. Ibadan: Ibadan University Press, 1970.
Faulkner, W. *The Sound and the Fury*, 1946.

Ferster, C. B., & Skinner, B. F. *Schedules of reinforcement.* New York: Appleton-Century-Crofts, 1957.

Fight over fluoride. *Time,* March 10, 1952, *59,* 46-47.

Firth, R. The theory of "cargo" cults: A note on Tikopia. *Man,* 1955, *55,* 130-132.

Fischer, L. *The life of Lenin.* New York: Harper & Row, Pub., 1964.

Frankfort, H., Frankfort, H. A., Wilson, J. A., & Jacobsen, T. *The intellectual adventure of ancient man.* Chicago: University of Chicago Press, 1946.

Frazer, J. G. *The golden bough.* New York: Macmillan, 1922.

Freud, S. *Totem and Taboo.* New York: Moffat, Yard and Company, 1918.

Freud, S. *The interpretation of dreams.* New York: Random House, 1950.

Gans, H. J. *The urban villagers.* New York: Free Press, 1962.

Gans, H. J. *The Levittowners.* New York: Vintage Books, 1967.

Gearing, F. *Priests and warriors: Social structures for Cherokee politics in the 18th century.* Washington, D.C.: American Anthropological Association (Memoir 93), 1962.

Geertz, C. *The social history of an Indonesian town.* Cambridge, Mass.: M.I.T. Press, 1965.

Geertz, C. *The interpretation of cultures.* New York: Basic Books, 1973.

Gillin, J. P. Some signposts for policy. In *Social Change in Latin America Today.* New York: Harper, 1960.

Glenn, E. S. Semantic difficulties in international communication. *ETC,* 1954, *11.* (Reprinted in S. I. Hayakawa, Ed., *Our language and our World,* New York: Harper & Bros., 1959. Also in *The use and misuse of language,* Greenwich, Conn.: Fawcett Books Group–CBS Publications, 1962.)

Glenn, E. S. Translation as a tool of research. In R. H. Weinstein, Ed., *Report on the Sixth Round Table Meeting on Linguistics and Language, Teaching.* Washington, D.C.: Georgetown University, 1955, pp.

Glenn, E. S. Review of V. A. Zvegincev's *Semasiologija, Language,* 1959, *35.*

Glenn, E. S. Meaning and behavior, communication and culture. *Journal of Communication,* 1966, *16.* (Reprinted in Samovar & Porter, *Intercultural communication: A reader,* Belmont, Ca.: Wadsworth, 1972.)

Glenn, E. S. New left or new right? In G. R. Weaver & J. H. Weaver, Eds., *The university and revolution.* Englewood Cliffs, N.J.: Prentice-Hall, 1969.

Glenn, E. S. The two faces of nationalism. *Comparative Political Studies,* 1970, *3.* (a)

Glenn, E. S. Cohen's "Conceptual Styles," a comment. *American Anthropologist,* 1970, *72.* (b)

Glenn, E. S. The symbolic function, particularly in language. *Semiotica,* 1973, *8.*

Glenn, E. S. Theory of meaning and some cognitive considerations for the analysis of differences between cultures. *Communication and Cognition,* 1974, pp. 000. (Special issue on Cognitive Anthropology)

Glenn, E. S., Johnson, R. H., Kimmel, P. R., & Wedge, B. A cognitive model to analyze culture conflict in international relations. *Journal of Conflict Resolution,* 1970, *14.*

Goldstein, K. Concerning the concept of "primitivity." In S. Diamond, Ed., *Culture in history: Essays in honor of Paul Radin.* New York: Columbia University Press, 1960.

Goldstein, K. *The organism: A holistic approach to biology derived from psychological data in man.* Boston: Beacon Press, 1963.

Granet, M. *La Pensée Chinoise.* Paris: Albin Michel, 1950.

Gregor, A. J. *The ideology of fascism, the rationale of totalitarianism.* New York: Free Press, 1969.

Groos, K. *The play of animals.* New York: D. Appleton and Company, 1898.

Groos, K. *The play of man.* New York: D. Appleton and Company, 1901.

Hallowell, A. I. Ojibwa metaphysics of being and the perception of persons. In R. Tagiuri & L. Petrullo, Eds., *Person perception and international behavior.* Stanford, Ca.: Stanford University Press, 1958.

Hamady, S. *Temperament and character of the Arabs.* New York: Twayne Publishers, 1960.

Harrison, T. *Savage civilization.* New York: Knopf, 1937.

Herring, H. *A history of Latin America.* New York: Knopf, 1961.

Hoffer, E. *The true believer.* New York: Harper & Row, Pub., 1951.

Hoijer, H. The Sapir-Whorf hypothesis. In H. Hoijer, Ed., *Language in culture.* Chicago: University of Chicago Press, 1954.

Horowitz, I. L. *Radicalism and the revolt against reason.* Carbondale, Ill.: Southern Illinois University Press, 1968.

Hsu, F. L. K. *Clan caste and club.* Princeton, N.J.: D. Von Nostrand, 1963.

Hsu, F. L. K. Psychosocial homeostasis and jen: Conceptual tools for advancing psychological anthropology. *American Anthropologist,* 1971, *73.*

Inkeles, A. The totalitarian mystique. In C. J. Friedrich, Ed., *Totalitarianism.* Cambridge: Harvard University Press, 1954.

Inkeles, A., & Smith, D. H. *Becoming modern.* Cambridge: Harvard University Press, 1974.

Ittelson, W. H., & Kilpatrick, F. P. The monocular and binocular distorted rooms. In F. P. Kilpatrick, *Explorations in transactional psychology.* New York: New York University Press, 1961.

James, W. *Principles of psychology.* New York: Henry Holt Co., 1890.

Jensen, A. R. Patterns of mental ability and socio-economic status. *Proceedings of the National Academy of Sciences,* 1968, *60.*

Jensen, A. R. A two-factor theory of familial mental retardation. *Proceedings of the 4th International Congress of Human Genetics,* 1971, Paris,

Kagan, J., Moss, H. A., & Siegel, I. E. Psychological significance of styles of conceptualization. *Monographs of the Society for Research in Child Development,* 1963, *28,* No. 2.

Kaiser, R. Gl, & Morgan, D. *The Soviet Union & Eastern Europe: New paths, old ruts.* New York: Foreign Policy Association, 1973.

Ken Ling. *The revenge of heaven.* New York: Putnam's, 1972.

Keniston, K. *Young radicals.* New York: Harcourt Brace & World, 1968.

Kilpatrick, F. P. Two processes in perceptual learning. *Journal of Experimental Psychology,* 1954, *47.*

Kilpatrick, F. P. *Explorations in transactional psychology.* New York: New York University Press, 1961.

Kluckholn, F., & Strodbeck, F. L. *Variations in value orientations.* Evanston, Ill.: Row, Peterson, 1961.

Kohlberg, L. Stage and sequence: The cognitive-developmental approach to socialization. In D. A. Goslin, Ed., *Handbook of socialization theory and research.* Chicago: Rand McNally, 1969.

Kohlberg, L. From is to ought. In T. Michael, Ed., *Cognitive development and epistemology.* New York: Academic Press, 1971.

Kohn, H. *The idea of nationalism.* New York: Macmillan, 1944.

Kohn, H. *The mind of Germany.* New York: Scribner's, 1960.

Krader, L. Buryat religion and society. *Southwestern Journal of Anthropology,* 1954, *10.*

Krader, L. A nativistic movement in Western Siberia. *American Anthropologist,* 1956, *58.*

Kroeber, A. The superorganic. *American Anthropologist,* 1917, *19.*

Kuhn, T. S. *The structure of scientific revolutions.* Chicago: University of Chicago Press, 1973.

Kulpe O. Versuch über Abstraktion. In *Bericht über den ersten Kongress für experimentelle Psychologie,* Leipzig: J. A. Barth, 1904.

Labov, W. Some sources of reading problems for Negro speakers of nonstandard English. In J. C. Baratz & R. W. Shuy, Eds., *Teaching Black children to read.* Washington, D.C.: Center for Applied Linguistics, 1969.

Labov, W. The logic of nonstandard English. In F. Williams, Ed., *Language and poverty.* Chicago, Ill.: Markham Publishing Company, 1970.

Lanternari, V. *The religions of the oppressed.* New York: Knopf, 1963.

Laswell, H. D. The psychology of Hitlerism. *The political Quarterly,* 1933, *4.*

Lawrence, T. E. *Seven pillars of wisdom.* London: Jonathan Cape, 1940.

Leacock, E. B., Ed. *The culture of poverty: A critique.* New York: Simon & Schuster, 1971.

Leeds, A. The concept of "culture of poverty": Conceptual, logical, and empirical problems with perspectives from Brazil and Peru. In E. B. Leacock, Ed., *The culture of poverty: A critique.* New York: Simon & Schuster, 1971.

Lenin, V. I. *Materialism and empirio-criticism.* New York: International Publishers, 1927.

Lennenberg, E. H. Cognition in ethnolinguistics. *Language*, 1953, *29*.

Lerner, D. Interviewing Frenchmen. *American Journal of Sociology*, 1956, *62*.

Lerner, D., with Pevsner, L. W. *The passing of traditional society*. Glencoe, Ill.: Free Press, 1958.

Lévi-Strauss, C. *La Pensée sauvage*. Paris: Plon, 1962. (a)

Lévi-Strauss, C. *Le Totémisme aujourd'hui*. Paris: Presses Universitaires de France, 1962. (b)

Levine, R. A. *Culture, behavior, and personality*. Chicago: Aldine, 1973.

Lévy-Bruhl, L. *Les Fonctions mentales dans les sociétés inférieures*. Paris: Felix Alcan, 1910.

Lévy-Bruhl, L. *Mentalite Primitive*. Paris: Alcan, 1922.

Lewis, O. *La Vida*. New York: Random House, 1966.

Lifton, R. J. *Revolutionary immortality: Mao Tse-tung and the Chinese cultural revolution*. New York: Random House, 1966.

Lifton, R. J. *History and human survival*. New York: Random House, 1971.

Lipset, S. M. *Political man*, Expanded second edition, John Hopkins University Press, 1981.

Loevinger, L. Measuring personality patterns in women. *Genetic Psychology Monographs*, 1962, *65*, 241-251.

Luria, A. R. *Cognitive development, its cultural and social foundations*. Cambridge: Harvard University Press, 1976.

Lynd, H. M. *On shame and the search for identity*. New York: Harcourt Brace Jovanovitch, Inc., 1970.

McClelland, D. C. *The roots of consciousness*. Princeton, N.J.: D. Van Nostrand, 1964.

Maier, N. R. F. *Studies of abnormal behavior in the rat*. New York: Harper & Row, Pub., 1939.

Maine, Sir Henry. *Ancient law: Its connection with the early history of society, and its relation to modern ideas*. London: L. J. Murray, 1861.

Malinowski, B. The problem of meaning in primitive languages. In C. K. Ogden & I. A. Richards, *The meaning of meaning*. New York, Harcourt Brace, 1923.

Malinowski, B. *Argonauts of the Western Pacific*. New York: Dutton, 1961.

Mausner, B., & Mausner, J. A study of the anti-scientific attitude. *Scientific American*, 1955, *192*, No. 2.

Mead, G. H. *Mind, self, & society*. Chicago: University of Chicago Press, 1934.

Mead, M. *New lives for old*. New York: Morrow, 1956.

Mead, M. *Soviet attitudes toward authority*. New York: Schocken, 1966.

Mehnert, K. *Soviet man and his world*. New York: F. A. Praeger, 1962.

Métraux, R. B. Interview with a Chinese scholar. In M. Mead & R. B. Métraux, Eds., *The study of culture at a distance*. Chicago: University of Chicago Press, 1953.

Métraux, R. B. & Mead, M. Excerpts from "Themes in French Culture," by Rhoda Métraux, in *Themes in French Culture, A Preface to the Study of the French Community*, by Rhoda Métraux and Margaret Mead, Hoover Institute, Stanford University Press, 1954.

Michael, F., & Chang Chung-Li. *The Taiping rebellion, history and documents*. Seattle: University of Washington Press, 1966.

Milgram, S. Some conditions of obedience and disobedience in the presence of authority. *Human Relations*, 1965, *18*.

Miller, S. M., & Riessman, F. The working class subculture: A new view. In A. L. Grey, Ed., *Class and personality in society*. New York: Atherton, 1969.

Mukařovski, J. Foregrounding and backgrounding. In P. Garvin, Ed., *A Prague school reader*. Washington, D.C.: Linguistic Circle of Washington, 1953.

Muller, H. J. *Freedom in the ancient world*. New York: Harper, 1961.

Mumford, L. *The city in history*. New York: Harcourt, Brace & World, 1961.

Nair, K. *Blossoms in the dust*. New York: Praeger, 1962.

Nakamura, H. *Ways of thinking of eastern peoples*. Tokyo: Japanese National Commission for UNESCO, 1960.

Nakane, G. *Japanese society*. Berkeley: University of California Press, 1970.

Neisser, U. *Cognitive psychology*. New York: Appleton-Century-Crofts, 1967.

Newfield, J. In defense of student radicals. In G. R. Weaver & J. H. Weaver, Eds., *The university and revolution*. Englewood Cliffs, N.J.: Prentice-Hall, 1969.

Northrop, F. S. C. *The meeting of east and west*. New York: Macmillan, 1953.

Opler, M. E. *Apache odyssey: A journey between two worlds.* New York: Holt, Rinehart & Winston, 1969.
Pares, B. *A history of Russia.* New York: Knopf, 1937.
Parsons, T., & Shils, E. A., Eds. *Towards a general theory of action.* Cambridge: Harvard University Press, 1950.
Patai, R. *The Arab mind.* New York: Scribner's, 1973.
Pavlov, I. P. *Lectures on conditioned reflexes.* New York: International Publishers, 1928.
Perry, W. *Forms of intellectual and ethical development in the college years.* New York: Holt, Rinehart & Winston, 1968.
Piaget, J. *Le Développement de la notion de temps chez l'enfant.* Paris: Presses Universitaires de France, 1946.
Piaget, J. *The child's conception of physical causality.* Paterson, N.J.: Littlefield, Adams & Company, 1960.
Piaget, J. *Play, dreams, and imitation in childhood.* New York: W. W. Norton, 1962.
Piaget, J. *The moral judgment of the child.* Glencoe, Ill.: Free Press, 1966.
Piaget, J. *The mechanisms of perception.* New York: Basic Books, 1969.
Piaget, J. *Genetic epistemology.* New York: Columbia University Press, 1970.
Piaget, J., & Inhelder, B. *The psychology of the child.* New York: Basic Books, 1969.
Plato. *The dialogues of Plato* (B. Jowett, trans.). New York: Charles Scribner & Company, 1871.
Polansky, N. A., Borgman, R. D., & De Saix, C. *The roots of futility.* San Francisco: Jossey-Bass, 1972.
Popper, K. R. *The open society and its enemies.* New York: Harper & Row, Pub., 1962.
Présence africaine, 1959. Proceedings of the Second Congress of Black Writers and Artists, No. 5.
Pribram, K. *Conflicting patterns of thought.* Washington, D.C.: Public Affairs Press, 1945.
Quispel, G. *Gnosis als Weltreligion.* Zurich: Origo, 1951.
Radcliffe-Brown, A. R. The comparative method in social anthropology. *Journal of the Royal Anthropological Institute,* 1952, *81.*
Radhakrishnan, S. *The Hindu view of life.* New York: Macmillan, 1962.
Radin, P. *The world of primitive man.* New York: Henry Schuman, 1953.
Reclus, J. *La Revolte des Tai-Ping.* Paris: Roger Maria, 1972.
Reinmer, V. Is flouridation a Marxist plot? *The Reporter,* June 16, 1955, *12.*
Rosenhahn, D. L. Learning theory and pro-social behavior. *Journal of Social Issues,* 1972, *28,* 151-163.
Roszak, T. *The making of a counter-culture.* Garden City, N.Y.: Doubleday, 1969.
Roszak, T. *Where the wasteland ends.* Garden City, N.Y.: Doubleday, 1973.
Royce, J. R. *The encapsulated man.* Princeton, N.J.: D. Van Nostrand, 1964.
Sakharov, L. O Metodakh Isledovanija Ponjatij. *Psikhologija,* 1930, *3,* No. 1,
Schneider, L., & Lysgaard, S. The deferred gratification pattern: A preliminary study. *American Sociological Review,* 1953, *18,* 142-149.
Scribner, S. Mode of thinking and ways of speaking: Culture and logic reconsidered. In R. Freedle, Ed., *New directions in discourse processing.* Norwood, N.J.: Ablex Publishing Corporation, 1979.
Shelley, P. B. *The Boat.*
Shouby, E. The influence of the Arabic language on the psychology of the Arabs. *The Middle East Journal,* 1951, *5.*
Skinner, B. F. "Superstition" in the pigeon. *Journal of Experimental Psychology,* 1948, *38,* 168-172.
Smith, A. H. *China in convulsion.* New York: Fleming H. Revell Company, 1901.
Steed, H. W. Preface. In A. Kolnai, *War against the West.* New York: Viking, 1938.
Stern, F. *The politics of cultural despair.* Garden City, N.Y.: Doubleday, 1965.
Stewart, E. C. *American cultural patterns: A cross-cultural perspective.* Pittsburgh: The Regional Council for International Education, 1971.
Suttles, G. D. *The social order of the slum.* Chicago: University of Chicago Press, 1968.
Suzuki, D. T. Lectures on Zen Buddhism. In E. Fromm, Ed., *Zen Buddhism and psychoanalysis.* New York: Harper & Brothers, 1960.

Szalay, L. B., Moon, W. T., & Bryson, J. A. *Communication lexicon on three South Korean audiences*. Kensington, Md.: American Institute for Research, 1971.

Taper, B. Letter from Caracas. *The New Yorker*, March 6, 1965, pp. 101-143.

Thorne, J. P. Generative grammar and stylistic analysis. In J. Lyons, Ed., *New horizons in linguistics*. Baltimore: Penguin, 1970.

Thrasher, F. M. *The gang*. Chicago: University of Chicago Press, 1927.

Tocqueville, A., C. H. M. C. de. *Democracy in America*. New York: Knopf, 1945.

Tönnies, F. *Gemeinschaft and Gesellschaft*. Tübingen: Mohr 1837. C. P. Loomis, trans., *Fundamental concepts of sociology*. New York: American Book, 1940.

Triandis, H. C., with Vassiliou, V., Vassiliou, G., Tanaka, Y., & Shanmugam, A. V. *The analysis of subjective culture*. New York: John Wiley, 1972.

Tröltsch, E. *Deutscher Geist und Westeuropa*. Tübingen: Mohr, 1925.

Tucker, R. C. *The Soviet political mind*. New York: Praeger, 1963.

Viereck, P. *Metapolitics: The roots of the Nazi mind*. New York: Capricorn, 1965.

Vinay, J. P., & Darbelnet, J. *Stylistique Comparée du Française et de l'Anglais*. Paris: Didier, 1960.

Vygotsky, L. S. *Thought and language*. Cambridge, Mass.: M.I.T. Press, 1962. (Original Russian published in 1934)

Waley, A. *Three ways of thought in ancient China*. Garden City, N.Y.: Doubleday, 1939.

Wallace, A. F. C. Revitalization movements. *American Anthropologist*, 1956, *58*, 264-281.

Weber, M. *Wirtschaft und Gesellschaft*. Tübingen: Mohr, 1922.

Weber, M. *The religion of China: Confucianism and Taoism*. Glencoe, Ill.: Free Press, 1951.

Weber, M. *The religion of India*. Glencoe, Ill.: Free Press, 1958.

Wedge, B. Communication analysis and comprehensive diplomacy. In A. S. Hoffman, Ed., *International communication and new diplomacy*. Bloomington, Ind.: Indiana University Press, 1968.

Wedge, B., & Muromcew, C. Psychological factors in Soviet disarmament negotiations. *Journal of Conflict Resolution*, 1965, *9*, 18-36.

Werner, H. *Comparative psychology of mental development*. New York: Science Editions, 1961.

White, L. A. *The science of culture*. New York: Grove Press, 1949.

Whorf, B. L. *Language, thought and reality, selected writings* (J. B. Carroll, Ed.). Cambridge, Mass.: M.I.T. Press, 1956.

Whyte, W. F. *Street corner society*. Chicago: University of Chicago Press, 1943.

Wieder, D. L., & Zimmerman, D. H. Generational experience and the development of freak culture. *Journal of Social Issues*, 1974, *30*.

Willey, B. *The seventeenth century background*. Garden City, N.Y.: Doubleday Anchor, 1953.

Witkin, H. A., Lewis, H. B., Hartzman, M., Machover, K., Meissner, P. B., & Wapner, S. *Persoanlity through perception*. New York: Harper, 1954.

Witkin, H. A., Dyk, R. B., Paterson, H. F., Goodenough, D. R., & Karp, S. A. *Psychological differentiation*. New York: John Wiley, 1962.

Wolfenstein, N. The Soviet image of corruption. In M. Mead & R. Métraux, Eds., *The study of culture at a distance*. Chicago: University of Chicago Press, 1953.

Worsley, P. *The trumpet shall sound*. New York: Shocken, 1970.

Wright, R. H. The stranger mentality and the culture of poverty. In E. B. Leacock, Ed., *The culture of poverty: A critique*. New York: Simon & Schuster, 1971.

Wylie, L. *Village in the Vaucluse*. New York: Harvard University Press, 1964.

Yablonsky, L. *The violent gang*. New York: Macmillan, 1962.

Yablonsky, L. *The hippie trip*. New York: Western Publishing Company, 1968.

Zablocki, B. *The joyful community*. Baltimore: Penguin, 1971.

Zijderveld, A. C. *The abstract society*. Garden City, N.Y.: Doubleday, 1970.

Author Index

A

Albert, E. M., 86, *319*
Allport, G. W., 70, 94, *319*
Almond, G., 208, *319*

B

Babbitt, I., 172, 174, 175, 239, 240, *319*
Balandier, G., 137, 229, *319*
Bally, C., 88, *319*
Banfield, E. C., 97, 100, 105, 108, 109, 111, *319*
Bartlett, F. C., 50, 57, *319*
Bateson, G., 61, *319*
Bell, D., 193, *319*
Benedict, R., 24, 243, *319*
Berger, C. R., 152, *319*
Berman, H. T., 291, *319*
Bernstein, B., 12, 77, 87, *319*
Bever, T., 54, *319*
Bridgman, P. W., 29, *319*
Bronfenbrenner, U., 162, 286, *319*
Bruner, J. S., 35, 57, 58, 59, *319*
Burridge, K., 127, *319*

C

Calabrese, R. J., 152, *319*
Canaday, J., 173, *319*
Cantril, H., 41, 50, 105, 131, 151, 152, *319*
Cassiver, E., 140, 141, *320*
Cayton, H. R., 101, *320*
Chang, Chung-Li, 149, *323*
Chang, Tung-sen, 236, *320*
Chesnoff, R. Z., 270, *320*
Cheyney, E. P., 144, *320*
Chomsky, N., 54, *320*
Chu, V., 238, *320*
Cleaver, E., 35, *320*

D

Da Cunha, E., 150, *320*
Darbelnet, J., 90, *325*
Davis, A., 101, *320*
de Custine, 280, 282, *320*
Decter, M., 188, *320*
Deese, J., 68, *320*
d'Haucourt, G., 285, 300, *320*
Descartes, R., 275, *320*
Deutsch, K. W., 171, *320*
Deutsch, M., 87, *320*
Diaz del Castillo, 284, *320*
Diop, Aliune, 170
Dollard, J., 101, *320*
Domenach, J. M., 300, 301, *320*
Drake, S. C., 101, *320*
Durkheim, E., 16, 94, 104, 126, *320*
Duvall, E. M., 95, *320*

E

Eliade, M., 37, *320*
Erickson, F. D., 17, *320*

F

Fadipe, N. A., 117, *320*
Fanon, F., 171
Faulkner, W., 33, *320*
Ferster, C. B., 61, *321*
Firth, R., 134, *321*
Fischer, L., 197, *321*

Cobban etc.

Cobban, A., 166, *320*
Cohen, R. A., 77, 87, 278, 303, 311, *320*
Cohn, N., 142, 143, 145, 148, *320*
Cole, M., 64, 219, 220, 221, 222, 312, *320*
Coleman, J. S., 110, *320*
Condon, J. C., 1, *320*

SUBJECT INDEX